HENRY VIII
The Mask of Royalty

2/23
$2—

HENRY VIII, 1491–1547. *After Holbein*

HENRY VIII
The Mask of Royalty

LACEY
BALDWIN SMITH

JONATHAN CAPE
THIRTY BEDFORD SQUARE LONDON

FIRST PUBLISHED 1971
© 1971 BY LACEY BALDWIN SMITH

JONATHAN CAPE LTD
30 BEDFORD SQUARE, LONDON WCI

ISBN 0 224 00523 5

The extract from Robert Bolt's *A Man for all Seasons* is
quoted by permission of Heinemann Educational Books Ltd.

PRINTED AND BOUND IN GREAT BRITAIN
BY BUTLER & TANNER LTD, FROME AND LONDON

CONTENTS

ILLUSTRATIONS

To
J. R. S.
and
Timi in conjunction with
Mac and Dennie

It might be argued that this book was almost as complex in the making as its subject—Henry VIII. Suffice it to say that my wife's time, patience and industry were indispensable; my graduate students were long-suffering and co-operative; and the Fulbright Act, Northwestern University and the John Simon Guggenheim Foundation generously subsidized the research. Bits and pieces of the study have been appearing in article form for nearly a decade, the most recent being the genesis of Chapter 5, which was published in *Action and Conviction in Early Modern Europe,* a series of essays in honour of E. Harris Harbison, the man who first excited my interest in Tudor England and Henry VIII.

L. B. S.

1

The Faces of Death

Weep not, my wanton, smile upon my knee;
When thou art old, there's grief enough for thee!
Robert Greene, *Menaphon* (1589)

That 'serene and invincible prince', Henry VIII, lay dying; pomp
and pride had been laid aside for the naked end of life where 'worms
shall lie under thee, and worms shall be thy covering'.[1] As a demigod
he lived but as a man he died. Everywhere the vulgar indecencies of
death were evident: the heavy scent of rose oil and ambergris to
cloak the stench of sickness, the window tapestries to keep out the
night dampness, and the chamber fire to purge the 'pestilential airs'
and 'evil vapours'.[2] Doctors Owen, Wendye and Huycke, with their
urine flasks, cathartic prescriptions and astrological charts, were
patiently waiting for what they knew must come before another
dawn.* Patrec, the King's own flute-player, ministered the only kind
of relief possible: soft music, 'the medicine of the soul'. Everywhere
were subdued voices, whispered conversations, which had once
stirred the King to frenzy but now could no longer touch him.
Physician, councillor, musician, friend, each according to his nature,
made plans for the morning when 'the King that was' would be gone
and a nine-year-old boy would sit upon the throne of England.
  Of those who ministered, watched and waited, the doctors faced
the most pressing dilemma. It was clear that Henry's 'robust

* It is not clear who attended upon the dying monarch. The death of a sovereign was a public spectacle, but with Henry there was a deliberate effort to
keep his declining health and approaching death as secret as possible (*Span.
Cal.*, VIII, 475, pp. 330–31). Since the King's will in all likelihood was not
signed until the evening of his death (see pp. 267–272), those who witnessed
the document may also have watched him die. There were eleven in all: John
Gate(s), the first signer, was a gentleman of the Privy Chamber; David
Vincent, Henry Nevell, Edmond Harman, Wyllyam Sayntbarbe and Richard
Coke were grooms of the chamber; George Owen, Thomas Wendye and Robert
Huycke were doctors; Patrec was a musician; and William Clerk was clerk of
the Privy Council and private secretary to the King. Who else waited in the
bedchamber and ante-room is impossible to say. The only names of which we
can be certain are Paget, Seymour, Denney and Cranmer.

13

constitution', which had once wearied eight horses in a single day and turned hunting into a martyrdom for his less vigorous companions, was rapidly failing. Fifty-five years before, fire and water, those primordial elements so essential to the medieval explanation of creation, had conjoined to produce a monarch of extreme sanguine temperament: body fleshy, arteries large, 'hair plenty and red', cheeks ruddy and set off by delicate white skin, 'pulse great and full, digestion perfect, anger short, sweat abundant', and inclination hopeful, lusty and amorous.[3] By constant examination of the royal urine, stools and sputum, and by careful cupping and blood-letting in accordance with the phases of the moon, Henry's internal humours had been kept in tune, but now all was in discord, and 'liver, brain and heart, these sovereign thrones', were in hopeless disarray.[4] For months the medical expenses of the Privy Chamber had been soaring: £4 17s. 6d. in August, £13 11s. 2d. in September, £25 0s. 4d. in December; and, judging from the increasing amounts spent on rhubarb—a sure specific for the excessive yellow bile of a choleric disposition—the King's physicians were struggling with an enraged patient racked by the furies of pain and disease.[5] But now such remedies no longer sufficed. Modern specialists may speculate on what ultimately killed Henry Tudor at the age of fifty-five,* but for the sixteenth century there was no need to water-cast or consult the stars to perceive that the King's swollen body was no longer a fit place for his 'life-soul'.

The immediate problem was to tell a King who 'was loath to hear any mention of death' that he should prepare to die.[6] To do so was not only medically unwise, since priest and physician held firmly to the injunction that hope must be offered 'to the sufferer even if the symptoms point to a fatal issue',[7] but worse, it was potential treason to imagine the King's demise. Prudently, the doctors suggested that Sir Anthony Denney, long a gentleman of the bedchamber and friend of the sovereign, should convey the news.† Sir Anthony approached the King and quietly spoke the truth. In 'man's judgment', he told Henry, he was 'not like to live'. Then he exhorted his sovereign 'to prepare himself for death' and to recall the sins of his former life, 'as becometh every good Christian man to do'. Henry was a specialist when it came to sin, both in himself and in others, and the chronicler

---

* See pp. 231–3.
† The story comes from John Foxe, *Acts and Monuments*, V, p. 689. Exactly how much of it is to be accepted is largely a matter of religious taste. The *D.N.B.* (article 'Anthony Browne') claims that Sir Anthony Browne, Master of the Horse and Squire of the King's Body, with 'good courage and conscience' told Henry he was approaching his end.

John Foxe reported that he responded in the odour of pure Protestant sanctity: the mercy of Christ is 'able to pardon me all my sins, though they were greater than they be'. Exactly what he said during those final hours is more a matter of legend than of reality, but for physician and friend alike the job was done. Henceforth the King had need of none but a priest, and in a little while he called upon the divine who knew and loved him best—Thomas Cranmer, Archbishop of Canterbury.

Monarchs cannot afford simply to die and be done with it. The political and theological implications of their passing are legion. What Henry saw, or should have seen, as eternity closed about him is an issue of historic dispute which is more a mirror of man's imagination than of God's judgment. One story depicts Thomas Cranmer arriving too late and a King lying speechless, already beyond help. When the prelate grasped the cold hand and begged his sovereign to give some token of dying 'in the faith of Christ', legend records that the fingers gave a last spasm of pressure and farewell.[8] The *Spanish Chronicle* is more confident of the serenity with which Henry faced his maker and redeemer. Calling the Queen to his bedside, he bade Catherine Parr a touching farewell, assuring her that 'it is God's will that we should part'. Then, at peace with the world, 'he confessed and took the holy sacrament and commended his soul to God'.[9] John Foxe paints a less domestic but equally edifying scene. Perceiving that his moment was at hand, the King firmly stated his confidence in Christ's willingness to cleanse his soul, and, setting aside the ritual of the old Church, said that he would 'take a little sleep' ere he called his Archbishop, and thus fearlessly passed into oblivion.[10]

Henry was gone, but 'this, however, consoles us, that he is now in heaven, and that he hath gone out of this miserable world into happy and everlasting blessedness'.[11] The words are those of the small boy who was now King. His certainty as to his father's spiritual residence is touching, but others were equally positive that the old King had found a home in the sulphureous pit. Such authorities present a picture of tortured conscience, of frantic oscillation between terror of divine retribution and bold defiance, as the dying monarch called loudly for a bowl of white wine, gabbled about monks and clerics, and shouted the agonizing words: 'All is lost.'[12]

Modern writers, without committing themselves as to the King's final destination, have made it perfectly clear in more secular terms where they think Henry should have ended. A 'disgrace to human nature, and a blot of blood and grease upon the history of England', cried Charles Dickens; 'the real blood-guilt lies with the King,' said

G. R. Elton; 'cold-blooded, deliberate cruelty mark not only his advancing years but his whole reign,' wrote Sir Charles Oman; and the most vindictive of all, the verdict pronounced by the Danish doctor, Ove Brinch: 'The egotistic, brutal and reckless features of his character prevailed, and eventually he appears a psychopath of the boasting, swaggering, self-maintaining and self-glorifying type who, with transparent hypocrisy and meanness, calls upon everybody to inform him of other people's supposed heresy with the sole purpose of advancing his own personal aims.'[13]

The faces of Henry Tudor are not all satanic; shift the historical lighting and other images emerge. 'He sought the greatness of England, and he spared no toil in the quest ... Surrounded by faint hearts and fearful minds he neither faltered nor failed'; so wrote A. F. Pollard.[14] In the eyes of his Lord Chancellor, Henry was 'a most gentle gentleman, his nature so benign and pleasant that I think till this day no man hath heard many angry words pass his mouth'.[15] For the generation which followed, Henry was a great king, and they gave thanks for the very ruthlessness which so shocked later observers. 'If in any point he seemed more severe than just towards his high subjects, let us unfeignedly hold him excused, yielding him thanks even in his sepulchre, for by it we possess public tranquillity to this day.'[16] The fairest judgment of all is the one which leaves the verdict open. 'He was undoubtedly the rarest man that lived in his time. But I say not this to make him a god, nor in all his doings I will not say he hath been a saint ... He did many evil things as the publican sinner, but not as a cruel tyrant or as a Pharisaical hypocrite ... I wot not where in all the histories I have read to find one private king equal to him.'[17]

Whatever the picture, heinous or heroic, neither friend nor foe ever accused Henry Tudor of want of trying. Nor did they associate the English King with the chilly sensation of failure and futility which surrounded the final days of Martin Luther when he perceived the worm at the core of life and wondered whether all his works were dust, 'vanity and vexation of spirit'. Even if Henry shouted 'All is lost,' there was no suggestion that the battle had not been worth the fighting. Instead, there is the feeling that, given a second chance, the King would have done it all again. Nowhere is there the sense of exhaustion and doubt implicit in Luther's answer to the Dowager Electress of Saxony when she wished him many more years of life. 'Madame', he sighed, 'rather than live forty years more, I would give up my chance of Paradise.'[18] Henry Tudor would have been shocked by such a bargain; in fact, one suspects that on that January day, he would have happily bartered his soul for forty more years in which to dominate the rash and contentious men who were silently watching him die.

The King's ultimate end may be a point of considerable theological interest and doubtless was a matter of great consolation for those who loved or hated their sovereign, but the need to survive makes pragmatists of us all, and those highly secular and astute gentlemen, the King's 'well-beloved councillors', viewed Henry's death as a tangled and dangerous problem in political survival. For half a decade they had seen age dig deep trenches in a face once pink and polished, while the reddish-gold beard turned to coarse white, the muscular belly became a sagging deformity of fifty-four inches, and pain, disease and the ravages of suspicion consumed a superb constitution and a fine mind. Time had not been kind to Henry VIII, but such had been the vitality and dogged determination of his will to live that it was now difficult to realize the end was at hand. Thrice within the year—in March, October and December—the inflamed ulcers on his leg had sent great javelins of pain and fever through his body, and each time he had survived. Only a fortnight before, the King had been reasonably well; now he was *in extremis,* and the pillar upon which his ministers had built their lives was crumbling.[19] For as long as any man in that room could remember, he had been schooled to picture Henry as a god on earth, to defer to his royal judgment, and to make a distinction between 'his Highness' earnest request' and his own fond fancy.[20]

No one could stand in his place. Divinity now resided in a child king, 'a vessel apt to receive all goodness and learning',[21] but charisma had vanished with the 'old man'. Authority rested with sixteen councillors, all excellent lieutenants and servants, but lacking the magnetism and magic of leadership. Mr Secretary Paget was an efficient and honest clerk, trusted by his monarch and liked by his colleagues, but his pedigree was too fresh and the varnish on his coat of arms too sticky. He could stage-manage the succession in quiet consultation with the Earl of Hertford as efficiently as he had organized the business of the dying King's government, but he lacked the vision, ruthlessness and social standing to rule a kingdom.[22] Anthony Browne, the Master of the Horse, was too old, older than the King, and already sick unto death. John Dudley, Lord Lisle, was a rising star and a sound soldier, but he was frank to confess his foolishness when it came to matters of money and politics.[23] Sir Thomas Wriothesley, the Lord Chancellor, though his office stood next in rank to that of the Archbishop of Canterbury, was not popular. George Blagge of the Privy Chamber detested him and scurrilously penned: 'By false deceit, by craft and subtle ways,' cruelty had 'crept full high, borne up by sundry stays'.[24] Sir Richard Morrison was scarcely more complimentary, noting that he had known the Lord Chancellor as 'an earnest follower of whatsoever he took in hand, and did very seldom miss where either wit or travail were able to bring his purposes to pass'.[25] Wriothesley was beyond doubt a useful servant to his master, but for this very reason he seems to have had few friends, and in the new reign he was jettisoned as soon as possible. Of the sixteen men named in Henry's last will and testament to have 'the government of our most dear son' and the rule of all his 'realms, dominions and subjects', only the King's brother-in-law Edward Seymour, Earl of Hertford, qualified as a man of 'fit age and ability' to govern in the name of his royal nephew.[26]

Men do not willingly rush into an unknown future; they prefer the well-understood horrors of today to the nightmares of tomorrow, and though there was relief among the spectators that they had survived the ordeal of Henry's declining years, there was none of the vulgar rejoicing which attended the death of Francis I of France. No one stood in the antechamber gleefully reporting: 'The lady-killer is going.'[27] Henry, for all his legendary amours, could not be dismissed so lightly, and friend and foe alike felt little but deep foreboding as death dropped a pebble and to the farthest limits the circle spread.

Eustace Chapuys, the Imperial Ambassador, who could list Henry's failings by the dozens, warned the Emperor Charles V that the King's death might be a disaster to the Imperial cause in Europe.[28] A frantic Protestant minister wrote his friends at court asking: 'What think your worships they [the secret Catholics about the monarch] would attempt if his Majesty were at God's mercy?'[29] The astute and conservative Bishop of Winchester was equally apprehensive of what would happen 'when those that now be young' shall take over the reigns of government.[30] In Europe foreign observers speculated whether the Lady Mary might try to unseat her youthful half-brother and whether the Emperor might be persuaded to help her.[31] Only the French Privy Council was publicly sanguine, and it met three times in secret and emergency session to debate whether 'so good an opening for war would not be allowed to pass'.[32]

It was an accepted principle of monarchy that, as death closed in upon a long-reigning prince, 'discontented minds or wits starved for want of employment' would begin to voice 'new projects, suits, inventions and infinite complaints'.[33] The 'new projects' had been long in the making, and every man saw Henry's passing from his own perspective. Councillor, wife, daughter, son, servant and prelate— each judged the expanding circle of consequences in his own terms. For Hertford and Sir William Paget, who had sat the evening through at their master's bedside and later whispered together in the long gallery out of hearing of King and colleagues, there was no 'want of employment', only 'infinite complaints' about the existing state of affairs.*

Neither man had cause to criticize the King's bounty, for those who stood close to royalty were handsomely rewarded in his last will and testament: £3,000 annually for the Princesses Elizabeth and Mary; £1,000 in cash to Catherine the Queen; 500 marks each to Cranmer, Wriothesley, Hertford and Lisle; £300 to Browne, Denney and Paget; £100 to doctors Owen and Wendye (but, strangely, nothing for Huycke); 100 marks to Patrec; and £50 apiece for the four gentlemen ushers of the chamber.† Generosity, however, was not enough. Title, land and income, those essential sixteenth-century attributes of political responsibility, had been omitted. The sovereign himself had been aware that the peace and tranquillity of his realm rested on 'the maintenance and good continuance of the nobility' and the 'gratifying and rewarding' of loyal servants. Just before he died he ordered a fat book of new titles and manors to be devised, and courtiers and ministers hoped to profit from the fall of the House of Howard and the expected execution of the Duke of Norfolk; but Henry had hesitated for reasons of his own, and now he was dead.[34] Worse yet, the King died without naming his real successor. Though Henry, very likely at Paget's urging, had honoured his brother-in-law by making him the custodian of his testament, the will was a deep disappointment to the man who was of the same blood as the young Prince.[35] Power had been made collective and distributed equally among sixteen councillors, and Hertford was only one among a headless cadre. Both instinct and nature rebelled at the thought that there should be no cap to the social pyramid, no highest level of appeal, no single will behind which the kingdom could unite, and no governor who could answer on terms of equality the threats and greetings of foreign kings. Finally, and most serious of all, the will was unsigned. Henry had delayed too long and death had caught

---

* Exactly what Paget and Hertford said in their quiet conversation in the gallery at Westminster is, of course, pure speculation. We do know, however, that the Earl promised Mr Secretary to follow his advice in all his 'proceedings more than any other man's' (P.R.O., S.P. 10, vol. 8, f. 4, or B.M., Cotton MSS, Titus F III, f. 274 [277]).

† One mark equalled 13s. 4d. Consequently 500 marks was worth £333 6s. 8d. and 100 marks £66 13s. 4d. In all there were sixty-five bequests, plus 100 marks for the poor, and manors and rents worth £600 yearly which were presented to St George's Chapel at Windsor Castle to be spent for masses and obits for the King's soul, alms to be given out in his name, support for thirteen 'poor knights', and a sermon every Sunday in perpetuity.

him unawares, for the document bore not the signature of the King
but a facsimile, a dry stamp witnessed by Sir Anthony Denney, Mr
John Gate and William Clerk, the King's private secretary. It was
perfectly legal, but scarcely a propitious document on which to construct a new regime.

There were other questions to be discussed in the long gallery.
Who should fetch the young Prince and when? Which portions of
the will could safely be made public?[36] How long could Henry's
death be kept secret to give time for planning and security? What
excuses could be offered for the closing of the ports and the cancelling
of all sailings, so that foreign ambassadors could not report their
suspicions?[37] What military precautions should be taken at home, on
the Scottish border, and above all in Calais and Boulogne to forestall
a possible French attack? What should be the fate of the Duke of
Norfolk, imprisoned in the Tower and hourly expecting execution?
What had been the King's plans for the old Duke, and now that
Henry was dead was it legal, or more to the point expedient, to carry
them out?

Then there was the matter of an inventory, the incredible task of
accounting for thirty-eight years of clutter and debris collected in
fourteen or so manors, castles and palaces throughout the kingdom.
Even before the breath was out of the old King, minions were busy
recording, inspecting, detailing each cup, carpet and clock, every
pillow, vestment, harness and culverin. The five close-stools at
Hampton Court were minutely described (one was in 'green velvet
fringed with Venice gold and green silk embroidered with the King's
arms and badges') and even the ostrich-plumes for military helmets
were carefully listed under the separate heading—'feathers at Westminster'. For almost four decades a mountain of 'stuff' had been
secreted about, and probably not even Henry himself with his command of minutiae could have said exactly where it all was: the small
sums of money found 'in his secret jewel house at the end of the
gallery by the privy gardens' at Westminster, the maps and pictures
in the 'secret study called the Chaier House', the coffers, tills and
bags of writings, the regals, virginals and lutes stored in the 'little
study called the New Library'.[38] Henry had always been dangerously
aware of what pertained to the Crown and had lavished the same
attention on the exact disposal of the imprisoned Bishop of
Chichester's best mule as he had on the inventories of goods and
jewels belonging to his various wives.[39] It was not that many of the
King's domestics were blatantly dishonest, but it was difficult to
prove ownership or distinguish between what was public or private,
and officials tended to attach themselves to various articles of value.

Now that the master was gone, Secretary Paget and Mr Thomas Cheyney, the Treasurer of the Household, were too well trained not to look after the interests of the son, even if the job took almost three years. Dying involved a great deal of work for yeoman, sergeant and gentleman, and Sir William Paget had much to consider and discuss with his friend the Earl of Hertford.

Farther afield, other men and women waited upon the King's death and speculated. As Archbishop Cranmer wept for what was past even though he knew that Henry 'saw not perfectly God's truth', and as Bishop Stephen Gardiner prepared the funeral oration, in which he spoke of that 'pitiful and dolorous loss', Queen Catherine Parr had her own private grief and furtive joys.[40] Parliamentary statute protected her jointure and dowry, and her husband's will expressly bade those in charge of the final inventory to reserve her £3,000 in plate and 'such apparel as it shall please her to take', but henceforth she was a childless dowager, as politically stale as yesterday's obituary. Marriage to the King three and a half years before had interfered with a quiet romance with Sir Thomas Seymour, brother of the Earl of Hertford and junior uncle to the young Prince. In January 1547 he was still available, and in the dangerously short time of four months the two were secretly joined in matrimony. For Sir Thomas the Queen was second best—he aspired after a real princess, not a shop-worn royal widow—but Catherine could not be particular. She was a lady three times married and she wanted her Seymour for many reasons, not least because it gave her status in a man's world and would enrage her chief rival, Lady Hertford, who, as soon as her husband had set aside the King's testament and established himself as Lord Protector, would be ruling at court and claiming precedence over a dowager queen.

Catherine Parr's stepdaughter, the fading Princess Mary, found no such consolation in her father's passing. There had once been a time when she might have rejoiced to see him in hell. She had always known that 'while her father lived she would be only the Lady Mary, the most unhappy lady in Christendom',[41] but during the last five years Henry had grown kinder to his daughter, and she had learned to love the King, her father. Now that he was gone, she deeply resented Catherine's proposed marriage to the handsome Sir Thomas; she sensed an insult to the old man's memory and a cruel reminder that at thirty she herself was even further from marriage than she had been while her father lived. When Seymour begged her to forward his courtship with the Queen, she answered that 'if the remembrance of the King's Majesty my father (whose soul God pardon) will not suffer her to grant your suit, I am nothing able to persuade her to forget the loss of him who is as yet very ripe in mine own remembrance'.[42] Not the wife but the daughter, who had suffered so much at his hands, was the King's true mourner.

Two others grieved, but for different reasons. 'A little manikin' was now a king, and, though Edward knew his duty, being a monarch was a very worrisome thing.[43] All his short life he had been told that his princely task was 'to satisfy the good expectations of the King's Majesty', and he assured his father that he was 'worthy to be tortured with stripes of ignominy, if through negligence, I should omit even the smallest particle of my duty'.[44] Edward always did his best, but he was never quite convinced that the best was enough. Only four months before his royal obligations began in earnest, he participated in his first state function, the official welcome of the Admiral of France who had come to conclude peace between the two countries. In a frenzy of anxiety he wrote his stepmother to ask how well the Admiral spoke Latin; if he turned out to be a classical scholar, then Edward wanted to learn his lines more carefully.[45] Now the rehearsal was over. Henceforth a small boy with a starched, if precocious, mind would be expected to live up to the words pencilled across his famous Holbein portrait: 'Equal your renowned father in greatness; no man can wish for more.' At the other end of the royal spectrum stood another king, old, diseased and dying. When Francis I of France heard the tidings, he sighed for the memory of young sovereigns wrestling upon a cloth of gold. He was melancholy, for the two royal brothers were 'almost of an age and of the same constitution; and he feared that he must soon follow'.[46]

It was difficult to realize that a reign of thirty-eight years was over, that a new and unprecedented regime was beginning. From the children of the scullery to the yeomen of the ewery, from the grooms of the stable to the clerks of the greencloth, each one translated the crisis into personal and petty anxieties and aspirations. Was his office at stake? Would the new masters economize now that a boy king ruled without wife or need of pomp and circumstance? Would the servants of the Prince's household replace those of his father? Would the guard be reduced? What would happen to the Dowager Queen's household—the seven gentlemen and thirteen yeomen of her privy chamber, her maids of honour and the servants of her wardrobe and bed? Would the establishments of Elizabeth and Mary be enlarged or curtailed? Who would control court and government patronage in the name of an innocent sovereign? And the most crucial query of all—which of that council of sixteen would eventually secure the mantle of the old King's authority? Only one thing was certain: rival factions at the top might come and go, but administra-

tive habits, especially bad ones, would go on for ever. For each in
turn, Henry's death would make a difference. Kin, friend, colleague,
servant, subject, so the widening sphere expanded till it encompassed
even the nagging fears of minor clerks and inefficient minions, whose
faceless voices speak only through the endless rhythm of demographic data.

The moment of Henry's passing, viewed as a vital statistic, stands
in sterile isolation, a detail devoid of compassion and vacant of
meaning to be recorded as precisely as possible: close to two a.m. on
the morning of Friday, January 28th, 1547.[47] When Martin Luther
died, scarcely ten months before the English monarch, that event
was noted by hired observers with the same clinical objectivity: 'A
few days now past died Martin Luther,' a thing 'not of much
moment'. They added, however, a crucial codicil: 'Yet by reason of
the great fame that goeth of it in this country, we could do no less
than advertise your majesty.'[48] By the same token the King's demise
was also a moment of 'great fame'; for the doctor it was a gripping
study in pathology, for the priest a tense drama in theology, for the
councillor a baffling lesson in politics, and for the biographer a crisis
to which fifty-five years of life had been but a prologue. The end of
life is in fact the beginning of the old King's story.

If the conclusions of geriatrics are correct, it is during the final
stages of life that man casts off a portion of the protective shield
hammered out during childhood and adolescence and reveals the
raw personality beneath.[49] For Henry Tudor the concluding period,
the half-decade after 1542, was scarcely heroic, and he stumbled
towards goals which seem puerile and fatuous compared to the giant
strides and historic achievements of the middle years of his reign.
But the very fact that there were no distracting issues, no great
decisions and no *alter rex* makes these years crucial to the biographer
of a monumental old monarch and the lesser men who surrounded
him.

It is a strange vagary of history that the documents left by the
accident of time are so intimate, yet so perverse, that they reveal
Henry's love for baked lampreys, his passion for clocks (in three
years he spent over a hundred pounds on those mechanical wonders
of his day and maintained a professional clock expert at the cost of
forty shillings a year) and the names of his French chef and his
private laundress,* but not the underlying purpose of his French
wars, his notion of cosmology, his concept of kingship, or whether in
the end he died a Protestant or a Catholic. The results of a man's life

* The 'yeoman cook for the king's mouth' was Pero Doux or Perot Le Doulce
(see *L.P.*, XIV [1], 781; XV, 1032, p. 541). The laundress was Anne Harris,

preserved in stone and statute are easy enough to record, but the structure of his mind, the subliminal assumptions which set the frame of reference for his actions, and the unreason which may lie behind motivation, are the very devil to extract. How can the historian hope to sound the secret chambers of a mentality such as Henry's which was devoid of speculative thinking and engrossed in all the petty considerations of a filing clerk, and reach down to what William James called the 'experience of individual men in their solitude'?[50] The inner personalities of a Luther, a Thomas More, even a Napoleon, are revealed a hundred times over in action and writing; but Henry was a great pompous Prometheus, chained by the narrowness of a mind which accepted the standards of his age as so self-evident that they required neither defence nor articulation .

Leonardo da Vinci voiced the dilemma when he pointed out that 'a good painter has two chief objects, to paint man and the intention of his soul; the former is easy, the latter is hard, because he has to represent it by the attitudes and movements of the limbs.'[51] A portrait of the old sovereign, then, must be constructed out of the outward actions of the man. The artist, however, is at an advantage; he need only reveal life, not resurrect it. The historian must conjure up the dead, raising not only the body of the past but its mind as well. Psychology out of cultural context is worse than no psychology at all. Henry Tudor may indeed have been the hapless victim of a host of Freudian monsters, a neurotic, possibly even a psychotic in the modern clinical sense of the term, but if he was, he was a sixteenth-century neurotic and, even more important, a royal one. Each personality is a part of the cultural sea which sustains and envelops it. The giants of history, like icebergs, stand in frozen isolation; one-seventh emerges above the ebb and flow of time, six-sevenths remain hidden, the result of ageless conditioning of the inner recesses of mind and soul. Analyse an iceberg and it turns to water; subject Henry's character to study and it too may vanish. Yet scrutiny, especially of the obscure regions of the King's mind, is exactly what is needed if the man as well as his soul are to be revealed.

G. K. Chesterton once argued that a landlady did better to note her boarder's approach to God than inquire into his financial resources.[52] On the same principle Henry's biographers are advised to investigate the structure of the King's mind, the system by which he

---

who received £20 a year in wages and fees but had to provide her own sweet-smelling herbs and powder, fuel for her fire, soap, and two chests for the clean and dirty linen (Nicolas, *Privy Purse Expenses*, pp. 51, 62, 91, 109, 130, 189, 209).

organized the human, physical and moral relationships around him, and the manner in which he conceived of his office, his God and his universe. How did a divine-right monarch respond to eternity in a society which described heaven in anthropomorphic terms and assured all true believers that they would be kings in paradise—a matter of understandable concern to a man who was already a king on earth? How did a sovereign who spoke for God and by the very logic of his office could do no wrong justify and explain failure in himself or in his policies? And, equally revealing, what were the needs and motives which formed his character and shaped his vision of royalty, his sense of honour and the operation of his conscience?

Henry was no consciously historic animal, deliberately acting upon his knowledge and fear of the past; nor was he an economic being, aware of the market-mechanics and commercial trends of his age; nor was he a secular man, accepting as the purpose of life the physical welfare of mankind; nor was his a rational mind, clearly distinguishing between the real and the imaginary. Instead, the King was a baffling composite of shifting silhouettes. As a sovereign filled with the spirit of divine duty, modelling his royal stance on the actions of Old Testament kings, he appears with one face. As a Christian of excessively tender conscience, who knows he must eventually make a very special reckoning with God, he reveals another image. As a man of honour, a warrior knight and noble gentleman who lived a dream drawn from Arthurian legend and shared by every sovereign and nobleman of Europe, he is something else again. Finally, as a ruler and manipulator of men, for whom power was not so much a tool of political life as a mantle in which to wrap his own private fears and inadequacies, he presents still another mask.

The final portrait of an old man in whom age has opened windows into the closet of mind and soul may not be pretty, but it may be well to remember that the years rarely bring out the best in any of us; men, deprived of the masks with which they confront the world, become, so to speak, 'caricatures of themselves'.[53] In defence, Henry, who knew himself no better than his historians do, might have answered with Walt Whitman:

> Do I contradict myself?
> Very well then I contradict myself,
> (I am large, I contain multitudes.)
> (*Song of Myself* [51])

2

The 'Old Man'

'All I say is, kings is kings, and you got to make allowances.
Take them all round, they're a mighty ornery lot. It's the
way they're raised.'

Mark Twain, *Huckleberry Finn*

The dignity and honour of the dead King, the Princess Mary had said, was 'ripe in mine own remembrance', and, as the new reign broke into a babble of discord and dissension, that memory began to sharpen and emerge as the mirror of those things 'that are worthy a prince'.[1] The members of the council of regency had been unanimous in their determination to project their colleague, Edward Seymour, Earl of Hertford, into the seat of authority, on the grounds that a protectorate was 'the surest kind of government and most fit' for a commonwealth,[2] but in doing so they learned something about their late master: unlike the Earl, he had known to perfection the role of kingship. With that lesson before him, Sir Anthony Browne drew the inescapable conclusion that 'princes with their majesty may be oft envied and hated; without it they are always scorned and condemned'.[3] Desperately Sir William Paget urged the new Lord Protector to recall that he was no longer a private subject but a man who supplied the 'place of a king', and he offered the gratuitous counsel: 'Then, sir, for a king do like a king.'[4] The admonition was sound, but the application hazardous.

Paget could point to a perfect model of monarchy: the massive Holbein fresco of Henry which dominated the Privy Chamber at Whitehall Palace. Here was the shrine before which subjects worshipped, for the entire Tudor dynasty—Henry, his father, his mother, and Jane Seymour, the only wife to bear him a legal son—were clustered around a central monumental pillar in the traditional style of the Holy Family about the altar. Though the scene was designed to celebrate ancestral continuity, the dominating figure was that of the second Tudor, rendered five feet ten inches tall, three feet across the shoulders and seeming to bend the wall with his weight. Portrayed for all to see was a high and mighty prince who kept 'his

26

subjects from the highest to the lowest in due obedience' and who
somehow contrived to cloak his most outrageous acts in the mantle
of majesty. The Lord Protector, who knew his Henry every bit as
well as did Paget, might well have asked: how was it done? In
answer, Sir William could only talk fulsomely about those citadels
of public order—law and religion—lacking which, 'farewell all just
society, farewell king, government, justice and all other virtue'.[5] The
Principal Secretary sensed the mystery but like so many bureaucrats
he missed the point: law and religion were deadening without style;
they needed the sure hand of royal leadership to make them bear-
able.

Power is a state of mind, a delicate balance between the will to
rule and the desire to obey. It can be institutionalized into a rigid
chain of command, metamorphosed into a social habit, justifide on
grounds of lofty idealism or crude necessity, and utilized to achieve
any purpose under heaven or hell, but what the Earl of Hertford
failed to grasp was that power can only be measured in terms of
human contacts and must start with the domination of those closest
to the source of authority. Henry's own definition of his majesty was
refreshingly simple and unquestioningly biblical. He accepted without reservation the formula laid down in Scripture: 'Where the word
of a king is, there is power: and who may say unto him, What doest
thou?'[6] He was, he told the Bishop of Winchester, the 'old man' and
'had been directed in the mean way of truth, and therefore was meet
to be arbiter between the others to reduce them to the truth'.[7] There
is a whole universe of ideas locked within those words, but the essence
of power for Henry was the control and manipulation of people, and
their subordination to the will of the monarch.

Paget and others might mouth political platitudes about civil and
religious obedience, but the 'old man's ' dearest desire was 'to proceed
in all our acts and doings, as may be most acceptable to the pleasure
of Almighty God, our Creator, and to the wealth [and] honour of us,
our succession, and posterity, and the surety of our realms and subjects within the same'.[8] The order is significant if shocking to
twentieth-century sensibilities schooled in the conviction that royalty
is but the scullery-maid of social utility. It seems monstrous that
personal wealth and honour should be allowed to stand before the
security of the kingdom, yet Henry was adamant on this very point.
When his bishops suggested the startling proposition that kings were
expected to foster the material prosperity of their subjects as well as
to guard the true faith, defend the realm, administer justice and
show a 'fatherly pity' to all, he was horrified, and struck out with his
own pen the offending words: 'to provide and care for them [his

people] that all things necessary for them may be plenteous'.[9] For Henry the betterment of mankind stemmed from the welfare of princes, not the wealth of subjects; his prelates, not he, were in danger of putting the cart before the horse. 'In all your doings', advised Roger Edwardes, 'remember the majesty of your person, wherein consisteth the politique life of all your people, and eke [increase] the health of your state and theirs.'[10] This advice was directed to Elizabeth, but Edwardes had learned his social philosophy under her father.

Henry was well aware that he owed weighty duties to God and man, but his foremost obligation was to his own royal person. His princely honour demanded not so much unthinking obedience on the part of subjects as absolute freedom from restraint for himself. He warned the captains sent out to crush the Yorkshire rebels in December 1536 that he would never negotiate with traitors, for 'our honour should be touched in such sort, as it were by a constraint, to grant them their desire therein, or to permit you in any wise to common with them ...'[11] Almost from the start of the reign, he announced that he did 'not choose any one to have it in his power to command me, nor will I ever suffer it'.[12] A generation later he was boasting that he was 'too old to allow himself to be governed', and the Imperial Ambassador reported that the King was determined, no matter the cost, to 'show his absolute power and his independence of anyone'.[13]

Henry's notion of domination was never the cold exercise of a political abstraction but the intensely personal pleasure of manipulating other men. His techniques for achieving 'his independence of anyone' were neither intellectual nor organizational but psychological, striking at the emotions, nurturing fear and insecurity, catering to each man's secret aspiration, searching out hidden envy and spite, and confusing the rational operation of his Council by calculated caprice. His weapons combined devastating charm and sweet reasonableness with close attention to detail and the deliberate demoralization of those closest to the seat of power. The strategic principles on which he operated were, first, that 'fear begets obedience'[14] and, second, that in every heart resides secret malice. Exactly how far the King was ready to go in this mental warfare at which he was so adept is demonstrated in three stories which present Henry in such a hideous light that it is difficult to believe that they ever took place. Truth, however, is a fickle damsel; she may be wedded to historical accuracy, but as often as not she consorts with legend, and though the details are doubtless embroidered, the tales nevertheless reveal the mind of a sovereign determined to be master in his own house, and, unlike Hertford, well versed in how to get his way.

The first tale is a familiar one and concerns Thomas Cranmer, Archbishop of Canterbury.[15] During the spring of 1543 the conservative members of the Council were increasingly alarmed by the steady drift towards heresy, especially in high court circles, and with reason they suspected that the Archbishop and his 'learned men' were the source of much of the infection. Tactfully they broached the matter to Henry in terms he understood best: religious deviation led straight to social revolution. They also pointed out that Cranmer was inviolable because he was a member of the Privy Council and no man dared bring evidence against him. Only if the prelate were safely put away would men 'be bold to tell the truth and say their consciences'. 'Upon this persuasion', Henry gave secret orders that the unsuspecting ecclesiastic should be taken into custody when he appeared next morning at the regular meeting of the Council.

After the conspiracy had been carefully devised and the plotters had departed, Henry proceeded to behave in an extraordinary fashion. 'At night about 11 of the clock', he sent Anthony Denney post-haste to Lambeth Palace, demanding the Archbishop's immediate presence at Whitehall. 'My lord being abed rose straight way, and went to the King,' who revealed to the astonished prelate what was in store for him. Henry was obviously enjoying himself hugely and ended by asking: had he 'done well or no, what say you, my lord?' Unbelievably, the Archbishop thanked his sovereign for the warning and the chance of a fair 'trial of his doctrine', for, he said, 'he doubted not but that his majesty would see him so to be used'. The innocence of Cranmer's answer left Henry almost speechless. Due obedience and humility were right and proper but this was unadulterated folly, and the King burst out: 'Oh Lord God! What fond simplicity have you: so to permit yourself to be imprisoned, that every enemy of yours may take advantage against you.' Thereupon he presented Cranmer with a ring, lectured him on the art of political survival in the sixteenth century, and told him exactly how to behave when confronted by his enemies on the Council. The Archbishop was to demand his right to face his accusers. If this were refused and his colleagues sought to commit him to the Tower, he was to display the King's ring, 'by the which', Henry explained, 'they shall well understand that I have taken your cause into my hand from them'. Armed with this excellent advice Cranmer departed to wait upon events; the fox had suddenly become the hound.

It is not difficult to imagine what transpired next morning at eight o'clock. The Council, happily assuming that they were doing their master's bidding, ordered the prelate to appear before them, keeping him waiting for three-quarters of an hour in the antechamber among 'serving men and lackeys'. When word of this humiliation was brought to the King, he was outraged and exclaimed: 'Have they [the councillors] served me so? It is well enough; I shall talk with them bye and bye'; but strangely he made no effort to inform them of his decision or end the farce.

'Anon my lord Cranmer was called into the council.' He was accused of infecting the whole realm with heresy and told that it was the sovereign's pleasure that he should be committed to the Tower and examined as a common heretic. Still feigning humility, the Archbishop begged that he should be confronted with his accusers, and when this was denied and he was about to be dragged away, he turned and said: 'I am sorry, my lords, that you drive me unto this exigent to appeal from you to the King's Majesty.' Then at the dramatic moment he revealed the King's ring to a Council struck dumb with dismay. Instantly the recriminations began, and Lord John Russell, the Lord Privy Seal, reminded his colleagues that he had warned them 'what would come of this matter. I knew right well that the King would never permit my Lord of Canterbury to have such a blemish as to be imprisoned, unless it were for high treason.'

It was clear to all that they had blundered and as a body they rushed to excuse themselves like so many schoolboys caught in the jam-cupboard. Henry scolded them accordingly. 'Ah, my lords, I had thought that I had had a discreet and wise council, but now I perceive that I am deceived;' and he berated them for having treated an archbishop like 'a slave, shutting him out of the council-chamber among serving men'. The fact that Henry himself had ordered them to do exactly as they had done was of no importance; presumably the Council was expected to know the sovereign's secret mind as well as his spoken word. When the Duke of Norfolk offered by way of justification the fatuous excuse that the Council had desired the imprisonment of Cranmer only so that he might 'after his trial be set at liberty to his more glory', Henry brushed the fragile argument aside, saying: 'Well, I pray you use not my friends so.' And finally, in an orgy of righteous indignation, he lashed out: 'I perceive now well enough how the world goeth among you. There remaineth malice among you one to another; let it be avoided out of hand, I would advise you.' The story is indeed marvellous, not the least wonder being that the narrator, Ralph Morice, Cranmer's secretary, found the monarch's actions in no way strange.

A single example of perversity and mental sadism might be dis-

missed either as the action of a senile and foolish monarch, hopelessly
forgetful and pathetically inconsistent, or as a parasitical legend of
the kind that attaches itself to any flamboyant and controversial
personality; but the same plot reappeared less than a year later. This
time the victim was Cranmer's rival, Stephen Gardiner, Bishop of
Winchester, who belonged to the conservative faction at court.[16] The
shoe was now on the other foot, for the radical, pseudo-Protestant
members of the Council hoped to engineer the Bishop's destruction.
The occasion was the execution in March 1544 of the prelate's
nephew and secretary, Germain Gardiner, for denying the royal
supremacy. Charles Brandon, Duke of Suffolk, in league with the
Archbishop, the Earl of Hertford and John Dudley, Lord Lisle,[17]
persuaded Henry that Winchester must be guilty by association; for
they argued that the Bishop's secretary 'would never stand so stiff
in defence of the bishop of Rome's usurped power and authority
without his said master's both advice, knowledge and persuasion'.
Henry concurred and obligingly permitted the Duke to have
Gardiner 'committed to the Tower to answer to such things as may
be objected against him'. As with Cranmer, the decision was made
in the evening, and the Council was ready to act the next morning.
Unfortunately, however, the 'talk was not so secret' but that some
of Winchester's friends in the Privy Chamber sent him word.[18]
Immediately Gardiner repaired to Westminster, using as his excuse
'some matter to minister unto the King'. Though presumably Henry
had not sent for the Bishop, he did exactly as he had done with the
Archbishop: he revealed all, saying that it was 'thought that you are
not all clear in this offence, but that you are of the same opinion with
him [Germain Gardiner]; and, therefore, my lord, be plain with me,
and let me know if you be that way infected or no. If you will tell
me the truth, I will rather pardon the fault; but if you halt or dissemble with me, look for no favour at my hands.'

At this admonition, Winchester wisely fell to his knees, confessing
that he had once harboured some of the evil views of his secretary
but promising 'from that day forward to reform his opinion, and
become a new man'. The technique was somewhat different from his
rival's, but the humble submission had much the same effect. Henry
granted a full pardon on the spot, but again he did not see fit to inform the Duke or the Council. The next morning, when Suffolk
heard that the Bishop had escaped his enemies, he stormed into the
royal presence, complaining that Henry had 'prevented our commission which I and others had from your grace, concerning my Lord of
Winchester's committing to the Tower'. 'Wot you what', was the
King's abrupt reply, 'you know what my nature and custom hath

been in such matters, evermore to pardon them that will not dissemble, but confess their faults.'

Henry may have found Cranmer's resilient simplicity touching and Suffolk's belligerent methods a mirror of his own tactics, but Stephen Gardiner was closest to him in his pragmatic and political approach to matters of Church discipline and doctrine, and it was not long before the Bishop was again basking in the pleasant glow of the King's confidence. In time he found occasion for revenge, but when the conservatives sought to strike at what they viewed as galloping heresy at court by poisoning Henry's mind against his spouse, Gardiner wisely allowed the Lord Chancellor, Thomas Wriothesley, to arrange the plot.[19] As John Foxe tells the story, Queen Catherine Parr was not only 'very zealous toward the gospel', but also careless enough to risk theological discussion as a way of entertaining her ageing and difficult husband. Henry listened to Catherine's disturbing ideas; then politely ordered her from his chamber, bidding her 'farewell, sweetheart', which Foxe assures his readers was his usual term to the Queen when giving her leave to depart. The moment she was out of hearing, Henry burst into loud indignation and sarcastically announced: 'A good hearing it is, when women become such clerks; and a thing much to my comfort, to come in mine old days to be taught by my wife.' Then on Gardiner's recommendation he issued a warrant to investigate Catherine's heretical activities and search her rooms. Should any damning evidence be found, the Queen was to be seized and 'carried by night unto the Tower'.

Shortly before the day of the arrest, Henry was up to his usual tricks and disclosed the entire scheme to Dr Wendye, loudly exclaiming that 'he intended not any longer to be troubled with such a doctress as she was' and 'charging him with all, upon peril of his life, not to utter it to any creature living'. Then, in proper fairy-tale fashion, the warrant for the Queen's arrest was 'accidentally' dropped by one of the members of the King's Council, opportunely picked up by 'some godly person' and taken to Catherine, who immediately 'fell incontinent into a great melancholy and agony'. On hearing of his wife's state of mind, Henry sent the same Dr Wendye, to whom he had already revealed the plan, to attend upon the Queen and comfort her. The doctor's prescription was to advise Catherine to hide her heretical books, to throw herself upon the King's mercy and to assure him that she had only appeared to differ from him in religion so as to entertain him during the 'painful time' of his infirmity and to profit herself from his greater theological expertise. The counsel was excellent, for Henry was delighted by his wife's humble and tactful remarks, and declared that they were once more 'perfect friends'. Unfortunately he again failed to make this important fact known to Lord Chancellor Wriothesley. Instead, he carefully arranged to be with the Queen at the moment of her arrest.

With immense glee John Foxe describes the concluding scene of his story. 'The day and almost the hour appointed being come, the King being disposed in the afternoon to take the air,' sent for Catherine. There in the privacy of the garden he made himself 'as pleasant as ever he was in all his life before'. Suddenly, 'in the midst of their mirth', appeared the unsuspecting Lord Chancellor with forty of the King's guards at his heels, 'with purpose indeed to have taken the Queen ... even then unto the Tower'. Henry was outraged, and 'stepping a little aside called the Chancellor unto him'. Exactly what was said, Foxe grudgingly admits he does not know, but he assures his avid readers that Wriothesley fell to his knees while the King shouted: 'Arrant-knave! beast! and fool!' The tirade over, the unfortunate councillor was dismissed, and 'thus departed the Lord Chancellor out of the King's presence ... with all his train; the whole mould of all his device being utterly broken'.

The conclusions to be drawn from these tales are legion. For some there is evidence of a psychotic mind operating in a universe of its own, where reality has been lost and where the logic behind action is the closely guarded secret of an apparently irrational mentality. Others detect signs of a perverted personality, which takes pleasure in the public embarrassment and discomfiture of ministers who cannot defend themselves. Still others perceive a weak and gullible man, so emotionally unstable that he oscillates helplessly between extremes of over-action and regret. Possibly the stories reveal nothing at all except the sad picture of a diseased and senile old man, forgetful, irritable and floundering in a world which was passing him by. Or again the sceptic might argue that all three episodes are scandalous fabrications in which a tired plot has been utilized thrice over for reasons of religious and political bias.

There is in fact far too much corroborative evidence indicating that Cranmer, Gardiner and the Queen were indeed in grave trouble to dismiss the stories as mere legend,[20] but whatever the verdict a single fact stands out: the consistency of the King's behaviour. Henry himself was the directing and controlling force in each incident, and his script was invariably the same—quietly to foster animosity and jealousy within his Council, to appear to encourage the majority faction and become a partner in an elaborate plot, then to warn the intended victim of his impending fate, thereby turning the tables, to allow the unsuspecting Council to walk into the trap, and finally to indulge in a splendid display of Tudor temper and outraged morality.

B

What then was Henry's purpose? Why these complicated and humiliating farces? Clearly all three stories cry out for psychiatric analysis, but before the old King is placed on the couch, John Foxe must have his say. His explanation is simple, rational and essentially political, but it squarely hits the mark of both Henry's character and the nature of his office: 'like a wise, politic prince', Henry ordered the arrest of Catherine Parr 'not upon any evil mind' to be done with her, but 'rather closely dissembling' to 'try out the uttermost of Winchester's fetches'.[21] The monarch's purpose, then, was to test, to probe, to search out secret malice, and above all to 'show his absolute power and independence'.

Distrust was inherent in the royal office, and instinctively Henry sensed the warning that 'in old and infirm years' a prince 'may be ruled over by a new train of hungry councillors'.[22] That was the central problem of those final years: how to maintain his control. It was a political and psychological necessity, and he warned his ministers in 1541 that he had ways of discerning 'the good servants from the flatterers' and of guarding against advisers who temporized 'for their own profit' and traitors who hid their poison behind 'fair and pleasant words'.[23] The King had many means of sifting the chaff from the grain, but certainly one method of trying 'out the uttermost fetches' of those closest to him was to arrange intricate traps and then watch his victims squirm. There is no better way of probing the truth about a man than to observe his reaction to the unexpected.

Not only did Henry throw dust in his councillors' eyes and tell tales behind their backs; he also sought to isolate them, inventing means to minimize any sense of conciliar solidarity. Sometimes he set snares to catch them, but just as often he endeavoured to divide them with flattering words and the marvellous magnetism which so rarely left him. The King, Sir Thomas More shrewdly pointed out, had a gift for making each man believe that he alone enjoyed his 'special favour'.[24] He would call foreign ambassadors aside, bidding them be seated so that the two of them could have a private tête-à-tête about Continental affairs.[25] Sometimes, to the dismay of the more staid members of his court, he would allow his cronies to become 'so familiar and homely with him ... that they forgot themselves'.[26] He had pet names for the gentlemen of his bedchamber and called George Blagge his 'pig',[27] and whosoever touched his heart invariably received a kindness—money for a poor woman to redeem her husband from debtor's prison, a gift to his jester 'for his surgery when sick in London', a present to a blind harpist, a token to a poor man with thirteen children, and twenty-eight shillings to Thomas, his footman, 'to relieve him in his sickness'.[28] He would take ministers into his privy closet and comfort them, as he did with Bishop Gardiner, if he thought his treatment had been too harsh, saying that 'his displeasure' was directed not so much at the man as at the issue under discussion.[29] So successful was he in cultivating this happy illusion of special concern and favour that in a report drawn up shortly after his death, Sir William Paget assured the lords of the Council that his late master 'used to open his pleasure to me alone in many things'. Yet scarcely three pages further on in the same document Sir Anthony Denney and Sir William Herbert, both gentlemen of the bedchamber, announced that Henry 'would always when Mr Secretary was gone tell us what had passed between them'.[30]

Essentially the same technique of divide and rule was used in public theological debates. The monarch, Cranmer reported, 'is wont to hand over' controversial books 'to one of his lords in waiting for perusal, from whom he may afterwards learn their content. He then takes them back, and presently gives them to be examined by some one else, of an entirely opposite way of thinking to the former party. Thus, when he has made himself master of their opinions, and sufficiently ascertained both what they commend and what they find fault with, he at length openly declares his own judgment respecting the same point.'[31] The Archbishop loyally declared his sovereign to be 'an astute and vigilant observer', which was the only tactful thing to say about a man who fancied himself 'meet to be arbiter between the others to reduce them to the truth', but Cranmer failed to perceive the secret purpose behind the procedure. Not only did the system save work, but it also told Henry exactly where everybody stood.

Years later, towards the end of the century, Sir Thomas Wilson painted a picture of Elizabeth's court that was far more reminiscent of Henry's reign than his daughter's. 'In all great offices and places of charge', he said, 'they do always place two persons of contrary factions ... to the end, each having his enemy's eye to overlook him, it may make him look the warilier to his charge, and that if any body should incline to any unfaithfulness ... it might be spied before it be brought to any dangerous head ... This is seen in ye Tower, the place of the most trust, where the Lieutenant and Steward, Master of the Ordinance and Lieutenant of the same, have been ever in my remembrance vowed enemies ...'[32] Evidently Elizabeth had learned her political skills from her father.

Secrecy was indispensable to Henry's purpose, and the conclusion to be drawn from the King's correspondence is that his notion of successful diplomatic and political policy was secret covenants secretly arrived at. He regarded Sir Thomas Wyatt, the English Ambassador in Spain, as being both foolish and delinquent in failing to seal his official letters, thereby permitting Bishop Gardiner to read his dispatches before forwarding them to London.[33] The monarch who conspired behind his Council's back could never willingly permit his ministers to consort with one another even by accident, for it undermined the rock upon which his entire grasp of government was based: 'Three may keep counsel, if two be away; and if I thought that my cap knew my counsel, I would cast it into the fire and burn it.'[34]

The most spectacular case of deliberate deception occurred immediately following the outbreak of peace between England and France in the autumn of 1546, and reveals the King operating in diplomacy along lines identical to his chosen methods at home—deceiving, demoralizing and dividing his ministers. Just before the end of the war, the French had begun the construction of a fort designed to dominate the English citadel of Boulogne. The town had been won two years before, and by the terms of the treaty Henry was permitted to keep it for eight years. The French ramparts, having been started during the war, were not affected by the treaty, and, to the dismay of the English garrison, construction was continued after the peace. At the urging of Lord Grey of Wilton, the English commander at Boulogne, Henry asked his Council what should be done, and with a single voice they informed him that any attempt to stop the French would be a flagrant breach of the peace. Mr Secretary Paget was accordingly commanded to draw up a letter to Lord Grey ordering him to leave the fortifications strictly alone, 'the which the King himself did sign'. Sir Thomas Palmer was sent with the Council's instructions to Boulogne, but, before his going, Henry secretly 'sent for him into his privy chamber', and bade him carry to Grey a private message instructing him to ignore the official communiqué and destroy the French fort. 'This my message', said Henry, 'shall be his clearing therein, and the service gratefully accepted.' Sir Thomas was anything but happy, and reminded his sovereign that it was unlikely that anyone would credit the word of a simple knight which was in flat contradiction to 'the import of his majesty's writing'. Abruptly, the King cut short the plea. 'Deliver thou the message,' he said, and leave Lord Grey to decide 'the executing thereof'.

When Palmer arrived at Boulogne and presented his contradictory messages, Lord Grey faced an embarrassing dilemma—to follow the advice of his own council, which unanimously warned him to obey the written word, or to deny every bureaucratic and military instinct and accept the spoken, informal and dangerous command of his sovereign. Protecting himself as best he could by requiring Palmer to repeat the King's words verbatim, while a clerk wrote them down, and by ordering Sir Thomas to sign the statement and the council to witness it, Lord Grey proceeded to do as the King required. That night he sallied forth and overthrew in four hours what it had taken the French three months to raise and 'so in great quietness returned into the town', and dispatched Palmer back to London with the news.

As Sir Thomas entered the presence-chamber, Henry spotted him even before he could make 'his reverencies', and shouted: 'What, will he do it or no?' And so anxious was he to hear the report that he refused to read the written dispatches and impatiently demanded that Palmer speak up then and there. When the King heard what Grey had done, he smiled and turned to his Council, quietly asking: 'How say ye, my lords? Chastilion, the new fort, is laid as flat as this flower.' One minister was unwary enough to walk into the trap and answered that whoever 'had done it was worthy to lose his head'. Straightway Henry contradicted him, announcing 'that he had rather lose a dozen such heads as his that so judged than one such servant that had done it'.[35]

Such language was typical Henrician hyperbole, for the King was for ever indulging in displays of bad temper, 'beknaving' Thomas Cromwell 'twice a week' and sometimes knocking 'him well about the pate', or savagely lashing out in what Stephen Gardiner described as 'whetting', a most unpleasant experience.[36] Histrionics, however, did not necessarily mean much, for in a century of experts Henry was a master in the rich and lusty style of his day: he referred to Luther as 'this weed, this dilapidated, sick and evil-minded sheep' and 'sooty wicket of hell', to Louis XII of France as a lacerator of 'the seamless garment of Christ', and to papists as 'barking preachers' and 'false prophets and sheep-cloaked wolves'.[37] Even the tough hide of Bishop Gardiner, however, could be pierced by such verbal tirades, and it was fortunate for the unknown minister who had brought upon himself the pregnant words about losing heads that there was no chance to test the statement, for the King was dead within the year.

Of all the instruments of political coercion, information is the most fundamental, for without it none of the others—taxation, law, police—can operate; each in turn is dependent upon precise and intimate data concerning numbers, incomes, actions and beliefs. It therefore behoved the King, as the father and nurse of his people, to know all. Knowledge, Henry sensed, was the indispensable hand-maiden of authority, and, when united with hard work and close attention to detail, it was the rock upon which his power rested. The gods of political success can only be propitiated by endless hours of clerical labour, and the power to manipulate one's fellow man varies directly with the sacrifices made in terms of eye-strain, long hours and mastery of detail. What every executive, royal or plebeian, seeks to achieve is a maximum of control with a minimum of effort. The trivia of power—a requisition for 'six score oaks' for the great hall at Westminster, an order to deliver saddles to Lady Elizabeth's stable, a warrant for William Goldsmith to be usher and door-ward of the mint in Bristol at ten pounds a year, passports, payments, pardons, pensions and promotions—were details which might safely be delegated,[38] but ultimate control had to be retained if the sovereign's authority was to be his own.

In the exercise of power appearances are deceptive, and, administratively speaking, Henry has had a singularly unfriendly press over the centuries. Modern historians, enchanted by the twentieth-century managerial man who is regular in his business habits and has read Max Weber on bureaucracy and power, have toppled the soldier, saint and sage from their place of honour in history. The picture treasured by every schoolboy is the image of Cardinal Wolsey groaning under his 'outrageous charge and labour' and suffering from 'a cold stomach, little sleep, pale visage and a thin belly', while bluff King Hal, with sophomoric disregard for business affairs and most of the worst features of a Bluebeard combined with an Old King Cole, idled away his time in extravagant locker-room frivolities.[39] The laments of foreign diplomats have been accepted uncritically when they grumbled about the King's intense delight in the hunt to the exclusion of sensible administrative pastimes, or complained of the cavalier fashion in which bureaucratic routine was swept aside by royal whim and ill-temper. Marillac reported that, as the King grew in years, so did he 'in loving rest and fleeing troubles', and Chapuys's sense of business was outraged by the thought of Henry spending his days 'in the field to divert his ill humour' and not attending to matters of state.[40] Some of this criticism is simply irritation on the part of men who had to chase after a perambulating prince no matter what the state of their health, but most of it is a reflection of the fact that the tempo of government varied tremendously, especially during the winter months when there was plenty of time for relaxation. The portrait of a wan and exhausted Wolsey is an early war-time exception, and as the years slipped by the great Cardinal found occasion to wax fat and florid. At a post as important as Calais, the Lord Deputy, Lord Berners, spent his days translating Froissart, *The Golden Book* of Marcus Aurelius and three

other works, largely because he did not have enough to do. The
French Ambassador confessed that 'often for fifteen to twenty days
there is no talk of state affairs' because cold and snow had brought
war and diplomacy to a halt, and in November 1545 Paget reported
that he was left alone, the rest gone, 'some home, some to the term,
some a hawking and some a hunting'.[41]

To make matters worse, Henry's work habits were scarcely commendable to either modern historian or sixteenth-century diplomat.
He preferred late hours, dedicating the morning to the chase and the
early afternoon to eating, and he interviewed foreign ambassadors
on impulse and at erratic times, often postponing the real work of
government until midnight.[42] Moreover, he liked short cuts and out-
lines. If a letter was too long, he would not take the pains to read
it;[43] if a report was not in capsule form—clear, concise and full of
pertinent suggestions—he complained, scolding Norfolk for his
letters full of 'extreme and desperate mischiefs' but remiss in 'honest
remedy', and congratulating Cranmer for precise theological answers
to the royal queries.[44]

Under the tinsel and trappings, the gay routine of dog-tricks, wild-
boar hunts and carousing on the Thames, and the vast sums spent
on gambling and jewellery,* there was an observant and cautious
administrator who never relaxed his vigil, pried into the most trivial
detail of state, and scrutinized with suspicious care every cog of the
machinery designed to relieve him of the drudgery of power. The
right to 'forge' the King's name was granted to a handful of chosen
intimates of the chamber—Anthony Denney, William Herbert, William Paget, William Clerk, John Gate and others—but the procedure
was prudently circumscribed: only three men ever received such
authority at any given time; an impression of the King's signature
was pressed upon a document and the indentation was carefully outlined in ink by one of the three while the other two looked on;
regularly the three men had to be pardoned 'of all treasons concerning the counterfeiting, impression and writing of the king's sign
manual'; and every document so signed had to be described and
listed in a book, each page of which was initialled by Henry
monthly.[45] Since the King was the fountain of all that was good or
evil, everything from a pardon for murder to a recommendation for
marriage required his signature. The right to pardon belonged to the
Crown alone but the mechanics of mercy could be left to others, and
Joan Lucas, who had attacked her sister-in-law Joan Gowme with a

* Between November 1529 and December 1532 Henry spent £10,801 8s. 9d. on
jewellery and £3,243 5s. 10d. on cards, dice, tennis and wagers (Nicolas, *Privy
Purse Expenses*, pp. xxiv, xxix).

'bed-staff ... inflicting mortal wounds whereof she languished' for twenty days and then finished her off by breaking her neck 'with both her hands', received her reprieve signed with the dry stamp. Likewise Roland Hunt, groom of the chamber, when he asked his royal master to write the widow Alice Moore praising his matrimonial qualifications, had to make do with William Clerk's 'forgery' of the King's signature.[46]

The regular and routine matters of state were largely handled by the Council, but again conciliar action was scrupulously inspected by the monarch. On Sunday evenings Henry was presented with a list of the Council's business for the following week, and he himself drew up the agenda. On Fridays the Principal Secretary would summarize the week's work and next day present each item for the sovereign's approval or seek his decision on open questions. If an issue required immediate attention and could not wait until Saturday, the Council would send the Lord Chancellor or Sir William Paget directly to the King's closet for royal action,[47] and regularly Henry made his secretary write marginal comments on the Council's deliberations: 'The King likes these articles and desireth you to go through with them,' The King is pleased,' 'The King has given to him and his heirs one hundred marks by the year,' or 'Order shall be given on knowing what the sum is and to whom payable.'[48]

The Council was an adjunct of kingship, the trumpet through which royalty spoke, and in theory there was no limit to its competence. It was the Privy Council which issued orders for prayers for the success of the Emperor's army against the Turks, wrote out harsh decrees against horse-stealing, arranged for provisions to be sent to the Scottish border, organized flood-relief for Ely, cared for the King's timber in the north, established the price of fuel in London, decided whether a band of Portuguese immigrants were godly Christian merchants or despicable Jewish money-lenders, settled a particularly scandalous marital dispute between William Bulmer and his wife Jane, and scolded the wife of Mr Huick for lewd and unfaithful behaviour.[49] But in all their proceedings there is scarcely a hint of policy-making, and the most significant words of the Privy Council are those confessing that the lords of the Council were 'loath to offend' their master by 'doing too much or too little'.[50] Henry never dignified his Council with his presence; instead he remained aloof, the puppeteer pulling the strings of government, all of which were gathered in his hands.

The monarch's command of the minutiae of power was prodigious. He was endowed with an encyclopedic memory and could recall the hundreds of gifts, annuities and offices bestowed upon the hordes of petitioners who attached themselves to the royal bounty.[51] He inspected with care his wife's household, maintained a book signed with his own hand listing every government servant who had entry into his chamber, along with their diets and accommodations at court, kept a 'check roll' of all those who attended upon his son, and perused each land deal or government licence in which a minister was a partner, haggling over the terms and protecting the Crown's interests.[52]

Henry Tudor was an incorrigible annotator and editor, and he had a passion for clarity and order. The evidence, at least in the closing years of his life, of the care with which he reviewed the critical documents of his rule is overwhelming.[53] He systematically outlined the reports of his ambassadors as a schoolboy might underline his textbook, underscoring sentences and placing subject headings in the margins.[54] Wherever a word inadvertently chosen by his Council touched his honour, he jumped on it. When clerks drafted a proclamation announcing the need for uniformity in religion and spoke of the 'terrible' laws by which diversity would be rooted out he changed 'terrible' to 'good and just' laws.[55] When his bishops suggested that not even princes could kill or use bodily coercion except 'according to the just order of their laws', he replaced 'princes' with 'inferior rulers'.[56] Even when his self-esteem was not involved, he was for ever improving on his servants' words, spelling out the sense of their sentences, concerning himself with quibbles, and probing for possible misinterpretations. When his theologians introduced their discussion of the first article of the Creed ('I believe in God the Father Almighty') by simply saying 'for the plain understanding of this article', Henry felt obliged to add: 'ye must understand that we intend to declare every material word of the same.'[57] In the sixth article the thorough sovereign, who delighted in supplying the reader with clear road-signs, added to the statement that Christ was the sole mediator between God and man the words: 'according as hereafter in this book it shall more largely appear'. In all he did, the King sought to maintain exactly that level of precision. He sent detailed instructions and maps for the defence of Boulogne with orders to construct a shooting-gallery 'twelve foot wide within' and boarded with planks 'of two inches thick' and made 'so full of holes that a great number may stand and shoot out of them at one time'.[58] Laboriously he studied the military procedures for Hull and signed the monthly pay schedule. With painstaking and redundant care he insisted that the master mason and master carpenter should sit with the paymaster on pay-day 'if they be not sick', and that the paymaster should receive sixpence a day for a clerk 'to help to write his book'.[59] The same pedantic elaborations can be found in his doctoring of *The Bishops' Book* and the Six Articles of 1539. He felt it insufficient that the Articles should limit his title of Supreme Head to 'this church of England', and he enlarged the jurisdiction to encompass 'this whole church and congregation of England'. He regarded the fourth article deficient when it spoke only of vows of chastity and, just to be on the safe side, included 'widowhood'. Finally, when his prelates compared Jesus's conquest of hell to Samson's slaying of 'the mighty lion', exactness required that he note that Samson's 'powers be not comparable' to Christ's.[60]

It is sometimes said that Henry preferred to work through a secretary,[61] but if he did, such assistance saved him little effort. His labours in theology and the formulation of doctrine, though random and often contradictory, are an impressive edifice of marginalia, corrections, queries, additions and citations. He read and corrected the Ten Articles of 1536; the following year he annotated and criticized at length *The Bishops' Book*; he wrote Bishop Tunstal in 1539 a long and learned treatise on auricular confession and he composed his own defence of purgatory; he rewrote the Six Articles of 1539; he scrutinized with recondite care the answers of his clerics to questions regarding the true nature of the sacraments; and large sections of the final religious formula of his reign, *The King's Book*, which reflected the Supreme Head's most mature views on what his Christian subjects should believe, are in his own hand.[62]

In matters of state the same hard-working enthusiasm is apparent. Henry kept tight control over diplomatic affairs, holding at least 108 audiences with foreign emissaries between 1538 and 1546.[63] He wrote personally to the Privy Council about Gering, the overseer of the works for Nonsuch Palace, to discover the truth of the man's claim that he had been away from his job at the Council's bidding.[64] He acknowledged Lord Cobham's request for venison to help him maintain the hospitality and dignity of his office of Lord Deputy of Calais,[65] and he even interested himself in the matrimonial difficulties of Stephen Vaughan, his financial expert at Antwerp. Mr Vaughan had lost his wife and wrote to both Wriothesley and Paget to help him locate a new spouse, England being, he said, 'full of widows' and 'the King's Majesty' being 'my gracious good lord'. The unfortunate man was highly particular in his feminine tastes, and reminded his friends that he was 'declining now towards age' and that 'an honest woman that feareth God is above all riches'. If Paget could discover a candidate who was neither 'sharp, foolish, drunk' nor 'sluttish', he was to 'keep her in store'. The lady eventually chosen turned out to be only moderately wealthy, but this defect was more than balanced by her honest demeanour, godly reputation and domestic qualities as a stepmother for his many children. The King, however, was more concerned with Vaughan's efforts to borrow money from the Fuggers on behalf of the Crown than with his marital negotiations and refused to allow him to leave his post, but he did bless the union by permitting the lady to travel to Calais. Moreover, he responded favourably to Vaughan's plea that they be licensed 'to marry there without banns' and without the permission of the Archbishop of Canterbury, 'who therein will make no small scruple'.[66] God's royal vicar on earth was considerably more understanding of the needs of busy financial agents than the Archbishop, and was quite ready to circumvent Cranmer's spiritual authority in the name of governmental convenience.

Henry maintained the same careful watch in the privacy of his closet, requiring his secretaries, Sir William Petre and Paget—and before them Wriothesley—to submit their drafts to him with two-and-a-half-inch margins and inch-wide spacing between the lines so that he could scribble his corrections.[67] The records are riddled with references to instructions, devices and letters in 'his own handwriting', and in 1529 Erasmus noted the care with which the King commented, suppressed, corrected and altered his own epistles. 'You might recognize the first drafting of a letter,' he said, 'and you might make out the second and third and sometimes even the fourth correction: but whatever was revised or added was in the same handwriting.'[68] There is an Elizabethan legend that when Secretary Petre was mortified by his master's brutal handling of his prose—the King 'crossed and blotted out many things'—Henry kindly turned to him and bade him recall that 'it is I that made both Cromwell, Wriothesley and Paget good secretaries, and so must I do to thee'. Tactfully he explained that princes 'know best their own meaning, and there must be time and experience to acquaint' their secretaries 'with their humours before a man can do any acceptable service'.[69]

The King's humours, unfortunately, were often without humour, for he took his office with deadly seriousness, and fancied himself as a combined father-confessor and inspector-general. Henry could be generous and considerate to a Vaughan, but he refused to comply with Catherine of Aragon's bequest of her clothes and personal property until he had seen 'what the robes and furs were like', and he denied her a queen's burial at St Paul's on the grounds that the cost would be more 'than was either requisite or needful'.[70] He was outraged with Lord Lisle, captain of Boulogne, at the thought that his officers were squandering military supplies, and he grumbled that 'if such excessive waste continues it will avail little to be at such charges for keeping and fortifying the town' [71] With Sir Richard Riche, the treasurer of the English army in France, he was even sharper, and when Sir Richard reported that 8,000 men in fourteen days had gone through £55,348 17s. 3d., a sum which the King darkly noted should have been sufficient for an army of 42,000, he directed that Riche submit 'a more plain and more certain declaration'.[72] By the winter of the 'old man's' life, the lavish prince of story-book fame, if he ever existed, had long since been transformed into a monarch who kept careful count of pounds, shillings and pence.[73]

'There was no movement made anywhere, however secret, of which he had not notice ... ',[74] and the gospel according to King Henry was a pedant's delight: be informed of everything. His servants were carefully schooled in the creed, and Paget confessed that in his diplomatic correspondence he was always careful to include 'matters of no great importance', for he thought 'it meet that his majesty should know all'.[75] When Sir William Petre made the mistake of generalizing about French affairs, he was quickly told to write 'not generally' but in detail exactly what the French King 'likes or mislikes, that we may not mistake his resolution'.[76] Nor was it sufficient that English diplomats directed their letters to Wriothesley or Paget on the ground that there was no news worthy of reading by the monarch.[77] No matter how trifling the subject, Henry wanted to know directly, and he spared no expense either in extracting information through bribery or in maintaining a post which could handle messages at breakneck speed.[78] Dispatches dated December 29th, 1545, from Paget in Calais were received and answered the following day by the Privy Council, after consultation with the King.[79] Marillac was astonished that Henry knew of the fall of Castelnuovo to the Turks two days before the news arrived in France, and he concluded that 'there is not a single bruit anywhere which he does not hear among the first, be it false or true, even to little private matters which princes care but little to hear. He speaks as if he knew not only kings and lords but their ministers, armed forces, families, designs and exploits ... as if he had men all over the world who did nothing but write to him.'[80] Doubtless Henry was posing for the French Ambassador's benefit, for it flattered his vanity that he should be the best-informed sovereign in Europe. Information, however, was something more than a diplomatic convenience; the King had a mind that required and thrived upon detailed knowledge.

The German sociologist Max Weber many years ago exposed the central issue surrounding the exercise of political power within the modern state when he pointed out the tension resulting from a dilettante prince or any head of state seeking to maintain his independence of action in the face of the ever-increasing preponderance of trained technicians.[81] Specialized knowledge, be it in medicine, law or theology, is almost impossible for the layman to refute, and most of the tragedies of state policy stem from the collision between the well-meaning follies of amateurs and the comic profundities of professionals. Henry, however, confounds the Weber thesis, standing it on its head. He was a virtuoso who dominated by the sheer weight of his erudition a Cabinet composed of confused, if hard-working, amateurs. The sovereign was, in the words of an admiring contemporary, 'a perfect theologian, a good philosopher, and a strong man at arms, a jeweller, a perfect builder as well of fortresses as of pleasant palaces, and from one to another there was no necessary kind of knowledge, from a King's degree to a carter's, but he had an honest sight of it'.[82] The statement is more than egregious adulation. The monarch knew his Church Fathers better than most ecclesiastics, and Erasmus noted that he had been soundly schooled in history by his father.[83] His library at Westminster alone contained almost a thousand volumes, for the most part annotated Bibles, concordances and glosses; Church histories, chronicles and the early patristic scholars; Aristotle, Cicero and Thucydides; manuals on hunting, hawking and chivalry; and, above all, the great schoolmen— Aquinas, Albertus Magnus, Bonaventura, John of Salisbury, Abelard and others.[84] Campeggio, the Papal Legate, admitted during the long theological dispute over the legality of the King's marriage that Henry had done his homework so diligently 'that I believe in this case he knows more than a great theologian or jurist'.[85]

Long before the divorce placed a premium on total theological recall, the King's omnivorous thirst for trivia compelled him to master every facet of the strict ritual surrounding the joust, state functions and religious pageants.[86] Later, the same attention to and methodical analysis of copious detail and the careful absorption of information were applied to war. Henry's military competence ranged from archery, ballistics, fortifications and logistics to surveying, strategy and tactics, and he proved himself a better authority on French tidal waters than even the specialists. His evaluation of the effectiveness of Ambleteuse as a victualling port for Boulogne was vindicated in the face of the expert advice on which Hertford was relying.[87] Early in the reign, the Venetian Ambassador was astounded that Henry, when he visited the Venetian merchant fleet at Southampton, 'had all the guns fired again and again, marking their range, as he is very curious about such matters'.[88] The same love of precision appeared later in life when the King demanded of the busy Earl of Hertford a technical report on the performance and speed of a new ship he had sent to the fleet.[89] The result was that even a Lord Admiral, albeit a somewhat amateurish one, accepted his master's greater naval knowledge without reservation. At Portsmouth during the French war Lord Lisle was fulsome in his humility in the face of royal expertise, assuring his master that he would attempt nothing against the French fleet anchored outside the harbour until he had made the King privy to every plan and had received the benefit of his instructions. Indeed, the commander confessed that he had learned all he knew from Henry himself, and it was little joy 'being so near the fountain' to 'die for thirst'.[90] Even a veteran campaigner such as Hertford remarked that he would happily go into debt a thousand marks more than he was 'on condition that the King's Majesty were here but for one hour, where his grave and prudent advice' would be indispensable.[91] The flattery is transparent but there remains a residuum of truth—the eighth Henry was an excellent technician.

The picture of that mountain of quiddities, technical files and biblical quotations is pedantic but not totally displeasing. Henry admired and enjoyed scholarship and the camaraderie of intellectual discovery, and, as the Spanish Ambassador perceived, he was always 'more accessible to persuasion than to threat'.[92] At one time he had discussed geometry, mathematics and astronomy with Sir Thomas More, and at night they had watched together 'the diversities, courses, notions and operations of the stars and planets', and had speculated on the marvels of the cosmos.[93] As late as 1529, even as the theological and polemical war surrounding the divorce was mounting, Erasmus could write: 'The king has never given up the pursuits of the mind, and as often as the business of his realm permits, he either reads or discusses. He is a man of great friendliness, and gentle in debate; he acts more like a companion than a king.'[94] It was easy enough for a monarch of great personal charm who possessed an encyclopedic memory, tightly packed with scriptural and military data, temporarily to divest himself of his divinity and rest his argument and superior authority on his own expertise.

The King approached scholarship with a respect born of five hundred years of scholastic tradition. Training in syllogistic reasoning and emphasis upon historic authority came early in life, and young Prince Edward was a master of the syllogism at the age of nine, treating his father to the argument: 'As war brings on noise and tumult, so does peace usher in tranquillity. Noise and riot is an evil; therefore war is an evil. Rest is a blessing; therefore peace is a blessing.'[95] Henry himself was an expert in the same kind of debate, and he did not hesitate to bring the heavy sword of logic to bear on the enemies of God: matrimony, he maintained, is accepted as a worldly concern, and priests are not to involve themselves in secular negotiations, ergo no priest should marry.[96] Like any sound scholastic the King's notion of winning an argument was to call in the massive artillery of erudition and to engage in a pedantic duel of quotations drawn from history, scripture or the Church Fathers. His longest theological treatise, *The Defence of the Seven Sacraments*, a refutation of the heretic Luther, is exactly this—one hundred references from thirty books of the Bible and seventy quotations from the Church Fathers—one-third from St Augustine, one-third from Jerome, Ambrose and Gregory, and the rest from other patristic authors.[97] The sovereign's long, dull, dry defence of his title to the throne of Scotland is a scholastic marvel of ancient histories which he called 'the light of truth and the life of memory', and of obscure instruments of homage and 'registers and records, judiciously and authentically made'.[98] He even went so far as to urge the Archbishop of York to search his archives for further authorities and precedents. His answer to Bishop Tunstal's defence of auricular confession was typical of his style of debate. It irritated him that Tunstal, after all his texts and authorities had been answered by Cranmer and the King in a public display of mental gymnastics, should have sought to continue the argument in private. With mock servility he accused the prelate of attacking him when he stood defenceless without his theologians about him and 'so by mine ignorant answers to win the field'. Then, marshalling his wits, which he confessed were 'not the wiseliest', he proceeded to bury Tunstal's position under a mountain of patristic citations.[99]

Martin Luther, who had suffered from Henry's ponderous scholastic tactics, rudely dismissed the English sovereign as a 'comic jester', a 'miserable scribbler' and a petty 'glossator, colouring everything with glosses and illusions' and for ever missing or ignoring the point.[100] Henry never forgot or forgave those words, for they struck at the core of his thinking, dismissing as trifles the intellectual pillars on which all his actions rested: 'to search, examine and inquire' into the truth of a proposition and to judge it on grounds of logic or historic and divine authority.[101]

As the years pressed in upon a monarch who liked to confound his subjects with his learning, and as younger men grew restless in the face of royal scholarship which had failed to change with the times, Henry sought to strengthen his professional standing by appeal to that most irritating and unanswerable of authorities: old age. More and more the past was viewed as a useful storehouse of memories and experiences which could be brought out, dusted off and displayed for the benefit of the present. The process involved a convenient amount of forgetting, fabricating and falsifying, so that the dreary and unpleasant facts of yesterday could become the rosy fictions of today. 'Thus is woven that vast and tangled web of error, prejudice and special pleading we call history.'[102] Henry was for ever attesting to 'the white hairs in his beard' and boasting of the wisdom that comes with years. To his nephew James V of Scotland he sadly observed that 'being a king ... these thirty years' had given him understanding into 'the general state and proceeding of Christendom'; to the Spanish Ambassador he sighed and said that he had been a prince for forty years 'and no man could say that he had ever acted otherwise than sincerely and openly'; and to Paget he spoke about 'knowing by experience the practices of the world'. As he grew older he indulged more and more in the old man's fancy that age is wiser than youth. He told the Yorkshire rebels in 1536 that 'seeing we have been these twenty-eight years your king' he knew better now than when he had commenced his reign 'what were the commonwealth and what were not'.[103]

Towards the end, the coarse hide of obstinacy, toughened by advancing years and professional vanity, made the King, in the words of John Foxe, 'very stern and opinionate'.[104] Even Thomas Cranmer with all his theological training was careful to acknowledge his monarch's greater skill and not to cross his will, and at the conclusion of his discussion on the nature of the seven sacraments he wrote: 'This is mine opinion and sentence at this present, which I do not temerariously define, and do remit the judgment thereof wholly unto your majesty.'[105] Three years later in 1543 Henry disputed at length with his Archbishop the question of justification by faith alone, until Cranmer finally retreated before the King's erudition.[106] When expertise was fortified with a marvellous memory for detail, a clear if simplistic sense of logic and great personal magnetism, and when it was utilized as an instrument of authority, subjects did well to make a distinction between their own fond fancies and his majesty's greater knowledge. The distinction, however, was not simply a question of political prudence. In the final analysis the quality of Henry's learning was more important than the quantity. No matter how technical the debate, the King held the trump card. His knowledge was special, for it stemmed from God Himself; he was always 'Harry with the Crown'. Paget might speak of 'law and religion', Cranmer might cite a host of theological precedents, and Hertford could display his impressive title of Lord Protector, but nothing could substitute for the divinity that 'doth hedge a king'.

Throughout the long reign, power never stood alone and naked; it was always adorned in the gorgeous gowns of divinity. It was Henry's ability to live a dream, to maintain the myth that royal authority and learning stemmed from on high, which transformed the petty tyrannies of an opinionated old man into the majesty of a king, so that Paget could sincerely exclaim: 'Our Lord save him in which in this world, next God, is the cause of my comfort, of my joy and of all felicity.'[107] The difference between what is real and what is make-believe is not always clear, and occasionally a touch of paranoia is useful to both men and society. The spy, for instance, who has a highly developed persecution complex, and really believes that he is being shot at, may be better suited for survival in a world of espionage than a more normal individual. On the same grounds, Henry's intense conceit that he spoke for God was essential to his survival as a sovereign in a society which found it necessary for its own well-being to believe in the direct interference of the deity in the affairs of men.

3

The Emperor's New Clothes

Upon the King! let us our lives, our souls,
Our debts, our careful wives,
Our children, and our sins lay on the King!
We must bear all. O hard condition!
... What infinite heart's ease
Must Kings neglect that private men enjoy!
And what have Kings that privates have not too,
Save ceremony, save general ceremony?
Henry V, IV, i

It is well to remember—Mr John Hales wrote to Sir Anthony Browne —that in approaching royalty Englishmen had 'not to do with man but with a more excellent and divine estate', and such was the majesty which surrounded a prince that it was difficult to stand before a king without trembling.[1] It is not easy for the twentieth century to reconstruct the mentality of a generation which grovelled before that immense bag of windy conceit that claimed to speak for God, and it is possible to maintain that the extravagant adoration of Henry's 'divine prudence' was either prodigal flattery or meaningless jargon mouthed by everybody but believed by nobody. On the other hand, those who require a more rational and socially oriented explanation can point to the words of the Bishop of Winchester, who knew all about the instruments by which the 'better part' of society sought to dominate the larger part. 'If we', he said, 'desire the name of king to be sacred, which all good men desire ... we must take care lest any stigma be cast upon this name by others.'[2] Presumably a deliberate social conspiracy was operating; the worshippers closest to the altar of monarchy appreciated that their own authority rested on translating theological fiction into ceremonial reality. As with the emperor and his new clothes, no one cared to reveal the King's true nakedness, for every Tudor official knew that the art of successful government resided as much in the meticulous staging of 'pompous circumstance' and the magic of political lighting as in the awkward axe of coercion. There is, however, more to divinity than meets the eye. The unadorned truth may have been a carefully concealed political secret, but the mantle of majesty with which every loyal

heart dressed its sovereign was very much in the eye of the be-
holder.

Possibly Lucien Febvre was correct in maintaining that the sixteenth century was visually retarded, and that it reacted more
directly to what was heard, smelled or touched than to what it saw.[3]
Subjects may indeed have responded to the trumpet-call of majesty
and to the odour of divine sanctity, but more important than any
ocular deficiency was Tudor England's absolute conviction that the
idea of majesty was more real than the physical trappings. When
Henry welcomed Anne of Cleves in January 1540 and rode with her
in state into Greenwich, the chronicler Edward Hall was unable to
see reality: a paunchy and middle-aged monarch disgusted by the
sight of his frumpy and pock-marked bride. Instead he lyrically
recorded a vision: 'Oh what a sight was this, to see so goodly a Prince
and so noble a King to ride so fair a lady of so goodly a stature
and so womanly a countenance, and in especial of so good qualities,
I think no creature could see them but his heart rejoiced.'[4]

The ability to separate the ideal from the real, and at the same
time to endow it with a reality of its own, was a deeply ingrained
mental habit which the sixteenth century owed to the philosophy of
Platonic realism developed by the schoolmen of medieval Europe.
Man's ontological imagination can be extraordinarily vivid: the
good, the courageous, the virtuous, the honourable and the evil are
for the Platonic mind no mere intellectual contrivances devised to
handle a multitude of particular actions, but are sensible realities in
their own right. They exist like 'some brooding omnipresence in the
sky', eternal metaphysical models which can be discovered but can
never be created by man since they belong to the domain of God.

Realism pervaded almost every facet of sixteenth-century thought,
conditioning its intellectual outlook and its emotional response to
life.[5] Page, groom, councillor, gentleman and king assumed that sin,
honour, glory and faith were actual entities. When Henry wrote of
searching for 'the culpe, blame, default and occasion of so many
evils' in society, he used those words not as convenient ways of
describing undesirable actions but as palpable realities to be discovered and rooted out like so much anthracite from a coal-mine.[6]
Honour and renown for the heroes of the sixteenth century were as
real as the Holy Grail. 'Good men of noble aspiration', it was said in
Spain, 'must seek life and must go from the good thing to the better
... and try to win honour.'[7] In England William Caxton told his
readers that 'it is most fair to men mortal to suffer labours and pain
for glory and fame immortal';[8] and Henry himself, old, gouty and
bald, wrote his brother-sovereign, the King of France, that 'you

greatly touch our honour, the which, as you are aware, having always guarded inviolably to this present, I will never consent in my old age that it shall be anyway distained'.[9] The King's view of his honour is perfectly clear: it was a reality, almost material in its substance, to be cherished and protected as closely as the most brilliant jewel in his treasury.

The war of rival truths which broke out when Martin Luther nailed his defiance to a Wittenberg church door was scarcely unique in the sixteenth century, but the conflict acquired an emotional intensity peculiar to a way of thinking which conceived of truth as a physical verity. Henry may have been indulging in the conceit of the expert scholar when he said that he was right on the issue of his divorce with Catherine of Aragon 'not because so many saith it, but because he, being learned, knoweth the matter to be right', but he was also voicing the general conviction of his generation when he concluded that he had found the truth 'so certain, so evident, so manifest, so open and approved' that it 'ought to be allowed and received' by all Christian men.[10] The truth for Henry and all his subjects was something to be discerned, defended and, if necessary, written down in blood. In understanding early Tudor England the twentieth century is at a disadvantage; it cannot see the emperor's new clothes or Henry's mantle of majesty; it cannot perceive the cloaks of virtue, the crowns of glory or the black gowns of evil.

The mind which fills the universe with lucid Platonic realities must also populate the earth with clear and rigid social models: the ideal cleric, the perfect knight, the true gentleman and the humble peasant. Most societies tend to think in terms of stereotypes, featureless figments possessing exaggerated group-characteristics—the avaricious Jew, the lewd Frenchman, the rich American, the fat banker, the Prince Charming. But these are imaginary short cuts which permit men to group their impressions into manageable units; the banker does not have to be fat to qualify for his profession, nor the prince charming. Platonic social types, on the other hand, are quite different. They are hollow containers filled with qualities suited to their shape. The Tudor social philosopher approached his subject as did the sixteenth-century physician. As the four humours found in varying proportions in man—the phlegmatic, the melancholic, the choleric, and the sanguine—were not simply metaphors to describe human character but physiological entities, so the ideas of courage, avarice, love, loyalty and honour found in the body politic were psychological realities.[11] As the complexion, colour and habits of the doctor's patient were thought to reveal his internal temperament, so a man's actions in society signified his inner disposition. The tree was known by its fruits: the good pastor could be discerned by his acts of piety, charity and love; and the perfect knight was revealed by his deeds of loyalty, courage and generosity. Men were frail vessels filled with virtues and vices, and Henry never doubted that 'if I know a man which liveth in adultery, I must judge him a lecherous and a carnal person; if I see a man boast and brag himself, I cannot but deem him a proud man'.[12] The possibility that the walls which man presents to the outside world, however transparent they may appear, can obscure and distort the reflection of the true character within, or the concept that bragging can be a sign of insecurity rather than of pride, was totally foreign.

Rarely did those about the King seek to analyse the nature of his office, nor did they conceive of kingship as a public corporation. Instead they beheld a series of royal stances—generous acts, honourable acts, just acts, courageous acts—each reflecting the idea of monarchy. As Paget said: 'For a king, do like a king'; and when Henry learned that James V of Scotland besmirched the role of clean-fingered royalty with the filthy profits of sheep-raising, he warned that such actions 'cannot stand well with the honour of his estate', and that they would surely 'cause his subjects to mutter and mutiny'.[13] Henry instinctively knew that princes could survive the hatred of their subjects but never their scorn.[14]

A sixteenth-century sovereign lived his life upon a public stage, where he could enact his kingly role and display his royal worth. The monarch who did nothing was as empty as the hero who stayed at home, but the king who did the wrong thing and stepped out of character brought upon himself the contempt of his subjects. The script by which princes lived was known to both actor and audience, for it had been written by God Himself. John Lyly's king was no idler, but 'goeth up and down, entreating, threatening, commanding ... but not losing the dignity of a Prince'.[15] Thomas Cromwell was overcome with the image of kingship in operation. 'It was a wonder to see', he wrote in 1537, 'how princely, with how excellent gravity, and inestimable majesty, His Majesty exercised' the office of supreme 'head of his Church of England'.[16] The same awe was voiced by William Petre in describing Henry's last emotion-packed speech to parliament. The King used words 'so sententiously, so kingly or rather fatherly', that they brought tears to the eyes, and Sir William confessed that the performance 'was such a joy and marvellous comfort as I reckon this day one of the happiest of my life'.[17] Petre and Cromwell were kindred spirits—efficient, scrupulous, rational and devoted administrators of the Crown—and both of them knew the biological realities of the master they served, but, like every other loyal subject, they presumed a greater reality: the majesty which encompassed the person of their sovereign.

Tudor England was well aware where the safety and security of the prince resided—not in 'outward humility and humble obeisance', not in kneeling bare-headed before the King, but in wishing him well 'with heart and mind'.[18] A carefully conditioned mind supported by an enthusiastic heart was a far surer prop to monarchy than a wall of statutes or an army of civil servants, for no amount of legislation could cleanse the disloyal breast, and all the tax-collectors in the world could not make generous the mean and avaricious. In later reigns English monarchs had cause to complain that loyalty, though fervently and eloquently spoken, did not always go as deep as a man's pocket-book. As the century grew longer, the subsidy rolls grew shorter, but under Henry VIII the Crown succeeded in an unprecedented fashion in unlocking a subject's purse as well as his heart. Moreover, the personal safety of the sovereign was never in question. Kings were for ever being blamed for the calamities of their age, and there were a few who held that therefore it made no difference if Henry 'were knocked or patted on the head'.[19] But these attacks came largely from the religious lunatic fringe, and were confined to words not deeds. For most Englishmen the myth of royal invulnerability still held, and the silver bullets, magic potions and sacred daggers from which later sovereigns had to be protected were never used against the shield of divine majesty which surrounded the Emperor Charles, Francis I and the eighth Henry. The royal taster was a ceremonial relic, the two hundred yeomen of the guard were largely for show, and the only security measure which Henry seems to have taken was to bring with him, when travelling on progress, his own bolts and rings for his chamber door.[20] Sixteenth-century subjects possessed a built-in restraint: if they harmed the King in thought or deed, Satan would surely gather them to hell. It was clearly written: God waited upon the King's health, keeping 'all his bones that not one of them shall be broken' and preserving him 'from all the crafty conspirations and subtle assaults of all his enemies'.[21]

Henry rarely spoke of his special association with God except when his authority was in question, but his letters and conversations were thick with allusions to the obvious: 'with God's help', 'if the grace of God forsake us not', and 'my discharge afore God'.[22] As a young man he had dreamed of an imperial crown equal to that of the Holy Roman Emperor, and he had taken seriously his descent from the legendary hero King Arthur and the Emperor Constantine.[23] He was also quite sure that only the divinely ordained king could have 'subjects'; the rest of society had to make do with 'inferiors'.[24] At his coronation God had been invoked to bestow on him 'the dew of heaven and the fatness of the earth and the plenty of the corn and wine'. His sceptre was a mystical staff; the canopy over his throne was the symbolic shield protecting his kingdom, and he had been anointed with the holy oil supposedly used by Edward the Confessor and rediscovered by Richard II.[25] No wonder Sir Francis Bryan is reported to have said: 'I would rather for my part stick to the devising of a King that hath *majesty* in him' than to a thousand Lutherans put together.[26]

Realism leads inevitably to anthropomorphism and animism. Virtues and vices were endowed with tongue, mind and body, and when Richard Cox urged his pupil, Prince Edward, to do battle with Ignorance and all his friends, to conquer Captain Will, that 'ungracious fellow', and to curb Captain Oblivion, he was not simply appealing to a small boy's imagination or indulging in a literary ploy.[27] He was displaying a habit of mind which preferred to equip abstractions with corporeal and social substance. The perceptual world in which Henry lived was in a constant state of flux, for animated abstractions did not have to comply with physical laws of this earth;[28] they were quite capable of changing their shapes. Hailstones the size of eggs fell from the sky with the faces of devils on them, rain turned to blood, animals behaved like men, decapitated traitors chased about the countryside holding their heads in their arms, and when a high wind blew down St Alkmund's church steeple, it was authoritatively reported that Satan had left as his trademark great talon scratches on the fourth bell.[29]

Animism could be dangerously superstitious when evil spirits were said to steal milk by turning themselves into hares and sucking the cows dry in the meadow, or when traitors sought the death of sovereigns by mutilating wax effigies of royalty.[30] *The Bishops' Book* spoke out against those who thought it 'unlucky to meet in a morning with certain kinds of beasts', and it condemned anyone who by 'astrology, divination, chattering of birds, physiognomy' and other means sought to foretell the future.[31] But the line between silly credulity and faith in God's miraculous ways was difficult to draw, and despite Thomas Cranmer's opposition the King insisted on removing astrology and physiognomy from the list of 'unlawful and superstitious crafts'.[32] Cranmer was scarcely in a strong position to oppose his master, for he had himself reported in October 1532 from Germany the spectacle of a blue cross above the moon and a great horse's head and flaming sword in the sky. 'What strange things these tokens do signify to come hereafter', he said, God alone knew, 'for they do not lightly appear, but against some great mutation'.[33] Possibly Henry felt that occupational jealousy was behind his prelate's position, for the King had a heavy investment in the stars; he maintained Nicholas Crazer as his Astronomer Royal at the cost of twenty pounds a year. It was well known that the celestial world was populated with highly corporeal and active inhabitants in the shape of cherubim and seraphim, intelligences and potentates, angels and archangels, many of whom conducted divine services 'all the day long' and took time off to listen to the appeals of men just 'before their matins and after their evensong'. Even the Pope was careful to synchronize his religious services with the portents of the stars.[34]

Much of the emotionalism so characteristic of the century was tied up with this animistic view of the world, for functions of state, war, politics and diplomacy were translated into anthropomorphic forms which could be directly and personally experienced. War was not an engagement of insensate social machines but a clash of heroes animated by hate, compassion and courage. Diplomacy was not the deliberate balancing of international power or the thoughtful calculation of foreign goals in terms of domestic means, but an encounter of individuals far more real than the power structures they represented. In the sixteenth century institutional authority devoid of princely features and personal responsibility was unimaginable. The modern Catholic, who in baffled outrage wonders whether Gardiner, Cranmer or Henry actually believed the 'blasphemous rubbish' that God's sovereignty could be transferred to a mortal king and a whole kingdom owe its salvation to the fanciful conscience of a single man,[35] confuses what is philosophically reasonable with what is psychologically possible. In an anthropomorphically orientated society, it is far easier to accept divinity in a man than to believe an institution to be divine. Of course, humility before God's royal or papal vicar on earth is not the same thing as the belief that he is the infallible channel through which the deity is obliged to speak. God has many vehicles by which to reveal His will, and it took no greater stretch of the imagination to believe that Henry spoke for God when he stood 'in his estate royal' conjoined in parliament with his subjects 'in one body politic' than to believe that the deity was present when the Pope spoke *ex cathedra*. The Renaissance world knew full well that Satan could take upon himself the face of prince or pontiff, but Henry's subjects held firmly to the creed that it was presumptuous to pass judgment upon the features of a king. It was sufficient that the symbol of majesty was that of Henry Tudor. For this reason, Bishop Gardiner bemoaned the destruction of religious images during the Reformation, for it weakened the ability to translate political abstractions into understandable human shapes, which he considered essential to the operation of good government. The illiterate peasant, he said, cannot comprehend the words imprinted on the king's great seal, 'yet he can read St George on horseback on the one side and the King sitting in his majesty on the other side; and readeth so much written in those images as, if he be an honest man, he will put off his cap'.[36]

The Bishop might have added that the same peasant, being a cautious as well as an honest man, would want to edit his thoughts before doffing his cap, for the ears and eyes of a king were as the ear and eye of God; they could see and hear into the secret hearts of subjects. 'Wish the king no evil in thy thought,' the pulpit warned, 'for a bird of the air shall betray thy voice, and with her feathers shall she betray thy words.'[37] Church and state were agreed that 'there is nothing hid that shall not come to light; neither is there any secret that shall not come to revelation', and Thomas Wriothesley warned all potential traitors that the King 'hath eyes and ears in the bottom of their bellies and the lining of their hearts'.[38] This truth was known to Mistress Catherine Howard, the King's fifth wife. When she cuckolded her royal spouse and indulged in her dangerous romance with Thomas Culpeper in the dark of the palace back-stairs, she sought to thwart God and escape the King's sharp ear by warning her lover not to give verbal shape, even in his mind, to their secret. Naively she begged him, when he went to confession, not to 'shrive him[self] of any such things as should pass betwixt her and him, for if he did, surely the King, being Supreme Head of the church, should have knowledge of it'.[39] The twentieth century will sweep the mystery aside and note that Tudor priests in and out of confessional were state spies, but a twenty-year-old Queen with a guilty conscience, who knew that angels kept their matins and evensong and God spoke intimately to kings, might have had a different explanation, even if she realized that in bed Henry behaved like any other man.

Majesty encased the living king like a tortoise-shell; without it he was a mortal man, and, as Catherine Howard knew, diseased and disgusting; with it the sovereign was a terrifying spectacle, a great lumbering Juggernaut before which the young Queen and all her generation prostrated themselves. Divinity was no more than the shine upon the shell, theological polish which enhanced the obvious—majesty and sovereignty were attributes of God Himself. Consequently it was necessary for a monarch to enact a role of kingship which was as close to the heavenly ideal as possible. The model was a composite of royalty, drawn largely from the wrathful personality

of Jehovah and the militant actions of Old Testament kings and
prophets. As the prophet Isaiah 'put on wrath instead of clothing and
took jealousy about him instead of a cloak', so also must royalty
dress.[40]

Punishment administered in blood was regarded in the sixteenth
century as sound politics, but the retribution which Henry visited
upon the luckless peasantry who defied his majesty during the
Pilgrimage of Grace was patterned directly after Jehovah. His
majestic anger made the Duke of Norfolk shudder when he was
ordered to 'cause such dreadful execution to be done upon a good
number of the inhabitants of every town, village and hamlet ... as
well by the hanging of them up on trees as by the quartering of them
and the setting of their heads and quarters in every town, great and
small ... as they may be a fearful spectacle to all others hereafter that
would practise any like matter; which we require you to do, without
any pity or respect'.[41]

Martin Luther's answer to peasant disobedience was just as bloody
as Henry's, but his style was that of a Thuringian coal-miner's son,
not of a king: 'A rebel is not worth answering with arguments, for he
does not accept them. The answer for such mouths is a fist that
brings blood from the nose.'[42] For Henry a bloody nose was not
enough, for

> ... to the king God hath his office lent
> Of dread, of justice, power, and command;
> Hath bid him rule, and wills you to obey.
> And, to add ampler majesty to this,
> He hath not only lent the king His figure,
> His throne and sword, but given him His own name,
> Calls him a god on earth. What do you then
> Rising 'gainst him that God Himself installs
> But rise 'gainst God?[43]

The Lord of lords, who bestowed upon Henry an 'ampler majesty'
and before whom he bowed down, was a God of wrath and vengeance,
but even Jehovah could be touched by mercy, 'for the Lord's hand
is not so shortened that it cannot help, neither is His ear so stopped
that it may not hear'.[44] The essence of sovereignty was not so much
the fixed exercise of stark retributive justice by which the good were
rewarded and the evil punished, as it was the quality of mercy un-
sullied by the claims of man. God is just, but He is also merciful in
order to prove the unconditional nature of His majesty. The very
capriciousness of His mercy is, in fact, the manifest proof of His
power. In both heavenly and earthly societies justice prevailed, but

subjects were not always asked to pay the full penalty for their sins. Policy demanded that a politically privileged nobility should be exempt from legislation designed to rule the vulgar multitude, but time and again it was the King's mercy, upon which no one could depend but on which all men might call, that stayed the operation of punitive law. As God saved as an act of will transcending justice, so Henry reprieved in order to prove his majesty and display his independence.

The essence of mercy is its unpredictability; in March 1542 the King let Mistress Margaret Davie boil for poisoning three members of the household where she worked, but three months later he pardoned Peter Mannying, a horse-leach, for murdering his pregnant wife by first wounding her with a sword and then throwing her down the stairs. That same year he saved a woman coin-clipper from death by burning even as she was being bound to the stake.[45] Again and again the King's mercy protected the privileged members of his chamber. Law-abiding citizens were shocked that Thomas Culpeper should be forgiven the violent rape of a park-keeper's wife and the murder of one of the villagers who sought to restrain him.[46] Court society thrilled when Sir Edmund Knyvet, who was condemned to lose his right hand for brawling with Sir Thomas Clere in the precincts of the royal court, was reprieved just as he placed his wrist upon the block and the knife was raised on high. As the French Ambassador drily commented, Sir Edmund was 'more frightened than hurt', and possibly this was the underlying purpose of a performance which was more a ritualistic punishment than an actual execution: the sergeant of the woodyard supplying the block, the King's master cook presenting the execution-knife and the sergeant of the poultry bringing the cock which 'should have his head smitten off upon the same block and with the same knife'.[47] But it was dangerous to presume too much; Culpeper might be pardoned of rape and murder outside the palace, but in November 1542 Mr Collins, gentleman, was hanged for manslaughter in the court grounds.[48]

The distinction between hope of benevolence and dependence on clemency was exquisitely subtle, for the man who placed no faith in the King's mercy dishonoured royalty as much as the man who felt that he had a claim upon it. In 1589 George Puttenham still judged that in 'a prince it is comely to give unasked, but in a subject to ask unbidden'; the first was a sign of a free and bountiful will, the latter of a loyal and confident heart, and he told the story of Henry VIII who was asked by one of his courtiers to remember Sir Anthony Rouse with some gift by way of recompense for the debts Sir Anthony had incurred in the royal service. The insult was twofold:

Rouse conceived of the King's mercy in terms of a reward for services rendered; worse, he was too proud and distrustful of the sovereign's generosity to petition for himself; and Henry answered: 'If he be ashamed to beg, we are ashamed to give.'[49]

It was difficult for a king to preserve the freedom essential to his majesty and at the same time it was tempting to indulge in the moral sadism of demanding abject confessions before extending the hand of mercy. The satisfaction which Henry received in assuring Wolsey that 'your faults acknowledged, there shall remain in me no spark of displeasure', or in telling Gardiner that it was his nature always 'to pardon them that will not dissemble but confess their faults' is transparent.[50] Though there was always the risk that the very act of submission might impose some claim upon the King's clemency, Henry knew that even God required that contrition precede pardon. Moreover, true sovereignty reserved the right of capricious choice; no matter how abject the confession, mercy might still be withheld, as those two elegant young gentlemen, John Mantell and Thomas Lord Dacre, discovered to their horror.

Thomas Fynes, Lord Dacre of the South, was a nobleman blessed with youth, estates and connections, while his brother-in-law John Mantell was a nephew by marriage of the Duke of Norfolk, and one of the 'handsomest and best bred men in England'. The two gentlemen with fourteen companions were accused of murder; in the words of their indictment, they illegally conspired to 'hunt the park' of Mr Nicholas Pelham 'with dogs and nets and other engines' and 'bound themselves to slay any of the King's lieges who might resist them'.[51] Mr Pelham did not take kindly to the ancient aristocratic code that a nobleman's cherished hunting rights stood above the claims of private property, and when his servants defended their master's lands one of their number was fatally wounded. It was obvious that none of the well-bred culprits regarded their actions as murder, but the council and the judges of the King's Bench thought that Dacre and his friends had sought to intimidate Mr Pelham and make an example of one of his park-keepers. Consequently on June 27th, 1541, Mantell and the other commoners were found guilty, accepting their sentences, according to Sir William Paget, 'very temperately and charitably'. Dacre, as a peer of the realm, was handled privately by the Council. One of the lords was so 'vehement and stiff' in his insistence that accidental manslaughter by aristocrats should not be construed as deliberate murder that Paget could hear the debate through two sets of closed doors. At first Dacre stuck to his story that he had intended no murder and demanded a trial by his peers. Eventually he changed his plea and 'upon hope of grace' confessed his indictment to be true. Paget was deeply moved by the spectacle of a young nobleman brought 'by his folly to such a care', and exclaimed that it was indeed joyful 'to hear him speak at the last so wisely and show himself so repentant'.

Just how repentant these well-bred delinquents were is disputable, since it was clear that the entire lot had been led to expect the King's mercy. The next day the Council went as a body to confer with the sovereign and ask pardon for the young men. Henry 'would not hear of it' and demanded their immediate execution. Later at dinner they read him Dacre's humble submission, 'hoping thereby to move His Majesty to pardon him'.[52] Henry remained adamant. Not only were the fourteen condemned to death, but Dacre's noble blood did not spare him the ignominy of hanging, and 'for greater shame' he was 'dragged through the streets to the place of execution' like a common criminal. Mantell, Dacre and two others were executed in London, but to the end neither the judges nor the populace, which gathered to view the event, believed that a reprieve would be denied youths who had every reason to claim the King's mercy. The expected did not transpire; the unexpected did. Despite the tears of the audience the aristocrats died, but the least deserving of the group were 'appointed to have the king's mercy'. John Cheyney, who had already been in trouble for a similar misdemeanour, and three others received pardons.[53] Policy may have entered into the calculation, for Cheyney was the son of the Treasurer of the Household, but the old nobility learned the lesson of equality under a law designed for all subjects. At the same time the quality of mercy most essential to sovereignty—its freedom—was preserved.

If vengeance and mercy wore the mask of a king but belonged to God, then power must needs be dedicated to the service of the deity. The Tudor state was no 'be-all and end-all of human existence',[54] but a hallowed vehicle through which God revealed His purpose. As such, it was more a moral force than a political entity, more a set of social habits reflecting the eternal battle between good and evil than a body of laws. When Bishop Bonner said that 'in matters of state, individuals were not to be so much regarded as the whole body of the citizens',[55] he had no notion of the modern secular Leviathan, which consciously organizes humanity along rational lines and generates its own justification for action. Instead, he was speaking of man's collective efforts to enact God's truth on earth. Society was a spiritual organism, not a political or economic contrivance, and John Rastel explained that the commonweal 'resteth neither in increasing of riches, power, nor honour, but in the increasing of good manners and conditions of men whereby they may be reduced to know God, to honour God and to love God, and to live in a continual love and tranquillity with their neighbours'.[56] The role of a king in such an enterprise was clear: 'To maintain virtue and to expulse vice; he will not only provide that he himself keep these commandments, but that all his subjects also keep them, even from the highest to the lowest.'[57]

In the preservation of his kingdom, Henry knew that 'fear hath, and ought to have, a great hand'; the hanging of one man could deter twenty from evil, 'for it is the nature of the many to be amenable to fear but not to a sense of honour'.[58] The realm, however, did not consist of the vulgar multitude alone; there always remained the better part, godfearing men and women who were susceptible to the call of honour. 'Love of virtue' and the virtuous example of princes, as well as 'fear of punishment', were the instruments by which the well-ordered community was to be constructed.[59] Ideally such a commonwealth was a model of the heavenly city, a society where all vice has been purged and the engines of coercion have withered away. Men of virtue obey because they are filled with God's grace and have achieved a perfect 'unity of will and mind'.[60] The social metaphor most often cited was the beehive, that marvellously arranged kingdom in which every insect, including the sovereign, is right-thinking, a living model of the ideal and perfectly virtuous bee which, like the good Christian, does its duty in that walk of life in which it has pleased God to place it.

In a sense, then, the purpose of Henry's rule was the annihilation of government: the attainment of the quintessence of harmony and tranquillity found in the virtuous commonwealth where the immutable perfection of God prevails. The King was clear as to his obligations; his appointed task was constantly to struggle against diversity and to inspire as well as coerce his subjects along the paths of righteousness. In his pontifical pronouncement to parliament in the winter of 1545 he not only acknowledged his duty to cultivate in himself the 'necessary virtues as a Prince or governor should or ought to have', but also berated those of his clergy who were filled with malice and discord. He warned the lords spiritual that if they could not find within themselves the love and charity necessary to live in concord, 'I whom God hath appointed His Vicar and high minister here, will see these divisions extinct, and these enormities corrected, according to my very duty, or else I am an unprofitable servant and untrue officer.'[61]

It is at this point that legend distorts the scene. The godly prince who maintains virtue in himself as well as in his subjects becomes the egregious hypocrite who squanders his patrimony, riots the night

through, wastes his time on senseless wars and idle ritual, and expects
posterity to believe him when he writes:

> Company with honesty
> Is virtue, vice to flee!
> Company is good and ill;
> But every man hath his free will!
> The best ensue!
> The worst eschew!
> My mind shall be
> Virtue to use,
> Vice to refuse!
> Thus shall I use me![62]

As long as the memory of Henry VIII endures, the myth of a
bacchanalian monarch will remain; it makes excellent copy, especially six wives and sixteenth-century table-manners. But virtue need
not be equated with fidelity or vice with over-eating. After all, most
of the King's matrimonial troubles were caused by his insistence on
the legality of marriage and divorce. Moreover, his marital record,
though sensational, was statistically not exceptional.* In his own
eyes and those of society King Hal was a monarch of rare virtue. The
court acrobats, mummeries, jousts, masques and cloths of gold were
part of the ritual of kingship, showmanship designed to place royalty
outside the normal standards of life. Thrift as a virtue, display as a
vice, are qualities associated more with Victorian England's *Thrifty
People and How They Thrive* than with the sixteenth century. Henry's
court, even his personal life, were models of virtue by the standards
of his age. In the entire annals of his reign it is difficult to find the
kind of childish rowdiness and brutal horseplay common in the
French court.

To the very end of his life the 'first gentleman of France', as
Francis I flatteringly called himself, loved boisterous brawling. The
Comte d'Enghien, his young favourite, was killed in a snowball fight,
instigated by the King himself, when some 'ill-advised' individual
tossed a linen chest out of the window on to the count's head.

---

* According to Peter Laslett (*The World We Have Lost*, p. 99), of the 72
husbands in the village of Clayworth in 1688, 21 married more than once and
of that group three married thrice, three four times and one tried it five times.
Further up the social scale and closer to Henry's generation, 28 per cent of the
aristocracy remarried between 1540 and 1660; 19 per cent of all their first
marriages were barren and 29 per cent produced no male heir; 48 per cent of
the second marriages were barren and 58 per cent produced no surviving male
heir (Stone, *Crisis of the Aristocracy*, pp. 167-9).

Francis himself bore the scar of a similar accident, inflicted years before when a log had struck him in the face during a mock assault on one of his own castles. It was considered a sign of particular renown and bravado for the King's son, the Duc d'Orléans, to defy fate and rush into a house infected with the plague, slash the bedding with his sword, scatter the feathers into the air and shout: 'Never yet hath a son of France died of the plague.'[63] He was dead within three days, but a mistake in judgment in no way lessened the honour of his action. French society thought it amusing when young gallants placed the bodies of hanged criminals in the beds of ladies of the court, and laughed when Orléans and his friends came close to fatally hanging one another in pretended anger. All Europe knew the reputation of Francis's court and the sexual conquests of the old sinner himself.

In contrast, the English royal household was a model of decorum. After a decade of Henry's rule, the King's councillors had made it clear that they disapproved of the likes of Nicholas Carew and Francis Bryan, who had ridden in the streets of Paris with the French King, 'throwing eggs, stones and other foolish trifles at the people', and had returned from France 'all French in eating, drinking and apparel, yea, and in French vices and brags'.[64] Sir Francis remained Henry's good friend, but any hint of duelling or violence near the royal palace when the King was in residence was a crime punishable —as in the case of Sir Edmund Knyvet—with the loss of the right hand.[65] The Earl of Surrey, in whose veins coursed Plantagenet blood as pure as the King's, was imprisoned in 1542 for throwing stones and breaking windows in the streets of London. The mock battles and sieges which Henry loved to stage in the jousting-yard were organized athletic rituals rather than acts of horseplay.[66] They were, however, extremely dangerous. At least once the King escaped death by a fraction of an inch when the Duke of Suffolk's lance struck his helmet; nine years later, at the age of forty-four, he was unhorsed and lay unconscious for two hours; but these were the risks entailed in enacting the part of a knight and a gentleman, not the results of unbridled violence.[67]

· If the English royal household was more restrained than its French counterpart, the explanation has much to do with the fact that Henry Tudor was far more inhibited than his Valois cousin. The possession of six wives obscures the issue, and even contemporaries could not help confusing matrimony with lust: 'Who,' wrote Richard Hilles to Henry Bullinger, 'judging of the King by his fruits, would ever believe him to be so chaste a character' as to leave Anne of Cleves a maiden after having been married to her for a month?[68] Yet

CATHERINE HOWARD, *c.*1520–42.

There is no positively identified portrait of Henry's
'Rose without a thorn'. *Miniature by Holbein*

ANNE OF CLEVES, 1515–57. *Miniature by Holbein*

HENRY VIII'S CHILDREN

above left
PRINCESS MARY, 1516–58.
Artist unknown

PRINCE EDWARD, 1537–53.
Attributed to Stretes

PRINCESS ELIZABETH, 1533–1603.
Artist unknown

Henry was neither ribald now bawdy nor particularly lusty. In fact the King was exceedingly touchy about his sex-life, answering the Imperial Ambassador's argument that perhaps God had ordained the succession to remain in the female line by shouting three times over: 'Am I not a man like others?'[69] The question for Henry was rhetorical, but later generations have had their doubts. Is the sovereign who goes through wives 'as some men go through socks' like other men? A single matrimonial catastrophe might be accepted as bad luck, but four marriages which end in disaster must have a common explanation. The psychologist J. C. Flugel may have been correct in saying that unconsciously the King was driven forward and at the same time repelled by his craving for sexual rivals, for incest and for chastity in his wives, thereby making his marriage-couch a nightmare of recriminations, fears and frustrations. All these 'desires,' says Flugel, 'are closely interconnected' and are 'derived from the primitive Oedipus complex'.[70] Or possibly it can be argued that the King knew or feared himself to be deficient in bed; certainly one of the rumoured charges directed against George Boleyn, the Queen's brother, was that he and his sister had gossiped about Henry's clumsiness as a lover and his lack of potency and staying-power.[71] Or again the explanation may be more brutally prosaic. As that excellent ecclesiastic of the Church of England, Bishop Stubbs, put it: the portraits of the monarch's many wives are, 'if not a justification, at least a colourable occasion for understanding the readiness with which he put them away'.[72] In truth, the question must be left unanswered. All that can be said is that the King did seem to have had a habit of involving himself in canonical incest by persistently marrying within the prohibited degree;* but whether by accident or unconscious design neither Henry nor, probably, his spiritual confessor could say.

Whatever the psychological speculations, there is evidence that Henry may not have been like most other men in that he was a

* Catherine of Aragon was his brother's widow; Anne Boleyn was his mistress's sister and had been pre-contracted to the Earl of Northumberland; Jane Seymour was a descendant of Edward III, therefore a distant cousin of the King, and Henry had to obtain a dispensation from Archbishop Cranmer from affinity in the third degree; Anne of Cleves had been pre-contracted to the son of the Duke of Lorraine; Catherine Howard was Anne Boleyn's first cousin and also the common-law wife of Francis Dereham; and Catherine Parr had been twice widowed before she married her sovereign. Nicolas, 'Descent of Henry the Eighth's Queens', p. 396, gives a table showing the degree of consanguinity of each of the wives to Henry, in which it is stated that Catherine of Aragon was a fifth cousin, Anne Boleyn was an eighth cousin, Jane Seymour a fifth cousin, Anne of Cleves a seventh cousin twice removed, Catherine Howard an eighth cousin, and Catherine Parr a third cousin once removed.

c

rather prudish individual, uncomfortable with smut and easily embarrassed by sex. In 1538 he was negotiating for a new wife and informed the French Ambassador that 'I will trust no one but myself; marriage touches a man too closely.' He wanted Francis, he said, to send to Calais an assortment of eligible French damsels so he could 'see them and enjoy their society before settling on one'. With wry Gallic humour, Castillon deliberately misunderstood, and asked the King whether he 'would perhaps like to try them all, one after the other, and keep for yourself the one who seems the sweetest. It was not thus, Sire, that the Knights of the Round Table treated their ladies in old times in this country.' Bluff King Hal is said to have blushed crimson and dropped the subject.[73]

There is a story that Henry enjoyed rhyming, and one day, while travelling on the river from Westminster to Greenwich to visit 'a fair lady whom he loved and lodged in the tower of the park', he challenged Sir Andrew Flamock to compose with him. The King wrote:

> Within this tower
> There lieth a flower
> That hath my heart.

Exactly what Sir Andrew replied has been kept discreetly hidden, but a version of his answer appeared in one of the worst plays of almost any century:

> Within this hour
> She pist full sower
> And let a fart.

Legend has it that the monarch was not amused and bid Flamock 'avant varlet' and begone.[74] The episode may just be evidence of sixteenth-century bawdy, but Sir William Paget, in a diplomatic dispatch from Paris in September 1542 felt obliged to apologize for the indelicate words of the French King, reporting that Francis was so anxious to engage the Emperor's army in battle that he had boasted 'he would give his daughter to be a strumpet of the bordel' if he could arrange the encounter. 'I beseech you, Sire,' Paget begged, 'to pardon mine unseemly terms, for the King spake them and worse.'[75] Possibly Bluff King Hal was more of a Victorian gentleman than we suspect. Certainly Paget seems to have taken seriously his sovereign's verse:

> My mind shall be
> Virtue to use,

Vice to refuse!
Thus shall I use me!

Whatever the truth about Henry's personal virtue, the secret of
the well-ordered commonwealth was known to all: true order
'standeth in ruling and obeying'.[76] Francis I expressed the same
conviction in more organic terms. 'Every properly established
monarchy and republic', he said, 'consists of only two parts—the
rightful rule of princes and superiors and the loyal obedience of subjects, in which, if one of the two is at fault, it is, as in the life of man,
the separation of the body and of the soul. Life lasts only as long as
the soul commands and the body obeys.'[77] Henry preferred a more
medical analogy and compared the rebellious subject to the dying
patient who out of sheer stubbornness will give no 'credit to his
physician' who 'knoweth the cause of the disease and the very
remedies thereof'.[78]

When the early sixteenth century spoke of order, it meant something far more than the common man's duty to obey. It postulated
a scheme of things which presumed that the heavens themselves
observed 'degree, priority and place', and visualized all relationships
—ethical as well as physical—as a series of fixed and tidy geometric
patterns. Henry's generation was moving away from the medieval
past with its visual straight-line diagrams, representing the polarity
of ideas such as humility and pride, but the physician's world was
still a linear arrangement balancing hot and cold, dry and moist. The
natural philosopher continued to think of air, fire, water and earth
as discrete categories conforming to the four points of a square. The
zodiac was still conceived of as a twelve-sided figure, the image of the
firmament remained a series of eleven concentric crystalline circles,
and above all the link reaching from the meanest beast to the god-
head itself was a straight-line 'chain of being' giving to all creation a
single geometric unity. Existence, moral as well as physical, was a
neat and enduring experience.

Disrespect, that cancer of all well-ordered societies, was an ethical
and political failing, for it introduced confusion into the designs of
both God and man. When Mr Rogers, the surveyor of the works at
Boulogne, used vile language to Lord Grey, the sovereign ordered his
Council to warn the man that the King demanded that respect for
rank 'should be known and observed', for it was an insult to royal
authority if 'his chief officer should be with words unfitting and
uncomely behaviour seem brought into contempt'.[79] The Lancaster
Herald paid with his life for his failure to understand the full
symbolism of his office: as the King's messenger it was judged treason

when he carried letters to Robert Aske in 1536 and knelt before the traitor.[80] Henry could accept with equanimity the existence of rebels, fools and misguided subjects, who like the poor were always present. What shocked him about the Pilgrimage of Grace, he said, was the 'shame to all you that note yourselves and have been taken of the nobility to suffer such a villain' as Robert Aske, 'a common pedlar in the law', with 'neither wit nor experience', to act 'as though he were your ruler and guide'. Indignantly he exclaimed: 'Where is your nobility become?'[81] The answer was clear. 'The lords of the soil', like God's vicar on earth, had as great an obligation to maintain and exercise civil authority as had the rank and file to obey it. By their inaction the nobility were defiling their own image and violating God's perfect hierarchy.

Henry's reaction to the Pilgrimage of Grace and to Robert Aske's treason was typical of his generation. No notion of social unrest, of seething mass-pressure, occurred to the King because society had no shape in his imagination outside the individual saints and sinners who composed it. In the early sixteenth century there could be no record of society, no real social analysis, no reform of the system. Instead, history was an extended moral homily upon the actions of men behaving rightly or wrongly.[82] Social science, even in the hands of Sir Thomas More, consisted largely of a chronicle of those human vices which contained the seeds of civil evils—avarice led to economic inflation, vanity resulted in theft and murder, and pride ended in treason. There was no doubt in Henry's mind that Aske had allowed pride to lead him into the ultimate treason of seizing power which did not rightfully belong to him, and that he had to be destroyed. The cure was invariably the same: the destruction of the evil-doer, not the mitigation of the forces behind social wrong. Only More in his *Utopia* was presumptuous enough to wish to improve on God's creation. At best society was an historical cage in which man enacted the divine drama of his existence; his doom was his own; society as a whole was guiltless. No one, least of all Henry, looked to the bright face of tomorrow, for a future which was not a monotonous repetition of the past was unthinkable. Fear of change filled the Tudor soul, and Sir Thomas Wyatt cried out in terror that in 'my bones there is no steadfastness: such is my dread of mutability'.[83] The power to control and manipulate nature, to change the world, belonged to the deity. Men could not shape a society which had been instituted by the Lord; they could only look into the mirror of the past, conform to the image of yesterday's heroes, and struggle to survive in the prison of today while accepting what fortune had reserved for tomorrow. The King, despite his sacrilege against the ancient faith and

the intense conviction with which he battered down the walls of
Rome, accepted the perversity of his stars, 'for whoso will struggle',
he said, 'against fate at such a point is full often the further off from
his desire'.[84]

Despite all the references to the harmony of the body politic, all
the appeals to the changeless and rigid order of the beehive, and all
the authoritarian efforts to subsume man into the larger totality of
family, parish, craft, estate and kingdom, there remained in the
sixteenth century an essential individualism which is lacking in
modern social systems: moral responsibility resided in man, not
society; in the individual, not the group. Tudor England was unaware of the twentieth-century nightmare of morally empty men,
transformed into statistical aberrations by the accident of social and
psychological pressure, blindly seeking to destroy the society which
spawned them. Evil still wore the terrible face of Judas burning in
hell, not the neutral smile of Lorenz recording the aggressive instincts of man. There was no such thing as a social disease called
rebellion, only rebellious subjects, no collective sickness known as
heresy, only obstinate and foolish heretics, no concept of social
delinquency, only whores, cutpurses and usurers.

The transformation of the inert body of some three and a half
million Englishmen, myopically concerned with the egotism, frustration and tedium of survival, into a virtuous kingdom breathing a
single purpose demanded an uneasy balance between the deadening
unity of total conformity, in which identity is annihilated and
obedience becomes a senseless social instinct, and the anarchy of
morally responsible men who choose or reject the path of righteousness. Where the usual instruments of coercion are lacking—a
vigilant police trained in mob psychology and criminal detection, a
complex and accurate information and filing system, and a highly
mobile military force—society must make do with the despotism of
the mind. If the state is technologically unable to force a man to do
right, it must teach him to want to do the right. The luxury of
diversity of opinion is really only possible when a community has a
reasonable chance of defending itself, either by offering so much
material well-being that its citizens will not risk rebellion, or by
detecting and isolating deviant behaviour before it can spread.
Tudor England possessed neither of these assets. The economy was
dangerously marginal, producing enough to feed but not to satisfy
all. Self-imposed social habits which compel good citizens to queue-
up, or call in the local constabulary in preference to taking the law
into their own hands, were almost non-existent. John Walker of
Griston was probably not exaggerating when he boasted that 'If

three or four good fellows would ride in the night, with every man a bell, and cry in every town they passed through, "to Swaffham! to Swaffham!" ' he could collect 10,000 men by morning.[85]

Fear of starvation kept the economic machine moving, giving grim reality to the scriptural injunction that it was man's duty as well as his fate to labour. Fear of torment in the bowels of hell or on the scaffold stayed the hand of the murderer, but it was the educational rod which whipped the mind into shape. 'The unity of the State', said Master Rypon, 'exists not merely in its houses or its streets, but, as all the philosophers testify, in the agreement of its minds.'[86] The will to obey was for ever being fostered in primer, pulpit and proclamation, for 'obedience is the principal virtue of all virtues, and indeed the very root of all virtues and the cause of all felicity'.[87] A B C and horn-book, Aesop's Tales and Solomon's Proverbs, Cato's advice to his son and the words of the catechism, had a single refrain: obey—obey God's commandments, obey father, mother and pastor, obey magistrate and master, obey the prince. The most tireless watchman society can possess resided deep within the soul of every subject—a sense of guilt. To know one's duty and to feel the lash of conscience were inner compulsions which no one could escape. Four times a year the general sentence and curse upon mankind was read from the pulpit: a detailed listing of all the sins of society from heresy to counterfeiting, from blasphemy to petty larceny, all denounced and shown for accursed before God and the entire heavenly host.[88] Every child, rich and poor, memorized and repeated the words of the catechism:

> ... To submit myself to all my governors, teachers, spiritual pastors and masters: To order myself lowly and reverently to all my betters: To hurt nobody by word nor deed: To be true and just in all my dealings: To bear no malice nor hatred in my heart: To keep my hands from picking and stealing, and my tongue from evil-speaking, lying and slandering: To keep my body in temperance, soberness, and chastity: Not to covet nor desire other men's goods; but to learn and labour truly to get mine own living, and to do my duty in that state of life, unto which it shall please God to call me.

The purpose behind this parroting was obvious: to scar the soul so that 'ye must needs obey, not for fear of vengeance only, but also because of conscience'.[89]

As the social scale was mounted, the consciousness of moral responsibility increased in direct ratio to the political power exercised. The greater the freedom of political action, the weightier the responsibility, until the royal pinnacle was reached and Henry could say to Charles V: 'Ubi spiritus domini, ibi libertas': where there is the spirit of God, there is freedom.[90] The free king was the responsible king, a prince who does his duty not from instinct but from choice. Henry, like all his generation, was a man of conscience; it had been drilled into him as part of the experience of living in a Christian world. But that conscience was far heavier than the didactic voice which spoke to common folk, for the sovereign above all other men possessed the power of free choice. 'Whoever has the dignity' of a king, Aquinas had written, 'has the burden attached',[91] a fact to be recalled in understanding that impressive and unyielding thing—the King's conscience.

Again and again Henry VIII has been accused of peculiar bloodthirstiness in the exercise of his authority, of not only behaving like an Old Testament king but also of hiding personal vengeance behind *raison d'état*. When he suggested to the Earl of Derby that the abbot and monks of Sawley be hung from a 'long piece of timber ... out of the steeple of their monastery',[92] it is said that he was dignifying sadism by calling it political justice. When he promised Robert Aske that the full measure of agony would not be demanded and that he would be hung 'full dead' before being cut down and disembowelled, the King kept his promise but is reported to have ordered that the wretched creature be hung alive in chains until dead, a process that took days, even weeks.[93] If the law had to be written in blood, why couldn't the victims of the royal supremacy be decently executed and be done with it? From a practical point of view the height of the gallows and the length of the rope were immaterial, but psychology working within the limits of prevailing theological assumptions, not technology, determined the dramatic details of the execution.

The twentieth century is appalled by human pain because for the first time in man's agonizing history physical anguish is unnecessary. It can be exorcized by the high priests of medicine and technology, and men need no longer make do with bell, book and candle. Today, if God is dead, it is because He has lost His cardinal purpose: to supply His creatures with an explanation for the suffering in their lives and to offer them relief in a world to come. Society has usurped His function, for it claims as its goal the bliss of paradise on earth. The saints of old who endured all for their faith are now forgotten. An Ignatius Loyola, who inflicted on himself the torments of the body so that he could strengthen his will in its determination to serve God, would be considered today more fit for the psychiatric couch than for spiritual office. It is no longer expected or considered desirable that man should have to or want to endure pain. Twentieth-century saints are those who accept hardship in order to relieve others of their afflictions. Their attainment is no longer judged by what they endure, but by the good which they do for society. There is no place for the individualistic world of the sixteenth century where Henry Tudor gave weekly alms of forty-four shillings seven pence,[94] not because he thought it socially desirable or because he knew full bellies made sound subjects, but because the act of giving was essential to his soul's salvation. Relief of suffering was only incidental to the act; the real benefit was the spiritual good accruing to the giver, not the material welfare redounding to the receiver.

For the sixteenth-century man, suffering was the corner-stone on which life itself rested, for the purpose of society was not man's happiness but his salvation, and only through suffering could man attain heaven. Tudor England was far too intimate with the agonies of life to ignore them. Since pain was the central and eternal ingredient of existence, there could be no indifference to what God Himself had ordained. The joys promised in the gospel were not open to the man who lived all his years in comfort. The ideal Christians were the martyrs of the Church, who by their suffering were swept into paradise. Quite literally the blood of the martyrs was the seed of the Church. When the condemned poisoner endured for three hours the pain of boiling to death, or when Thomas Wriothesley and Sir Richard Riche turned the handle of the rack on Anne Askew, these horrors could be identified with the normal agonies of daily life, and compared to the suffering reserved for the faithful: was the anguish comparable to that of the holy martyrs? Was it of a greater or lesser intensity than the Lord Chancellor himself had experienced with an abscessed tooth or bladder-stones, or the King had endured from gout and an ulcerous leg? The sadism which appears in modern literature and entertainment is without this anchor. The twentieth-century man who enjoys the thought of torture has no personal experience of it; the sixteenth-century man had. He was in part inured to it because he lived with it, but he could also measure the agony and place it in a scheme of things which removed the sadism.

Only in this framework of universal suffering does the stark horror of Tudor punishment and the King's vengeance become intelligible: the diseased tooth could not be extracted without pain, and the diseased soul of the criminal could not be purged without torture. The sixteenth-century traitor and the heretic not only deserved to die in pain, but their lingering anguish was the only possible way by which they could be cleansed of their offences. Indeed, it was essential that they die in agony, not only as Henry said 'for the example and terror of others'[95] but as a reward for the virtuous.

Heaven without hell, virtue without vice, punishment without reward, mercy without vengeance, were psychologically unthinkable.[96] The sight of a good hanging, drawing and quartering sent a pleasurable thrill through the audience because there was both identification with the pain and a heightened sense of righteousness. If the virtuous could not be rewarded on earth with material comforts and relief from affliction, they could at least enjoy the sight of the consequences of evil. It was only just that the pain should psychologically and symbolically fit the crime. As Judas, Cassius and Brutus endured an eternity encased in ice in Dante's hell as the appropriate punishment for the insensate pride which had led to treason, so Messrs Jones, Potter and Manering were hanged dressed in the King's livery, because they were his servants and had killed Roger Cholmeley out of pure malice.[97] Twenty thousand people gathered on a Sunday in July 1539 to watch the poetic justice of Cratwell, the London hangman, dancing on a gibbet for robbing a booth at Bartholomew Fair.[98] It was not so much that Henry's dignity required that the Abbot of Sawley swing high from his monastery spire, or that he gained a perverted satisfaction from being able to command such a death, as that the execution fitted the psychological and theological realities of the day.

If physical suffering is an eternal quality of life to be endured by all until death, there is the danger that pain as a social deterrent will lose its effect. Society, therefore, sought to enhance the magnitude of the punishment by humiliating the evil-doer. As Sir Thomas Wyatt warned his fifteen-year-old son, 'men punish with shame as [the] greatest punishment on earth; yea! greater than death'.[99] It was savage enough that John Wyot the carpenter who had slandered the King should be set upon the pillory and have one of his ears nailed to a board behind his head; it was humiliating that he should have to stand there with a dunce's cap on his head lettered 'for lewd words'; but it was deliberate degradation to require that the wretched man remain there until he found the courage either to cut or pull the ear off himself.[100]

All classes were exposed to humiliation and for each estate the punishment suited the social standing of the culprit as well as the nature of the crime. Whipping was the preferred correction for whores, urchins, servants, vagrants and school-children, but those who wore satin did not always escape ear-clipping, branding, jeering and the stocks.[101] Three gentlemen, a squire and two yeomen, were pilloried at Cheapside in December 1544 with signs written over each man's head announcing their 'wilful perjury and other devilish abominations'. Each was burned with a red-hot iron on the left cheek with the letter P, and relieved of the right ear. They were then returned to their respective counties, where they suffered the same public indignities on their right cheeks and left ears, and were imprisoned until they had paid an aggregate fine of £1,706. Probably only rank saved their lives, for their 'abominations', even by sixteenth-century standards, were indeed 'devilish'. They had committed arson by burning forests, coal-pits and houses; they had poached, stolen fish and destroyed the ponds; they had indulged in the malicious vandalism of stripping bark from trees, cutting tongues out of animals, amputating horses' tails, and slicing off men's ears; and they had committed treason by writing lewd political rhymes. Without doubt they deserved far worse than they got.[102]

A different kind of humiliation was reserved for the scholar. He was forced to confess his ignorance publicly, and Robert Warde was ordered to recant his 'folly and lewd behaviour' and admit himself to be a 'man of small experience, less wit and no learning, nor yet of any commendable qualities', who had 'in ale house and unmeet places' wrangled about scripture and spoken against the King's gospel.[103] The ultimate humiliation was reserved for the traitor, and only the King's mercy could save even a nobleman from the final physical and symbolic degradation of the hangman's dance, castration, disembowelment and the systematic butchering of the body as if it were a side of beef. The true horror of such a death was not so much the pain, which men knew how to endure, as the public mutilation of a man's good name. Not only did Robert Aske the man die in chains, but his honour also was strung up for all the world to observe as agony turned a gentleman into a beast. Tudor England sensed that the real mark of authority was not the ability to kill or to inflict economic and political sanctions, but the power to mortify and degrade, and this was exactly what Henry was doing, both as a man and a king, when he ruled those about him and made a laughing-stock of Wriothesley, Suffolk, Norfolk and the rest of his Council.

4

Behind the Mask

Above all things our royalty is to be reverenced, and if you
begin to poke about it you cannot reverence it. When there
is a select committee on the Queen, the charm of royalty
will be gone. Its mystery is its life. We must not let in
daylight upon magic.

Walter Bagehot, *The English Constitution*

Henry had become, in the rich but unflattering imagery of the French
Ambassador, 'not only a king to be obeyed on earth, but a veritable
idol to be worshipped'.[1] What Monsieur de Marillac did not perceive,
however, was that it is far easier to worship a statue than to obey
a flesh-and-blood monarch. In being transformed by society into
the graven image of majesty, Henry, as a man, was in effect the
first victim sacrificed upon the altar of his own divinity. Luther
missed the point when he said that 'Junker Heintz will be God and
does what he lusts'.[2] The gods are not free agents; they are owned
by their worshippers and are slaves to their reputations. The paradox was neatly presented by Stephen Gardiner for the benefit of
his sovereign when he wrote that 'increase of worldly things make
men poor and not rich, because every worldly thing hath a need
annexed unto it'.[3]

Royalty was a glasshouse, for the cloak of majesty could only be
seen when on display; remove the spotlight and kings stood nude
and quivering like other men. If the rules of adulation for the
devotees were minutely regulated, the behaviour of the idol was
even more carefully prescribed, and in the end Henry became the
prisoner of the mumbo-jumbo and liturgy designed to translate the
will of a man into the word of a god. That wonderful independence
and absolute power of which he boasted were figments of the
imagination. The divinity that doth hedge a king was dazzling silver
for those who viewed it from afar, but for the man within, the mask
was of iron. Power does not reside in the effigy; it belongs to the
servants who guard it, maintain it and transform its will into political and economic reality. The idol must oblige its high priests, and Sir
Thomas Cheyney, when he represented his master at the christening

of Francis I's granddaughter in July 1546, saw only a magnificent performance, not the agony standing in the wings. With lavish praise he reported to Henry how the French King, the Dauphin, the Admiral 'and a great company of ladies came under my chamber window in three little galleons, singing as sweetly as ever I heard, the King himself being one of them that sang. Such a triumph at a christening as I think was never seen nor heard of as this is like to be.'[4] Cheyney was blind to reality: a sick and syphilitic king in constant pain and fever, his groins a mass of abscesses,[5] and dead within the year. But the triumph demanded a king of 'high cheer', and, whatever the personal cost to Francis, that is what Sir Thomas saw.

At all times it was necessary for royalty to maintain appearances. Princes were not to rush about, to use bad language or seek petty revenge, and the Emperor's brother Ferdinand, the King of the Romans, was considered ill-mannered and unkingly because he demeaned his office by 'running upstairs at a nimble pace like a mean man'.[6] In speaking to a prince, said George Puttenham, 'the voice should be low and soft' as a sign of humility; in gaming with a king 'it is decent to let him sometimes win of purpose to keep him pleasant'; and in associating with him it is insolent to 'forgive him his losses', arrogant 'to give him great gifts', undutiful to refuse his bounty, and vain to 'feast him with excessive charge'.[7] By implication the converse was also true: kings should give more than they received, forgive their gambling debtors, grant favours unasked and entertain their subjects with exorbitant display.

Had kings really been, as Bishop Gardiner argued,[8] a breed apart, then their role might have been easier. What set kingship off from the rest of society was not the uniqueness of its virtues but the concentration of qualities found in more diluted form throughout the body politic. Hospitality, honour, extravagance and chivalry were no monopolies of the Crown; they were the essential attributes of men of good breeding. Francis I placed more value on his status as First Gentleman of France than on his Capetian blood. In England towards the end of the century William Segar organized society along the same aristocratic lines. 'Of gentlemen', he said, 'the first and principal is the king'; then followed in descending order princes, dukes, marquesses, earls and finally knights.[9] Royalty, then, was nobility on a grand scale, and every act of a king was measured by the standards of those lower in the ranks. If, as Sir Thomas Smith argued, a gentleman in order to 'be so accounted must go like a gentleman' and be judged more by the fashion of his spending than by the nature of his income, then monarchs had to do likewise.[10]

Henry could go nowhere and do nothing without dispensing gratuities. It was not so much that cash was a sounder basis for service than loyalty as that largesse was the expected attribute of power. If the sovereign boarded one of his own men-of-war, he distributed tips to the crew; if he listened to a Sunday sermon, he paid twenty shillings for the privilege. To the gardener who brought him a glass of water he offered sixpence, and to the man who fulfilled the boast that he could eat an entire buck at a single sitting he gave the handsome sum of forty shillings. The present of a porpoise cost him ten shillings, a lion £6 13s. 4d., and when he drew the line at a popinjay he still had to give away ten shillings.[11] The entire court expected New Year's gifts: £6 13s. 4d. for the sergeant and officers of the wardrobe, five pounds for the trumpeters, forty shillings for the porters of the gate, twenty shillings for the pages of the chamber, four pounds for the minstrels, two pounds apiece for the King's barber and clock-maker, and ten shillings each for the King's bowmen. Majesty could afford to overlook no one, however insignificant, and when 'divers poor men, women and children' presented their sovereign with 'capons, hens, books of wax, and other trifles', they were rewarded with £4 17s. 4d., and James Hubert who gave figs and raisins received forty shillings.[12]

In a sense kings were in constant competition with those below them. If Thomas Cromwell, a blacksmith's son, could support daily two hundred of the destitute and later in the century Edmund Earl of Derby's charity feed 50,000 annually, Henry's honour required that he do that much better.[13] His daily offerings totalled £115 18s. 4d. a year, and his gifts to the 'honest beggars' who clustered about the palace gates were sufficient to pay for at least 100,000 unappetizing meals.[14] In a century which was affluent in little but surplus labour, it became the mark of social distinction for a gentleman to invest himself with great swarms of serving-men 'as well to show his power as to grace his person'.[15] The Bishop of Ely managed with 100 servants; the Lord Chancellor only appeared in public with his 'family of gentlemen' before him and his yeomen dressed in velvet and chains of gold after him; the Earl of Northumberland retained 171 well-bred domestics; and Edward Seymour when he became Lord Protector supported 167.[16] Necessity more than vanity required that Henry match such pretension with his 50 aristocratic pensioners and 200 guards, and that he maintain an establishment suitable to his dignity, for 'after the deeds and exploits of war' a gentleman's household is 'the first thing that strikes the eye and which it is therefore most necessary to conduct and arrange well'.[17] If Cardinal Wolsey could entertain 400 guests at a

single sitting, fill 280 guest-rooms and boast a staff in excess of 400
at Hampton Court, royal hospitality, when Henry took over his
prelate's palace, demanded a more extravagant banqueting hall of
106 feet by 40 feet, a second great kitchen and a new beer cellar. If
six simple knights during the tournament of May 1540 could keep
open house for a week, feasting all comers, a gesture said to be much
'to the great honour of this realm of England',[18] it was only proper
that Henry should delay the reception of visiting celebrities until
he could 'gather his nobles and show his estate'.[19]

It is impossible to calculate with certainty the size of the royal
menage, for the court was all things to all men—the well-spring of
patronage, the seat of government, the heart of the kingdom, the
centre of society, the altar of sovereignty and the abode of kings. It
was larger, noisier, more crowded, probably smellier and certainly
more ridden with pettiness, privilege and peculation than more
humble manors, but these were matters of degree, not kind. The
King's palace still retained the essential functions of any gentleman's
household—a private residence, an economic and administrative
centre, and a symbolic pile of social authority and political prestige.

As a dwelling to house the royal family, the court is fairly easy to
compute. It consisted of the Privy Chamber, that inner layer of
service closest to the sovereign, numbering in the neighbourhood
of 80 privileged individuals, but this figure does not include the King's
physicians, surgeons and apothecaries, his messengers, minstrels
and musicians, his 9 cup-bearers, carvers and servers, his 4 squires
of the body, his 50 gentlemen pensioners, or the 80 yeomen who
guarded his rooms.[20] The outer layer, appropriately termed the
'below stairs', was infinitely larger and far more difficult to gauge,
for it encompassed everyone from the Lord Steward and Lord
Treasurer, the master cooks and their 33 children of the kitchen, to
the feather-maker, the King's fool, the librarian, the Astronomer
Royal and the grooms, ushers, pages, yeomen and sergeants of the
palace, not to mention the hen-taker and other hunters. The catering
staff in the pantry, kitchen, boiling-house, cellar and the like
numbered 274 plus 80 personal servants.[21] How many more were
needed to sweep, make the beds, clean out the jakes and cart off
the night-soil, catch the rats, maintain the stables, feed the hounds,
attend the falcons, care for the gardens and guard the grounds is
mere guesswork. Even if the scrupulous scholar tabulated the total,
including the Queen's household, the semi-independent establishments of the royal children, and the skeleton crews to maintain the
fourteen royal residences which Henry kept in various states of
repair, he would have to establish an arbitrary cut-off point for the

army of part-time servants, the unpaid labourers and the droves of freaks, acrobats, magicians, vendors, vagabonds, scallawags and scamps clamouring at the palace gates. Was, for instance, the minion of Mathew de Mantua, the King's studman, who received two pounds of his master's annual salary of £4 11s. 3d. and probably did most of the work, to be accounted one of the King's servants? In what category does one place Morgan Wolf the King's goldsmith, John Hopkyns his fishmonger, Ralph Stannowe the schoolmaster of his henchmen, Hans Holbein his painter, Vincent Aymer his cartographer, or the masters and yeomen of the mint, the post and the ordinance? A figure might be assigned—a cautious estimate of a thousand, or a bolder and more likely calculation of twice that number for the hordes of high- and low-born domestics who sustained royalty.* Even then another four to five hundred would have to be added to cover the clerks and bureaucrats who administered the King's laws, enforced his justice and collected his taxes.

There are better if more subjective ways of gauging magnitude than inaccurate head-counting. If Hampton Court is measured against modern governmental edifices, it sinks into insignificance. Compare it to Blenheim Palace, and Renaissance monarchy takes second place to eighteenth-century aristocracy; but contrast Henry's architectural conceit to old St Paul's Cathedral or the sprawling medieval palace of Westminster and it fills the mind with awe. Only Church and state could give the lie to mutability and mortality by building monuments to God's changeless design: the cathedral as man's gateway to eternity and the palace as God's high vicarage on earth. Here at Hampton Court was proof of majesty: an ungainly crowd squeezed into every nook and cranny and spilling over into the palace grounds, where tents were set up for the army of excess domestics who served those who served royalty. To attend upon a king without displaying the visible signs of social status was to disgrace the sovereign, and dukes, councillors and pages—each according to his estate—brought with them their own well-appointed and 'seemly servants'. Archbishop Cranmer was allowed nine beds for his retainers, Bishop Gardiner had to make do with six, Mr Denney

---

* This is not entirely guesswork. When Henry went on a state visit to France in 1532, according to Edward Seymour (*Seymour Papers*, p. 3), he took with him most of his court: 137 persons who belonged to his chamber, 253 who were of the 'below stairs', 134 Yeomen of the Guard and 66 of the stables, a total of 590. Accompanying this number were 2,139 servants—a ratio of 4 to 1! This does not include the Queen's chamber, which probably numbered close to 80, not counting servants (*L.P.*, XV, 21). Neville Williams (*Royal Residences*, p. 7) says that Whitehall Palace in its heyday could seat 1,500 guests at dinner.

of the Privy Chamber with three and the grooms of the closet with two beds for the three of them, while Mr Secretary Paget and his clerks had to fit themselves into a small room over the west gate.[22]

The magnitude of such a household, especially in an age which judged kings and commoners more by the conspicuousness of their consumption than by the weight of their money-bags, is best described in terms of the organizational confusion which engulfed royalty. There is a surface camouflage of order about Henry's court, a functional rationality which is deceiving. The five main divisions of any gentleman's dwelling were clearly and sensibly articulated—a place of worship, a hall for eating, a space in which to prepare meals, a storage area and procurement office, and, most important of all, a suite of rooms where the master slept and worked. A house was far more than a shelter. It was a communal home, a perfect image in microcosm of the entire kingdom. Degree, priority and place operated in miniature within the family even more rigidly than it did in the social hierarchy of the outside world. The master of the house was the father of his family; not only of his own children but also of the servants and the young scions of lesser folk who sent their sons and daughters to be educated in his residence. Children and domestics slept together, were whipped together and educated together. Youth stood while age sat; sons waited upon their fathers; daughters helped their mothers dress; and when Henry required that the chief clerk of his kitchen see that 'the King's dish be of the best and sweetest stuff that can be got, and in likewise for every estate ... according to their degrees',[23] he spoke not as a monarch demanding special treatment but as a father maintaining the necessary distinctions on which all authority rested.

At least once a day the Tudor household gathered in common worship; the master, his wife and children a little apart from the servants and minions, kneeling in prayer at a respectful distance. Kings were more isolated in their vaulted chapels, where the royal family knelt in a raised gallery opposite the altar while the rest of the staff stood on the stone floor below. Authority not only worshipped apart, it ate apart. The great hall fed the entire establishment, but the royal family, important guests and noble servants sat on a raised dais while the children, lesser functionaries and domestics made do with trestle tables running down the sides of the chamber.[24] With a fine sense of liturgical and administrative harmony, the dean of the chapel, the almoner, the king's carvers, the queen's servers, the master cofferer and the clerks of the greencloth sat together for dinner and supper.[25] On the scale necessary to royalty, this kind of communal existence tended to break down through sheer weight of numbers, and, except on state occasions, eating in the great hall was left to clerks and minions. The high-born crept off to private meals in their rooms, a custom which the catering departments deplored as inefficient and which angered the King as a violation of social and domestic theory.[26]

The administrative heart of the court was the board of the green-cloth, which was responsible for purchasing and preparing the food, servicing and cleaning the palace, regulating an army of servants, and scrutinizing every detail of household life.[27] Normally the Lord Steward headed the domestic staff, but real power resided with the treasurer and controller, the financial and administrative overseers of the court. Under them stood the cofferer, the four masters of the household, the clerks of the controller and the greencloth, and finally a small cadre of grooms and yeomen who scurried about the palace, running errands and collecting information. With the painstaking pride of confirmed list-makers and tabulators, the clerks of the greencloth laid bare every domestic secret: the sums spent for wood and rushes in the woodyard, charcoal in the scullery, wheat in the bakehouse and meat in the acatery; the charge for the King's armoury (in 1540, £611 12s. 8d.); and the cost of carting the royal household while on progress and the number of miles allowed between each palace (Greenwich to Westminster five miles, Richmond to Windsor fourteen miles, Westminster to Hampton Court eleven miles, computed at fourpence a mile).[28] All this punctilious accounting was designed to assure the smooth operation of the King's suite, with its rooms arranged in ever-decreasing size, moving from spacious public approachability to intimate, private seclusion. First came the great hall, open to all; behind it was the guardroom or waiting-chamber; then followed the presence-chamber containing the throne from which Henry held court; and behind that were the privy chamber, the king's closet and finally the retiring room with its eleven-foot-square bed and gold and silver canopy. Here resided the heart of majesty, 'the stately seats, the ladies bright of hue; the dances short, long tales of great delight'.[29]

The entire structure was beautifully arranged to sustain a myth, but it was mostly an illusion, a trick of organizational lighting that deceived the eye, for behind the façade of careful control by the board of the greencloth, behind the detailed listings of diets, duties and deficiencies, and behind the rational order of departmental divisions, lay a chaos of human sloth, bureaucratic inertia and financial confusion which smothered the King's will and made a mockery of his precious freedom.

Size and the perambulating nature of the household precluded any real possibility of efficiency. Throughout the year, and especially during the summer months, the court wandered from palace to palace, fouling its nest as it went. To move Elizabeth it took from four to six hundred carts and 2,400 horses loaded with furniture, bedding, tapestries, kitchen utensils, library books, animal fodder and the personal effects of each member of the household from the Queen to the court jester and the locksmith.[30] Every courtier, nobleman and councillor brought his own retainers, servants and pages, so that the total entourage was a small army on the march. When in May 1552 Edward VI went on progress 345 men-at-arms and 7 councillors were ordered to escort him, until it was discovered that the geometric progression of master to servant was such that the total would have approached 4,000 horse, which the young King himself noted 'were enough to eat up the country'. In the end the number of men-at-arms was cut to 150.[31]

Such a horde ate prodigiously. On a single day Henry's household, reduced in size for travel to Calais, tucked away in meat and poultry alone 6 oxen, 8 calves, 40 sheep, 12 pigs, 36 'capons gras', 96 'good capons', 7 swans, 20 storks, 34 pheasants, 192 partridges and the same number of cocks, 56 herons, 84 pullets, 720 larks, 240 pigeons, 24 peacocks, and 192 plovers and teals.[32] Elizabeth's establishment, virginal, economical and less prodigal than her father's (except in the stables), consumed annually 600,000 gallons of beer, 300 tuns of wine, 1,240 oxen, 8,200 sheep, 13,260 lambs, 2,752 dozen chicken, poultry and capons, 60,000 pounds of butter and 4,200,000 eggs.[33] Under Mary, the court at Richmond was serviced by eighteen kitchens in which the confusion was, according to a Spanish visitor, 'a veritable hell'. The company consumed daily nearly 100 sheep, 12 great oxen and 18 calves, besides vast quantities of game, poultry, venison, wild boar and rabbits, while the beer intake, he said, was 'more in summer than the river would hold at Valladolid'.[34]

No matter how arduous the inspection or how honest the clerks of the greencloth, peculation, confusion, waste and duplication were commonplaces in a household where food was consumed in huge quantities and where well-born domestics delegated their duties to servants who in turn passed them on to the urchins and rascals of the court. In both France and England the Crown fought prolonged but losing battles against the swarms of vagabonds, 'vile persons' and 'masterless' servants who lived off the droppings of majesty.[35] Theoretically, candle-ends and the remains of tallow were to be collected daily and sent back to the chandlery to be melted down; in fact they were purloined and sold outside the court. The sergeant

of the scullery was enjoined to 'make true provision' of all fuel
expended in his department, but no amount of book-keeping could
prevent the children of the scullery from pocketing bits of coal to
take home. The officers of the greencloth were ordered to 'view and
see that the meat be served forth wholly and entirely and in due
proportion ... without fraud, embezzling, or diminution', but no
proclamation could stop noblemen from maintaining their own cooks
in the royal kitchens or prevent servants from serving their lords with
more than their due. 'Relics and fragments' from the kitchen, the
pastry and the boiling-house were in theory collected by the almoner
and distributed to the poor at the outer gate of the palace, but in
fact the food vanished, either fed to the great mastiffs or taken home
by those who were not permitted to eat at court.[36]

Often petty thievery was legitimized by usage and built into the
system. The highest to the lowest exercised the cherished perquisite
of gleaning: the sergeant of the cellar claimed the dregs from the
wine-kegs; the sergeant of the chandlery was permitted to abscond
with the blankets, sheets, bolster and pillowcases used during the
installation of a Knight of the Bath; the warden of the fleet had a
right to all the old timber and cuttings of new timber from any repair
of the King's palaces and to the used rushes and straw that remained
when Henry moved from one building to another; and Henry
Neville, Lord Beryavenny, the hereditary larderer, claimed all the
left-over beef, mutton, venison and fish after a coronation dinner.[37]

Cleanliness was a state devoutly to be wished, but neither threats
nor cajolery could banish filth and neglect in a century which was
highly versed in matters of salvation but was deplorably weak on
plumbing. A certain level of hygiene in the presence of the sovereign
could be indoctrinated through ritual, and the ceremonies of filling
the King's cup, making his bed, setting his table, carving his meat
and cutting his hair were partially successful efforts at inculcating
hygienic habits by elevating them into a memorized and sacred
liturgy. The royal barber was instructed to keep himself 'pure and
clean' and not to consort with 'vile persons' or 'misguided women';
the monarch's well-bred domestics were reminded that their duty
was to maintain the chamber free 'of all manner of filthiness' and not
to delegate their tasks to pages and 'mean persons', but the stream
of orders bidding grooms and ushers clear away the dirty dishes and
'broken meat' is evidence enough that the number of even a
king's servants bore little relationship to the quality of the service
rendered.[38] Two hundred years later, Mr Soame Jenyns was still
observing that when at dinner a dog fouled the rug, nobody could
be found in the household menial enough to clear away the mess.

The will to rule in the sixteenth century was for ever being dulled by the prodigious effort it took to overcome inertia and redirect established customs, and it is doubtful whether Henry or any other master had real control over the operation of his house. Throughout the century Tudor efforts to reform the court proved to be transitory. The monarch was rarely able to economize, and it was difficult to dismiss a servant for theft, let alone inefficiency. The effectiveness of the king's will was in inverse ratio to the distance of the official from him. Exactly who controlled the thousands of positions at court is difficult to ascertain, but the further one moves into the sub-structure of the household the less consciously political and more instinctively clannish patronage becomes. Most posts were oral appointments on good behaviour, and, judging by the repetition of names, family in-breeding was high. Even on Henry's death, when all positions at court were technically in jeopardy and a clean sweep might have been expected as the household reorganized itself to meet the needs of a wifeless and childless monarch, the new Lord Protector found it easier to add to than to cut back on the size of the domestic staff. Though he seems to have tried to dismiss or pension off one hundred of the yeomen of the guard, in the end that body rose to the all time high of 207. The thirty-three gallopines, or children of the kitchen, became thirty-seven under Edward; Henry's musicians and minstrels were increased by twenty-four, almost double their number, probably because the young Prince's players were joined to those of his father;[39] and not one of the eight officers of the buttery under the father was removed to make room for the three men who had served the son; instead the authorized number was expanded first to ten and then to eleven.[40] As every bureaucrat knows, the law of survival is to increase and multiply, and no Tudor king and certainly no lord protector could restrain that growth.

A man bound by chains of tradition and inertia may be an unknowing captive. So conditioned were the natural leaders of society to the enervating service which surrounded them that Henry was probably unaware of the demands constantly being made upon his patience and privacy. When he requested a midnight snack, the process touched the cherished rights of dozens of underlings, which not even a monarch dared circumvent. A bit of bread and wine involved the gentleman usher of the bedchamber who instructed one of the grooms of the closet to inform the sergeants of the buttery and cellar to have the food delivered to the door of the chamber, where it was conveyed in reverse order to the monarch.[41] Time-consuming and frustrating as such protocol and ritual could be, it helped to shield royalty from pressure from below. If the King could not fully exercise his will upon the swarm of domestics and clerks who overwhelmed him, they in turn found it difficult to reach him or break through the wall of custom which protected his office.[42]

Henry could guard himself from the foe without, the lesser suitors and clamorous mountebanks whose thirsty loyalty could never drink deeply enough of the royal bounty. The real danger lay closer to the throne: the intimates of his closet, the gentlemen of his chamber, the valued advisers of his Council, and the companions of his pleasures, whose proximity to the sovereign offered unparalleled opportunity for manipulating royalty. That excellent Protestant John Foxe admitted that 'King Henry, according as his Council was about him, so was he led', and the Catholic propagandist Nicholas Sander gossiped that courtiers and ministers 'did never suggest unto him anything to the destruction of any man, or speak anything for their own benefit' except either in the evening when the King was comfortably filled with wine or 'when he had gone largely to the stool, for then he used to be very pleasant'.[43] Neither picture is edifying and both are dangerous exaggerations, but they give verisimilitude to the proposition that royalty is surrounded by a lie and that suspicion is inherent in kingship. As the anvil at which all men sought to hammer, 'some for money and some for favour',[44] Henry Tudor may indeed have had grounds for distrusting those closest to his power and cause to devise various means for dividing 'the good servants from the flatterers'.

There is no need to depend on Sander or Foxe to prove that there were servants who sought to blind the monarch with a mist of subtle influence so pervasive that he was scarcely aware of it. Regal authority could not be usurped except by coup d'état, but it could be confused by the deliberate concealment of information, by the judicious misrepresentation of facts, and above all by the secret possessed by every good secretary: an exact knowledge of his master's mind. According to George Puttenham the role of a royal adviser was an exceedingly delicate one, for 'princes may be led but not driven.' His recipe for success was to maintain the fine line between flattery which was servility and rough criticism which was dangerous; the ideal servant sought always 'to counsel and to admonish, gravely not grievously, sincerely not sourly'.[45] Of all the councillors, Sir William Paget was in the best position to lead the King, conditioning his mind with grave and sincere advice. Authority to open, sort, read and report on Henry's mail gave the Principal Secretary power to edit and adapt, a fact well understood by his colleagues who were for ever sending him messages to be shown the King 'if you think good'.[46] Even the Archbishop of Canterbury considered it politic to ask Mr Secretary to peruse and correct a letter he wanted signed by Henry and returned to him.[47]

Exactly how the Secretary used his power is impossible to say; he swore that only twice had he ever sought to influence the King for money, but he never denied that he could and did coax his sovereign to remember the Lord Chancellor 'with some cast-off house', Stephen Vaughan for an 'honest office of no charge', and Lord Lisle for chantry lands worth four hundred pounds a year.[48] Henry always had the final say, and no one could predict the outcome, but Paget controlled the vital flow of information and, though the procedure was dangerous, he could exercise a form of pocket veto. When Lord Cobham requested licence to leave his post at Calais, Sir William did not even bother to bring it to the King's attention, explaining that he could not 'honestly sue for it'.[49] With Lord William Grey the situation was different. Grey himself referred his petition to return from Boulogne to Paget's 'wisdom whether ye think it good to move the premises or no unto the King's Majesty'.[50] Only a confidant could guess when an irascible old man would be feeling generous.

Selecting the time and place to approach a master is the function of any good secretary; deliberately concealing or doctoring information is another matter, and far more difficult to judge. Who can say whether the meagreness of the evidence is proof of administrative integrity or a sign of successful dishonesty? Certainly Paget was not above a cautious amount of well-bred blackmail, especially when his own pocket-book was involved. His part in the transfer of a choice piece of monastic land, which required the Bishop of Durham's consent, was not above reproach. When Tunstal withheld his permission, the Secretary lashed out, announcing that he was loath to inform Henry of the Bishop's decision, 'not knowing how his Highness would take it'.[51] Only once does there seem to have been a deliberate conspiracy to conceal information lest the King be tempted into precipitous action of which the Council disapproved. The matter concerned a particularly valuable diamond appraised at a hundred thousand crowns, the purchase of which the Fuggers were urging in January 1546 as part of a larger loan. Stephen Vaughan, who thought his sovereign already possessed more jewels 'than most of the princes of Christendom' and considered it improper to put further temptation in his way, wrote Paget that he had not informed the King about the 'largeness of this diamond' and asked the Secretary to plug any leaks from other sources. Eventually Henry had to be informed, but the secret was well kept until Vaughan discovered that there was no way of negotiating the loan without confessing the existence of the gem.[52]

The only servant who openly admitted to tampering with dispatches was Thomas Wriothesley, who 'played the jolly courtier' and covered up for his friend Sir Thomas Wyatt, the English Ambassador to Spain in 1537. In those days Wriothesley was one of the clerks of the signet, and acted as secretary to both the King and Cromwell. Exactly what liberties he took are not clear, but he seems to have changed the address on one of Wyatt's letters and 'so handled' the King that he was no longer displeased with some fault in his ambassador. 'Write both to His Majesty and to my Lord [Cromwell],' Wriothesley warned his friend, 'as though you had never advertisement' of the matter.[53]

Far more pernicious and dangerous to the exercise of the King's control than politic efforts to suppress information or an occasional case of friendly forgery by a minor official were the efforts of ministers to act in concert. If Henry's purpose was to divide, isolate and humiliate, his victims in self-defence sought to protect themselves by clinging together and concealing any dissension in their ranks. Out of sight, out of mind was an ancient and well-tested adage, and the civil servant exiled in foreign or provincial parts had to guard himself against the butterflies who fluttered about the court. 'Ye see what it is to serve out of the king's majesty's sight,' sighed Stephen Vaughan to William Paget: those at court 'getteth a good office'.[54] Bishop Gardiner produced the remedy when he wrote to Sir William on behalf of his clerk Davye that 'we ambassadors ... must hold one with another'.[55] Winchester's admonition to stick together implied considerably more than persuading Secretary Paget to look after the legal interests of one of his employees. A certain amount of honour among thieves was needed if Gardiner, Paget, Cranmer, Wriothesley and the rest were to survive the King's sinister talents for humiliating and harassing them. Years later Winchester reminded the Archbishop of the time when they had placed conciliar unity above religious conviction. Henry had been at his most suspicious, and, in the presence of the Lord Chancellor, turned to Gardiner and asked him if he had 'any embittered feeling' towards Cranmer. 'How coldly I answered the King,' the Bishop recalled, 'lest he smell any dissension, I have Wriothesley himself as witness and my conscience before God.'[56]

Holding together and looking after one's friends were instinctive in the sixteenth century. If Paget favoured fellow civil servants, he did no more than Dr William Butts, Henry's physician, who supported the followers of the gospel, and, possibly even better than Paget, could gauge the timing of a suit to be made to the sovereign. The doctor once received a letter from Ralph Morice, Cranmer's secretary, on behalf of Richard Turner, whose pious but vehement activities against the papists in Kent had been represented to the King as rabble-rousing civil disobedience. The attack on Turner was part of a conservative effort to destroy the Archbishop's reputation, and the reformers turned to Butts for a remedy. 'And so spying his time', when Henry was having his beard washed and trimmed, the physician 'with some pleasant conceits to refresh and solace the King's mind' produced Morice's letter and demonstrated exactly how to manipulate royalty. 'Pleasantly and merrily' he began 'to insinuate unto the King the effect of the matter and so, at the King's commandment, read out the letter'. Henry ordered the epistle to be read twice, and after a short consideration 'so altered' his mind that 'whereas before he commanded the said Turner to be whipped out of the country, he now commanded him to be retained as a faithful subject'.[57]

Ministers and doctors knew their master, and the temptation to shape the sovereign's mind, to forward the affairs of a friend or thwart the plans of a foe was irresistible. The observant Imperial Ambassador sensed a little of what lay behind Tudor politics when he reported that Stephen Gardiner was the most successful of all English diplomats because he understood 'his master's nature' and therefore knew how to persuade the King to adopt other people's policies as his own.[58] There was, however, an important corollary to successfully manipulating royalty: it was perilous to be caught out at it. Henry was exceedingly watchful lest his servants temporized 'for their own profits', and Sir William Paget thought Bishop Gardiner 'too wise to take upon himself to govern the King'.[59] The Secretary was quite correct; 'Wily Winchester' was never obvious and the guiding principle of his political career was always to 'go with the King's Highness and as far as he', but never to 'enter any dangerous matters, not knowing certain, by himself, whether His Grace would after allow them or no'.[60] Sir Thomas Seymour, younger brother of the Earl of Hertford and an inexperienced gentleman of the chamber, would have done well to harken to the prelate's advice. When Seymour tried to set the King's mind against Archbishop Cranmer, he quickly learned that Henry was not easily fooled and, worse, was willing to wait weeks to exact his revenge.

Sir Thomas was fronting for a group of land speculators who sought to persuade the monarch 'to overthrow the honourable estate of the clergy' and to plunder ecclesiastical property as he had the monastic lands.[61] Their plan was to put 'into the king's head' the tale that Cranmer 'kept no hospitality or house' worthy of his revenues and dignity, but squandered his episcopal incomes to purchase estates for his wife and children. In order that Henry 'should with more facility believe this information', they acquired the services of Sir Thomas. Deliberately spreading the rumour among the gentlemen and members of the chamber, Seymour told his story to the monarch, pointing out that men of God should not be plagued with temporal and financial matters but should be placed on a salary and their incomes surrendered to the Crown. The King was unreceptive to the thought of clerical lands fattening his royal coffers but showed concern at the allegation that his Archbishop failed to maintain his episcopal dignity. Some weeks later Henry suddenly ordered Sir Thomas to go straight to Lambeth Palace with word that the King would speak to the Archbishop at two o'clock of the afternoon. When Seymour arrived with his message, he discovered Cranmer's great hall set for dinner in a style befitting a prince of the Church, and was promptly invited to partake of the prelate's hospitality.

The narrator of Seymour's embarrassment, Ralph Morice, is reluctant to accuse his sovereign of deliberate malice and simply says it is not known whether it was 'chance or of purpose' that Henry happened to send his servant to Lambeth just as the Archbishop was entertaining in grandeur, but, knowing the King's methods, one might hazard the guess that Cranmer had been forewarned. Obviously ill at ease and making but a short repast, Sir Thomas hurried back to Westminster to report that the Archbishop would wait upon his master at the time indicated Then Henry asked: 'Had my lord dined before ye came?'; and 'What cheer made he you?' Sir Thomas was sufficiently perceptive to catch the drift of the King's queries, and he promptly fell to his knees and 'besought the King's majesty of pardon'. Blandly Henry inquired: 'What is the matter?' and wisely Seymour answered: 'I told your highness that my lord of Canterbury kept no hospitality correspondent unto his dignity, and I now perceive that I did abuse your highness with an untruth.' As usual, Henry was delighted at this voluntary confession of fault, but was not well pleased when Seymour sought to exonerate himself by transferring the blame to informers who had seemed 'to be honest men'. He roughly lectured the unfortunate courtier: 'I know your purposes well enough; you have had among you the commodities of the abbeys ... and now you would have the bishops' lands and revenues to abuse likewise.' Then with typical Henrician logic he reversed the argument, stating that if the

Archbishop and other prelates, as Seymour had first informed him, maintained lean and meagre hospitality, then, far from confiscating their lands, the Crown should increase their revenues to help them sustain their social positions. 'Therefore', he concluded, 'set your heart at rest; there shall no such alteration be made while I live.' Seymour's mistake may have been that he did not approach the King in his cups or at his toilet, but the experience certainly taught the young man that Henry was a past master at turning the tables on any would-be conspirator, and that it was exceedingly hazardous to attempt to distract the monarch's 'eyes with mists'.

Ministers may indeed have enveloped their motives in a heavy fog of deception, and the inertia and privilege which permeated the household may have clogged the machinery of royalty with the grit of human guile, but these were evils against which Henry could wrestle and even defeat; it was the man within whom the King could not control. Every courtier and adviser appreciated that their master was a highly emotional man. The documents are thick with tear-stained evidence of the King's unrestrained griefs and un-paralleled joys. Power is not conducive to strict emotional control, and Henry got away with a degree of hysteria intolerable in lesser men. As the years slipped by, his grip on himself wore dangerously thin, but in fact all his life King Hal had carried his heart on his sleeve, his face a mirror of the turmoil within. Early in the reign the Venetian Ambassador reported that the young Prince went 'pale with anger' at evil tidings, and another Venetian remarked on the outbursts produced by any mention of the French King.[62] Henry eventually mastered diplomatic etiquette and became a stickler for the ritual essential to a proper functioning of international inter-course, but try as he might he never learned to mask his feelings completely, and Chapuys was for ever noting that the King sighed frequently, that his face expanded and his eyes glittered with plea-sure, or that his colour changed with indignation. Towards the end, the Ambassador said that 'either through his anger or forgetfulness, he got into a complete confusion and no one could set him straight', and on another occasion Van der Delft decided that 'it was high time for us to get clear of him ... in order to avoid offending him or irritating him further, having regard to his malady'.[63]

Matters which touched Henry deeply invariably produced tears and tantrums. In July 1535 the King's fool carelessly joked at the expense of Queen Anne Boleyn's morality and Princess Elizabeth's parentage, with results which almost cost him his life; the knave had to be hidden away till the King's wrath abated. A year later an emotional about-face occurred. If the Imperial Ambassador is to

be believed, Henry clasped his illegitimate son the Duke of Richmond to his breast and burst into tears, sobbing that God had saved
him and his half-sister Mary from their stepmother, 'the accursed
whore' who had plotted to poison them.[64] When yet another of his
wives did him wrong, and in November 1541 Catherine Howard
proved herself to be a delinquent bride and a cuckolding wife, he
lost all emotional control and put on a public and highly embarrassing display of tears and wild threats of terrible revenge.[65] Six months
later, Chapuys was still writing that he had never seen the sovereign
so 'sad, pensive, and sighing'. It was not until the news of the
miraculous English victory over the Scots at Solway Moss in November 1542 that the emotional pendulum swung violently to the other
side and there was gaiety again at court.[66]

Emotional imbalance may have been intensified by the opportunities for self-indulgence inherent in kingship, but the real responsibility lay less in the office than in the man, for Henry invariably over-reacted to any stimulus. He sealed his senses against
bad news and exulted at good. Reports in October 1523 of the
humiliating defeat of his splendid army of ten thousand men fifty
miles from the gates of Paris were dismissed as false until evidence
to the contrary was overwhelming.[67] Stories of Catherine Howard's
adulterous treason were denied as malicious gossip until no other
interpretation became possible. Word of Catherine of Aragon's
death was celebrated with masque, banquet and a ball where Henry,
cross-gartered in yellow hose, danced the night away with Anne
Boleyn. News of the overwhelming Imperial victory over the French
at Pavia in 1525, where Francis was ignominiously captured, produced shouts of glee and the jubilant assertion that 'all the enemies
of England are gone'.[68] Unfortunately the English King rarely
looked before he leaped, and never saw the dark of distant consequences for the pleasure of immediate relief. It was not that Henry,
in the medical parlance of his day, was of an incorrigibly sanguine
humour, but that he was for ever of the happy conviction that every
problem must have a direct and immediate solution. The battle of
Pavia meant the humiliation of his rival, the triumph of his ally
the Emperor, and the death of Richard de la Pole, the White Rose,
whose claim to the throne was a constant reminder that the Tudors
were royal parvenus. He could not see how disastrously the European
balance of power had been changed or how difficult it would be
henceforth for an English tail to wag the Imperial dog.

There is a singular lack of proportion to Henry's intellectual and
emotional approach to life which might have been acceptable in an
adolescent or understandable in an undergraduate but was terrifying

in royalty. He once told Thomas Wriothesley that he greatly admired the actions of a servant of his grandfather Edward IV, who begged his sovereign 'for a thousand oaks that he might only obtain twenty'.[69] Both in public and in private, Henry Tudor adopted the same exaggerated tactics. His solution for persuading the Pope to grant him a divorce in 1527 was all A-bomb and direct action: the sending of two thousand troops to Rome to 'liberate' Clement VII from Imperial influence so that he could do as the King commanded.[70] Six years later Francis I was complaining of the same heavy-handed methods, and informed Bishop Gardiner that 'as fast as I study to win the Pope, ye study to lose him'. His royal brother, he said, had clearly 'marred all'.[71] Possibly the tragedy of the divorce did in fact stem from Henry's character; he was too eager, too emotionally committed and too anxious to prove himself correct to realize that the infuriating web of legal and diplomatic quiddities spun by Imperial and papal jurists need not be brutally torn asunder: given time, Cardinal Wolsey, that master of legal deception, might have disentangled them.[72] What Henry VIII never learned was that the statesman who elects to use a battleship to do a row-boat's work may get the job done but he may also annihilate his objective.

As a result of his precipitate enthusiasms, Henry was destined to go through life eating his words. During the years when the King was a dutiful and eloquent son of the Church and was writing *The Defence of the Seven Sacraments*, Sir Thomas More warned him against over-stating the theory of papal supremacy on the ground that popes were political figures with whom monarchs might some day find themselves in conflict. 'I think it is best therefore that the part be amended, and his authority more lightly touched.' Henry, however, would have no such politic half-measure. 'Nay, quoth his Grace, that it shall not. We are so much bounden to the See of Rome that we cannot do too much honour to it.'[73] The same tank-like logic and blindness to consequences were revealed some eighteen years later in his approach to the dissolution of the monasteries. Those petrified old oaks were corrupt and rotten; ergo they should all, without exception, be cut down. Once they were destroyed, that was the end of the problem as far as the King was concerned, and he resolutely closed his mind to Bishop Latimer's argument that if 'the founding of monasteries argued Purgatory to be: so the pulling of them down argueth it not to be'. He firmly refused to see the theo-logical implications of his actions, and when the Bishop wrote that 'now it seemeth not convenient' for 'the Act of Parliament to preach one thing, and the pulpit another clean contrary', Henry refused to accept any such sophistry and coldly noted down in the margin: 'Why then do you?'[74] In his mind, if a proposition was good, it was wholly good, right not only for the moment but for all time, and half-measures were no substitute.

Clearly the King was an enthusiast in all he did, in both the intensity with which he held a position and the lengths to which he was willing to go to sustain it. He wrote *The Defence of the Seven Sacraments* in a month; he informed Anne Boleyn that his study of the theological justification for his divorce involved four uninterrupted hours a day of intensive work and had caused 'some pain in his head';[75] and when Anne of Cleves arrived in England the forty-eight-year-old sovereign could not wait to inspect her and rushed off in disguise to Rochester for a quick pre-view. The meeting was ludicrous and unpropitious. Henry burst in upon the astonished maiden, who was sitting at the window engrossed by bear-baiting in the courtyard below. Confronted with this boisterous intruder who kissed and embraced her, Anne was polite but uninterested, and much to the chagrin of the King kept on looking out the window. Annoyed but determined, he retired, cast off his disguise and returned to enjoy the lady's horrified confusion.[76] Henry was, it has been said, a man cursed with too much energy;[77] inevitably he overdid everything — eating, hunting, studying, editing, annotating, dancing, jousting and, it might be added, marrying. His enthusiasm was somehow disproportionate, and this is what makes him so difficult to follow. One moment he scampers off with the Protestant hare, the next he is running with the Catholic hounds; in one breath he is violently French in diplomacy, in the next he is all Imperial; one day he cannot wait to fondle Mistress Anne Boleyn's 'pretty duckys', the next he is capable of believing that she has committed adultery with a hundred men.[78] As Chapuys, who in quiet amusement spent his days watching Henry's erratic behaviour, summed it up: 'When this king decides on anything he goes the whole length' — a refrain which resounded throughout the sovereign's life.[79]

Henry may have gone the whole way in his emotional commitments, but intellectually he rarely got more than half-way. In spite of his expertise, his extraordinary mastery of detail and his encyclopedic memory, he was not an intellectual. His mind was quick and its filing system neat and efficient, but compilation and cataloguing were largely substitutes for thinking. Whatever the theological merits of *The Defence of the Seven Sacraments*[80] Henry never really answered Martin Luther because spiritually they had no common meeting-ground. Neither emotionally nor intellectually was the King equipped to comprehend the solitary nightmare of self-analysis which led the German monk to God. Typically Henry ignored the root and saw only the branches of Luther's argument. 'Why raises he this tumult?' The answer was direct and simple: to foster evil men who sought to escape punishment for their sins. The concept of faith based on despair without strict attention to good works and obedience to God's law was, for the English Moses, silly and dangerous. It was plain to all, the King explained, that there were 'ten to be found who sin in the too much confidence' of God's promise, for every 'one who despairs of obtaining pardon'.[81] What Henry could not see was that God's Word when it enters man's heart has little to do with the theological niceties of the past. Luther was right: Henry Tudor's book was 'based on words of men and the use of centuries'[82] about which the King was a specialist. The Defender of the Faith was always stronger when it came to ritualistic means than to spiritual ends.

Henry was happiest when engulfed in busy work—filing, arranging, studying diplomatic phraseology and calculating problems in logistics which were capable of clear answers. During the frenzied activity following the invasion of France and the siege of Boulogne in the summer of 1544, he found time to answer his wife's request for approval of her ladies-in-waiting. Even in the midst of his occupation 'in foreseeing and caring for everything ourself', he indicated that he remembered in detail each of the damsels. Catherine Parr was replacing some of her ladies because of sickness, and her husband astutely observed that he thought the new selection just as diseased and decrepit as the old, but he graciously added that 'we remit the accepting of them to your own choice, thinking, nevertheless, that though they shall not be meet to serve, yet you may, if you think so good, take them into your chamber to pass the time ... at play'. Then in his own hand he concluded: 'No more to you at this time, sweetheart, both for lack of time and great occupation of business.'[83] The routine of war, the 'great occupation of business' and the preciseness of a military campaign gave the King a marvellous sense of achievement and importance; his mind was taxed but not confused, and, old and ailing as he was, he knew himself to be in full control of the world about him. The sensation would not last, but for a brief moment Henry was content, and Chapuys commented that he had rarely seen him in such excellent spirits.[84]

As a man grows older, his behaviour tends to take exaggerated forms: fear becomes paranoia, single-mindedness degenerates into intolerance, wilfulness sinks into obstinacy, and insecurity is more and more tied to the spectre of mental and physical impotence and incompetence. Behind the imposing façade of detailed factual know-

ledge and love of pedantry was a very uncertain and insecure
sovereign. Possibly the Holbein portrait of a giant glowing with
beneficent self-confidence and inner health was placed in the King's
privy chamber, not in the presence-chamber where one might expect
to find such an icon, because an ageing sovereign had greater need
of the image of kingship than did his subjects. Certainly the effigy
was at odds with the living man. Henry was not the self-assured
decision-maker who, like the Red Queen, shouts 'Off with her head';
he approached most important decisions in the same fashion as his
daughter Elizabeth, reluctant and crab-like. He preferred to post-
pone and, it was reported in 1519, to 'sleep and dream upon the
matter and give an answer upon the morning'.[85] Seventeen years
later he was doing the same thing. The King, wrote Ralph Sadler to
Thomas Cromwell, 'first appointed me to come to him at mass time
to read the same unto his Grace, at which time when I came he said
he would take a time of more leisure, commanding me to tarry until
the evening, when he said he should have best leisure, because he
would maturely advise and peruse the said instructions'. Henry's
excuses did not fool Mr Sadler, for he significantly added: 'As ye
know his Grace is always loath to sign, and I think deferred the reading of the instructions at mass time because he was not willing to
sign.'[86]

Eventually kings must sign; that is their job, and Henry knew his
duty. His methods, however, were painfully pedestrian—if an issue
cannot be postponed, then devise a fixed procedure for making up
one's mind which will remove doubt and uncertainty by always
producing the right answer. If a mathematical theorem, when properly applied, will give the correct solution, then a mechanical approach to decision-making should relieve a man of responsibility
and induce a sense of inner confidence by substituting technical
expertise for real understanding. Almost without exception, the
King's handling of decisions was structured and ritualistic: scrutinize
every detail, study every authority, weigh all the evidence, make up
your mind slowly but surely, and then doggedly stick to your guns,
for those who speak for God cannot for ever be changing their minds.
The method, as applied to diplomacy and the iniquities of the French
King, was neatly outlined in 1525 by Henry himself in a letter to
Bishop Tunstal. In the accomplishment 'of his duty unto God and
the world', he said, he was 'bounden first to search, examine and
inquire where should rest the culpe, blame, default and occasion of
so many evils, to the intent that, the cause once removed and ex-
tirpated, the effects of the same may also be disappointed'.[87] It is
little wonder that Campeggio exclaimed that once the King had

made up his mind, 'if an angel was to descend from heaven, he would not be able to persuade him to the contrary'. Chapuys noted the same conviction when he reported that not all the sovereign's councillors combined can 'persuade him to follow a different course in politics unless the idea comes from him first', and Wolsey warned on his deathbed: 'Be well advised and assured what ye put in his head, for ye shall never pull it out again.'[88] Such inflexibility was not so much ingrown stubbornness as the necessary defence against doubt, the lingering terror, which Martin Luther was honest enough to admit when he cried: 'You alone know everything? But what if you were wrong, and if you should lead all these people into error and into eternal damnation?'[89]

For Henry Tudor, Luther's terrible question remained unasked; instead, there was the compulsion to be right, the thirst for flattery and hankering after approval. All his humble disclaimers—his 'simple judgment', 'ignorant answers' and 'lack of practice'—do not ring true; they provided opportunities for being told the contrary. Chapuys knew how to reach him by 'praising his prudence and experience and saying that ... he should be like a father to the Emperor'—a role the King fancied.[90] The same need to be convinced was evident during the divorce, and when Anne Boleyn first began to call herself Queen, Henry peered anxiously into the faces of his subjects, seeking their approval. He was, said Monsieur de Marillac, a man who 'wants to be in favour with everyone'.[91] It was Erasmus who cut through to the bedrock on which the King stood. Henry, he noted, 'possessed a lively mentality which reached for the stars, and he was able beyond measure to bring to perfection whatever task he undertook. He attempted nothing which he did not bring to a successful conclusion.'[92] The French Ambassador also guessed the truth but phrased it differently; this prince, he said, was 'as all the world knows, far from reckless and bets only on a sure thing'.[93] Throughout his life Henry Tudor attempted only what he could do superlatively well, for both as a man and a divine-right ruler he could not risk failure.

The King's least attractive quality, his refusal to accept responsibility, was part of the same mask, an effort to preserve his image in the looking-glass of his soul. Again and again Henry found cause to shift the blame to others. When early policy had gone wrong, the fault was never his but always belonged to the trusted servant who had told him 'all these things contrary'. Eventually the years of Wolsey's rule were dismissed as none of his doing: 'Those who had the reins of government in their hands deceived me; many things were done without my knowledge ... '[94] The statement was false—

THOMAS HOWARD,
DUKE OF NORFOLK, 1473–1554.
Holbein

SIR WILLIAM PAGET,

PRINCIPAL SECRETARY, 1505?–1563.
Anglo-German School

The Emperor Maximilian (1493–1519) kneeling before Christ.
Woodcut by Hans Springinklee

Henry knew and approved of most of what his Cardinal did; but royalty must be guiltless.[95] When in 1540 the King finally began to perceive that Cromwell's execution had been a blunder, it was necessary to sidestep the responsibility, and he placed the burden squarely on his Council who 'upon light pretexts, by false accusations' had 'made him put to death the most faithful servant he ever had'.[96] As for the calamities of his many spouses, he regretted 'his ill-luck in meeting with such ill-conditioned wives' and, with tears running down his face, accused his Council of having urged him into marriage with Catherine Howard.[97] In Henry Tudor, man's normal instinct to avoid blame was fortified by his peculiar relationship to God. Surely the cause of so much matrimonial misalliance must lie in evil counsel; it could not reside in God's vicar on earth. The crux of the matter was that the King could not have survived unless Tudor society had accepted the formula that 'outward esteem to a great man is as skin to fruit, which though a thin cover, preserveth it'.[98] The axiom was presented as a political principle, but for Henry it was a psychological imperative.

If there is a single theme which runs throughout Henry's life, from the moment the ten-year-old boy became the heir apparent, it was his fear of not being able to live up to the high standards expected of a divine-right monarch; standards, incidentally, which became both more difficult and more necessary to sustain after the break with Rome, when the monarch stood in direct and isolated relationship with his God. Divinity and dependence are incompatible; therefore it was for ever necessary for Henry Tudor to reassert his independence if only to hide his fear from himself. Boasting, bragging and flaunting power are common ways of covering up; projection is another. John Foxe may have been correct: Henry was simply displaying his political acumen when he arranged those humiliating scenes whereby he sought to 'try out the uttermost' of his ministers' 'fetches', but the King may have had other than political needs to satisfy. It is a great comfort to the nagging sense of failure to detect inadequacies in one's fellow man. It may have been necessary to the King's own self-esteem to make his servants look ridiculous, to pull the rug out from under them so that he could draw strength from the sight of their fear and discomfort. Possibly also the intense pleasure with which he listened to confessions of fault was not so much moral sadism as relief for his own insecurity, and a form of identification which exorcizes guilt by associating it, transferring it and confusing it with someone else's sins. Certainly his need to blame others and, as will shortly become apparent, the necessity of transferring responsibility to God are unmistakable. What kind of inner

D

anguish this divine-right King who could do no wrong may have suffered no one can say. The miracle is that he was capable of making decisions at all, if every royal decision had by definition to be right.

A lurking awareness of incompetence can be suppressed by dependence upon ritual as a substitute for thinking; it can also be dispelled by the methodical structuring of life so that the unexpected never takes place. Henry was a man almost without humour; he laughed, but only at others, never at himself, and he was for ever guarding against the possibility that the joke might be on him. The ministers and friends on whom he depended most were not merely administrators who could relieve the anguish of decision-making but servants who knew how to do so without humiliating their master. Anne and George Boleyn could not be forgiven their mockery, and Wolsey and Cromwell were destroyed exactly when they committed the unpardonable sin of making their sovereign look ridiculous: Wolsey at Blackfriars when the Papal Legate adjourned the divorce trial to Rome, and Cromwell when his diplomacy led Henry to play the stud to a Flemish mare. The men who survived—Paget, Lisle, Hertford and above all Cranmer—were not just tactful; they offered their sovereign the external support he required, and, strangely enough, because he seemed a child, they loved him all the better for it.

It was the man who may have loved his master best who sensed the full terror of the nightmare in which Henry Tudor lived. After the fall of Thomas Cromwell in 1540, Cranmer wrote his master that if such a councillor could not be believed, 'I wot not whom your grace may trust.'[99] The answer was self-evident: God's lieutenant on earth could trust only his own divine judgment, and Henry feared even that to be suspect. Here was the secret imp at the core of his personality that led him to seek self-assurance in strident boasting and fanfare, in hiding behind statistics, in shifting the blame and in discovering outside sources of evil which had somehow corrupted and thwarted his good intentions. If the source of the trouble could not be found in the world of man, it could always be sought for in the affairs of God, a subject on which the King was a specialist. The compulsive need to be right, the urge to cast out doubt can lead a man along many paths; it took Henry straight to God, and there we must seek to follow him.

5

'The Conscience of a King'

> MORE. In matter of conscience, the loyal subject is more
> bounden to be loyal to his conscience than to any other
> thing.
> CROMWELL. And so provide a noble motive for his fri-
> volous self-conceit!
> MORE. It is not so, Master Cromwell — very and pure
> necessity for respect of my own soul.
> CROMWELL. Your own self you mean!
> MORE. Yes, a man's soul is his self!
>
> Robert Bolt, *A Man for All Seasons*, Act II

Henry's religious progress, the erratic route he followed between a
malleable and ancient Catholicism untempered by the hot blast of
the Council of Trent and a new and shapeless Protestantism still
lacking the cold logic of John Calvin, leads through a theological
bog into which even the expert may sink without trace. The sign-
posts are few, and often untrustworthy. The old faith was a venerable
and complex corpus of belief which had endured for fifteen hundred
years because it was a spiritual synergism: a union of patristic
commentaries, scholarly glosses, papal decretals and time-honoured
custom conjoined with the revelation of scripture, all of which added
up to something more than the sum of its parts. The totality was a
monumental authority, but the components were rarely clear and
occasionally downright contradictory. It took Sir Thomas More
seven years to convince himself that the secular supremacy of the
Roman pontiff did in fact stem from divine prescription.[1] Time out
of mind, the sacrament of the mass had been both a re-sacrifice of
Christ's body on the cross and a commemoration of that historic
event, but whether it was more one than the other remained in doubt,
and ceremonial usage was not precise. The seven sacraments had
been sanctified by the centuries, but history still resounded with the
wrangle over the exact distinction between Baptism and Confirmation. Protestantism, on the other hand, had not yet been born; it
remained a vague muddle of traditional anti-clericalism, Erasmian
humanism and a theological medley of Luther, Melanchthon, Bucer

and Zwingli. Fortunately it is not necessary to chart the King's
doctrinal course as he floated about in this sea of religious uncertainty; it has been extensively handled elsewhere.[2] To the casual
observer the religious ingredients appear as whimsical as Gilbert's
recipe for a heavy dragoon—elements which were fusible only in
the crucible of Henry's imagination. The residuum was a unique
jumble of theological notions held with a tenacity which converted
rather banal tenets into a heavy-fisted creed. In a study of motivation, however, the conviction with which a body of belief is held is
more important than the doctrine itself. The King's approach to
God, his comprehension of evil and his explanation of existence
reveal far more about the operation of his mind than do the par-
ticulars of dogma.

The deities before whom men bend the knee in supplication, wrote
William James, are 'the gods we need and can use, the gods whose
demands on us are reinforcements of our demands on ourselves and
on one another'.[3] Henry would have indignantly refuted such a
formula as the blasphemous denial of the essence of the universe:
God, not man, was the measure of all things. But for the historian
the premise is indispensable. The surest way of knowing a divine-
right monarch is to study his concept of the King of Kings, for if
Henry Tudor expressed his own state of earthly royalty in terms of
the august chair of heavenly sovereignty, he also modelled his
spiritual overlord on himself. How else could a king have spoken on
terms of intimacy with the deity who had created him in His own
image?

Henry's faith came to him ready made; it was the product of
countless generations and was fully sanctioned by the weight of
history. It was implemented by the instinct of deference which had
been built into the mentality of his age and was centred upon the
doctrine of authority: Christ's life, death and redemption of mankind,
Peter's possession of the keys to the kingdom of heaven, God's Word
revealed in scripture, father over child, husband over wife, priest
over layman, king over subject. The universe and all it contained
was an awe-inspiring and harmonious hierarchy, with power ascend-
ing from level to level to the ultimate authority of the Godhead.
On earth 'every degree of people in their vocation, calling and office'
had been appointed from on high to do their duty; so also in the
heavenly ranks archangels, angels, saints and martyrs recognized
'degree, priority and place'.[4]

To sustain such a complex and perfectly balanced scheme, the
aim of medieval and Tudor religious education was severely cate-
chetical: to drill the mind in habits of piety and duty. Christian

happiness and religious contentment in this eternal hierarchy were based on simple arithmetical computation, in which righteousness and obedience were weighed against sinfulness and wilful rebellion. The Church was at pains to insist that a man's worth must be judged by the calculation of pluses and minuses recorded during his life. Each Christian was warned to keep constantly in mind that the end of life is not death but the eternity of heaven or hell. If, at the final reckoning, a man cared to be numbered among the saved, he must choose on earth the society of the righteous. Nothing was more central to the teaching of the medieval Church than the prick of conscience, for only a clean conscience could secure the Christian from the torments of hell, and it was regularly reiterated that 'the poor man in his hut, wealthy in conscience, sleeps safer upon earth than the rich man in his gold and purple'.[5]

If there is anything in the Freudian argument that the origins of conscience must be sought in the early shaping of the infant mind even before formal instruction has begun, then the Tudor historian faces an impossible task: no sixteenth-century parent, not even a royal one, considered the psychic or educational development of a child worth recording in detail. We know next to nothing about Henry's religious indoctrination, except that the final product was a conventional sovereign who, at the age of fifteen, parroted the accepted religious formula of his day: on the death of the King of Castile, he wrote Erasmus that 'those things which are decreed by Heaven are so to be accepted by mortal men'.[6] It is recorded that he read his Proverbs with their moral enjoinder to give obedience to father, magistrate and God, studied diligently the works of Thomas Aquinas, and was drilled by John Skelton in healthy respect for stern piety and a fear of the seven deadly sins which no amount of humanistic laughter or Renaissance anti-clericalism could dispel.[7] In the oft-quoted observation of the Venetian Ambassador, it was early noted that Henry had been thoroughly inculcated with orthodox habits, for he was 'very religious; heard three masses daily when he hunted, and sometimes five on other days' besides regularly attending vespers and compline.[8] The King's zeal for the faith is undeniable and only to be expected in a civilization which believed with St Jerome that 'in all my actions ... my mind is on four things: first, that my days be short; second, death draweth near; third, mine end is dubitable and doubtful; and the fourth, my departing, painful, and my reward, pain or joy'.[9]

Since the drama of salvation and damnation was the central theme and explanation for the existence of mankind, it behoved all good Christians to map clearly the dimensions of heaven and hell. Both were reflections of man's organizational mind—heaven being the state of exquisite order, hell that of perfect disorder—and both were symbolic representations of man's life on earth. Hell was the place where soft couches were transformed into beds 'more grievous and hard than all the nails and pikes in the world'; loving hugs became the embraces of loathsome devils; and the great retinues of kings and princes turned into a legion of worms and demons which tormented the sinner's body. Conversely, heaven was a bright and beautiful city, 'the hereditary stronghold of the Eternal King', and though God had become an indescribable spiritual essence, the heavenly host which inhabited the spacious halls, fields of joy, and green meadows filled with flowers and sweet odours, was a highly corporeal and active company[10]. At one time God's sanctuary had been populated with His faithful vassals who practised to perfection the virtues and ideals of medieval feudalism; by 1500 the residents of heaven were somewhat less feudally oriented but they remained firmly patriarchal and monarchical. God was the King of Kings with all the attributes of human sovereignty, for the sixteenth-century mind could not conceive of a deity without the heavy cruelty of retributive justice by which to prove His omnipotence.

Henry's relation to this spiritual world and his position as a potential citizen of the kingdom of God were unique. He was not a normal man but a sovereign by divine right, and this posed all sorts of difficulties when it came to participating in the eternal joys of a heavenly society in which all men were kings.[11] Rich and poor believed in the reality of paradise but with a distinction: the poor understandably assumed that God preferred their rustic virtues and would reward their pious patience, punishing the rich and blessing the downtrodden; the rich, on the other hand, argued that in heaven all men were equal but some were more equal than others. The whole of Tudor society knew that 'In my Father's house are many mansions,' and that God's abode, where peace reigned eternal, could not possibly do without rank and privilege. If 'all the pleasure of this world' was nothing 'compared to the least joy of heaven', then a special level of kingliness had to be reserved for God's lieutenants on earth, for, said Thomas Aquinas, kings have a heavier duty than other men and therefore can expect a greater reward and 'receive a high degree of heavenly happiness'.[12]

Henry's association with the world to come and his image of his heavenly master are difficult to assess, but it may not be too far from the truth to assume a direct and anthropomorphic picture. The King was critical of the way his bishops discussed the thorny problem of graven images and of their argument that God's form cannot 'be represented or expressed ... for He is no corporeal or bodily substance'. The prelates reluctantly admitted, as a concession to the 'dulness of man's wit', that representation of the King of heaven was permissible, but they quickly added that 'if the common people would duly conceive of the heavenly Father without any bodily representation, it were more seemly for Christian people ... ' The English monarch was not pleased with such an ethereal God-head; he liked to dress his deity in the material possessions of this earth. Much to Archbishop Cranmer's horror he struck out the offending sentence which urged subjects 'to be without all such images'.[13] He found the egalitarianism implicit in the Lord's Prayer even more distasteful, and when his clerics wrote that God 'equally and indifferently regardeth the rich and the poor' and that 'all Christian people be Christ's own brethren and the very co-inheritors and compartioners with Him in the kingdom of heaven', Henry made it perfectly clear that Christians were only 'co-inheritors' touching their souls in heaven and not their bodies on earth.[14]

If monarchs were in fact God's viceroys in this world, the assumption was, of course, that God was a captain, and therefore Henry's relationship was that of a lesser commander to his general. If the King's concept of heaven in any way reflected his generation, which viewed paradise by the standards of earth and translated human society into the after-life, then his world to come must have been replete with Christ as King of Kings, the Holy Family dressed in the height of Tudor fashion, a divine court with musicians, jesters and servants, and a privy chamber in which Henry Tudor knelt, neatly balancing subservience with a due appreciation of his own importance. He acknowledged his allegiance but at the same time claimed God as his ally. That Henry's contemporaries viewed divine-right kings in this fashion is clear from Hans Springinklee's woodcut of the Emperor Maximilian entering heaven. Christ stands at the portal in His regal garb; at His feet kneels the Emperor, his own insignia properly set aside but his dress every bit the equal of Christ's and quite putting to shame the attire of his heavenly sponsors. A woodcut from the Cranmer Bible of 1539 portraying Henry's close association with the deity, approaches the problem from a slightly different perspective. The King is shown sitting in majesty, and God is bestowing upon him divine wisdom from above. As God's vicar on earth, Henry presents the Word to his spiritual and temporal lords; they in turn transmit the truth as revealed by the sovereign to the laity, who dutifully sing—not God's praise, but 'Vivat Rex.'

A monarch's special claim, as God's faithful vassal, to a secure and prominent abode in paradise carried with it weighty obligations.

Doubtless the spirit of God, as Henry had boasted, brought freedom, but the free man is the responsible man, and the King knew
well what he owed to his deity. His authority stemmed from on
high, and he was determined to discharge his responsibility 'afore
God, being in the room that I am in'.[15] Again and again Henry
reiterated the doctrine of duty. When his clergy said that man is
saved by his faith in Christ's passion and death, he added 'I doing
my duty'; Christians, he said, were the inheritors of God's kingdom
only 'as long as I persevere in His precepts and laws'; and when it
was suggested that man's adversity should be attributed to God's
will, he insisted that misfortune stemmed from man's 'own desert'.[16]
A king's duty was in part to demand of his subjects the same obedience which he offered God, and to do unto his people as he would
have God do unto him: to punish sin, to rout out evil and reward
charity, concord and obedience. But royal responsibility involved
far more than the strict discipline of the magistrate; it behoved
Henry, as a Christian prince, to keep his spirit free from the taint
of sin.

The sixteenth century accepted as a fact of hierarchical life that
rulers, as Christ's high vicars on earth, should be 'judged more
severely in proportion to the great power entrusted' to them. 'For
if God do extremely punish men of base estate and of low degree ...
how severely will he punish kings and princes ... ?'[17] Lesser men,
Cromwell, Gardiner, Cranmer and the like, could always justify
their actions by the Erastian creed that the prince must be obeyed
at all costs, but Henry could hide behind no such sophistry. If God
'illuminated the eyes of the king', then royalty was bound to render
account. Henry could usually be relied on to overstate his case, but
when conscience touched him and he began to doubt the legality of
his marriage to Catherine of Aragon, he may possibly have been
voicing a fear peculiar to a man who took his office with deadly
seriousness. 'Think you my lords', he said, such doubts touch 'not
my body and soul; think you that these doings do not daily and
hourly trouble my conscience and vex my spirit'?[18] Henry, as the
'head and soul of us all,' by definition had to be a man of tender
conscience; and when he announced that he prayed 'for you my
members, that God may light you with His grace', he was simply
repeating the obvious—his unique relationship and obligation to
God.[19]

In a study of man's religious experience, especially that of a
divine-right monarch, it is important to ask what was the King's
understanding of and reaction to sin and evil. Henry's thinking is
clear; it was cast in the mould of William James's 'healthy-minded

man' whose 'contentment with the finite encases him like a lobster-shell and shields him from all morbid repining at his distance from the Infinite'.[20] The 'contented' man, such as Henry, finds security by avoiding the primordial query—what am I doing alone in the midst of cheerless eternity? He asks only the safer question—how does the divine pattern of things accord with the ultimate reality of my existence? and he settles his score with evil by declining to admit his association with it. He is an activist who strikes a blow for righteousness and disdains to spend his days dwelling upon evil, especially when confession and absolution exist to wipe the slate clean of old debts and past trespasses. For these happy few, evil is merely a 'mal-adjustment with *things*, a wrong correspondence of one's life with the environment'.[21]

No man is for ever healthy minded, any more than he needs always be sunk in the hopeless introspection of James's opposite type—'the sick soul'. Even the most determinedly 'contented' individual has his moments of despair and despondency, especially as age, sickness and the tomb approach, but wherever possible Henry wrapped him-self tightly in the warm belief that obedience to God's decrees and scrupulous piety were sure antidotes to evil and that heaven had reserved a special place of honour for the anointed king. His religion was a secure haven, rich with custom and ritual and garrisoned with historic law and hierarchic authority, a place where royalty could converse on terms of respectful familiarity with divinity. For Henry, as for most of the healthy-minded clan, it was essential never to allow a feeling of precariousness, never to admit the stench of the grave or confess the fear of not meriting the fatness of the earth and the serenity of salvation, for these agonies would have destroyed his sense of spiritual well-being and disrupted the cosy tidiness of his cosmic consciousness.

Evil and sin for the King were real enough, but they always re-mained outside him and were either to be avoided or exorcized. Henry was a faithful follower of the policy noted by William James: 'We divert our attention from disease and death as much as we can; and the slaughter-houses and indecencies without end on which our life is founded are huddled out of sight and never mentioned ... '[22] No one was more anxious than the King to escape sickness, and when plague and death approached he fled—partly from fear, partly on the time-honoured premise: out of sight, out of mind. When evil could not be willed out of existence, when it came so close that he could not ignore it, then he pulverized it, striking a blow for God and doing his spirit no end of good. He lectured his sister Margaret on the 'inevitable damnation' awaiting the adulteress. Margaret had

obtained a divorce from her second husband on the highly questionable grounds that the Earl of Angus had been involved in a pre-
contract, and on the even more extraordinary argument that her
first husband, James IV of Scotland, had not been killed at Flodden
Field but was still living at the time of her second marriage. Henry's
notions of decency were outraged by such flummery and he warned
his sister: 'What charge of conscience, what grudge and fretting
yea, what danger of damnation' she brought upon her soul unless
she, 'as in conscience ye are bound under peril of God's everlasting
indignation', relinquished 'the adulterer's company with him that
is not nor may not be of right your husband'.[23]

When evil could not be bullied or ignored, and when it entered
his own life, Henry translated it into one of the most normal and
universal of human reactions: he saw sin in terms of personal persecution. Why has this happened to me? What have I done to deserve ill fortune, sickness and frustration? How have I erred to
warrant God's wrath? And, most important of all: How can I rectify
the situation? The root of the problem lay in the external mechanics
of living. If his dynasty was barren and his first wife old and in-
fertile, if his later spouses proved unfaithful or his diplomacy inept,
the cause lay not in himself but in some inadvertent violation of
God's commandment which had incurred divine wrath. To sin unconsciously is not the same thing as to acknowledge the source of
sinfulness within yourself. Study and obey God's laws to the last
letter, follow in the path of duty and piety, and all would go as
'merry as a marriage bell' again.

The King's healthy-mindedness was doubtless a reflection of the
happy knowledge that heaven smiled upon earth, but operating in
him was another quality which was peculiarly developed in this
insecure but conventional monarch: he lived in the firm conviction
that God can be coaxed by prayer and ritual into granting the
wishes of man. There are three positions, it has been said, in which
man can stand in association with whatever he considers to be his
God—'moral, physical or ritual'.[24] Certainly the last is the most
common and instinctive of the three, for the essence of primitive
religious consciousness is the desire not to know God or to understand Him, but to use Him, 'sometimes as meat-purveyor, sometimes
as moral support, sometimes as friend, sometimes as an object of
love', but most of the time as a source of power.[25] A deity who does
not concern himself with the immediate welfare of his believers,
who fails to give them victory in war, answer their prayers, or cure
foot-and-mouth disease in their cattle is not much of a god. Henry's
God, it is true, could not be coerced, but He could be entreated. He

had long since ceased to react to burnt offerings or the sacrifice of the firstborn, but there remained a tacit understanding that the deity could and did interfere in the affairs of man, and that He did so on the basis of a *quid pro quo*. Passionate supplication in prayer, flattering promises about going on a pilgrimage or crusade, sharp attention to ceremonial detail, and above all absolute obedience to God's laws could assure for the scrupulous worshipper the good things of life.[26]

The sixteenth century presumed a great deal of its God. The youthful Henry grew up in a world assured of the efficacy of papal excommunications directed against traitors. When Cornishmen rose up against the first Tudor in 1497, the Pope received much praise for calling down the vengeance of heaven whereby 'all who eat grain garnered since the rebellion, or drink beer brewed with this year's crops, die as if they had taken poison, and hence it is publicly reported that the King is under the protection of God eternal'.[27] Henry VII's contemporary, Louis XI of France, expected an even greater return for his piety. After lavishly endowing chapels for the benefit of the Virgin, he was outraged when told that the English were once again invading his kingdom, and cried: 'Ah, Holy Mary; even now, when I have given thee fourteen hundred crowns, thou hast done nothing for me.'[28] The picture of a heavenly world populated with singularly militant and meddling, not to say vengeful, personalities who could be enticed to come to the aid of man and enhance his material well-being was only half the equation; Satan and his followers were even more interfering, and it was constantly necessary to call upon the army of righteousness to protect the godly and their possessions from the malice of the devil.

Religion as a magical power to influence the heavenly host and ward off evil recognized no denominational lines. As the Catholic peasant burned a candle to St Clement to protect his house from fire and to St Apollonia to cure a toothache, so the reformer William Tyndale thought that no one would 'dare deny St Anthony a fleece of wool for fear of his terrible fire or lest he send the pox among our sheep'.[29] During the first year of the King's marriage, Queen Catherine was delivered of a stillborn child, and she wrote her father that the calamity was surely the will of God but that she planned to propitiate His anger by giving one of her richest head-dresses to the Franciscan friars.[30] A generation later in 1552 the young Protestant Edward VI calmly informed his physicians, when they assured him that his friend and tutor John Cheke would die, that such was not the case: 'He will not die at this time, for this morning I begged his life from God in my prayers, and obtained it.'[31]

Henry was no worse than his age, only more exacting. When in 1512 a male child was born, alive but sickly, he sought to insure the infant's life by going on a secret and barefoot pilgrimage to Walsingham. Saint Cuthbert's hand was perceived at Flodden Field in July 1513, when an English army routed a Scottish force, killing ten thousand, and it was avowed that the defeat had been inflicted by the outraged saint because James IV had plundered his church. Queen Catherine preferred to acknowledge only God's interference in this instance, and wrote Henry that 'this matter is so marvellous that it seemeth to be of God's doing alone' and she trusted that 'the King shall remember to thank Him for it'. Henry not only agreed with his wife and did as she bid, but he went to his usual extremes, assuring the Pope that as God had given 'Saul power to slay 1,000 and David strength to kill 10,000' so He had made Henry even stronger.[32] In May 1521 the King was planning a pilgrimage in gratitude for his recovery from a serious fever, and during the early years of his courtship with Anne Boleyn it is clear that he thought the deity might be successfully petitioned to act the role of a divine pimp. He wrote Anne that as his heart was dedicated to her alone, so also was he 'greatly desirous' that his 'body could be as well, as God can bring to pass if it pleaseth Him, whom I entreat once each day for the accomplishment thereof, trusting that at length my prayer will be heard'.[33] Each of these episodes is an example of a cause-and-effect approach to religion, a ritualistic and ceremonial performance in which the deity is assumed to take delight in 'tapers and tinsel, costume and mumbling and mummery'.[34] When the words and actions of the formula have been performed to perfection, then it behoves God to fulfil his side of the bargain and grant power, wealth and peace of mind.

There is little doubt that Henry was a ritualist, or that he thought in terms of Old Testament justice. Early in the controversy with Martin Luther he stated a position which no amount of religious revolution ever changed; there is, he wrote, much greater need 'to contemplate the severe and inflexible justice of God' than the caprice of His mercy.[35] Almost two decades later in his correction of *The Bishops' Book* he was still voicing the same conviction: God keeps His promise to man provided man does his duty to God.[36] Religion was a bargain in which both sides knew the rules and penalties involved, and the King carefully added to the commandment which enjoins us not to covet our neighbour's wife, servant, ass or any of his goods, the excellent mercantile axiom: 'without due recompense'.[37] In his own life, he was outraged that past services should not have their future rewards, and during the divorce controversy he made it obvious to the Pope that 'the favour, which alone, and now for the first time, we ask of your holiness ... cannot justly be denied to our piety and our efforts and endeavours for the Catholic cause'.[38]

The same bartering was implicit in the King's concern for ritual. On Good Fridays he dutifully crept to the cross and served the priest at mass, 'his own person kneeling on his grace's knees'; he scrupulously received 'holy bread and holy water every Sunday' and daily used 'all other laudable ceremonies'.[39] His reverence for the sacrament of the mass, it was reported late in the reign, 'was always most profound', and when it was suggested that, because of 'his weakness and infirmity', he did not have to 'adore the body of Our Saviour' on his knees but could 'make his communion sitting in a chair', he answered that if 'I lay not only flat on the ground, yea, and put myself under the ground, yet in so doing I should not think that I have reverence sufficient unto His blessed sacrament'.[40] To the end of the reign there were candles at Candlemas, palms on Palm Sunday, ashes on Ash Wednesday, and even when early in 1546 he added creeping to the cross to the list of unnecessary ceremonies which Archbishop Cranmer had been commissioned to draw up,[41] he did so exactly at the moment when it was becoming almost impossible for his obese hulk with its ulcerated leg to reach the altar on hands and knees. Henry was nothing if not pragmatic about the terms of the bargain he was willing to negotiate with the Almighty.

Henry Tudor was not only a ritualist but also a high priest; a specialist who knew every word of the incantation, every gesture of the ceremony, every rule of the commandment, and who brought to matters of ritual the same detailed knowledge he applied to the joust, court pageantry and military affairs. It has been said of ritual that it 'attaches itself to the basic activities and events of life, which are naturally those that affect the emotions most deeply—eating, drinking, intercourse, birth and death'. It tends also to be repetitive, pedantic and precise, and 'when some detail is omitted, worry and a sense of impending danger follow'.[42] Henry's leaden sense of duty, his contractual approach to God and retributive understanding of divine justice were heavily influenced by Leviticus, one of the most popular books of religious instruction in the early sixteenth century, and certainly the most ritualistic. It is in effect a catalogue of taboos and prohibitions, a ferocious listing of the punishments in store for anyone who dares to disobey. It offers the basic explanation of Christian causation in history—'I am the Lord your God' and 'if ye will not hearken unto me, and will not do all these commandments', then

I will even appoint over you terror, consumption, and the burning ague ... and ye shall sow your seed in vain ... And I will
set my face against you ... And I will break the pride of your
power; and I will make your heaven as iron, and your earth as
brass: And your strength shall be spent in vain: for your land
shall not yield her increase, neither shall the trees of the land
yield their fruits. And if ye walk contrary unto me, and will
not hearken unto me; I will bring seven times more plagues
upon you according to your sins.

Lev. xxvi 14–21

The connection between the King of heaven and earthly sovereigns was manifest to Tudor eyes. 'As as father over his children is
both lord and judge', wrote William Tyndale in 1528, so the Lord
'hath put kings, governors and rulers in His own stead to rule the
world'. Whosoever 'resisteth them, resisteth God' and 'shall receive
their damnation', for it is written: "Keep my ordinances and laws,
which if a man keep, he shall live therein" (Lev. xviii 5).'[43] Henry
knew his God as a 'consuming fire, ever a jealous God', and therefore it was essential to avoid all those things 'which are forbidden
to be done by the commandments of the Lord'. For Henry, as for
most people, it was far better to believe in a God who punishes you
according to a known and published code than one who lets you
down or, worse, ignores you.

Firm in his knowledge of the nature of the deity and walking in
the fear of his Lord, Henry became something of a spiritual hypo-
chondriac. No one was more careful of his soul's welfare than the
King, no one more scrupulous in his exact conformity to the prescribed religious formula of the day, and during the height of the
divorce crisis in 1533 the Spanish Ambassador noted that 'the King
in his blindness feared no one but God'.[44] He was constantly testify-
ing 'his zeal for the faith' with all the 'resources of his mind and
body',[45] for his relationship with his God was sanguine if elementary:
in return for the punctilious fulfilment of his religious obligations,
God would reward him with material success and eternal salvation.
Very early in life Henry confessed to the Venetian Ambassador the
core of his faith and the crux of a healthy-minded approach to religion when he proclaimed he could not 'see that there is any faith
in the world, save in me, and therefore God Almighty, who knows
this, prospers my affairs'.[46] Twenty-one years later, when correcting
The Bishops' Book, he incorporated the same argument but in
reverse. It was not sufficient, he said, to maintain that a Christian
must believe that while God 'is my Lord and Governor and I under

his protection, neither sin, neither the devil, nor yet death, nor hell can do me any hurt'. Instead, the King made God's 'protection' conditional, adding: 'which I am void of while I continue in sin'.[47] It followed, therefore, that should God remove His blessings and plague him with misfortune, somehow, somewhere, Henry had involuntarily sinned by failing to propitiate the divine wrath.

If there is anything approaching a complete explanation of Henry's actions it lies in an amalgam of his compulsive need to wall out doubt by keeping conscience clear and placing blame on others and his absolute conviction that events are determined by a bargain struck between God and man. Here possibly is the central explanation for the King's behaviour during the crisis of his life when an apprehensive and wary monarch, who was 'anything but reckless', drove through his divorce with Catherine of Aragon in the face of Christian outrage and the threat of hell fire. The man of conscience, if he is also a ritualist set upon convincing himself of his innocence, can be far more ruthless than the lover blinded by passion or the statesman absolved of his crimes by state necessity.

From the start, the 'pernicious and inordinate carnal love' of a lustful prince who allowed his conscience to creep too near a lady of the court was a popular explanation for the King's matrimonial scruples.[48] Likewise, reason of state—the need to secure the succession in the male line—was reiterated *ad nauseam* by Henry himself;[49] but ultimately the King rested his case on 'the discharge of our conscience'.[50] In 1529 he wrote his nephew the Emperor Charles V that he could not 'quiet or appease his conscience remaining longer with the Queen, whom, for her nobleness of blood and other virtues, he had loved entirely as his wife, until he saw in Scripture that God had forbidden their union'. Then he pointedly asked whether Charles 'would wilfully destroy' his uncle's soul by refusing to support the dissolution of such an unlawful union.[51]

Sexually and politically the situation in 1527–8 was perfectly capable of solution. Catherine's daughter, the Princess Mary, could have been married to her first cousin, James V of Scotland, thereby achieving what we are so often told was the ultimate purpose of Henry's Scottish policy: the creation of Great Britain.[52] Or Henry could have adopted any one of the ingenious, if tawdry, expedients offered by a Pope desperately anxious to find a solution short of divorce. His Holiness had made known his willingness to sanction royal bigamy, to permit adultery by legitimizing any children of the King and Anne Boleyn, or to bless the marriage of Henry's bastard, the Duke of Richmond, with the Princess Mary.[53] Public

opinion, if Erasmus accurately reflected it, obviously preferred some
such 'arrangement', for he wrote that the English monarch 'should
take two Junos rather than put away one'.[54]

There was another way out of the King's difficulties—carnal as
well as dynastic—so apparent that it is extraordinary that it was
never whispered abroad: Catherine could have been quietly mur-
dered in her bed and no one would have been the wiser. Had Henry
really been a Machiavellian monster willing to sacrifice all upon the
altar of dynasty or lust, his easiest course would have been to take
a page from his ancestors' book and send for the assassin. This was
to be his daughter's preferred method of resolving the riddle of
what to do with Mary of Scotland,[55] and Henry himself in 1545
sanctioned the murder of Cardinal David Betoun, though he wisely
refused to put it in writing.[56] He knew full well that his subjects
were sufficient realists to accept the argument that 'it is no murder
in a King to end another's life to save his own', for 'if you fail, the
state doth whole default, the realm is rent in twain in such a loss'.[57]
Yet Henry would have no murder, no papal dispensation, and no
Scottish marriage. His representative in Rome in September 1530
dismissed the Pope's proposition that the King should take two
wives on the grounds that he 'did not know whether it would satisfy
your Majesty's conscience',[58] and nowhere is there any hint that the
easy solution—quietly to do away with Catherine—was ever considered. Instead he held out for annulment and remarriage.*

Tradition says that it was Anne Boleyn who kept Henry waiting
at her chamber door for six interminable years until she had won
herself a crown, but given the King's inordinate affection for ritual
and the structure of his thinking, it seems almost as probable that
it was the husband who insisted on legitimizing his adultery. For
Henry the matter was simple: 'All such issue males as I have received of the Queen died immediately after they were born; so that
I fear the punishment of God in that behalf.'[59] Under such circumstances it was far more important to propitiate the gods by sacrificing
Catherine than to appease his appetite by bedding down Mistress
Anne, who in the end did oblige her sovereign some six months before
the divorce and showed that she was willing to make do with the
title of Marquis of Pembroke and a thousand pounds a year.†

* Henry's 'divorce' was never in fact a divorce but an annulment, since the
King maintained that he had not been legally married to Catherine in the first
place.

† The time-table is: created Marquis of Pembroke September 1st, 1532;
conception early December; secret marriage January 25th, 1533; Henry's
divorce May 23rd; coronation June 1st; birth of Elizabeth September 7th,
1533. When Anne moved into the royal bed is anybody's guess.

When Catherine of Aragon failed to secure the succession by a male heir, Henry searched his conscience for the source of such obvious divine malediction, and discovered the cause in Leviticus: 'And if a man shall take his brother's wife, it is an unclean thing: he hath uncovered his brother's nakedness; they shall be childless' (xx 21). Even if the sin were unconscious, ignorance of God's law was no excuse, for it was clearly stated: 'though he wist it not, yet is he guilty, and shall bear his iniquity' (Lev. v 18). It was perfectly obvious to the King that here was the root of the difficulty, and not even the protestations of a wife whom he had once loved and still respected could outweigh the evidence of sin. Catherine's passionate oath that she had come to his bed 'a true maid without touch of man' had to be balanced against the fact that God had not only destroyed all but one girl-child of that union but had also punished Henry seven times over. It was plainly written in Deuteronomy for all to read: 'I set before you this day a blessing and a curse; A blessing, if ye obey the commandments of the Lord your God ... And a curse, if ye will not obey ... ' (xi 26–8).

As a ritualist the King stood firmly on the letter of the law stated in Leviticus, which he knew word for word,* and he accepted literally the curse in Deuteronomy. The fact that Anne Boleyn herself came within the same prohibited degree—she was the sister of Mary Boleyn, Henry's mistress during the early 1520s—was irrelevant; Leviticus makes no mention of mistresses' sisters, only of brothers' wives. God, presumably, was annoyed over one thing at a time; if male heirs were still withheld from the second marriage, there was time enough to investigate the cause of the trouble. Man's ability to compartmentalize his mind and close the shutters on logical parallels should never be underestimated. Henry was never one to permit the ultimate logic of his argument to befuddle the simplicity of the immediate problem. If God had saddled him with a middle-aged and barren spouse then he must ask himself: What have I done to deserve this? Having found the solution, no other would do, for that which achieves the immediate purpose of receiving God's blessings and deflecting His curses must, by definition, be good. When the Imperial Ambassador noted that if this English monarch decided on an undertaking, 'he goes the whole length',[60] he was simply recording a facet of Henry's personality which the King would have been proud to acknowledge. There was no question about where he stood or possible doubt as to his position, for 'the bowels

* Henry's *Defence of the Seven Sacraments* quotes Leviticus and Deuteronomy (pp. 194, 206), and a glossary of both books is listed in the King's Library at Westminster (B.M., Add. MSS, 4729).

of his conscience and heart' had spoken and could not be denied.[61]

Everywhere Henry looked there were fearful indications that the Lord had turned His face against him, and possibly it is here that we have a clue to that most thorny of all Henrician problems—the dating of the King's conscience. The question of timing has always plagued Tudor historians. The first documented evidence of a divorce justified on grounds of conscience does not appear until May 1527, but the possibility of a divorce goes back almost a decade. The Queen's last pregnancy was in 1518; the following year Henry proved where the fault of sterility lay by siring a son by his mistress Elizabeth Blount; and by 1524–5 he had ceased to cohabit with a wife who had reached her fortieth year and was 'long past the usual age of childbearing'.[62] It is clear that the King's troubled conscience did not spring fully armed with the verses of Leviticus from Henry's theological brow. The thought may have been lingering unformed and unexpressed for years before 1527, or it could have been implanted by Cardinal Wolsey some time during the winter of 1526–7.[63] Whatever the inspiration, the fact remains that the years 1524 to 1527 provided the most overwhelming evidence of God's displeasure: a series of terrible blows guaranteed to make any monarch wonder why he was being singled out and cursed with ill fortune.

In March 1524 Henry received a bad scare and dire warning. In his joust with the Duke of Suffolk the King entered the list with the visor of his helmet open. Though the horrified audience shouted to the Duke to hold, he could neither hear nor see, and Suffolk's lance struck and shattered against the King's helmet less than an inch from his exposed face.[64] A year later, while hawking, Henry had an even narrower escape. In running after his quarry he jumped a ditch, tripped, broke his jumping-pole, and fell head-first into the water, his face stuck firmly in the mud. Panting attendants arrived just in time to save their sovereign from a singularly undignified death.[65] On top of accidents came diplomatic insult: the Emperor Charles in June 1525 had the appalling effrontery to ask to be released from his contract to marry the Princess Mary. A month later the worst plague in a decade descended straight from heaven to chastise the kingdom. Fifty people a day died in London and not even the King himself was safe, for, no matter how far or fast he fled, death followed. In January 1526 two gentlemen of his household died,[66] and for the next two years the terrible disease was endemic.

'Fear of death', it has been said, 'is fatal to the peace of a guilty conscience, and it might well have made Henry pause in his pursuit after the divorce and Anne Boleyn.'[67] The logic, however, is specious; Henry refused to waver, not in defiance of the plague, but because of it. Each blow—the terrible winter of 1527 when the sea itself froze and half the flour in London was made of beans,[68] the diplomatic debacle of the Peace of Cambrai in August of 1529 by which England was isolated and humiliated, and the public fiasco of the divorce trial at Blackfriars—simply strengthened his conviction. They were all further confirmation of God's word; 'I will set my face against you'; and further evidence of the pressing need to make atonement by a sin-offering in the form of a formal dissolution of his marriage. On top of everything else came the first signs of age, that moment when the balance tips towards the aches and pains of advancing years. Henry was thirty-five in 1526 in a century which reckoned forty-five elderly and fifty-five approaching the grave. In 1521 he was struck down by fever and complained of sinus pains; in 1528 his chronic headaches were first recorded; and in 1532 came the earliest mention of gout. More than once the destinies of Europe would be twisted by the close association between the prick of conscience and the pain of gout, and everyone in the sixteenth century knew that sickness was a visitation sent by God as a warning or a chastisement.

To a pampered monarch resentful of misfortune, regarding it as a personal affliction ordained by heaven, and desperately anxious to deflect God's wrath by religious ritual, it was evident that sickness and plague, accident and diplomatic defeat were the wages of sin. It is little wonder, then, that Henry's conscience was deeply touched or that he refused to consider shoddy half measures or immoral substitutes. Atonement had to be made both for the sake of his own soul and for the welfare of his kingdom, and God as well as man held him strictly accountable.

Henry was unwilling to contemplate the murder of his wife, but he was ready to commit what his contemporaries held to be a far greater crime: the risk of his soul's salvation by defying the Pope and severing his kingdom from God's Church. His soul alone would pay the ultimate price if he were wrong and the Christian-Catholic world were right. Emotionally, politically and spiritually the defiance of Rome took extraordinary nerve, and neither the anti-clerical and humanistic currents of the century nor the fervent support of a small coterie of admirers could alter the fact that most Christians knew that 'the King will hang in Hell one day'. Henry obviously appreciated the spiritual danger of his actions, for he shied away from schism as long as he could. The two people who knew him best—his wife and his chief minister—thought that he would never risk his chances of paradise.[69] All his actions up to the very threshold of the break with Rome were those of a man wavering on the brink, fearful of taking the final irrevocable step. As late as March 31st, 1533, two months before Cranmer in defiance of Rome granted the divorce, Henry was still telling Chapuys that if the Pope would 'do his pleasure in this affair', he would be willing to reconsider.[70] Yet when the chips were down and his bluff, if it was a bluff, was called, his will alone gave legality to the Royal Supremacy and his soul alone would be held accountable in the final judgment.

In the end the King placed his fate on the quality of his conscience; he was right 'not because so many saith it', but because he 'knoweth the matter to be right'.[71] As in so many other matters the expert had spoken, but so also had that same inner voice of individualism which sustained Martin Luther. 'Though the law of every man's conscience', Henry confessed, 'be but a private court, yet it is the highest and supreme court for judgment or justice.'[72] Like Luther and Calvin, he took his stand on his nearness to God and the strength of his spiritual conviction, but with a difference—his was not the lonely individualism of the solitary Christian with nothing but his faith to clothe his nakedness, but the splendid isolation of a King who stood apart and knew himself to be filled with God's grace. For all their mutual animosity, however, the German monk and the English King were strangely alike: each placed personal judgment above doubt. With Luther the very intensity of belief made it seem that his will stemmed from on high and was not the product of his fancy, and he quoted from Galatians (i 8): 'though ... an angel from heaven preach any other gospel unto you than that which we have preached unto you, let him be accursed'.[73] At the height of the divorce crisis Henry wrote something very similar: 'The sincerity of the truth', he explained to Clement VII, 'prohibited us to keep silence ... for it toucheth not worldly things but divine, not frail but eternal in which things no feigned, false nor painted reasons, but only the truth shall obtain and take place.'[74] This confidence in absolute rightness engendered the spiritual enthusiasm and the 'inhibition-quenching fury' necessary for a rather timid man to risk public scandal and to do what he, as a Christian prince, knew to be right. If the historian is ready to dignify Luther's ego by calling it conscience, then perhaps the same honour should be accorded Henry.

The line between conscience and pride is an exceedingly tenuous one, and there are those who argue that rebellion took no great courage, for pride inured the King's heart to fear and remorse; conscience was dead and in its stead was nothing but the criminal's greed and the instinct to survive.[75] Doubtless the circle of Henry

Tudor's understanding was small and securely guarded, and he rested his case on the simple alliance between God and man. As he put it: 'God and his conscience were perfectly agreed on that point.'[76] But after the divorce and the break with Rome, Henry was more alone with his God than ever before; never again could he say: 'As for me, I well know and acknowledge that I am unable of myself to [come to] the understanding thereof, and therefore, calling for God's help, most humbly submit myself to the determination of Christ's Church and interpretation of the holy fathers ...'[77] Henceforth, like the Protestant from whom he was so alien in almost every other respect, he stood in direct confrontation with God. The thought of ten thousand papal excommunications had lost its terror, but the fear of God 'to whom account must be rendered of all our doings' remained.[78] The Almighty had laid upon him the moral leadership of his kingdom, and Henry dared not fail.

6

The Moral Commonwealth

Take away the wicked from before the king,
and his throne shall be established in righteousness.
                                                    Prov. xxv 5

'My King', pronounced the Protestant martyr Robert Barnes, 'does not care about religion.'[1] What kind of presumptuous nonsense was this that dismissed the Supreme Head of the English Church and Defender of its Faith as a Pharisee? How could a prince who had spent his life labouring in the Lord's vineyard, clipping and pruning the formularies of the true faith so that his subjects might live 'in one faith, one hope, one charity' and, best of all, in one perfect agreement, be lacking in religion?[2] How could the royal theologian who had, in his own words, 'travailed to purge and cleanse' his kingdom of hypocrisy, superstition and 'sinister understanding of Scripture' be wanting in faith?[3]

The root of the issue dividing the King from Barnes and all those who felt the devil's breath close upon them was essentially semantic. No one denied that man's life was a moral drama, but for the healthy-minded monarch morality was an organizational matter of external obedience to a prescribed code of righteousness, while for Barnes and the 'sick souls' of his world it was a question of internal spiritual contentment. In theory there should have been no conflict between the two definitions. If individual conscience is in harmony with the spiritual aspirations and institutional procedures of society, socially acceptable actions—joining pilgrimages or peace corps, founding monasteries or libraries, spreading the gospel or clearing the slums— will produce inner satisfaction. In fact, society rarely achieves such a perfect balance of ethical values and social techniques. Either the rules of right action become outmoded and therefore cease to satisfy, or the shield of apathy and pragmatism which protects most tender consciences gives way before the conviction that man's actions on earth must be in accord with a higher meaning in the universe.

It is intriguing to speculate whether a sense of spiritual alienation from the world is a contagious infection of the soul, which spreads and grows without direct relation to the corrupt ways of this earth, or a social malaise varying with time and circumstance. The medieval past had had its swarm of lost denizens, but for centuries the Christian world had been strong and flexible enough to silence the discontented with either the harshness of iron and fire or the sweetness of respectability. Now, however, in the early years of the sixteenth century, the intensity of spiritual anguish seemed, if not necessarily stronger, more highly placed and more vocal than in previous generations, and was concentrated in the two most sensitive centres of Christendom: the university and the monastery.

In Germany Martin Luther laboured earnestly at his monastic calling and yet found no peace of mind. 'If ever a monk got to heaven by his monkery', Luther avowed, 'it was I':[4] but, try as he would, the young man found fasting, prayer and self-discipline—that way of life reserved for the religious elite of the medieval world—to be a hollow and senseless mummery. In England his despair was echoed by a Cambridge scholar who also sought to shut out doubt and fear by doggedly conforming to the letter of the ancient formula. Thomas Bilney was just as scrupulous as the Saxon monk in his holiness. He 'reckoned himself bound so straitly to keep and observe the words of Christ after the very letter' that, because he had been taught to say his prayers in private, he thought it 'a sin to say his service abroad, and always would be sure to have his chamber door shut' when reciting his matins.[5]

Little Thomas Bilney found no more satisfaction than Luther. The similarity between their disenchantments was symptomatic of the failure throughout Europe of right actions to generate right thoughts, and their solutions were of a kind: the divorce of outward deeds from inward bliss. One day in 1515 Martin Luther was pondering anew the assurance of St Paul: 'The just shall live by faith.' Suddenly the entire edifice of the church seemed to fall away, and the monk who had travailed so diligently at monkery knew himself to be reborn and to have 'gone through open doors into paradise'.[6] It was no longer necessary to light candles, creep to the cross, endow chapels, offer alms, retreat into a monastery, or do good works in order to please God. Luther suddenly sensed that actions have nothing to do with salvation; heaven cannot be bought with deeds, for the gates of the Kingdom are opened by God's infinite mercy to all who have faith. A year later Thomas Bilney also found new strength in another promise offered by St Paul: 'It is a true saying, and worthy of all men to be embraced, that Christ Jesus came into the world to save sinners, of whom I am the chief and principal' (1 Tim. i 15). The same light that had filled Luther now flooded in upon the Trinity College scholar. Christ's sacrifice had been sufficient; there was no more Bilney could do but fall upon his knees and rejoice in God's love. The agony of scrupulous holiness, of seeking to enact the exact letter of the prescribed ritual, was useless. In giving up the struggle and admitting defeat, Bilney like Luther found 'marvellous comfort and quietness', and his 'bruised bones', which had worked so industriously to do the right thing, now 'leaped for joy'.[7]

The crux of Luther's and Bilney's experiences was their emotional response to faith: the physical sensation of rebirth. The Christian who knows himself to be at one with Christ lives on a plane far above that reached by most men. Those fortunate few require none of the ceremonial props and stage machinery necessary to sustain the average man's faith. The regenerated do not have to be instructed in righteousness, for they already glow with inward zeal. They do what is right because their faith leads them along the path of God. For Robert Barnes, Thomas Bilney, William Tyndale and John Lambert, every one of whom died rather than countenance a life of expediency, this was the only possible moral imperative, for it came from the heart and not from the mechanical canons of society which dictated what was right and what was wrong and then held all men to it.

For all his theological proficiency, Henry Tudor could never be numbered among these ardent souls whose spiritual enchantment converted the agony of life into the joy of living. From Barnes's point of view the King had only an empty faith, a simple belief in God's Word and Christ's sacrifice, conceived in the mind as an act of intellect but dead to the heart. The intensity of Henry's conviction, the surging confidence of his self-righteousness, were, in the eyes of the religious radicals, not to be accounted true faith, for they were grounded on fear of damnation, not on the certainty of salvation. The Supreme Head simply could not comprehend Tyndale's confident assertion that 'when we have [faith] we need no other thing more', or his equally repugnant warning that 'whosoever goeth about to make satisfaction for his sins' to God, saying to himself, 'this much have I sinned' and 'this-wise will I live to make amends', is 'damned in his deed-doing'.[8] Faith without physical proof of right-doing seemed to Henry to be the height of pretentiousness, and repentance of sin which did not result in outward correction of misdeeds was sheer hypocrisy. Actions spoke louder than words, and the monarch assured his subjects that when the final pronouncement was made, every Christian would be 'called to an account of his life'; he would be judged 'according to his works, good or bad, done in his lifetime', and those who 'persevere in well-doing' would be 'given life everlasting'.[9] There was not the slightest doubt where the prince stood when it came to right actions on the part of his people: Englishmen were to withstand 'presumption', expel 'malice', refrain from 'carnal liberty', and 'live quietly and charitably together, each one in his vocation'.[10]

'Deed-doing' and 'well-doing' lay at the root of the controversy. Call it what you may—healthy-minded conceit or the despair of a sick soul, merit-theology or the doctrine of immediate grace, ritualism or mysticism, low- or high-intensity religion—the central issue was always the same: religion was either a series of social actions by which the incomprehensibility of the universe was translated into an intellectually meaningful and satisfying formula for living and getting along here on earth, or the lonely introspection of men seeking to find an inner happiness which transcended the here and now and spoke to the heart, not the mind. This was the chasm that divided Tudor England far more than did the bitterness of rival dogmas. If an emotional spectrum of religious response were established, with James's overheated 'sick soul' at one extreme and the frosty 'healthy-minded' pragmatic man at the other, without exception the advisers and courtiers closest to the King during the last decade of his life, as well as the 'old man' himself, would fall into the cool, low-intensity half of the scale. They were men who countenanced the world largely because they were, as one disgusted religious idealist put it, 'earthly men' and therefore had 'an earthly God to serve'.[11]

Henry's 'well-beloved councillors' worshipped their earthly deity in many ways and with varying intensity. Some, like Stephen Gardiner, were blatant exponents of 'belly-wisdom', and his deadly ministerial argument that 'good is not good, when it is not well done, to which well-doing, time is a special circumstance'[12] brought down upon him the wrath of all who placed purity of life above political expediency. Does Winchester, they demanded, think that he is 'bringing a new philosophy down from heaven? Hitherto we have waged war with the old sophistry of the monks. Now a new sophistry is brought forward, with powerful supporters, who measure and corrupt religion by human prudence ... '[13] The appeal of political prudence was not confined to wily Winchester; it caught even Thomas Cranmer, who warned his sovereign in 1546 that if such ceremonies as creeping to the cross were abolished without sufficient instruction it might 'seem to many that be ignorant that the honour of Christ is taken away' and there might be 'murmuration and grutching'.[14] Others were frank pragmatists, men branded as 'neuter, being indifferent' and 'observing all things that are commanded outwardly' but in their hearts 'set wholly against the same'.[15] When in the summer of 1546 Anne Askew was interrogated and tortured in an effort to make her recant her sacramentarian heresy and reveal the names of her friends at court, she accused Lord Lisle of counselling her to comply even though he knew it was contrary to God's will, and she scornfully rejected Sir William Paget's 'glorious words' to conform her faith to the fashion of the day on the ground that she could always 'deny it again if need were'.[16] Another of Anne's tormentors, Sir Richard Riche, who helped Lord Chancellor Wriothesley turn the handle of the rack, practised what his friend the Principal Secretary preached: he became an excellent gospeller under Edward VI, recanted and founded a Catholic boy's school under Mary, and returned to the new faith on the succession of Elizabeth, personally demolishing the popish ornaments with which he had endowed his academy. It might be said that Sir Richard was a time-server, studying to obtain the good will of all parties, but Edward Seymour, Earl of Hertford, a man of considerable principle, abided by Gardiner's advice 'to be noted neither on the one side nor the other', and his wife seems to have been able to keep the friendship of the Princess Mary while associating with the humanistic and dangerous doctrines of Queen Catherine Parr.[17]

How many bore the whips and ills of today so as to work from within, fearing to speak out lest they lose their influence, is mere guesswork. Richard Cox and John Cheke, the tutors of young Prince Edward, became ardent Protestants, the former the prickly Bishop of Ely under Elizabeth and the latter the clerk of the Edwardian Council, but during Henry Tudor's rule they were known as moderate and indifferent men, and Cox was one of those who wrote the interpretation of the sacrament of the mass which Anne Askew disdainfully refused to sign.[18]

Doubtless many were confused and uncertain as to the truth, and in their confusion accepted Bishop Richard Sampson's satisfying dictum: 'The word of God is to obey the King and not the bishop of Rome.'[19] After Henry's death, Thomas Cranmer had no answer to Stephen Gardiner's probing question—why had the Archbishop pliantly obeyed the old King if he really thought their late master was being seduced by popery? Surely to leave the monarch in error was to endanger his royal 'soul and the souls of others'. If, declared the Bishop, Cranmer gave as his excuse that he 'durst not say the truth', such a confession not only spoke ill for the quality of the prelate's faith but also was 'a marvellous allegation to the condemnation' of their sovereign.[20] Under Catholic Mary, Thomas Cranmer would eventually prove his metal, and with Latimer,

Hooper and Ridley 'play the man' on Smithfield meadow, but under his old master he wore the mask of an archbishop, and like the Duke of Norfolk believed simply that when the sovereign 'had distinctly declared his will more for one thing than the other, he was bound to support him'.[21] But many certainly crept into their holes and kept silent out of dread. The sight in July 1540 of Robert Barnes and two other heretics dying in agony for the gospel, and on the same day the spectacle of three priests mutilated and butchered for popery, was enough to win the earthly god of belly-wisdom a multitude of converts.

A man's position on the religious scale, regardless of whether he wore the ancient livery of Catholicism or the mod styles of Protestantism, did not have to be consistent. The discontented soul, who asks what in life has purpose that death does not destroy, may not find the answer immediately forthcoming or he may elect for years to accept the soothing arguments of healthy-minded men. Certainly Archbishop Cranmer, Bishops Bonner and Tunstal and even Stephen Gardiner himself moved from outward conformity, accommodating themselves 'to the conscience and opinion' of the majority,[22] to the greater consolation of inner conviction. But one man ruthlessly and persistently continued to judge religion in terms of the political myth of a kingdom swelling with well-doing, right-thinking, obedient and contented subjects: the King himself. Once the superstitious shell of unthinking and exaggerated obedience to the old creed had been cracked by his defiance of Rome, Henry was quite capable of entertaining a host of novel ideas, many of which were in tune with Lutheran doctrines, but emotionally he had neither understanding nor respect for the zeal of sick souls, be they Catholic or Protestant. He was, in the scornful language of Martin Luther, a man 'who has no love for the clear truth' and instead turns and twists, thereby rending 'his mouth like the fish trying to escape from the hook'.[23]

For almost fifteen years Henry carried on a doctrinal dance with the German Protestants, a religious minuet in which both parties bowed and swayed to the theological melody of Wittenburg but rarely touched hands, let alone danced cheek to cheek. It is deceptively easy to detect in this stately motion a steady and conscious movement towards Lutheranism and heresy. Diplomatic and theological discussions with the Germans began in earnest in 1534 and continued with varying degrees of sincerity throughout the reign. The point of closest understanding was reached in 1536, when the doctrinal drift away from Catholicism was dramatized by the publication of the Ten Articles. The entente continued on the same level during the following year, and then proceeded to blow hot or cold depending on diplomatic and domestic considerations. It fluctuated erratically during the winter and summer of 1538–9, collapsed in 1540, and warmed up somewhat during the last year and a half of the King's life. There can be no doubt that Henry knew about and sanctioned the dogmatic diet being offered his subjects, and that diplomatically he was anxious to maintain a foot in the Lutheran camp, even if it cost him a certain amount in theological consistency.[24] Heavy doses of Lutheranism were borrowed from the Augsburg Confession and Luther's Catechism and injected into the Ten Articles and later *The Bishops' Book*. This does not mean, however, that the King was a Lutheran, for his heresy stemmed not from any inner need to reorient his faith, but from a combination of humanistic anti-clericalism, compulsive anti-papism and confidence in his own theological expertise.

Early in his career, the young monarch learned the language, if not the message, of Christian humanism. Henry's approach to religion was far too mechanical and precipitous to grasp the import of Erasmus's philosophy of Christ, which enjoins man to revere the mind of St Paul preserved in his writings and not his bones encased in a shrine; but humanistic quips against sterile institutional religion and distaste for the 'fine-spun trifles' of professional theologians began to have their effect on a sovereign who liked to be told that his court was 'a temple of the muses'.[25] When humanists spoke of 'lordly bishops' and 'tyrannical prelates', or denounced hypocritical 'priests as 'dumb dogs who fear the layman with a Bible', it was not long before Englishmen came to applaud Bishop Latimer's polemical picture of clerics 'munching in their mangers, and moiling in their gay manors and mansions, and so troubled with loitering in their lordships' that they had no time for God's simple folk.[26] The moment the King's outraged conscience smashed his atavistic respect for the Holy Father and he accepted with his usual enthusiasm Sir Thomas More's warning that popes were political figures against whom princes might some day find themselves at odds, Henry, as was his wont, went the whole way. If the Bishop of Rome was merely a political creature, might not all bishops be so too?

Anti-clericalism and royal conscience coalesced to produce a sovereign deeply suspicious of priestly authority, and the Defender of the Faith became all Lutheran on the subject of Holy Orders. When in *The Bishops' Book* of 1537 his prelates proclaimed that 'it belongeth unto the jurisdiction of priests or bishops' to determine and regulate the ceremonial life of the Church, he inserted the secular warning that clerical authority was not a divine right but merely a social convenience, 'thought requisite and right necessary'. Then he added for good measure the practical postscript, 'which being overseen and approved by the King's Highness and his Council in Parliament, the subject shall be bound to obey'.[27] With excruciating care he crossed out any suggestion of special authority stemming from God, and much to Archbishop Cranmer's indignation deleted the bishops' injunction to obey our priestly father, 'by whom we be spiritually regenerated', substituting the more temporal command to honour the clergy and 'all other governors and rulers'.[28] Clearly the Supreme Head saw his clergy as civil servants of a Crown imbued with divine spirit. He was ready to defend their worldly dignity on the ground that their authority flowed from the fountain of royal power, but he was for ever watchful of any claim to spiritual pre-eminence. Even his stand in favour of clerical celibacy was more a peculiar manifestation of anti-clericalism than a sign of doctrinal orthodoxy. He opposed clerical marriages on the argument that married 'priests would so increase in numbers by affinity and descent' that they would soon tyrannize over all temporal authority, both princely and aristocratic, and would make their benefices hereditary.[29]

The most extraordinary example of the royal theologian's willingness to flirt with heresy and revamp the fundamental tenets of his inherited faith came during the closing months of his life. In August 1546, when the French Admiral Claude d'Annebaut was at Hampton Court for the concluding ceremonies establishing peace between the two kingdoms, Henry calmly suggested that England and France change the mass into a communion service, cast out the Bishop of Rome with all his popery, and unite to force the Emperor to do the same or 'break off with him'.[30] The Admiral was astonished, Cranmer could scarcely believe his ears, and historians ever since have wondered whether the story wasn't in fact a deliberate fabrication by John Foxe in order to place the old man firmly on the side of the Protestant angels. The evidence, however, indicates that the words were indeed spoken; nor were they out of character in a ritualist and a theological expert who had broken the ceremonial habits of his youth and had indulged his appetite for doctrinal debate. Ritualism is after all more a state of mind than a predilection for a consistent body of ceremony. The ritualist assumes a mechanical approach to religion, enacting the exact motions and words of the service, and, like the snake-charmer with his flute, expects the deity to sway and dance in response. Once the ritualist has been emancipated from a particular liturgy, he is quite capable, especially if he is highly proficient in the history and form of the rite, of changing both the philosophical explanation behind the ceremony and the forms themselves.

Henry could rarely leave well enough alone; his enthusiasm invariably carried him to extremes the implications of which he seldom saw. What he was up to in August 1546 may simply have been a calculated diplomatic indiscretion — shock treatment for the benefit of a militantly Catholic and suspicious Frenchman—or it may have been a momentous step in the total reworking of the ancient formula. During the previous spring and winter the King had been in a peculiarly excitable religious mood, and in early January he had appointed an ecclesiastical commission to inspect the ceremonies of his Church and indicate all those worthy of being abolished as either superstitious or abused. Unexpectedly, and on his own initiative, he added creeping to the cross to the list, and precipitately ordered that ringing bells on Allhallows' Eve, covering images during Lent, and kneeling before the cross on Palm Sunday should 'cease from henceforth and be abolished'. Diplomatic expediency and a long, politic letter from Bishop Gardiner had quickly cooled the sovereign's reforming ardour and most of the old ceremonies had been left intact,[31] but it is quite possible to argue that by late summer Henry was ready to pick up where he had left off. Those who perceive in the affair of the French Admiral evidence that the King had cast his lot with the new faith and set his kingdom upon a heretical course should remember that, although he was willing to change Catholicism until it was beyond recognition, he never stepped into the Protestant camp on the two crucial doctrines of good works and free will, nor ever accepted the starting-point of all Protestant theology: the slug of corruption which resides in every Christian soul and the ecstacy of despair which leads to God.

Henry never forsook his healthy-minded and organizational view of religion. From the start he discerned that Lutheranism 'robs princes and prelates of all power and authority; for what shall a king or prelate do, if he cannot appoint any law, or execute the law which is appointed, but even like a ship without a rudder suffer his people to float from the land?'[32] The venom, he warned, had as its purpose 'no other end than to instigate the people to make war on the nobles while the enemies of Christ look on with laughter'.[33] Commotion, sedition and revolution were the wages of heresy; and history abounded with clear proof of the consequences of placing God's word in the dirty hands of the multitude. English peasants had been led into rebellion through the heresy of John Wycliffe in the fourteenth century; insurrection arose in Bohemia in the fifteenth century as a result of the evil teachings of John Huss; and civil war had followed in the wake of Martin Luther's pernicious doctrines in Germany. Again and again the refrain was repeated: 'The common people have compelled the rulers to follow them, who, if they had taken heed in time, they might have ruled and led.'[34] The past was a sure mirror to the future and it warned the King to take heed.

The surest way of stampeding the King into action was to call a man a sacramentarian or an anabaptist and link his heresy with sedition. When Stephen Gardiner 'with his crafty fetches' sought to persuade his master to close the floodgates of reform in England in 1539, he crept 'into the king's ear' by warning him 'of civil tumults and commotions here within this realm' which must follow in the wake of religious innovation.[35] A year later when Thomas Cromwell fell from power, his crime, as represented to the King, was sacramentarianism by implication. It was reported that he had once said that if England turned against God's truth, 'I would fight in the field in mine own person with my sword in my hand' against the King 'and all others'.[36] The same argument was presented when the conservatives sought to destroy Archbishop Cranmer. They cautioned the sovereign that Cranmer's doctrines would prove dangerous, being likely to produce 'horrible commotion and uproars' as had recently sprung up in Germany.[37] The process was repeated against Catherine Parr, whose quiet humanistic mysticism had brought her to the edge of heresy and into the company of sacramentarians. Her religion, 'so stiffly maintained', it was said, not only 'dissolved the policy and politics' of princely governments 'but also taught the people that all things ought to be in common'.[38]

If Henry Tudor was not pedantically dotting his prelate's stylistic i's and crossing their theological t's, he was searching out the social implications of their advice to the faithful. The Supreme Head was suspicious of the injunction that Christians must 'heartily forgive' those who trespass against them, preferring the sound social dictum: we 'must eradicate and take away all rancour, malice, and will to revenge out of our heart, and commit the punishment of the offenders (being contrary to God or the princes' laws) to the order of justice'.[39] To his sensitive political ear, his bishops had inadvertently threatened the foundations of family and magisterial authority by suggesting that the duty of children and inferiors to their parents and superiors was not a one-way street; the Fifth Commandment, they said, 'comprised the office and duty of the parents and superiors' to those under them. The royal father struck out any such hint of reciprocity.[40] He was also particularly careful with the civic implications of the Lord's Prayer, especially the suggestion that 'our daily bread' might be the fruits of God's grace and not man's labour. The prelates had interpreted these words as meaning that the husbandman who 'tilleth and soweth his ground' should put his trust in God,

giving little worldly care for tomorrow, for the Lord would see that
he 'shall not lack things necessary'. Henry felt such advice to be an
invitation to laziness and rephrased the paragraph, making honest
labour a condition of paradise. 'The true labouring man', he noted,
'doing truly his office whereto he is called, shall attain salvation as
surely as any other creature, and they that do contrary shall be in
jeopardy of damnation.'[41] Political prudence required that subjects
be advised that industry is agreeable to the Lord and the road to
hell is paved with idleness. Puritan ministers had no monopoly over
what would one day be called the ethical tenets of capitalism when
it came to maintaining the properly ordered commonwealth.

Charity was the keystone of the King's definition of proper Christian behaviour, but he carefully explained that charity did not include leading his subjects into indolence or endangering their souls
by accustoming them to live by begging. 'One thing herein is to be
noted,' the King cautioned: there were many folk who would rather
live 'by the craft of begging slothfully than either work or labour
for their living'. It was no virtue in the benefactor or profit to the
realm to give alms to those who 'should be compelled by one means
or another to serve the world with their bodily labour'.[42] Even in
his final testament Henry could not resist lecturing his executors on
false charity, and when he instructed that alms be given to 'the most
poor and needy people that may be found', he added: 'common
beggars as much as may be avoided'.[43]

Theologically Henry never wavered from the doctrine of good
works and free will. Though almost every other religious tenet was
tainted with heresy, he held to the old faith in his conviction that
men must choose and labour to achieve their salvation.* Without
good works and free will there could be no moral responsibility,
without responsibility there could be no punishment, and without
punishment there could be no order within the commonwealth.
Predestination, said Stephen Gardiner, 'fixed and fastened' man

---

* The King's orthodoxy as it was expressed in *The King's Book* has been
scrutinized by Philip Hughes (*Reformation in England*, I, pp. 46–57), who
maintains that even when Henry was dealing with the subject of free will and
good works he was not really Catholic. The opinion is based on expert knowledge and may indeed be correct, but it is easier for the twentieth century to
detect theological deviation than for the sixteenth, and one wonders how
Father Hughes would have categorized the teachings of Erasmus or Cardinal
Contarini. Whatever else may be said, *The King's Book* is more Catholic than
Protestant, if such a statement has any meaning, and Cardinal Pole was willing
to use an expurgated version under Catholic Mary (Constant, *Reformation in
England*, I, p. 429). Certainly Henry would have called himself, and thought
himself to be, Catholic, which, after all, is the crucial point.

THOMAS CRANMER, 1489–1556.
Artist unknown

STEPHEN GARDINER,
BISHOP OF WINCHESTER, 1493–1555.
Artist unknown

Frontispiece of the Cranmer Bible, 1541

'with nails riveted and clenched with mere necessity', degrading his dignity and depriving society of the moral whip which excites all 'good direction and endeavour either to godly exercise or politic behaviour'; for how can kings blame a subject 'for what he cannot eschew' or chastise him for what 'he cannot avoid'?[44] Protestants, of course, answered that positive faith in God's mercy is a far more efficient compulsion to do right than the negative voice of a guilty conscience or the fear of divine vengeance, but a King who suffered from 'a conscience grieved' and who made 'satisfaction for his sins' to God with 'deed-doing' had little faith in such an argument. Men, said the Lord's vicar on earth, were inheritors of the kingdom of heaven only as long as they persevered in God's precepts and laws, and divine grace lighted their footsteps only if they 'willingly and wilfully reject not' that illumination.[45] The monarch whom God had appointed His high minister and who laboured with all the 'resources of his mind' to see divisions extinct, according to his very duty, could hardly allow his subjects the rewards of paradise without the merits of having lived in this world 'soberly, justly and devoutly'. When Henry came to issue the formulary which bears his name, *The King's Book* of 1543, he saw to it that his prelates concluded with the social homily that *soberly* meant 'all abstinence and temperance, and our duty touching our body', *justly* included 'all works of charity towards our neighbour with due obedience to our princes, heads and governors', and *devoutly* comprehended 'all our works spiritual which be done immediately unto God'.[46]

Religious reality accorded ill with the King's vision of a kingdom filled with sober and obedient Christians. The papist pot called the Lutheran kettle black, subjects ignored the King's politic and wholesome doctrine which neither savoured of the corruption of Rome nor smelled of 'the new naughty traditions', and, worst of all, now that the Supreme Head was in the business of expounding religious truth, the King himself was being spattered with the mud and filth of polemical dispute, and it was publicly being said that his pronouncements were not worth 'a fart'.[47] Henry faced an emotional revolution in which the old morality of instinctive obedience had been sadly weakened but not destroyed, while the new morality had not yet been disciplined by society into an acceptable code of behaviour. The success of any organization which seeks to convert religious zeal into institutional routine depends largely on the eclectic appeal of its doctrines and the ruthlessness and skill of its leaders. The weakest element in the King's healthy dogma was that it was never a composite faith, constantly drawing strength from a multitude of spiritual sources. Instead, it was an administrative

E

emasculation of Catholicism without the Pope, purgatory without the chantries, clerical chastity without monks or nuns, and a miraculous priesthood without an independent Church. There is a suspended quality about Henrician Anglicanism which did not go unnoticed even as the King sought to maintain his *via media*. Nicholas Harpsfield described Henry as 'one that would throw down a man headlong from the top of a high tower and bid him stay when he was half way down', and the French Ambassador remarked that it was difficult, to say the least, to maintain a Church which was doctrinally pure but at the same time passionately hated the Pope and always did 'what the King commanded'.[48] The settlement eventually collapsed because Henry sought to harness the intense zeal of sick souls to an ancient organizational structure for which they had little respect.

Religious change was operating on at least four different levels. Institutionally the Church of England was cut away from the international ecclesia centred at Rome, its monasteries demolished, and its revenues and jurisdiction commandeered by a Supreme Head in London. So long as the ancient rituals and the ribbons and wrappings of the old faith were retained, constitutional change meant little, for an Italian papacy living off English taxes seemed scarcely worth preserving. Change, however, was also taking place in the technology of religion, in the manner by which Christians spoke to God—taking communion in one or two kinds, venerating images or worshipping in silent prayer, seeing the story of a common religious heritage told in coloured glass or hearing it read from the Bible. These were often small surface matters, but once sacred habits had been tampered with, violent emotional responses were aroused. George Day, the moderate Bishop of Chichester, was willing to give up his theological belief in transubstantiation for the sake of religious unity under Edward VI, but he renounced his see and accepted imprisonment rather than consent to the government's order to replace the altars of his diocese with tables. The substance of an altar in terms of 'stone or wood', he admitted, was in theory indifferent, but to make an altar into a table drove home the inescapable fact that the sacrificial mass was being turned into a communion of the Lord's supper.[49]

Surprising changes in doctrine can be introduced so long as the physical habits of worship are left untouched, and theological change, the intellectual premises on which men rationalize their faith and justify ceremony, was creeping into Henry's Church even while he sought to maintain the outward trappings of Catholicism. On all fronts the old tenets were in debate: the mass as a communion or a sacrifice, priests as teachers or as a sacerdotal order, free will or predestination, and salvation by faith alone or conjoined with good works. Finally change was taking place in man's emotional reaction to ritual. Ceremonies which for centuries had been able to inspire inner contentment now produced a degree of repulsion which drove the King's subjects to violence. Images become idols to be smashed, dead pieces of stone and wood of less value than 'a living ape'. Abuses of ritual which had once engendered only tired cynicism about man's failings now excited a hatred and a sense of impending disaster which impelled Christians to pull down the entire edifice of their faith to remedy a single rotten beam.

It was a sad commentary on a century which had begun with Erasmus's prediction that his generation 'promised to be an age of gold, if ever there was one', that one of the oldest campaigners, John Frederick, Duke of Saxony, had to admit that 'of all things the most difficult is to settle religious differences, especially at this advanced age of the world when everyone thinks he has found the truth.'[50] What made matters worse in England was that young men were tramping the countryside saying that they knew 'the King's mind'.[51] The statement was not only presumptuous, since Henry's theological mind was scarcely clear, but it recorded the fact that the habit of obedience was breaking down. The indoctrinated habits, which Bishop Gardiner referred to when he warned that the destruction of religious images would weaken respect for a nobleman's coat of arms or the King's features on a royal seal, were imperilled. If the dutiful child who has learned to kneel before the statue becomes the man who destroys the idol, then what about other childhood habits— respect for elders, fathers, magistrates, priests and King? Condone the smashing of religious effigies and the burning of seditious books advocating the Antichrist of Rome, weaken the self-imposed restraints inculcated from birth by giving subjects a taste for licence, and then, as Gardiner warned Thomas Cranmer, 'the vehemence of novelty will flow further than your Grace would admit'.[52]

Everywhere authority, morality and charity seemed to be on the wane. In Coventry, drapers, mercers and cardmakers were impudently and sacrilegiously claiming that they 'as lief be confessed to a post as to a priest', and one went so far as to say he thought so little of the sacrament of the altar that he would 'as lief turn his arse to it as his face'.[53] In Essex, John Ellys 'did give his dog holy bread', and John Makyn and his wife refused to go to church and spent their days 'bowling and gulling'. The parson of Bradwell kept a woman, and the vicar of Kelvedon was found in bed with a whore by 'the watchman, constable and other honest men'.[54] Blasphemous fellows were maintaining that ditch-water was as miraculous as font-water and that holy water was 'a very good medicine for a horse with a galled back'. Others argued that churches were 'made for no other purpose but to keep people from wind and rain', that nothing was 'to be believed except it can be proved expressly by scripture', that 'no human constitutions or laws do bind a Christian man but such as be in the gospels,' and, most pernicious of all, that 'all things ought to be in common.'[55] Throughout the kingdom priests were delinquent and their flocks impious, and Christians were wasting their time 'arrogantly and superstitiously' arguing and disputing 'in churches, alehouses, taverns and other places'.[56] 'Zelly preachers' were filling the King's 'simple loving subjects' with dangerous bits and pieces of Scripture quoted out of context, saying that Christians 'are not subject to princes in any other way than for the sake of God', and that 'all outward things have been founded and instituted in a heavenly way for the sake of man'. Such assertions, Bishop Gardiner sighed, were particularly dangerous, for they were not altogether false but were 'spoken in such a way as to seem in favour of the people and to tend to anarchy'.[57]

Most of this ribaldry came from the lunatic fringe—the ranting of sacramentaries and anabaptists—but the current of social unrest ran deep and the appeal of an establishment of saints in which the golden days of the apostles would replace the golden chalices of avaricious priests was a powerful vision for all who placed faith above human law. The man who wished that the gospel might be read in all places, even in a brothel,[58] was undoubtedly an optimist, but he was also an activist, posing questions about the meaning of human life not readily answered in terms of an inherited framework which accepted evil as part of the human predicament and offered the sacrament of penance to make it tolerable. The militant extremes were deplored by Luther and Henry alike, but the energy and conviction which sustained them were symptomatic of a spirit common to all religious malcontents: a sense of alienation and lack of respect for the ethical aspirations of established society. It was not that such men wanted to reform the commonwealth by restating its laws, or even that they resented the economic and political injustices of a system which cast Christians into debtor's prison and tolerated the nobleman who had 'enough given him from God yet is not content there withal'.[59] These were peripheral to their thinking. Instead, they started from a completely different premise as to what society was all about. They believed in brotherly love and faith in God, and any community which was not based on these virtues and did not give free expression to them was rotten at its core. Obedience,

authority and order which did not stem from inner faith were worse
than trumpery; they were evil and distorted.

When Robert Wisdom exhorted his flock to take the gospel into
'the alehouse and talk and converse and reason of it', the Bishop of
London was appalled; religion and alcohol simply did not mix, and
he was quite sure that nothing but mischief would come of it. The
excellent Mr Wisdom retorted that by having 'scripture in their
hands' Christians would recall 'the fear of God' and abstain 'from
excess and drunkenship'. Then he stated the radical social argument
in its most extreme form: 'What is the cause of so many drunkards?'
Why are subjects 'so covetous, so puffed up, such shameful hypo-
crites, such horrible swearers, so cursed tongued', and 'so disobedient
to their parents'? Why are Englishmen 'such traitors and so false-
hearted to their prince, so heady in all mischief, so blown up, such
flatterers and liars, followers of beastly lust rather than the love of
God'? The answer for Mr Wisdom was clear: Englishmen had 'thrown
from them the word of God and there is *no wisdom* in them'.[60]
Whether practical men intent on ecclesiastical administration found
the pun or the egotism more repugnant is difficult to say, but they
had no confidence in a non-political theory of society, nor any
understanding of the love-soaked prophets of a better world who
believed passionately that 'every doctrine that the heavenly father
hath not ordained must be pulled up by the roots and cast
away'.[61]

To conservative minds, godliness and love were simply excuses
for loutishness, disrespect and violence, and governmental hysteria
was discernible when Bishop Gardiner wrote asking loyal Englishmen
to consider the terrible realities of life. 'The very dregs of humanity',
he said, were hurling themselves against the defences of Christendom,
putting on 'a theatrical mask of piety', and pretending 'to be vigorously banishing vices and renewing and restoring religion'. Such
people 'flatter the world with [a] licentious doctrine', offering to
pull from the necks of the multitude 'all such yokes' as have ever
been imagined 'either in thought or deed'. For the debtor they translate St Paul as saying that 'we owe nothing to no man but love';
for the covetous master they promise to pull down all holy days so
that 'he may have more work done him for his year's wages'; for
the servant they do away with all fasting and abstinence; for the
priest they offer 'wives to wed'; and for the people they speak of
'liberty of all things'. Winchester's fears have a modern ring when
he concludes that these 'abandoned men' interpret 'gentleness,
mildness, moderation, courteous speech in their opponents as
cowardness and lack of confidence'; they persuade 'their followers

to take nothing rightly'; and they secretly seek to overthrow all 'established practices'.[62]

The greatest disadvantage which the religious idealist had to face was the government's conviction that heresy and sedition were two sides of the same coin. The energy of Mr Swynnerton, who preached even on workdays, was disconcerting enough to elderly and conservative ecclesiastics, but his zeal and even his impudence in claiming to know the King's mind might have been forgiven him if the authorities had not feared that he was consorting with 'light people', filling their idle minds with dangerous ideas and providing religious justification for civil disobedience.[63] Behind ribaldry and sacrilege lurked the spectre of social revolution. The crazed Mr Collins was imprisoned because he defamed the crucifix by shooting an arrow at the figure of Christ and shouting out to the effigy 'to defend itself', but he died at the stake in 1538 because he was 'wont to exclaim against the nobility and great men of the kingdom, and rashly to bring forward against them many passages of holy Scripture'.[64] Religious discontent and civil rebellion were obviously walking hand in hand when William Turner dared speak out against the King's proclamation of 1543 limiting the reading of the Bible to men of social standing. What kind of ungodly belly-wisdom was it, he demanded, to say that 'rich men and the nobles are wiser than the poor people'? Then Turner sent shudders down respectable English spines by asserting that 'there are more gentle fools' in the realm 'than yeoman fools, number compared to number'.[65]

A chasm was opening up between an older generation which respected the traditions of the past but was willing to reform much that was abused, and younger men who had little respect for authority, longed to restore 'the simple and sincere verity contained in God's word',[66] and in their haste did not care whether they threw out the baby with the bath-water. Sadly John Skip, Bishop of Hereford, wrote to Matthew Parker, then the young Dean of Stokes, acknowledging the gulf between youthful idealists and elderly realists. 'Ye be hot and hasty,' he said, 'we be cold and tardy. We think that a great quantity of our qualities would do much amongst you, and a little of your qualities were enough for us.'[67] There was no common area of understanding. No matter what the issue—theological, constitutional, ceremonial or psychological—each side drew its own conclusions because, as Bishop Skip pointed out to Master Parker, the differences in their approach led them to 'proceed diversely'.

Even the folklore and merry tales of the century reveal the gulf between the two groups. There is the story of the Welsh highwayman (the butt of most sixteenth-century English jokes) who confessed to his curate that he had killed a friar and asked for absolution. When forgiveness was denied, the Welshman retorted: 'Marry, there were two friars and I might have slain them both if I had list, but I let the one escape. Therefore, master curate, set the one against the other and then the offence is not so great but ye may absolve me well enough.'[68] Stupidity and conceit are rarely edifying, even in a Welsh sophist, and the John Skips of this world would doubtless have sympathized with the curate who had to listen to such blasphemy, but to the exponents of justfication by faith the story involved much more than the abuse of the confessional. It was the logical culmination of a barter theology: murderers sought to enter heaven by hiding behind a balance-sheet morality which ticked off good deeds and bad deeds like so many bags of grain in a merchant's account-book. On the other side of the ledger was the confessor who ordered a poor man to say in penance every day for a year: 'The lamb of God have mercy upon me.' Twelve months later the man returned to confession and was asked whether he had done his penance. 'Yea, sir, thank God I have,' he replied. 'I have said thus today and so daily: "The sheep of God have mercy upon me." ' But, exclaimed the confessor, that was not correct. 'Yea sir,' quoth the penitent, 'ye say truth. That was the last year, but now it is at twelve months since, and it is a sheep by this time.' However much such simplistic 'deed-doing' might shock the tender conscience of a Robert Barnes, the lesson to be learned by the conservatives was that 'if holy scripture be expounded to lewd lay people only in the literal sense',[69] this was the kind of nonsense one could expect.

Erasmus's prediction in 1530 that the 'long war of words and writings will terminate in blows' was coming true when a growing spiral of distrust left little room for anything except recriminations and abusive language.[70] All was 'roses and sweetness' or 'black as pitch', and the polarization of positions was complete in 1537 when it was said: 'We must either [be] on God's party or else on the Devil's.'[71] Since 'gentleness, mildness and moderation' were construed as cowardliness and lack of confidence, and the doctrinal compromise expressed first in the Ten Articles and then in *The Bishops' Book* was unable to arouse the enthusiasm of either side, the Supreme Head during the winter of 1538 took a long look at his moral commonwealth and decided it was in immediate need of rejuvenation and discipline. Evil-doers, he said, had taken advantage of his 'liberality', and 'much contrary to his Highness' expectations' had disputed arrogantly against each other, slandering and railing.

Some were set upon restoring 'the old devotion to the usurped power of the Bishop of Rome' while others sought to subvert and overturn both the sacraments of the holy Church and 'the power and authority of princes and magistrates'.[72] On the politic ground that it was 'much better [for] no laws to be made, than, when many be well made, none to be kept',[73] Henry came down heavily in favour not so much of Catholic orthodoxy as of belly-wisdom, willing his preachers to agree and his subjects to obey.

'By long experience', the King had known 'that religion bears the greatest sway in the administration of public affairs and is likewise of no small importance in the commonwealth', and by 1538 his duty was clear: once again he would sing with the Prophets: 'I hated the wicked and loved your laws.'[74] His aim, as he informed the Governor of Scotland some five years later, was by great labour, constant vigil and God's grace to whip his Church 'to perfection' and 'to establish such a certain doctrine as is maintainable by the mere truth, and such as no man shall be able to impugn or disallow'.[75] Henry's mood in the midst of religious discord and civil disobedience was dramatically revealed in November 1538 when he faced his moral responsibilities and determined the fate of John Lambert.[76]

Lambert was an outspoken and dogmatic Lutheran, who had originally learned his faith from Thomas Bilney but had strayed into the sacramentarian camp by his long-winded and scholarly denunciation of transubstantiation. With a contempt for personal safety which made up in conviction what it lacked in worldly wisdom, he embarrassed his radical friends at court by disputing in public with Dr Taylor, one of the more liberal of the government's spokesmen, and then proceeded to carry his argument up the ecclesiastical ladder to Barnes, Cranmer and finally the King himself. When called upon to act, the Supreme Head put on a magnificent display. Clothed all in white, with his bishops and clerks in purple gowns on one side and his peers, justices and gentlemen of the chamber on the other, plus a full complement of guards to lend majesty to the occasion, he listened with 'brows bent unto severity' to the heretic Lambert, who had been brought heavily guarded from prison 'even as a lamb to fight with many lions'. The proceedings began with an address by George Day, Bishop of Chichester, who explained to the assembled multitude the sovereign's purpose. His Highness, he said, was loath to have it rumoured that he ignored his duty as Defender of the Faith or that he gave 'liberty unto heretics to perturb and trouble the churches of England'. As a statement of charges in an impartial trial, the Bishop's words left much to be desired; but as an impeachment of heresy and declaration of government policy it was a clarion call to action.

The inquiry got off to a bad start when Henry rose, turned to the prisoner, and said: 'Ho! good fellow; what is thy name?' and Lambert answered: 'My name is John Nicholson, although of many I be called Lambert.' The sovereign was not pleased. Simple, loving subjects had only one name; trouble-makers, who had something to hide, had two; and he crossly sat down, saying: 'I would not trust you, having two names, although you were my brother.' Lambert then sought to mollify his monarch with a panegyric, saying that the 'eternal King of kings' had 'inspired and stirred up the King's mind' to acts of extraordinary piety and honour. Unfortunately these words only added to Henry's irritation, and he roughly informed the prisoner that he had not come hither 'to hear mine own praises thus painted out in my presence'. He ordered the unfortunate man to come to the point; did he or did he not believe that the body of Christ was actually in the sacrament of the altar? The King made dramatically clear what answer he expected, for he 'lifted up his cap' as he referred to the Eucharist. Lambert, however, temporized and, quoting St Augustine, suggested that it was Christ's body 'after a certain manner'. Henry brusquely commanded him to forget about St Augustine and state 'plainly whether thou sayeth it is the body of Christ or no'. Forced to the wall, Lambert boldly exclaimed: 'I deny it'; and the Supreme Head forthwith refuted him. 'Mark well,' he said, 'for now thou shalt be condemned even by Christ's own words, *hoc est corpus meum.*'

For the King the trial was over: the heretic had been answered by irrefutable authority. Since Lambert continued obstinate there could be only one conclusion, which Henry delivered five interminable hours later when he called a halt to the endless arguments of his theologians and the scholarly answers of the prisoner. 'What saith thou now,' he exclaimed, 'after all these great labours which thou hast taken upon thee and all the reasons and instructions of these learned men? Art thou not yet satisfied?' Then he put the case to Lambert with his usual terrifying simplicity: 'Wilt thou live or die? What sayest thou? Thou hast yet free choice.' Wearily Lambert answered that he yielded himself wholly to the King's will. Henry considered the answer both irreverent and unfair, and ordered him to commit himself 'unto the hands of God, and not unto mine'. Lambert refused to accept the responsibility, saying that he commended his soul to God but his body to the King's mercy. That being the case, the King retorted, 'you must die, for I will not be a patron unto heretics.'

The uncompromising monarch and the contemptuous heretic had met and completely misunderstood each other, for one spoke the language of obedience, the other of spiritual contentment. Henry had said that the choice of life or death belonged to Lambert: obey the law or die. Lambert had answered that the choice in fact lay with Henry: destroy his body if he wished, but his soul belonged to God. He had abandoned the theological struggle and had fallen back on an intuitive truth which transcended formal reason, allowing himself to be carried wherever God ordained.

Lambert's horrible death by slow fire on November 22nd was the first of a series of royal warnings that 'living in a commonwealth, men must conform themselves to the more part in authority'.[77] In a kingdom where Church and state had joined into an instrument designed to establish a single moral community, the truth was no longer the monopoly of the ecclesia to be proclaimed by priest and bishop, it was now the secular thunder of the Defender of the Faith. Henry presiding with his lords spiritual and temporal at the trial of John Lambert was the prelude to king in parliament determining the true faith for all Englishmen. The decision to 'proceed to a full order and resolution to extinct all such diversities of opinion by *good and just* laws' made by the authority of parliament came in the spring of 1539, and on May 5th the Lord Chancellor informed the Lords and Commons that 'his majesty desires above all things that diversity of religion should be banished from his dominions'.[78] A committee of the upper house was appointed to devise means to end the shrill scolding of so many tongues and re-establish sobriety of mind and action in the King's loving subjects. The commission, essentially ecclesiastical in composition, wrangled ineffectually for ten days, until the Duke of Norfolk introduced six of the most disputed theological points into the House of Lords for debate. Henry lent his royal wisdom to the discussion and in the record space of three days the lords agreed. The only obstinate dissenter from these 'godly proceedings' was that 'lewd fool', Bishop Shaxton of Salisbury, who was conveniently kept from the House on the day of the final vote on the excuse that his household was infected with the plague.[79]

The Act for Abolishing Diversity of Opinion, better known to its supporters as the Six Articles, and more picturesquely to its opponents as 'the whip with six strings', received the King's assent on June 28th, and was clearly the product of his mind as well as his hand.[80] It gave a strongly Catholic interpretation to the central theological issues dividing the Henrician position from that held by the religious radicals. It was commanded that all of the King's subjects should henceforth believe that the bread and wine of the sacrament of the mass actually became the 'substance' of the body and blood of Christ after its consecration; that communion was to be in one kind; that priests were not to marry; that vows of chastity were to be accepted as part of the law of God; that private masses were agreeable both to the deity and the Church of England; and that auricular confession was to be regarded as necessary and expedient. More important than the theological truths laid down by the collective and infallible voice of King, Lords and Commons were the 'whips' attached to the bill by secular law-makers, determined to restore respect for civil and religious authority. Death at the stake without chance of recantation was decreed for those who by word or writing denied the real presence in the mass. Imprisonment and confiscation of property was the penalty for subjects who acted or spoke contrary to the other tenets of the act, and if they persisted in their error, burning was the punishment for a second offence.

Popular reaction to the bill and its royal sponsor was mixed. The German Protestants were disgusted and Martin Luther railed against the English Defender of the Faith saying that 'the devil sits astride this king so that he vexes and plagues Christ', and that 'money makes him so frivolous that he thinks he is worthy of adoration and that God could no longer manage without him'.[81] Englishmen were somewhat less severe; the sight of the King 'so wise, learned and Catholic' in the midst of parliament was impressive, and one eyewitness described the resulting legislation as 'the wholesomest act ever passed'.[82] The French Ambassador recorded that 'the people show great joy at the King's declaration touching the sacrament, being much more inclined to the old religion than to the new opinions'.[83] Whether this was true, considering the furore which the bill produced in Commons, is a matter of dispute. Dislike of heretical, militant and ill-mannered extremists, and fear of the possible social implications of sacramentarianism, should not be confused with devotion to the old faith. There was one point on which all shades of religious healthy-mindedness, be they Lutheran, Henrician, Catholic or humanist, could invariably agree—disrespect for established authority was dangerous. The bill was enacted as a moral lash to whip the religious community into respectfulness, not as a statement of doctrinal orthodoxy, and as such it received widespread support.

It has been pointed out more than once that the subsequent history of the statute supports this explanation.[84] The whip with its six strings produced a great deal of smoke but relatively little fire. The stalwarts of history, the men and women who faced bodily torment rather than the internal torture of conformity to an empty creed, make exciting copy, but the records show that, for each one who accepted death by fire, hundreds recanted, some with slight prodding, some with a taste of prison diet, and others under the threat of the stake. Almost five hundred persons came to the attention of the government during the first year of the great heresy hunt, and all were promptly pardoned. The following year, 1541, Bishop Bonner of London rounded up more than two hundred heretics, mostly unscrubbed and disobedient scoffers who had ignored the King's urgent appeal to charity. A few were accused of being sacramentarians but most were simple trouble-makers: the bored, the misfit, the obsessed, the selfish, the argumentative and the impulsive, who exist in all societies and are swept up by any cause giving meaning and freshness to their lives. Some were 'meddlers', 'babblers' and 'jesters'; others refused to go to church or, if they went, disturbed the service; and still others stole the holy bread and fed it to their dogs, read the Bible in church so loudly as to annoy their fellow worshippers, or argued and fought with their wives over matters of ritual.[85] Only a handful had stomachs for martyrdom—the threat of appearing before the lords of the Council was enough to teach the overwhelming majority good manners.

The pathetic victims of the first hunt were minnows for whom society felt little sympathy; the next sweep of the net in 1543, however, caught more important fish close to the throne itself. When a gentleman of the Privy Chamber, the master of the revels, the King's barber, his cook, three of his singers and composers, one of the masters of his household, the Dean of Exeter, a Windsor lawyer and a tailor-cum-churchwarden were charged with heresy,[86] the upper classes began to have second thoughts as to the comprehensive nature of the bill. Henry protected his own, and only the tailor, a priest named Anthony Peerson, and Robert Testwood, a choir singer in St George's Chapel, were actually burnt, but the natural leaders of the realm had discovered that a dangerous weapon had been placed in the hands of zealots who made no distinction between rascals and gentlemen in their determination to cleanse the kingdom. Within six months the claws of the Six Articles were twice trimmed, first by permitting recantation as a means of escaping the flames and limiting the death-penalty to the clergy, who were evidently expected to accept burning as an occupational hazard, and second by requiring that accusations be presented by twelve men under oath, that first and second offences be committed within a twelve-month period, and that no indictment be made except by two members of the Privy Council.[87]

The central pillar on which Henrician Anglicanism rested after 1543 was *The King's Book*, published in May and rather hopefully described as *A Necessary Doctrine and Erudition for any Christian Man*. Even though Henry announced that his book was a 'perfect and sufficient doctrine'[88] for the attainment of salvation, it clarified few of the points in dispute except free will and good works, both of which were expanded and explained in terms of man's responsibility to prove by his own efforts the true quality of his faith. As a pronouncement on proper Christian behaviour, however, it was a triumph of Tudor social ingenuity, incorporating most of the Supreme Head's criticisms of *The Bishops' Book*. Phrases which might be offered as justification for rebellion were systematically expunged or carefully circumscribed, and it was made clear that the appeal to God to forgive us our trespasses did not mean that 'laws of princes should be broken, condemned or not executed'.[89] Under the command 'Thou shalt not steal' the government methodically listed every social deviation a Tudor administrator could imagine, from bribery, counterfeiting and extortion to simony, usury and vagabondage. Even the indolent labourer who does 'not apply' his 'business', the attorney who takes too large a stipend or by 'negligence mars good causes', the receiver of stolen goods, and 'generally all covetous men' were included in the government list.[90] Any hint of social equality, either in heaven or on earth, was omitted, and the phrase that God 'equally and indifferently regardeth the rich and the poor' was replaced by the vapid assurance that the deity 'fatherly regardeth all'.[91] The King had a 'fatherly pity' and regard for his people without condoning any dangerous nonsense about equality. Should not God do likewise?

Henry was extremely touchy, both domestically and internationally, about his public image and the reputation of his government, and after 1539 the Council worked diligently to re-establish respect for the servants of the Crown as well as to enforce God's law. In recantation after recantation heretics were required not only to confess their religious lapses and social errors but also to reaffirm the image of governmental authority. In 1540 William Jerome was told to renounce his belief in justification by faith alone, publicly reaffirm the right of rulers to bind 'men's conscience', and retract his scurrilous description of members of parliament as 'butterflies, dissemblers and knaves'.[92] Three years later Robert Wisdom, who had once advocated the reading of scripture in alehouse and tavern, was ordered to reconsider his words, profess his sorrow at defaming 'the charity of the ministers of justice', and confess that Tudor England was 'a realm of justice and of no persecution of them that be good'.[93] Robert Singleton's confession was equally humiliating and even more damaging to the reputation of heretical scholarship. 'I am', he avowed, 'an unlearned fantastical fool; such hath been my preaching and such hath been my writing, which I here before you all tear in pieces.'[94] Sir John Olde was no less penitent and, after a verbal lashing by the Privy Council in July 1546, promised 'unfainedly to receive the King's Majesty's doctrine' and to conduct himself honestly and soberly.[95] The Council had no doubt what honest behaviour entailed; only seven months before, Henry had explained to his lords spiritual and temporal and his commons assembled that it was a priest's duty to 'set forth God's word both by true preaching and good example giving'.[96]

The vermin of society, urged on by religious fanatics, may have been gnawing at the cellar door, but the Supreme Head and all his loyal subjects knew that a far greater menace was pounding at the front entrance. No one, least of all the King, whose theological and spiritual reputation was at stake, could forget that the real danger was from Satan himself in the guise of the papal Whore of Babylon. The soldiers of Antichrist were everywhere: hidden at home behind masks of fulsome loyalty, crusading openly in Europe against the faithful, and only waiting to invade England until diplomatic events brought together the overwhelming military forces of a Most Christian King of France, the Most Catholic Majesty of Spain and His Holiness in Rome. In all the King's religious discussions, his handling of heresy at home and his involved diplomatic manœuvres abroad, a single, inescapable truth loomed above all others: Henry himself was a rebel, a proclaimed schismatic, and in the eyes of many a loathsome heretic. Christendom could not ignore such a fundamental fact. The habit of thought of ten centuries made it impossible to regard religious heterodoxy as other than ridiculous, or accept schism except as a fearful rending of the seamless cloak of Christ. The Emperor Charles had expressed the rooted conviction of the majority of Christians when in 1521 he listened to the presumptuous babbling of the heretic Luther and categorically pronounced that 'a single monk who goes counter to all Christianity for a thousand years must be wrong'.[97] Twenty-five years later it still seemed preposterous that Lutheranism and Anglicanism could be anything more than temporary aberrations. Europe remained confident that German heresy and English schism would shortly be healed and the truth restored, and in 1546 the Emperor wrote his son, who would some day send a Catholic armada against a Tudor Jezebel, that he expected soon to bring the German Protestants 'back to the true faith' and force them to 'abandon their opinions', a task 'to which we are so especially bound by the dignity to which God has elevated us'.[98]

It is easy for the armchair analyst, knowing that the hopes of Catholics were mere fantasies and the fears of Protestants needless, to forget that Henry regarded resurgent papal Catholicism as a far greater threat to his Church and his royal person than weak and faltering Protestantism. The lesson of the Pilgrimage of Grace had been well learned, and religious reformers did not hesitate to point out that 'the real cause' of the rebellion was not their doing 'but the papistical doctrine which taught the Lincolnshire rustics to take arms against their King'.[99] No one knew for certain how deep the old loyalties went or how much the King's subjects would risk for their faith. On the surface the break with Rome had been accomplished and the Royal Supremacy introduced with little opposition. It seemed as if the martyred seed of the old Church had fallen on barren soil, but Secretary Paget was quite sure that the new faith, purged of its papal poison, was 'not yet printed in the stomachs of the eleven of the twelve parts in the realm', and according to Bishop Bonner men obeyed out of fear, 'otherwise there had been no way but one'.[100] That one way was martyrdom, the path taken by the select band of fifty men and women who are venerated today by the Catholic Church: four laymen including Sir Thomas More, one cardinal, thirty-three monastics, eleven priests and the Countess of Salisbury.[101] Martyrdom, however, can be contagious, and no one could guess how many men, like Bishop Stokesley of London, wished they had taken their stand with Cardinal Fisher and More, or, like the Abbot of Woburn, kept their abbeys' papal bulls hidden against the day when the Pope would return to England.[102] Henry could never be certain that thousands of secret traitors, ready to welcome the Catholic armies of the Emperor, did not lurk in obscure English homes, and Charles V was astute enough to comment that his English brother would never permit him or his son to marry the Princess Mary, 'mistrusting what he would attempt in that realm if he had my lady Mary'.[103]

For all his vaunted independence, for all his bragging about 'mere truth' standing half-way between the corruption of Rome and the dreams of inferior people, Henry had never really had a choice. If his Royal Supremacy were to remain supreme and his kingdom were successfully to shut its gates to the papal dragon, the Supreme Head had to accept the argument offered by Cranmer's secretary: the King's supremacy would 'lie post alone, hidden in the Act of Parliament and not in the hearts of his subjects', unless he supported 'godly preachers' whose hatred of the papacy was a matter of faith, not politics.[104] Men touched with the frying-pan had one redeeming quality which Henry could not overlook: their loyalty to his supremacy in the face of secret papal unrest at home and overt threats from abroad. Their loathing for Mistress Rose of Rome had very different origins from their sovereign's, but it was just as intense. This factor alone was enough to atone for their naughty ways, for if the King had an arch-enemy whom he knew worked night and day to destroy his soul as well as his kingdom, it was that septuagenarian Renaissance gentleman, Alessandro Farnese, who sat upon St Peter's throne as Paul III.

Time and time again Henry had been offered the chance to heal the schism and return to the bosom of the Church without loss of honour or monastic lands, but invariably he had declined.[105] Possibly he was too proud to confess his faults; possibly the old religious habits of his youth had been damaged beyond repair; or possibly 'a conscience grieved' which had led him into schism in the first place would not now permit him to traffic with evil. As it was reported on the Continent, the English Defender of the Faith abhorred popes in general and detested Paul III in particular.[106] It was far too late to forgive the pontiff who had presented Fisher with a cardinal's hat, blessed the Pilgrimage of Grace, befriended the traitor Reginald Pole, threatened to use 'the branding-iron' on Henry, and spent the better part of ten years seeking to persuade Francis and Charles to do their sacred duty and deliver Rome's punishment upon England and her heretical King.[107] Everywhere the sly old sovereign looked, militant Catholicism seemed to be the primary menace to the future of his Church, the security of his dynasty and the safety of his realm. Paris, Madrid, Antwerp, Edinburgh and, above all, Rome, not Wittenberg, were Henry's real concerns, for these were the international arenas where his Christian conscience had to be defended, his royal honour guarded and his imperial independence displayed.

7

In Search of a Moral

> 'I quite agree with you,' said the Duchess; 'and the moral
> of that is—"Be what you would seem to be"—or, if you'd
> like it put more simply—"Never imagine yourself not to
> be otherwise than what it might appear to others that
> what you were or might have been was not otherwise than
> what you had been would have appeared to them to be
> otherwise." '
>
> Lewis Carroll, *Alice's Adventures in Wonderland*

Diplomacy: the word sits like an undigested pudding upon a rebellious stomach; the hypocrisy, monotonous verbiage, deliberate
obfuscation and, above all, the monumental triviality engender a
sodden feeling in even the most avid enthusiast for the sixteenth
century. Yet diplomacy, along with her champion war, were the
paramount preoccupations of kings, and they took the lion's share
of their working hours. The kettledrums of war, the staking out of
rival dynastic claims, the exchange of royal greetings and, most
sacred of all, the defence of honour: these were the proper concerns
of sovereigns, not those 'ruiners of home life' and muddiers of the
mind, the quiddities of theology and the trifles of trade and finance.
Crudely but unmistakably, Henry made the point clear: Cromwell,
he informed the French Ambassador in May 1538, was 'a good household manager, but not fit to intermeddle in the affairs of kings'.[1]

Ponderously and myopically, Henry looked about the diplomatic
board and made his moves, and no one has ever described the results
as outstandingly successful. Mistaken or inept are the kindest words
to describe the King's diplomatic and military labours during the
1540s, and more often than not the chorus of condemnation includes
wanton, extravagant, frivolous, stupid, and even criminal, culminating in a crescendo of might-have-beens. What wonders Henry Tudor
might have achieved for state, Church and humanity had he listened
to the sensible humanistic appeal to bestow the wealth of the
monasteries upon education and scholarship! What diplomatic
triumphs had he stayed out of the senseless Habsburg–Valois conflict for the control of Italy, conserved his insular strength for the

New World, and turned his back upon the feudal masquerading of
the Old! What a marvel of statesmanship had he successfully wooed
Scotland, forging a new Britannia and anticipating history by sixty
years! Instead, vainglory, peevishness and a desire for revenge
induced him to destroy his one real chance of bringing the two halves
of the island together when James V, melancholic and prematurely
aged, unexpectedly died in December 1542 and left as his heir a
week-old daughter. Henry's clumsy courtship brought not peace and
marriage between his son Edward and the infant Mary of Scotland
but a legacy of hate and a decade of sickening wars of reprisal. In
Europe he plunged into the madly extravagant concern of kings—
the quest for military glory—and squandered two-thirds of the
monastic wealth on a war which produced as its only military laurel
the conquest of Boulogne, a third-rate French port, which was volun-
tarily returned six years later, having cost over one million pounds
to seize, to hold and finally to give up. War, inflation, debasement
of the currency, debt and near-bankruptcy were the legacies of his
foreign adventures, and history has pronounced the unkindest judgment of all—his policies were inconsequential. The capture of
Boulogne in September 1544 is scarcely noted in even the most
detailed accounts of the Habsburg–Valois struggle, for it had almost
no effect on the final settlement between Charles and Francis. The
Treaty of Greenwich by which the Scots promised in ten years' time
to wed their queen to Henry's son was repudiated within six months
of its signing, and by the time Mary reached her tenth birthday
Prince Edward was dead and Scotland was more French than ever.
Only in the prodigious sale of monastic lands, by which estates valued
at £799,310 were transferred to courtiers, councillors, gentlemen and
merchants, was history made, and Henry's wars helped shape the
future by depriving his Stuart heirs of the means with which to
sustain their costly Tudor inheritance.[2]

By almost any standard the King's diplomatic and military
adventures were undistinguished, but to call his policies a failure is
to moralize in terms of historical consequences. Henry and most of
his contemporaries would have been content to let his record stand.
Given the structure of Christendom, the expectations of Tudor
society and the aspirations of its ruling elite, the King's performance
on the international stage, though often crude and wooden, was
greeted with applause. What the twentieth century cannot tolerate
is the script itself. Tudor England, however, was perfectly willing to
accept the worth of the King's purpose. 'There is nothing, after the
glory of Almighty God, in this world so much to be rendered by
kings, princes or any honest persons, or so highly to be regarded and

defended, as their honour, estimation, good fame, and name, which whosoever neglecteth is to be esteemed unnatural ... ' [3] The words are Sir Ralph Sadler's introductory remarks to James of Scotland but the Ambassador was the vehicle through whom Henry Tudor delighted in lecturing his nephew on the importance of a monarch's reputation in the eyes of those who really counted—the other sovereigns and princes of Christendom.

Christendom was a paradox. It was shattered beyond repair and yet it remained a reality. It was a geographic expression which had never really possessed a common law, language, economy, or even, by the sixteenth century, a common faith; yet it stubbornly retained the dream of political unity, enjoyed a language spoken by all educated men, and was well aware of its cultural and spiritual uniqueness. It could never succeed in an effective and collective defence against the infidel, yet it sincerely believed that a crusade against Islam was the noblest purpose for which a man could lay down his life. Its members fiercely hated one another, but no one thought it strange that an English sovereign should boast of his title to the Valois throne of France, that a French monarch should claim the Duchy of Milan and designate himself successor to the last Roman Emperor, or that a king of Spain should insist upon his historic rights to the Burgundian territories of France. The distinguishing features of statehood were clearly evident in England, Spain, France, Portugal and Venice, yet the concept of nationality was still imprecise. Even in England, historically one of the most introverted and self-conscious members of the European community, the quality of Englishness had not entirely subsumed all other perfections; actions remained heroic, godly, Christian, noble or kingly— universals which belonged to the entire Christian clan and not just to Englishmen. For all its discordant factions, Christendom still possessed enough substance to evoke a deep response. To Sir Thomas More, Europe was greater than the sum of its princely parts; it was a sense of membership in a common historic and spiritual experience, and he could not 'perceive how any member thereof may, without the common assent of the body, depart from the common head'. [4] The Emperor Charles V was even more captivated by the dream of a Christian organism possessed of one faith, one law, one head, and united in a single-hearted crusade to recover Constantinople from the Infidel. He accepted with quiet conviction the prophecy of his chancellor that God had set him 'on the way towards a world monarchy, towards the uniting of all Christendom under a single shepherd'. [5]

The Emperor was the primary prince of Europe, weaving three

dynastic threads into a single cord which stretched from Gibraltar
to Vienna and back to Antwerp, and Charles knew that each strand
was part of God's design in the struggle against Islam. His pedigree
read like an international *Who's Who* of royalty. Claiming direct male
descent from Adam, he was related to the Valois kings of France
three times over, and could boast within his immediate ancestry the
best blood of Europe—Flemish, Italian, Polish, German, Lithuanian,
Portuguese, Castilian and English-Plantagenet. As heir to the Habsburg estates in southern Germany, the Tyrol and Austria, he faced
the Turkish armies of Suleiman the Magnificent, which were batter-
ing at the eastern ramparts of Europe—overrunning Hungary, sack-
ing Budapest and reaching the gates of Vienna in 1529. As the
descendant of the Valois dukes of Burgundy, who had once been
accounted the first noblemen of Europe and had styled themselves
'dukes by the grace of God', Charles controlled the riches of the
Netherlands, the economic jewel of his empire, and inherited the
chivalric and crusading tradition of his Burgundian forefathers.
Finally, as king of the united realms of Aragon and Castile he possessed not only the best infantry in Christendom and the treasures of
the New World but also a kingdom which itself had been cut from
the Infidel's grasp and now dreamt of carrying the faith, 'so catholic,
so firm and so true', to the very walls of Constantinople. But the
most sublime crown of all, which not even two centuries of political
impotence could tarnish, was the imperial dignity, an honour which
outshone 'all other worldly titles', for it had been instituted by God
Himself in His war against the heretic within and the pagan without the Christian fold.

In men's minds such a constellation of honours represented either
a divine vision of universal monarchy or a satanic threat to the
liberties of the Christian community and a disastrous upset of the
traditional balance of power.[6] Either way, Charles's empire was
always more a fantasy than a political and economic reality. On
paper his financial resources seemed endless, but they were in fact
devoured by a hydra of obligations. Every addition that the Imperial
shepherd made to his wayward flock brought forth a new wolf. He
was master of Naples, Sardinia, Sicily and Tunisia, but southern
Italy and the western Mediterranean had to be defended from the
Sultan's ablest naval commander, Khair ad-Dīn Barbarossa. The
Archduchy of Austria carried with it the heavy burden of guarding
Vienna from the Turks and supporting the Emperor's brother
Ferdinand in his claim to the crown of Hungary. The Burgundian
wealth of the Lowlands was consumed in wars against Guelders and
defence against French designs on Artois and Flanders. The Imperial

title embroiled Charles in the religious and political strife of Germany, where Lutheran and princely ambitions joined in defiance of the Imperial authority; and, most costly of all, the fief of Milan obliged him to shield all of northern Italy from the dynastic ambitions of the King of France.

The Habsburg–Valois struggle poisoned Christian Europe, befuddling the noblest aspirations of priest and preacher, and bedevilling the best-laid plans of diplomats. The rivalry was too steeped in ancient hatreds to be contained or pacified. Neither side could forget the legacy of Louis XI of France who had destroyed Charles the Bold of Burgundy and absorbed his possessions into an enlarged France. No Habsburg ruler could ignore the encroachment of a kingdom which was systematically pushing into every interstice of Europe, expanding south-east into Savoy, Piedmont and Nice, claiming the southern kingdom of Navarre, edging into the Rhine valley, and pressing its feudal rights to Flanders and Artois. Nor could any Valois king overlook the dynastic ring cast around France by the Habsburg union of Spain, Burgundy and Austria. The clash of personalities sharpened the conflict, and both King and Emperor sought for economic reasons to control the affluent and cultural cities of the Po valley and northern Italy, but for Francis I Milan was more than an economic gem or even a family right; it was an obsession, for which all Europe knew 'he would give his soul'.[7]

Wherever Francis looked, the Habsburg complex obscured his Valois vision. The Imperial title had gone to Charles despite Francis's best financial and diplomatic efforts. The Emperor was the first and most dangerous vassal of France, holding his counties of Artois and Flanders from the French Crown, and claiming the lost duchy of Burgundy. Then there was Navarre, seized by Charles's grandfather in 1512 but still considered by Francis as properly belonging to France; and finally there was Milan, gloriously conquered in 1515 and lost at the disaster of Pavia in 1525, where ten thousand French soldiers died and Francis himself was taken prisoner. Charles had been neither gracious nor lenient in his triumph, and had shut his captive away for six months in a Castilian cell. At Pavia Francis had lost all save his honour and his life; and for a moment it seemed that the Emperor would require even these, for he demanded the feudal dismemberment of France and the return of Burgundy. The French King sought to abdicate; he indignantly refused his enemy's conditions; he fell desperately ill; but eventually he signed and gave his two sons as hostages, a guarantee that the first gentleman of France would keep his promise. King and Emperor met, and Charles took his pound of flesh: 'Give me your word', he said, 'that you will faithfully fulfil your pledges.' Francis had no choice but to perjure himself and answer: 'I swear to you I will keep my word.' Neither prince ever forgot or forgave those words. The French King kept his Burgundian duchy, received absolution from the Pope for breaking his oath, renewed his war against the Emperor, and sacrificed his sons to four years in a Spanish prison. Charles branded Francis a liar and a coward, and informed the French Ambassador that his master had 'acted neither as a knight nor as a nobleman, but basely'.[8] Then he challenged Francis to a duel.*

After Pavia no holds were barred; not only did the Most Christian King of France subsidize the Emperor's heretical subjects in Germany, but he shocked all Christendom by calling upon the forces of Islam, harbouring Barbarossa's navy at Toulon in 1543 and allying himself to the Caliph of All True Believers. Francis made no attempt to cloak dynastic self-interest in decent Christian morality, and the rest of Europe found his behaviour morally repulsive. But by drawing the Sublime Porte into the Christian community, the French King redressed the European balance of power and thereby established the conditions essential for English foreign policy during the 1540s.

The realities of international life were not lost on Henry Tudor, who fancied himself to be a political pundit and liked nothing better than to lecture his royal brothers on how to conduct their diplomatic and military affairs. Unerringly he went to the geographic root of the Emperor's political weakness, commenting that it was 'a great incommodity' that the parts of his empire did 'not lie together, but far asunder one from another'. He predicted that since the Imperial title was elective, Charles could some day expect difficulty in persuading German princes to accept his Spanish-speaking and Iberian-educated son as Emperor, and he warned that France would always cause trouble in Italy because Italians were fearful lest the Emperor seek to become 'the monarch of all Italy, which above all things they detest and fear'. Only on the subject of the Emperor's domestic difficulties in Spain did the King generously admit that he 'had no practice in those affairs these many years', and acknowledge that Charles and his council were 'a thousand times' better equipped to handle them than he.[9] No amount of gratuitous lecturing, however, could conceal Henry Tudor's dilemma: a small north-westerly island on the geographic and political periphery of the mainland could

---

* Peace was finally re-established in 1529. Francis technically gave up his rights to northern Italy, Flanders and Artois, married the Emperor's sister Eleanor, and paid two million crowns ransom money; Charles returned the two princes and promised not to press his claims to Burgundy for the time being. War broke out twice more, in 1536–8 and 1542–4.

afford neither splendid isolation nor Continental involvement. If Henry wanted to play the international game, he could not afford to stand aside, yet it was questionable whether his kingdom had the strength to sustain an active military role, and Chapuys thought it quite possible that King Hal would 'put off both belligerents with fine words that he may reap the greater advantage when both are exhausted, avoiding expense himself'.[10]

The unpleasant fact was that England was a second-rate power. The memory of the triumphs of Crécy and Agincourt might still distort the vision of Englishmen, but Charles and Francis had no such delusions. Henry's insular kingdom, really only 'half an island', was commercially dependent upon the wool trade with Flanders, industrially not even able to satisfy the domestic demand for pins, financially limited to an income one-third that of either Charles or Francis, religiously tainted in the eyes of every major kingdom of Europe, and militarily of the same magnitude as the papacy. As Thomas Wriothesley succinctly put it, she was 'but a morsel among those choppers'.[11]

War was the luxury of kings, the price of which was escalating far faster than their revenues. Artillery pieces which in the days of Agincourt had been mere children of three or four feet had grown into twenty-foot brutes pulled by teams of fifteen to twenty horses, and armies of ten thousand which had once won whole kingdoms had swelled to monstrosities of fifty thousand and more. Three months of campaigning in France in 1544 with an army of forty-two thousand cost King Hal £586,718 12s. 3d., but at the best he could depend on only £200,000 from his normal peace-time revenues and possibly another £200,000 from emergency parliamentary financing. Even victory proved prohibitively expensive—it cost another £426,306 19s. 5d. to defend Boulogne. Per capita Henry may well have been one of the wealthiest monarchs in Europe and his credit was excellent, but a kingdom of little more than three million could scarcely compete with sixteen million French, eight million Spanish and possibly twenty million Dutch, Flemish and Germans who owed taxes to the Emperor.[12]

Henry could be hopelessly irresponsible and extravagant in matters of money, squandering his capital and mortgaging his future for a military chimera, but he was fully aware of the advice given Louis XII of France: in war 'three things must be made ready— money, money and, once again, money'; and he was not happy about the price. Chapuys was for ever commenting on the King's unprincely avarice,[13] and Stephen Gardiner went to the pecuniary heart of the problem when he drily informed the Imperial Ambassador that honour in war was a glorious but also an expensive commodity. Chapuys replied with splendid chivalric disdain: 'How can worldly honour be increased without cost?' [14] Like the wealthy American financier who asked John Pierpont Morgan how much his yacht cost and was told that if he had to ask he could not afford one, Henry did not belong in that elite group who could afford war—the Holy Roman Emperor, the Most Christian King of France, and Suleiman I, the spiritual and temporal leader of Islam. In the end both Charles and Francis went bankrupt playing the costly game. They impoverished their people, pawned their plate, bartered government offices and titles of nobility, sold Crown lands, legitimized priests' children for a generous fee, and Charles grew so desperate that he literally lived off his creditors, who dared not see him go under. War, however, remained the badge of great-power status, and great kings were not expected to concern themselves with the sordid means by which the military monster was fed. Compared to the Emperor's desperate monetary extractions, Henry's squandering of his monastic wealth, the £270,000 extracted from his subjects in 'benevolent loans', the £272,000 borrowed from the Fugger money-lenders, and the £363,000 realized from the debasement of the coinage, were but the half measures of a poor cousin who was never quite willing or able to pay the price of military glory. [15]

The King was not only short of money, he was deficient in the dynastic sinews of diplomacy as well. Marriage held Europe together. An imperium of daughters, cousins, nephews and bastards, not political conquest or economic union, was at the core of the Emperor's dream of world hegemony. [16] He had at his disposal a son, two daughters and two illegitimate children, as well as his sisters and the thirteen siblings of that most prolific of all Habsburg studs, his brother Ferdinand. Francis I was equally well endowed—three sons and three daughters, plus the children of various collateral Valois lines. In contrast Henry Tudor was meagrely equipped: a sickly son whom the chanceries of Europe regarded as unpromising, two daughters both of whom had been bastardized, one illegitimate son (who was dead by 1536), his Scottish niece Margaret Douglas, and the children of his sister Mary who had married a social upstart and divorcé. By 1542 the King himself was scarcely more eligible. He had grown somewhat long in the tooth, his health was a matter of diplomatic concern, and international heiresses were skittish when it came to sharing the marriage-couch with a husband of whom it was said he 'either putteth away or killeth his wives'. [17]

Despite his posing, boasting and gratuitous lessons in diplomacy, King Hal had to admit that he stood only a cut above the dozens of sovereign princes and territorial bishops who cluttered the European chessboard, and could not possibly match the regal power of Charles or Francis. Rather plaintively Henry told the French Ambassador in 1542 that 'it was true that when the [French] King and the Emperor were on terms of agreement', as they had been three years before, 'they had pushed him into a narrow corner, but, thank God, he was still alive and not so little a king as had been supposed'.[18] The Emperor, however, was not convinced, and when Henry tact-lessly referred to his Imperial nephew as a most 'ungrateful' monarch, Charles coldly remarked that the term could be applied only to an equal or inferior, never to a superior, and he exclaimed that the English King would never have dared use such language 'were it not for that broad ditch between him and me'.[19]

It was galling but inescapable; Henry was a little king. Worse, he was not always taken seriously. When Sir Thomas Wyatt com-plained to the Emperor that nothing was being done to stop malicious tongues from defaming the King's character in Spain, Charles merely answered: 'If men give cause to be spoken of, they will be spoken of.' [20] The King's repudiation of Catherine of Aragon had been bad enough, and the Emperor for years enjoyed reminding Henry of the legitimacy of that union by addressing him as his 'good uncle', but the succession of wives who followed made the English King the laughing-stock of Christendom. One of the women most favourably inclined towards Henry—Charles's sister, Regent of the Lowlands— set the tone by remarking after the execution of Anne Boleyn and the King's precipitate marriage to Jane Seymour that 'when he is tired of this one he will find some occasion of getting rid of her'. Then she acidly added: 'I think wives will hardly be well contented if such customs become general.' [21] Henry never lived down his reputation as a Bluebeard, and only a few years before his death sporting gentlemen in Antwerp were laying bets that the English Lothario would divorce and marry once again.[22]

Then there was the matter of religion. Disrespect for and even defiance of the Pope could be condoned by a generation brought up on Erasmus's question: 'How long is it to be suffered that the Pope should ally himself first with one prince and then with another, until peace becomes hopeless?';[23] but the execution of More, Fisher and the Carthusian monks was regarded as an act of barbarism which placed Henry beyond the pale of Christian civilization. The English observer in Venice reported that he had never seen 'Italians break out so vehemently at anything; it seemed so strange and so much against their stomach', and the Bishop of Faenza spoke for most of Catholic Europe when he said: 'These are truly the most monstrous things seen in our times.' [24] A decade later Henry's spiritual credit was no better, especially among the lesser folk of Europe; it was still being said that 'the King had done what would give him a warm arse one day.'[25] Even the German Protestants considered him a doubtful ally, and Luther, who had never wasted any love or respect on the English Defender of the Faith, concluded that he was a dreadful old man and would some day 'come to grief' as he justly deserved.[26]

Henry's eventual destination was a matter of considerable diplomatic importance. Not only did the papacy pronounce him accursed in the eyes of man and God, and brand his loyal subjects as worse than infidels, but all Christendom was absolved of any oath which touched the person of this schismatic prince. The Catholic sovereigns of Europe rarely permitted conscience to stand in the way of self-interest, but in their dealings with Henry they possessed a heaven-blessed excuse for doing what came naturally; as Charles remarked, no pledge or treaty offered the English King 'would hold good' and the Pope could always be depended upon to annul any diplomatic promise whenever convenient.[27] Possibly Henry had sound cause to speak endlessly about 'the trust and credit between princes', if only because his own spiritual credit was so small.[28]

Rome was loud in her fulminations against the English prince of heretics, but Henry remained an essential, if detestable, member of the European community, and so long as Francis and Charles were diplomatic schizophrenics, preferring to divorce religious scruples from international politics, the King, his conscience and his kingdom were safe. A certain amount of compartmentalization was recognized as a diplomatic necessity, and most of Europe understood the logic behind Francis's warning to his Protestant allies in Germany to stop complaining about his ferocious persecution of heretics in France. He was, he assured them, determined to 'maintain the religion he received from his ancestors, and his friendship with these states did not affect it'.[29] Few pragmatists were willing to accept the conclusion that 'whosoever do make a peace or treaty with a Turk, he is also a Turk', or by the same token that the sovereign who allied himself with Henry became a heretic by association.[30] Smaller states might be able to indulge their consciences, and Venice sanctimoniously denied Henry diplomatic recognition after the break with Rome, but the great powers were hungry cannibals who preferred earthly expediency to heavenly reward. They were well aware of the economic and political realities of their diet, even though they were sufficiently well-bred to say grace before devouring their neighbour.

Fortunately for England the facts of European power politics were discernible to all, and Charles, Francis and Henry each knew exactly where the others stood; England would for ever foster Habsburg–Valois bitterness, France would sow hatred and discord on the Anglo-Scottish frontier, and Charles and Henry would always hesitate to disrupt the Antwerp–London commercial axis so essential to the financial welfare of both. Francis himself summed up the predatory nature of great-power diplomacy when he incautiously said: 'Of one thing you may be assured: that a king of France will never suffer a king of Scotland to be oppressed,' any more 'than a king of England will suffer an emperor or a French king to be over-come one of another', but will 'keep them in an equality'.[31] Henry agreed, and assured the Imperial Ambassador that he 'had no fear of being annoyed or troubled by anyone in the world, so long as a perfect amity did not exist between' Charles and Francis.[32] As for Scotland, it was an axiom of French policy to maintain a hold over that unruly outpost of Catholicism. A divided Britain was worth a dozen armies on the mainland and the surest guarantee that England would refrain from recovering her lost provinces on the Continent. At the same time Englishmen liked to recite:

> Who that intendeth France to win,
> With Scotland let him begin.[33]

There is a nonsense quality about the sixteenth-century inter-national scene reminiscent of an armed band of children playing at war, mimicking the secrecy, espionage and *Realpolitik* of adult diplomacy, but possessed of a dangerously short attention-span, incapable of dissociating problems from personalities, and living in a world where everything seems possible. The marvellous scheme of May 1516, whereby Henry was to be adopted by the Emperor Maximilian, invade Europe with an army of 2,000 horse and 4,000 archers and parade gloriously across Flanders and Northern France to Trèves where the Emperor would resign the Empire to him and present him with the Duchy of Milan,[34] might be dismissed as the dream of an addleheaded boy-king and a senile Emperor, except for the fact that most of the other sovereigns of Europe were swept up in the same kind of fantasy. Against Prince Hal's fervent desire 'to strike a blow for Christendom,' and dedicate his 'very blood and body' to the godly purpose of leading an army of 20,000 soldiers, 70 ships and 15,000 sailors against the Infidel, must be set Francis's boast that if he were elected Emperor, 'three years after his election he would be in Constantinople or his grave'.[35] Charles V was equally affected with the crusading itch. As an adult of thirty-eight he seriously considered it feasible to restore the Byzantine Empire with

200 sail and 60,000 troops, when he could not even take Paris with twice that army.[36]

For all their differences in style, Charles, Francis and Henry possessed one diplomatic quality in common: they rarely permitted any practical consideration to stand in the way of their dreams. Henry Tudor took seriously his feudal rights to the overlordship of Scotland and thought it reasonable that a kingdom which had spent five centuries defending its independence should recognize him as heir to the Scottish throne. His expectations were no more bizarre than the vision of his Imperial nephew, whose cherished ambition was to reconquer his ancestral lands in France. Charles V never flew the banners of Castile or displayed the flags of his Imperial office; instead he wore the colours of Burgundy, and until he died Europe went along with the myth that Imperial armies, manned by Dutch, German, Flemish, Castilian and Italian peasants, were in fact the forces of Burgundy temporarily deprived of their French orientation.[37] The English monarch may have been straining the limits of diplomatic credulity when, after the victory of Solway Moss in 1542, he loaded his Scottish prisoners with gifts, bound them with sacred oaths, and packed them off to their lochs and moors in the happy belief that they would actively support his claim to the Crown, but compared to the Emperor's extravagant behaviour after his triumph at Pavia, Henry's pretensions and methods seem modestly realistic. Charles forced his ancient enemy, after six months in a Spanish prison, to sign a peace treaty by which Francis swore on his honour not only to restore all of the possessions of Duke Charles the Bold of Burgundy but also to abandon his feudal claims to Flanders and Artois, marry the Emperor's sister, resign his rights to Milan, Genoa and Naples, provide a French fleet to escort Charles to his Imperial coronation in Rome, return all the estates of the most dangerous and traitorous feudal noble of France—Charles Bourbon—and finally join the Emperor in person on a crusade against the Infidel and the German Lutherans. Having extracted these concessions, Charles, against the overwhelming advice of his council, set his royal prisoner free in the fond expectation that Francis would abide by his pledge.[38]

One of the most persistent notions of sixteenth-century diplomacy was that by a wave of the diplomatic wand states could be dissolved, joined and rearranged into any shape ingenious ambassadorial minds could conceive. For almost a decade English diplomats lived with the nightmare that the Emperor would actually marry his daughter to the youngest of Francis's sons, Charles Duc d'Orléans, and present them with an independent state consisting of the Netherlands,

Burgundy and Guelders, or, equally incredible, that he might elevate Milan into a sovereign principality and present it to Orléans as a dowry for his niece, the Archduchess Anna of Austria. Neither of these political monstrosities was born, but no one doubted that the map of Europe could be redrawn without concern for local customs, economic ties or national prejudices. As Mr Secretary Paget said of the rival claims of England and France to Normandy and Aquitaine, lands and titles were the inheritance of kings, and 'princes be not wont to make an account to their people in such cases'.[39] Henry agreed whole-heartedly and saw no reason why the unification of England and Scotland could not be achieved by the magic of marriage, without serious regard to ties of economic self-interest or the bonds of a common faith; it certainly seemed just as feasible as the union of French Burgundy and Habsburg Netherlands into a single viable state.

Fantasy went deeper than the dynastic ambitions of princes; it stood at the root of all diplomatic and military convention. Nothing was too improbable for the story-book script of international politics and protocol. Lions were exchanged between sovereigns; and great pies, made from the largest boar ever killed in France and cooked by Francis himself, were shipped across the Channel to Henry, who found them 'marvellous good'. Implied chivalric insults were carefully staged as when Prince Hal sent his brother of France a sword of Arthurian proportions with the message that he possessed one even more weighty, and Francis replied that the instrument was archaic and scarcely 'maniable'. Even the military took seriously the report of a new invention with which to spy on the French—a great mirror on the top of Dover Castle in which, it was said, could be seen the naval activity of Dieppe harbour.[40]

To the modern mind the activities of sixteenth-century kings are worse than frivolous; they are utterly inconsequential. Endless time and labour were expended on supplying armies, estimating costs and planning complicated campaigns, but when the moment of battle came the cost made a mockery of the estimates of even the most experienced bureaucrats, the weather was invariably too hot, too cold, too wet or the wind 'contrarious and the sea very misty', armies proved to be ill-supplied and lacked staying-power, and peace negotiations were commenced almost the moment the war started.[41] Troops were regularly decimated by disease but only rarely routed by the sword, and though giant siege-guns could demolish almost any baronial castle, they were more than matched by the earthworks and trenches which protected most of the strategic centres of Europe. Battles, even miraculous triumphs of the magnitude of

Solway Moss, where the English army routed a Scottish host, were inconclusive, and most military chronicles sound as if they had been written by romantic juveniles. During the Imperial–French war, which broke out in 1542 and grew to include the English by the summer of 1543, it is difficult to ascertain any accurate deployment of troops, any precise idea of casualties or rational plan of attack. The accounts are diaries of gallantry spiced with the grotesque, wondrous narratives of how the King crossed the sea in a ship with golden sails and went forth to battle in full armour astride a mighty charger, of how Henry's smith was killed at his forge and Messrs Gooddolphin, Harper and Culpeper were blown to bits with a single cannon-shot, of how the walls of Boulogne were mined with such thoroughness that the King and his company were endangered by the flying rock, and finally of how on September 4th there arose a storm of 'marvellous lightning, thunder and rain' which lasted two hours.[42] The war involved hundreds of thousands of soldiers, three years of constant campaigning, and the near-bankruptcy of the belligerents, yet the results were minuscule. Charles defeated the Duke of Cleves and seized the French town of St Dizier, Francis won a glorious victory over the Emperor at Cérisoles, and Henry captured the French coastal city of Boulogne, but in the end Boulogne and St Dizier were returned, Cérisoles was forgotten and the Duke of Cleves was pardoned.

At sea the fighting was even more inconclusive. A Turkish fleet burned Nice but failed to take the citadel, wintered at Toulon and returned home taking with it a sizable percentage of the French population as galley-slaves. Farther north, in the Channel, the French invasion of England with two hundred sail resulted only in the accidental destruction of two capital ships—the French flagship which burned while at dock and the *Mary Rose* which sank before Henry's eyes in Portsmouth harbour.[43] The two naval disasters were symbolic. Despite the careless expenditure of life and the staggering financial outlay, the contestants were like so many male ruminants: their aggressive instincts and magnificent horns notwithstanding, they rarely hurt one another except by accident.

Of all the nonsensical actions of a sensible monarch who was 'far from reckless', loved his money-bags and was loath to part with them, the most extraordinary was Henry's decision to squander his resources on the capture of the small French city of Boulogne in the summer of 1544. By rights such a massive undertaking, when England was already at war on the Scottish front, should have had causes commensurate to the necessary fiscal and human sacrifice, and should be intelligible in terms of strategic and power concepts.

The historian should be able to say that the city was necessary to the defence of Calais, that it had to be seized before English armies could sweep on to Paris, or that it was a port from which Henry's ships could cut the all-important sea route between Scotland and France. But it is not at all clear that any of these rational explanations entered the sovereign's mind.[44] The entire French campaign was a wildly improbable enterprise, and both of those well-informed and astute political observers, the French and Imperial Ambassadors, were amazed that a monarch who was 'at peace with all his neighbours' and was 'profiting by their dissension' should have been willing 'to throw himself into a maze of difficulties for the service of God and the welfare of Christendom'.[45] Yet he did exactly that, and on an unparalleled scale.

What was the fascination of an unlovely French 'dog-hole' which outshone the military renown to be earned in Scotland or the political gain to be won from his enemies' discomfort? Doubtless matters of strategy entered into the King's calculation, but his entry into Boulogne had more to do with day-dreams than with *raison d'état*. If twentieth-century rationality is sought, the scholar is quickly thrown back on the conclusion that 'the most obvious feature of the age was the near-absence of any coherent set of principles against which policy could be measured'.[46] However, as the medievally inclined Duchess in Alice's Wonderland insisted, 'Everything's got a moral, if only you can find it.' A set of principles existed, but, like the Duchess's baby, one is never sure whether it will turn out to be a howling infant or a squealing pig.

Economic determinism, the struggle for markets, national aggrandizement and domestic political pressures do not cause war; they simply set the frame of reference in which the struggle will be fought. What produces conflict is man's emotional response to violence and the way society pictures war. If war is accepted as a way of life, as a stage on which man can achieve an essential part of his purpose in living, or as a testing-ground by which individuals, nations, and races can realize their superiority, then causes become irrelevant. As Chapuys noted, conflict was so much a part of English-Scottish existence that border-people were not accustomed to declare war; it was peace that had to be proclaimed as an act of calculated policy.[47] Elsewhere aggression was more decorously garbed in socially acceptable excuses. War was for the sake of God, for the revenge of honour, or in defence of just rights, and the English were regarded as quaintly archaic in holding it 'a point of honour not to begin war without defiance'.[48]

When Henry, bare-headed, delivered his challenge to his brother

of France in May 1543, and declared his intention of waging war, he
presented a list of 'justifications' which were meaningful to his
generation, but which had little to do with the actual cause of the
fighting. He challenged Francis to break off his scandalous understanding with the Sultan, to cease his aggressions against the
Emperor, to acknowledge his obligation to pay Henry's yearly
pension of 102,104 crowns (approximately £2,000), of which not a
penny had been seen for nine years, and to deliver as security for
these just debts and all future pensions several hundred square miles
of the French coast. Then for good measure Henry insisted that his
French brother hand over for English justice the son of a cobbler
who styled himself 'la Blanche Rose' and boasted that he was the
rightful king of England, stop his efforts to incite Scotland to war,
release all of the King's subjects cruelly and rigorously imprisoned,
and finally join England and the Empire in expelling the Turks from
Europe. If Francis refused, then his kingdom would be dismembered
and Charles as duke of Burgundy and Henry as king of France would
demand their full feudal and historic rights.[49] Out of such an
imaginative array of international grievances, it is tempting to
isolate the 'true' cause and discard the rest as rhetorical fluff, but in
effect the entire challenge was window-dressing, merely a formal
recognition that a 'just' war could only be waged between sovereign
princes.[50] The actual fighting needed no more justification than a
fox-hunt, and something akin to the spirit of the hunt prevailed in
the sixteenth century's approach to war. There were, of course, a
handful of fuzzy-minded intellectuals who deplored 'the open manslaughter' and senseless glorification of homicide, as there are those
today who cavil about blood sports or feel sorry for the fox.[51] These,
however, were mean and narrow men who could not understand their
King when he wrote that, 'being a prince of such honour', he could
never give up Boulogne 'which we have royally conquered in our
just wars'.[52]

A prince of honour, a royal conquest and a just war were three
phrases with but a single refrain. Even a bishop knew that the first
concern of war was the pursuit of honour and renown; after these
had been achieved, matters of strategy and politics could be discussed. 'I esteem nothing Boulogne', said Bishop Stephen Gardiner,
'in comparison of the mastery we have won in keeping of it, and
defending our realm alone. Boulogne in process may be lost [in]
many ways; the name, fame, honour and renown gotten by it can
never decay, if it be now established by a peace.' Winchester felt
obliged to dress any mention of peace in the armour of chivalry, and
he quickly added that he had heard such honour spoken of English

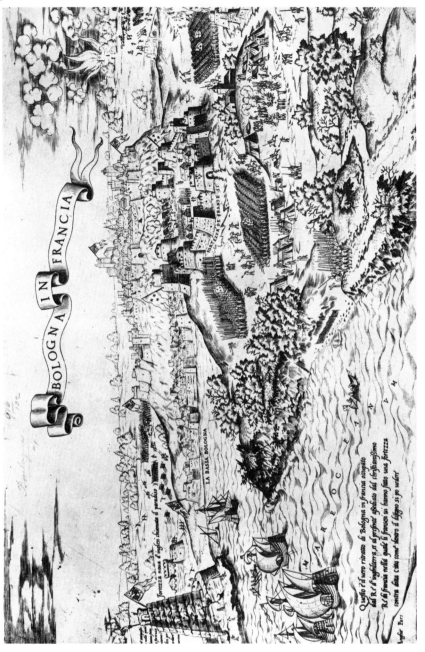

Plan of Boulogne; a view of the siege of the town in September 1544
(*executed c.*1550)

JAMES V, 1513–42.
Artist unknown

EDWARD SEYMOUR,
EARL OF HERTFORD, *c.*1506–52.
Corneille De Lyon

arms, even by Italians, that he was 'afraid of further war for losing any piece of it'.[53]

Charles, Francis and Henry were all caught up in a dream: three ludicrous and rusty White Knights enveloped in a youthful vision of chivalry so vivid that gouty old age seemed immaterial. It made no difference that councillors reminded the Emperor, when he spoke of crusading for the sake of God's honour, that he was a middle-aged gentleman who should eschew 'enterprises fit only for young lord-lings', or that advisers implored Henry not to endanger his life by accompanying his armies to Europe but to stay at home in bed. Neither sovereign had any intention of following such vulgar advice, for both appreciated that honour was 'an ardent heat which en-flameth the mind of man to glorious enterprises'.[54] Instinctively each sensed that if honour were taken away, 'where is our reverence? take away reverence, what are our laws? And take away law, and man is nothing but a gross mass of all impiety.' [55]

Honour stood at the root of Henry Tudor's personality. Next to conscience it was the term he used most often—'it cannot stand with my honour', honour requires that our armies be 'last in the field', 'touching our honour' which we 'will not have stained in our old age'—and no more than conscience was it a pretence which hid self-interest and pride.[56] When Henry Tudor was born, knighthood was in its sunset, but its afterglow was more intense than its high noon, for it touched a wider public. The printing press had usurped the place of the minstrel, and the exploits of Jason, Hector, Charle-magne, Lancelot and Galahad had become the household possessions of a Coventry mason as well as the clean-fingered gentleman. By 1491, the year of the King's birth, a score of books had left William Caxton's press to enchant an entire generation into living a chivalric ideal which had probably never conformed to actual life but was, in the sixteenth century, perversely and passionately valued. Its very artificiality gave it meaning.[57]

The romance of chivalry was fashioned by a host of unknown craftsmen out of three great literary traditions—the songs of Charlemagne and his noble captains, the romance of Troy with its unpredictable heroes, and the Arthurian cycle touched with the sin of Lancelot. These three embodied the childhood aspirations of most of Europe, and Englishmen liked to add the legend of their last warrior king, Henry V, 'the flower and glory of all knighthood'. Charles V neglected his classical education, read avidly the incredible deeds of Oliver and Roland, and dreamt of jousts and crusades. Late in life he sought to relive the chivalric glory of his Burgundian fore-fathers, and he spent almost two weeks immersing himself in the

F

ritual of the Order of the Golden Fleece and feasting its knightly companions. Only Bishop Gardiner thought the action anachronistic, irreverently commenting that the world was 'so far out of order as there is small cause to make any feast'.[58] On the other side of the Channel, Henry commissioned the first life of Henry V; proudly displayed the 'original round table' at Winchester to visiting dignitaries; and encouraged his friend Lord Berners to translate Froissart's *Chronicles* so that 'his worthy subjects, seeing in history the very famous deeds' of their ancestors, might be inspired to like virtues and manhood.[59]

Roger Ascham had nothing but contempt for all this play-acting, and warned that it was dangerous to fill young minds—royal, imperial or common—with a military creed which sought to transform wanton violence into a social sacrament.[60] Simple carnage, however, was not the primary appeal of the heroic way of life. The chivalric posture required a public stage, a military setting, and actors who were 'worthy to be known' because of their noble hearts. The action was muscular and brutal, but the magic of make-believe transformed senseless manslaughter into a fairy-tale. What motivated the hero was not so much a desire to emulate the marvels of the past as the conviction that style makes both the man and the occasion; the manner in which a deed is done is more important than the achievement itself.

The medieval bachelor knights who swore to cover one eye with a patch until they had accomplished some notable exploit were held in great esteem, for their determination to achieve renown was considered far more important than the odds they faced by fighting half-blind. Even a thirteenth-century cleric was outraged when it was suggested that an English king should journey forth to war armed with money, not men, thereby treating him as if he were 'a money-changer, a banker or a peddler, rather than a king and leader of knights and magnificent preceptor'.[61] Three hundred years later Castiglione was still insisting on much the same thing: 'You know in great matters and adventures in wars the true provocation is glory; and who so for lucres sake or for any other consideration taketh it in hand ... deserveth not the name of a gentleman, but is a most vile merchant.'[62] No wonder Henry entered his first excursion into the Continental military arena in 1513 not for political or economic gain but, as it was said, to 'create such a fine opinion about his valour among all men that they could clearly understand that his ambition was not merely to equal but indeed to excel the glorious deeds of his ancestors'.[63] It was essential to his role, during the wet night after the first day's march into France, that he should model himself on

Henry V on the eve of Agincourt. Refusing to undress, he rode about the camp until three in the morning encouraging his men, and assuring them that now 'we have suffered in the beginning, fortune promises us better things, God willing'.[64]

Honour could be displayed in any walk of life, but no one doubted that war was the special condition of society most heavily steeped in glory. Honour, however, had its drawbacks when it came to winning battles. The intensely personal nature of the creed justified such histrionics and disdain for military discipline that it is surprising wars were won at all, even by accident. If lieutenants, as Henry learned to his extreme irritation, did not ignore express instructions because they considered them pedestrian or dull, they sulked in their tents over some slight to their reputations or challenged the enemy to personal duels. The King was outraged when his Vice-Admiral, Sir Thomas Seymour, ignored his precise orders to convoy the supply barges between Dover and Boulogne and instead went kiting off in quest of glory and seventeen great French men-of-war anchored at Dieppe. Henry had cause for annoyance: Seymour had left his supply ships unprotected, had been unable to find them when he returned and had ended up in Portsmouth harbour sans honour and obedience.[65] James V of Scotland fared even worse when honour, or perhaps simply clannish churlishness, helped to destroy his whole army at Solway Moss. For reasons still uncertain, the Scottish King placed in command of his invading troops a court favourite whom the chieftains refused to obey; the result was a staggering defeat.

Quality always stood paramount, and victory did not necessarily go to the side which had killed the most men or had achieved its tactical purpose. By the standards of his day, the Earl of Surrey was clearly defeated in January 1546 and 'thereby lost greatly in reputation' when his foot-soldiers inexplicably panicked, fourteen well-bred captains lost their lives and two of their ensigns fell to the French, despite the fact that the enemy lost three times as many men, gave up the field of battle, were thwarted in their military plans, and lost ninety baggage-carts. It was the quality of 'the young gentlemen' who fell, especially George Pollard of the King's gentlemen pensioners and Edward Poynings, captain of the guard at Boulogne, that gave the French cause to brag, for Henry's honour had been touched. England's chivalry, not her military strength, had been defeated, and only some noble exploit of arms could avenge such a disgrace.[66]

The satisfaction of honour was a sacred duty, a matter understood by every European sovereign. When Francis gave as his justification for war against the Emperor in July 1542 the murder by

Imperial agents of two French ambassadors en route to Constantinople, Henry indicated to 'his dearest brother' that he appreciated
the need 'to proceed to the revenge' of honour.[67] It was fortunate
that he did, because within the year the King was to have double
cause to avenge his own reputation in Scotland. By August 1542
English-Scottish border relations, always bloody at best, had deteri-
orated to such a point that Sir Robert Bowes, Warden of the Middle
Marshes, led an 'unofficial' punitive raid into Scotland in pursuit of
border raiders and promptly fell into a well-planned ambush.[68] The
encounter was a frontier skirmish of little strategic importance except
that it sustained the cherished principle of Anglo-Celtic relations—
one outrage deserved another. What transformed the defeat, which
scarcely counted since it had been achieved by trickery, into a
matter of supreme importance was that Sir Robert, his brother and
a half-dozen other gentlemen were captured, a disgrace to English
arms far more humiliating than the seventy dead or the four to five
hundred common soldiers captured. Scotland had meddled 'with the
most noble prince and father of wisdom of all the world', who would
'not be trifled withal in no case'.[69] Henry's honour had been touched,
and over and over again he preached the necessity of some 'notable
exploit', some 'honourable enterprise', to purge the disgrace of
Bowes's defeat.[70] When a month later two of the King's heralds
were assassinated while returning from James's court, Henry was
even more shocked than his French brother had been, calling the
murder a slaughter 'so abominable and so barbarous' that it was an
outrage upon 'humane society'.[71] Only after Solway Moss, where the
capture of two Scottish earls, five barons and five hundred lairds
and gentlemen, as well as some seven hundred other prisoners, more
than rectified the chivalric balance, did the King feel that his
reputation had been restored and his spirits begin to revive.

Style, in both victory and defeat, bemused reality, transforming
simple slaughter into a theatrical display more real than the agony
and waste which accompanied it. Fantasy was for ever being mixed
with scenes of mass inhumanity. On one day Sir John Wallop's
small army burnt Beaulieu Abbey for the sheer joy of destruction;
on the next Sir John, an old friend of the French commander at
Terouenne, delivered a challenge demanding that six of the French
captain's noblest warriors 'might run with six gentlemen of our
army for life and death', and all military operations ceased to watch
the spectacle.[72] A similar piece of chivalric nonsense occurred when
the Emperor's army passed Châlons without attacking it and a
cadre of French gallants rode out 'wishing to have a skirmish and
break lances for the love of their ladies'. Rather unfairly the Imperial

Army, with a vastly superior force, brushed them aside, leaving only dead heroes behind.[73]

In almost all descriptions of early-sixteenth-century war the approach is medieval—a studied unconcern for the fighting, its purpose or its aftermath, but a passionate interest in the feats of individual warriors, 'hardly breaking' their maces and staffs upon the unfortunate heads of the enemy or capturing tall young men in open combat.[74] The French boasted that they were not 'accustomed to make war by military artifices, but with banners waving, particularly when we have for [a] general a valiant king, who ought to inspire the greatest poltroons to combat bravely'.[75] For his part Henry Tudor reacted in much the same fashion; he concurred with Lord Lisle after the premature death of James V that there was no longer any honour in continuing the fight against 'a dead body, or upon a widow or on a young suckling'.[76] The entire Scottish campaign, in fact, was described in heroic terms almost as imaginative as those used to dress royalty. Reality on the border was plain enough: 'Only women, children and impotent creatures' survived; they lived in wretched hovels which were systematically burnt and just as regularly rebuilt in a single day, and they eked out a miserable living by stealing forth at night 'to manure the ground and to sow corn'.[77] Yet after the Earl of Hertford's paralysing but 'prosperous adventure' into Scotland, during which he gutted some fifty towns, abbeys, chapels, nunneries and castles, the chronicler Edward Hall loyally and without a hint of remorse recorded the exact number of buildings demolished so that such a 'great exploit' might 'be the better known'.[78] Interestingly enough, the only suggestion that burning Scottish dunghills and carving up women and children were feats of doubtful honour came from the King himself, who informed the Emperor by way of Mr Secretary Paget that it was 'more convenable ... for a lieutenant to spoil and waste a country' than a monarch. Hertford's raid on Scotland was much to Henry's 'honour and reputation', but if he had gone in person and returned without achieving some major exploit of arms, the world would have thought he had 'done little for so great a charge'.[79] Honour, it seemed, was a capricious damsel, and her insatiable demands varied according to the worth of her lover.

Should a more discerning, if no more humane, twentieth century ask why such wanton barbarism did not at least anger the Scots, the answer is that it did, but a demand for revenge is not the same as a sense of moral outrage. After all, Scottish gentlemen were no kinder to their own peasants, and it was said that a highland laird 'set not by the hurt of the poor folk but laughs at the same'.[80] What is shocking is not man's inhumanity to man; why should Henry, who endured daily torture with his ulcerated leg, or Charles, who suffered an agony of gout and arthritis, concern themselves with the miseries of this world: they had plenty of their own. What is horrifying is the perversity of the indifference. It was essential to his Majesty's honour that his soldiers and sailors should have splendid new coats of gorgeous colours before setting off to do battle in France, but no one thought it unreasonable that fifteen hundred common labourers should be carted off to Boulogne without food or lodging and expected to lie in open trenches exposed to enemy fire.[81] Such men were born to die, some in a London gutter, others in a French ditch, but nothing was too good for the chosen few. At Boulogne it was necessary that the deputy lieutenant, the captain, the marshal, the treasurer, the controller, the chief porter, the surveyor and the auditor deport themselves as they had always lived —as gentlemen. A captain received £365 plus wages for 30 household servants, 4 horsemen and 6 men-at-arms, besides a free house and 100 acres of the country. In all, the sixteen chief officers did magnificently, considering the irrelevant fact that a war was being waged; they received £4,420 17s. 4d. in diets and wages and 1,080 acres of land, a statistic that explains why the knight-porter of Calais was captured by the French while out rabbit hunting![82]

The accusation might be made that any reconstruction of sixteenth-century war in which honour is presented as an end in itself is an anachronism excusing man's most brutal inanity—his urge to destroy—by converting it into a vision which nobody believed but everybody used for their own purposes. The charge is not without merit, but the argument misses the point. Today men trained in a military tradition tend to approach social conflict with a built-in prejudice: wars, if they must be fought, should be won. This does not mean that military leaders do not make good peace negotiators, or will not stop short of total victory for reasons of international politics. It does mean, however, that they prefer—all things being equal—to win a war as quickly as possible with all the instruments available to them. In the sixteenth century, Henry, Francis and Charles viewed military conflict only incidentally in terms of territorial acquisition, strategic gain or economic advantage. Instead, they saw it as an adventure which it was their duty to sustain. Old, diseased and ridiculous as they were, they accepted without question a proposition still regarded as sound three generations later: 'In a Prince there is nothing so glorious as to be called a great captain or a worthy soldier.'[83]

The purpose of society was paradoxical. In one breath sovereigns were God's instruments on earth, His hammers to construct the ark of salvation; in the next, they were the architects of war in which men of honour could display their worth and gain immortality on earth. Society could no longer countenance the prospect of knights errant blundering about the countryside in quest of a military dream. Armour, charger, spear and squire were far too costly;* the clumsy boiler-plated heroes of the past were too vulnerable, and public opinion too intolerant of private war. The state had to take over from private enterprise and supply the sword and buckler as well as the justification for war, so that Castiglione's courtier could be 'seen in open shows', be 'known among all men', and be 'esteemed among the best'.[84] If honour demanded that 'things well done' be publicly done and enacted even 'before the very eyes' of the King,[85] then it behoved monarchs to supply the military stage on which honour could be displayed, reputations won, immortality achieved and the heroic ideal transformed into a reality.

In 1542 Henry Tudor was ready to listen to the voice of chivalry and the advice of would-be heroes; as the new year waxed he had need of good will and great renown, for his heart was sore, his pride was hurt, and his honour both as a man and as a king was sadly tarnished.

---

* Tilting armour cost between £10 and £12 and field armour £8 in an age which regarded £2 10s. as a yearly living wage (*L.P.*, XX [1], 558).

8

Honour Saved

> Rightly to be great
> Is not to stir without great argument,
> But greatly to find quarrel in a straw
> When honour's at the stake.'
> *Hamlet*, IV, iv

The thirty-second year of the King's reign was not a success. If the misfortunes of 1525–7 had been sufficient to send Henry in search of the cause of God's malediction, those of 1541 were enough to smash all illusions, leaving only a bitter, sick old man. The giant who had dominated the matrimonial stage of Europe for the last fifteen years and could not doubt the physical magnetism of his royal person was in November held up before all Christendom as the cuckolded husband. The new year had augured no such calamity. It had begun as a perfect Indian summer, a moment of golden health and spiritual satisfaction when the domestic and international affairs of the sovereign prospered mightily. Abroad, the key to England's international well-being, mistrust among the major powers, was unlocking the door to further Habsburg–Valois discord. The diplomatic heavens, so long in perilous harmony, were returning to their warlike formation. For two years the King had lived with the nightmare that Charles and Francis might forget their hatred, come to terms over Burgundy and Milan, and unite to crush sin and schism throughout Europe, but even since the Emperor had bestowed Milan upon his son in October 1540 it was clear that the giants of the international system were safely back on a collision course. At home, the embarrassing six-months' comedy of the King's fourth marriage to Anne of Cleves was mercifully over. In her stead reigned Henry's 'rose without a thorn', Mistress Catherine Howard, who since July 28th, 1540, had been vigorously fulfilling her marriage vows 'to be bonair and buxom in bed and at board, till death us do part'.

At fifty Henry Tudor was still magnificent. True, the puffed-sleeved, fiercely corseted and tightly hosed colossus immortalized by Holbein four years earlier was giving way to an elderly Titan, dressed in rich fustian gown and warm collar, who was having trouble with his leg and preferred to spend his days 'in loving rest and fleeing trouble', but for the moment the younger, more vigorous image prevailed, and the French Ambassador remarked that he had seldom 'seen the King in such good spirits or in so good a humour'.[1] Throughout the summer and winter of 1540 youth returned to the court and the twenty-year-old Queen reigned supreme. The monarch, it was said, 'had no wife who made him spend so much money in dresses and jewels', and every day there was 'some fresh caprice' which the besotted husband sought to satisfy.[2] Another man might have been content with a costly courtesan, but not so a prince of conscience who was wont to 'go the whole length'. Henry preferred legality in all that he did, and sex was no exception; he took literally his marriage promise: 'With my body I thee worship, and with all my worldly chattels I thee endow.'[3] The apple of the King's eye obligingly chose as her motto 'No other wish save his',[4] an expression of endearment and wifely concern which the ageing monarch accepted as no more than his due. As the year progressed, however, the court began to note that the spoiled bride was behaving in a singularly improper fashion for one who had no other wish than to serve her husband.

Henry's Indian summer was short-lived. In March 1541 the King discovered that he was more in need of a companion beside his sick-bed than a symbol of his vanished youth. During the early spring the ulcer on his leg closed, and he lay with blackened features and raging fever, conscious that sickness and suffering were sent by God as either a warning or a chastisement. It was said that the King was depressed and suffered from a 'mal d'esprit', and every mirror of the privy chamber disclosed that he was growing bald, paunchy and wrinkled. He vented his irritation on his ministers, calling them profiteers and flatterers, and raging that 'if God lent him health' again he would shortly see to their correction. His subjects, he complained, were 'an unhappy people' who harboured sedition in their hearts, and he would soon make them so poor that they would no longer have the time or energy to indulge their disobedience.[5] His peevishness was so intense that he closed his household to all music and entertainment during the Lenten festivals and even barred his door to his prattling and irresponsible wife.

Henry recovered and so eventually did his disposition, and throughout the spring he plunged into a therapeutic frenzy of activity, arranging the most spectacular progress of his reign, a triumphal journey northward to receive the accolades of loyal subjects who had never before set eyes upon their lord. As if staging a full-scale invasion, the King sent five thousand mounted troops to herald his arrival and ordered furniture, bedding, tapestries and two hundred sumptuous tents carted to York to impress the local inhabitants and serve his court, while he himself set forth with a thousand retainers, officers and companions.[6] Disloyally the weather refused to co-operate. Rain turned the roads into a quagmire of mud and delays, and for nearly three weeks the cavalcade was bogged down scarcely three days' march from London. At York worse irritations were awaiting the King when he finally arrived on September 16th. James of Scotland had given the English to understand that he would meet Henry for a discussion of the mounting tension between their two kingdoms. For weeks fifteen hundred workers had been labouring mightily to rebuild the great abbey hall of St Mary's, and refurbish it with paintings and plate sent from Westminster as a setting befit an encounter between sovereigns.[7] Alas, the royal uncle waited nine days in vain, and St Mary's was left vacant, embarrassing testimony that the King of England had been publicly jilted.

The insult rankled, but it had not been altogether unexpected, and domestically the progress was a spectacular success.[8] Yorkshire men were gratifyingly vocal in their fidelity and at great financial pains to make amends for the disloyalty of five years before, when an army of traitors had called themselves the Pilgrimage of Grace and taken as their badge of rebellion the five wounds of Christ. King Hal was in excellent spirits as he slowly retraced his steps to London. His health was reasonably good as it so often was when on the move, a fact which the King attributed to the country air, the relaxation of the hunt and the excitement of constant change; and his Queen, though alas not yet pregnant, was the embodiment of youth and vivacity. With a glad heart and gratitude to God for the 'good life he led and trusted to lead', he returned to Hampton Court to be told that his son was desperately sick with quartan fever and was 'so fat and unhealthy' that he could not long survive.[9] Three days later, on November 2nd, he was handed a letter disclosing that his pampered bride had been behaving like a common whore.

The truth about Catherine Howard can never be known.[10] Almost everything recorded about the girl comes from political or religious ill-wishers and personal associates frantic to disentangle themselves from her disgrace, but out of the lies, half-truths, malicious gossip and uncertain memories emerged three indisputable facts: Catherine was not a virgin at the time of her marriage to the King and she may technically have been the common-law wife of Francis Dereham, a gentleman of her grandmother's household; her behaviour while Queen was worse than silly: it was probably adulterous; and finally, in proper story-book fashion, her cuckolded husband was the last person to know or to suspect.

Catherine was raised in the vast, lax and old-fashioned entourage of her step-grandmother, the Dowager Duchess of Norfolk, and educated for little else than to catch a young man's fancy. Suddenly, however, a girl of few prospects was transformed by the magic of her uncle's influence at court; in December 1539 the Duke of Norfolk arranged for her appointment as one of the twelve maids-in-waiting to Anne of Cleves. Catherine was never more than an instrument of family and factional politics by which the Duke and his ecclesiastical ally, the Bishop of Winchester, sought to destroy Thomas Cromwell and direct the policies of the kingdom more to their religious and political liking. A Howard in the King's bed, carefully punctuating whispered endearments with favours for her friends and relations, was a priceless political weapon, for it was an axiom of family survival that there was more to marriage than 'four bare legs in bed'. From the moment that Henry 'did cast a fantasy' towards this Howard pawn, Cinderella was carefully schooled on 'how to behave', 'in what sort to entertain the King's Highness', how to dress, and what to say.[11] The sovereign was made welcome at the Dowager's house across the river at Lambeth, and Stephen Gardiner sought to advance the courtship by inviting Mistress Catherine to dine with the King at his episcopal palace. She learned her part well, and Henry spent his days and nights rowing back and forth across the Thames. By June he was hopelessly trapped, captivated by a nineteen-year-old girl who wisely refrained from mentioning that she was somewhat more experienced in the ways of love than was becoming a virgin-bride. And why should she have confessed her childhood failings? Neither the Dowager Duchess nor any other member of the Howard clan had seen fit to spoil the royal romance by introducing the name of Henry Manox or Francis Dereham.

It had all started some five years before at Horsham, the Dowager's country estate in Sussex. There, in the communal life under the titular guidance of the short-tempered but tolerant old matriarch, Catherine was reared with other Howard cousins and friends. Life was too short at Horsham to inquire strictly into what went on after the children were locked in the dormitory at night, and there was certainly a good deal of flirting which the Duchess countenanced so long as it was not too blatant. At fourteen Catherine was one of the more 'forward virgins' and she was soon doing more than finger-exercises with Mr Henry Manox, her instructor on the virginal. The liaison continued when the Duchess moved her household to the family's suburban residence at Lambeth, and their intimacies had gone far enough for Manox to boast that Catherine had promised him 'her maidenhead though it be painful to her'.[12] The young man, however, was neither sufficiently well born nor attractive enough to hold a Howard for long, and he was soon replaced by a far more flamboyant lover, Francis Dereham esquire, who made himself at home in the 'maidens' chamber', even though the door was technic- ally locked. Dereham was not alone in scaling the walls of the girls' dormitory or bringing with him 'wine, strawberries, apples and other things to make good cheer' during the midnight hours, but what eventually proved fatal was the inevitable move from flirting in doublet and hose to 'naked bed'. There was absolutely no doubt, said one of the married inmates of the chamber, 'what belonged to that puffing and blowing'.[13] More than once the couple were caught kiss- ing in the great gallery by the Dowager, who indignantly wanted to know whether Catherine thought she was at Henry's dissolute court. Dowager Duchesses were always critical of the younger generation, but Lord William Howard, Catherine's uncle, was more relaxed. When the jilted Manox sought to stir up scandal by informing the Duchess of what was going on behind her back, Lord William simply lectured his niece on tactics, not on morality: 'What mad wenches! Can you not be merry amongst yourselves but you must thus fall out?'[14]

By the time Catherine left Lambeth in December of 1539 she was, in the eyes of the Church, Francis Dereham's common-law wife, calling him husband and making almost no effort to conceal their sexual relationship. Had not the Duke's influence taken her to court she would probably have married the dashing Mr Dereham, who, though scarcely a spectacular matrimonial catch, was a gentle- man of independent means and a great favourite with the Dowager. None of this, of course, came out until it became politically profitable to recall that 'puffing and blowing', but what cost Catherine her head was not only her past indiscretions but also her present follies. From the moment she became Queen she was deluged with pleas to remember her friends of yesterday, and doubtless it was diplomatic to find places in her royal chamber for the ladies who had shared her bed and her secret at Lambeth. It was, however, the height of imprudence to take as her private secretary Mr Francis Dereham, who boasted that if the King were dead he was sure he would be able to marry her and who continued to brag about the special favour the Queen conferred upon him.[15] Possibly Catherine might even have survived importing an ex-lover into her household had she stopped there. Unfortunately she never understood that what might be con- doned in a girls' dormitory was high treason in a queen's apartment,

and she now turned her attention to Mr Thomas Culpeper, a gentleman of her husband's Privy Chamber, whom the French Ambassador
caustically described as a young man who shared the King's couch
and now 'wished to share the Queen's too'.[16]

Thomas Culpeper's intentions can only be surmised, since adultery
was never proved, despite the fact that he and Catherine met
regularly during the King's illness in March and continued their
assignations throughout the summer progress of 1541. In theory a
modicum of respectability was preserved by Lady Rochford, who
acted as procuress and chaperon, but she always remained discreetly
at the far end of the chamber and at least once obligingly fell asleep.
Culpeper was typical of a growing element about the King: boisterous, militant and well-connected. He belonged to a select body of
young men who could speak informally to their sovereign and did
not hesitate to impose upon his friendship, a privilege which Culpeper
successfully utilized when he became involved in an ugly case of rape
that resulted in murder while resisting arrest.[17] Whatever Catherine
saw in him—the grace of a courtier, the obvious sex-appeal or the
scarcely veiled wantonness—Thomas soon became her 'little sweet
fool' and the court began to ring with their doings.

Even then, it was not just diddling the King in his own bedchamber which caught up with Catherine Howard but her past, for
the companions of her Lambeth days began to gossip. Inevitably
their talk was heard by those who detested the Howards and owed
it to their prince to ferret out the truth. Thus, while Henry was
returning from the north, giving thanks to God for the good things
of life and especially his pretty wife, the Council in London learned
about Francis Dereham and 'weighed the matter and deeply pon-
dered the gravity thereof'.[18] The King had to be told, but nobody
wanted to be the bearer of such tidings, and eventually a very
reluctant Thomas Cranmer was nominated to break the news. While
the monarch was at mass the Archbishop slipped him a letter with
the plea to read it in private; then he hurried away.

The King would not or could not believe what he read and dismissed the evidence as a tissue of lies. In order to protect his wife's
reputation, not to test her virtue, he ordered the Council to search
out the truth of what he was sure was a political plot against her
good name. Suddenly his world caved in; the Council rounded up
Manox and Dereham for interrogation and the whole sordid secret
came pouring out—how the music teacher 'had commonly used to
feel the secrets and other parts of the Queen's body' and how the
secretary 'had known her carnally many times, both in doublet and
hose between the sheets and in naked bed'.[19] Henry, however, still

would not accept the truth, and he slipped away from Hampton
Court to attend an all-night emergency session of the Council held
at Bishop Gardiner's London residence. There he learned the full
sink and puddle of Catherine's betrayal, and in front of all his
ministers he raged, so much that it was feared that he might be
going mad. He swore a terrible revenge, calling for a sword and
exulting in the thought that the faithless slut would never have 'such
delight in her lechery as she should have pain and torture in her
death'. Then, to the intense embarrassment of his councillors, he
wept, 'which was strange in [one of] his courage'. There were, of
course, the usual efforts to save the rags of his tattered self-esteem
and to shift the blame to others. Passionately he decried his 'ill-luck
in meeting with such ill-conditioned wives' and reproached his
ministers for 'this last mischief', but no amount of self-deception
could restore the image of youth.[20]

The King of the Holbein portrait was dead, and after that one
single outburst he sank into self-pity and melancholy. There was none
of the unremitting hatred with which he had hunted down and
destroyed his other 'adulterous' spouse. Only five and a half years
before, he had delighted in Anne Boleyn's death and had waited
impatiently for the cannon to proclaim the severing of her neck. In
those days, of course, there had been another lady waiting in the
wings; the end of life had signified a fresh start, and within the hour
of Anne's execution he was on his way to visit Mistress Jane Seymour. Now, however, things were sadly different; as the Imperial
Ambassador explained to his master, the King was like the woman
who lamented the death of her tenth husband more bitterly than all
the others put together because 'she had never buried one of them
without being sure of the next, but after the tenth husband she had
no other one in view'.[21]

Catherine might yet have escaped with her life—bigamy, after all,
was not adultery—and Henry might have accepted an annulment of
his marriage based on the Queen's betrothal to Dereham, but soon
the Council was on to Mr Thomas Culpeper. No one spoke of mercy
after that unfortunate man confessed that 'he intended and meant to
do ill with the Queen and that in like wise the Queen so minded to do
with him'.[22] It made no difference that overt adultery was never
proved; Tudor treason laws operated on the judicious proposition
that the evil thought must precede the seditious act, and in purging
the secret malice of the heart, the government was simply nipping
treason in the bud. Catherine, Dereham and Culpeper had been disloyal in their thoughts, and, as the French Ambassador reported,
Culpeper was condemned to die for having fornicated with the

Queen even though 'he had not passed beyond words', for 'his intentions were so loathsome and dishonest' that they deserved death.[23]

Execution came in December. For Culpeper it was merciful; Henry, against the advice of his Council, preserved the one-time companion of his bedchamber from the degradation of partial hanging, castration, disembowelment and quartering. He died on the block on December 10th, 1541, but Dereham lacked influence and endured the full horror of a traitor's death. Two months later, Catherine Howard died a queen. Though she eventually admitted the promiscuity of her early conduct she denied any pre-contract which might jeopardize the legality of her marriage to the King, and to that single point she clung. In the end Henry honoured her wish, a death befitting her regal dignity. On February 10th, 1542, a small flotilla of vessels escorted her for the last time down the river to the Tower where she was received with all the honour due to a queen. Two days later she was ordered to dispose her soul and prepare for death, and the following morning, along with Lady Rochford, she was helped up the scaffold, where both ladies acknowledged the justice of their deserts for having sinned against God 'in breaking all his commandments, and also against the King's royal Majesty very dangerously'.[24]

No one doubted that Henry had been sorely wronged, and from the start his Council sought ways 'to make him forget his grief' and even spared him the anguish of signing his wife's bill of attainder, which was done *in absentia* by letters patent.[25] Henry could be protected from reading the 'wicked facts of the case' as publicly presented in the Act, but he must have known that his wife's behaviour, and his own discomfort made marvellous gossip in every court in Europe. Sir William Paget was in Paris in December and was ordered to keep the matter to himself unless expressly asked, but both Chapuys and de Marillac were soon reporting the lurid details, and Sir William had to explain to Francis exactly how Catherine had 'wonderfully abused the King'. She had, he said, found 'means not only to train' Francis Dereham but had also retained as her chamberer one of the women who had shared their bed at Lambeth. Francis was fascinated, and, laying his hand to his heart, announced by his faith as a gentleman, 'she hath done wondrous naughty'. Later he wrote to console his English brother, dramatically avowing that he felt Henry's grief as his own, and more sincerely reminding him that 'the lightness of women cannot bind the honour of men'.[26] This was cold comfort indeed, and Henry felt the shame deeply. Christmas was a bleak season devoid of music and laughter and, though the court eventually returned to something like normal and by mid-January Henry was once again entertaining the ladies, he remained 'very old and grey' and ignored his ministers' pleas to take yet another wife. Never before had the sighs and lamentations been so prolonged nor had the old resilience taken so long to reassert itself. For an entire year the King maintained the social amenities of court in a listless, perfunctory fashion, taking little pleasure in public display and entertainment.[27] He kept to his chamber, nursed his injured pride, and listened to the voice of those who sought to distract him with the trumpet's martial sound.

For a time the life-expectancy of the Howard clan, which had knowingly sold him a frivolous piglet in a courtly poke, was in doubt. All were rounded up save the Duke, who discreetly stayed away from London but made it known that he thought his niece should be burned for her sins, and the Tower was so full of Howards and their retainers that accommodation had to be found elsewhere. Those closest to Catherine seemed on the verge of total destruction and were found guilty of misprision, but the King's fury lacked staying power and by August the Dowager Duchess, Lord William and the rest had been released and forgiven. Brother George kept his place among the King's gentlemen-pensioners, brother Henry received a pension from the Crown within a month of his sister's execution, and brother Charles, after a tactful sojourn in Venice, was back in time to receive a knighthood for his part in the 1544 amphibious invasion of Scotland.[28]

The Howards escaped, but James of Scotland did not. An old man might be able to forgive the family of his faithless wife, but not the insult to his honour administered by a disrespectful nephew who had left his uncle waiting at York. The image of youth was smashed beyond repair, but the make-believe of war could continue, and honour, so sadly soiled at home, might yet be redeemed abroad.

It would be intellectually satisfying to say that there was a direct connection between Catherine's death on Tower Hill in February 1542 and the outbreak of military operations less than a year later, and to argue that Henry in his melancholy turned to international adventure as the only outlet left him. It would be even more dramatic to perceive a war conspiracy staged by a military clique in search of glory and urged on by speculators anxious to protect their investments in surplus stallions and monopolies in saltpetre. Alas, except for the calculated self-interest displayed by the Duke of Norfolk, who had political fences to mend and held to war as the only way he could maintain his reputation, there is no documented link between Catherine Howard's death and the mounting war-tension during the summer and autumn of 1542.[29] Nor is there clear evidence of a military cabal set upon violence for its own gain, if only because it is

impossible to distinguish the hawks from the doves in a ruling elite
which accepted the heroic mystique as its code and made no distinction between military and civilian authority. Henry's Council
had its share of civilians—Paget, Wriothesley, Gardiner, Riche,
career-men who exercised immense power in Church and state—but
their authority was no greater than that of the Duke of Suffolk, the
Earl of Hertford, Lord Lisle or Sir Anthony Browne, all of whom
were essentially military men who entered into questions of state as
readily as civilians contributed to discussions of war. Soldiers in peace
were no chimneys in summer; they simply burned a different kind
of fuel. There could be no notion of civilian-master and soldier-
servant in a society which, except for its humanistic and clerical
fringes, accepted war as a way of life, not as an instrument of state
policy.

If there was no war party at court, there was a discernible increase
in the number of young and aggressive men about the King after
1540. The older war-horses—the Dukes of Norfolk and Suffolk, the
Earl of Southampton, Sir Francis Bryan and Sir Anthony Browne,
who spoke of campaigns already a generation old—were joined by
younger warriors anxious to display their mettle: the Seymour
brothers, a fresh crop of Howard progeny, various Pastons and
Carews, six of whom had entrée to the monarch's closet, Richard
Long and Thomas Darcy, both of whom became gentlemen of the
Privy Chamber, Sir John Dudley, with whom Henry enjoyed an
evening of cards and who was shortly created Viscount Lisle, and a
host of others.[30] The intimates of the King's chamber imbibed the
air of chivalry, rejoiced in the joust and engaged in honourable displays of martial prowess. They were touchy of honour, careless of
consequences and ready to sing:

> A master of art is not worth a fart
> Except he be in schools.
> A bachelor of law is not worth a straw
> Except he be among fools.

During the international joust of 1540 six of these young gallants,
including Sir John Dudley, Sir George Carew and Sir Thomas
Seymour, challenged all comers for a year and a day, and during the
first week of May they kept open house while the Earl of Surrey,
Lord William Howard, Lord Clinton and twenty-five others defended
the honour of England.[31]

The military atmosphere was further heightened the same year by
the addition of fifty well-bred gentlemen-pensioners, who enhanced
the King's reputation by their birth and prowess and infused the

court with young blood. Sir Anthony Browne landed the office of captain, but the company consisted largely of younger sons and relations of politically important families pressing for military distinction and posts close to the throne. The decision to introduce an elite guard of honour may have reflected Henry's concern for royal appearances and his desire to ape his brother of France, who sported two hundred such well-born young cavaliers,[32] but more probably it was a political response to social pressure. A generation later the path to social and political success lay through parliament, and under Elizabeth the number of seats in the House of Commons grew accordingly, but under Henry the way to profit and prestige took the ambitious man to court, close to a monarch whose revenues, thanks to Thomas Cromwell, were now sufficient to satisfy his subjects' thirst for recognition.

The King knew full well what inspired the young men of his court; he said himself they were 'desirous both of spoil and glory'.[33] The true hero had to be careful not to place too great a monetary value upon honour lest he be judged a merchant, not a gentleman; nevertheless the profits of battle were ever present in his mind. If the number of knighthoods and high military posts bestowed upon the gentlemen of the Chamber in 1544 is any indication of the potential gain to be extracted from war, then those closest to the sovereign had every reason to urge an aggressive policy.[34] Victory could be a highly lucrative enterprise, especially ransom money, which was carefully worked out between England and France in 1544 with a nice regard for social amenities and a discerning capitalistic eye: a thousand crowns for a king's lieutenant, a quarter's pay for the gentlemen and officers of the royal households, and the same for 'other gentlemen coming to war for pleasure or honest ransoms'.[35] At sea a man could do even better, and, much to the French Ambassador's irritation, Clement Paston of the gentlemen-pensioners, who commanded the 400-ton, 250-man *Anne Gallaunt*, was awarded seven thousand crowns for the capture of Baron de St Blancard, captain of the French galley *Blaunchered*, while his colleagues Sir John Clere and William Broke received all the apparel, plate, money and furniture from the vessel's poop deck and officers' quarters. Paston's take, however, was not all clear profit. The Baron had to be maintained at his captor's expense in a style befitting his rank—a matter of two thousand crowns.[36] The cost of keeping a prisoner was a sore point, and low-born captives imprisoned at Canterbury were ordered to labour for their food, the work to be sufficiently arduous to cause them to 'make the more earnest speed to procure their ransom'.[37]

Economic gain through warfare looked far better when presented as a social and political necessity. Peace, it was said, corroded the commonwealth, fostered political dissension and engendered cowardice and vice, while war toughened the moral fibre, bred domestic concord and relieved the kingdom of its 'ill-affected members'.[38] The argument that war was sound politics was an old one, and seventy years earlier, Henry's grandfather, Edward IV, had sought to justify his invasion of France on grounds of state expediency. His Archbishop of Canterbury had explained to parliament that the realm had experienced a generation of civil war, oppression and lawlessness, and in order to ship the trouble-makers out of the realm the King was urging 'war outward' so that gentlemen and younger sons might find profit in foreign conquests, common soldiers might earn a livelihood, and the derelicts of society might be exported out of the land.[39] Three generations later the lesson was not lost on Henry's government. The Privy Council was concerned that soldiers in Ireland be chosen out of the most 'wild and savage sort whose absence would do good', and at home orders were issued that all 'ruffians, vagabonds, masterless men, common players and evil-disposed persons' should be commandeered to serve in the King's galleys, thereby enhancing the war effort and ridding the kingdom of its least desirable elements.[40]

On a more august level the French Ambassador voiced much the same argument but in reverse, indicating in January 1541 that 'as long as the English are making war on each other they will undertake nothing against the King of France'. The implication was obvious: internal peace, so badly shattered after the destruction of Cromwell in June 1540 that foreign observers thought the kingdom was heading for sedition, might yet be purchased at the price of military glory.[41] Religious and political revolution might yet be bridled if court factions could unite against a common enemy. With Hertford, Lisle, Browne, Norfolk and Suffolk fighting an 'outward war' and Gardiner and Wriothesley busily supplying them with the instruments thereof, there would be little time for political intrigue, religious feuding or personal animosity.

War, expensive as it was, was slight ransom to pay if it stilled domestic discord, restored the health of the kingdom and purged the body politic of private brawls and moral flabbiness. The moral commonwealth for which Henry held himself responsible was not merely a matter of legislating right-thinking and a proper respect for God and magistrate; it was, as the King himself had said, the eradiction of 'all rancour, malice and will to revenge'.[42] Only the therapy of war and the quest for glory 'without respect for riches or reward' could transform rivals into brothers, and petty factions into ranks of single-hearted subjects, for in battle, it was said, men looked into the mirror of their souls.[43] It was exactly this lesson which Henry sought to teach the disloyal Mr Richard Read, alderman of the city of London, whose greedy merchant heart refused the sovereign's appeal for a 'benevolent' loan with which to defend the kingdom's honour. Since the man would not part with his riches his prince thought it fitting that such an ungrateful subject should risk his body and serve on the Scottish frontier as a captain at his own charge, so that he might feel the 'sharp discipline' of military life and smart for his follies.[44]

In 1542 Henry was a widower, disillusioned and ailing. He had had his fill of falseness and was ready to listen to the argument that foreign war, 'like a potion of rhubarb', could cleanse 'choler from the body of the realm' as well as from the heart.[45] There were plenty of young gentlemen lounging in his chamber who were willing enough to picture war as a purgation, a time of camaraderie when heroes could be judged by their true merits and not by the base standards of society, and throughout the spring and summer of 1542 the military motif swelled. The government began hoarding saltpetre and lead, listing the artillery in the Tower, stocking its stud farms, inspecting the defences of Hull, and during April Henry himself travelled to view the fortifications of Dover.[46]

Despite military preparations, no one could say whether Henry had set his heart on some notable exploit in the north against the Scots or across the Channel in France, and de Marillac confessed that the English kept their designs so secret that they could only be 'understood by conjecture'.[47] In early April he reported that Norfolk was languishing in political disgrace, but ten weeks later he wrote that the Duke was now being caressed and 'all men who have heretofore served in war are ordinarily at his house reckoning to be soon employed'.[48] Norfolk's return to favour augured war in the north, where the memory of his father's victory over the Scots at Flodden Field was still strong, but the French Ambassador was certain that France was Henry's ultimate goal. During July and August French ships in the Channel were treated as if they were pirates, English students were ordered home from Paris, French merchants made hasty preparations to leave England, border incidents along the Calais pale multiplied, and indignation against the French increased so fast that de Marillac predicted: 'In the end this boil must burst.' Even in September, when English forces were marching towards the Scottish frontier, the French Ambassador was still unconvinced, warning that beneath Henry's sweet words of friendship there was 'much poison hidden', and cautioning his master to remember that the English held the 'maxim that to hurt Francis in the future they must either overthrow or greatly enfeeble the Scots in order that, while occupied elsewhere, the Scots should not be able to harass them'.[49]

Perhaps the French Ambassador was correct. The English had been deliberately goading James V throughout the summer of 1542, and from the first week of July the level of atrocity and counter-atrocity along the border escalated at an alarming rate.[50] Possibly Henry had in fact determined on a campaign to secure his northern frontier, but preventive war quickly became punitive war when on August 24th Sir Robert Bowes marched into Scotland and promptly got himself captured at Haddon Ridge, along with six other gentlemen and nearly five hundred of his men. Such a defeat, and especially the rumour that a superior English force had refused to fight and had fled, demanded immediate vengeance.[51] Though Henry continued to maintain a smoke-screen of peace negotiations, he was busily preparing for an autumn invasion.[52] As for James, he deftly stalled, pretending to consider his uncle's scarcely veiled command to attend him at York and apologizing that his wife's forthcoming confinement made the visit impossible. The Scottish sovereign had no intention of forsaking his firm and ancient ally France, or leaguing with an old devil whose horns were all the sharper for being English, but he had little to lose by talking well into October, when, it was hoped, the weather would chill his uncle's aggressive ardour.[53] Henry, however, had determined on war no matter what the cost or the season, and by the middle of the month spies were reporting an accumulation of war-material and an army of a hundred thousand designed to strike fear into the stoutest Celtic breast.[54]

There was no dearth of excellent excuses for invasion besides the immediate cause—the disgrace of Haddon Ridge—which Henry delicately referred to as the warlike deeds of the King of Scots that 'could not in respect of our honour be passed over unreformed'.[55] The English monarch claimed with some justification to be the feudal suzerain of Scotland; therefore James had failed in his duty as a loyal nephew and vassal. Henry, however, did not insist on his legal rights; he merely reminded James of his subordinate feudal status and satisfied his own passion for legality by composing an elaborate and pedantic statement of his ancient rights. More serious than forsworn fealty was James's absolute refusal to purify his Church and forsake the Pope. Then there was the insult delivered at York the previous year, which Henry pointed out was the final 'delusion' in a long list of injuries involving border squabbles and political asylum that he had been suffering patiently for over a decade.[56] Possibly none of these excuses was a particularly convincing reason for war, but, as Sir William Paget told the French King, they were considerably better than those which Francis had concocted for his quarrel with the Emperor; indeed, 'if these be matters of no importance, nor lawful for to move war upon, I cannot see how any war is lawful'.[57]

The strategic results of the Scottish campaign were scarcely worth the diplomatic and logistic effort. The administrative mountain laboured and brought forth a military mouse. Norfolk proved to be a chronic and ineffectual complainer; the weather was atrocious; the 'incredible quantity' of military supplies rotted in the holds of water-logged ships long before they reached the frontier; there was more than a hint of dishonesty on the part of the victuallers; and the grand army of 100,000 shrank in reality to scarcely 10,000 ill-fed and demoralized men.[58] Originally Norfolk had boasted that he would 'make such a smoke' as should not be soon forgotten, but almost at once he and his colleagues were writing that the ordnance was defective and the wind contrary, and the navy had failed to intercept sixteen French ships hurrying to the defence of Edinburgh. Throughout the campaign the supply wagons broke down, the troops went without beer, nobody bothered to build a mill at Berwick to grind the wheat, and the horses turned out to be 'naughty nags'. In an agony of mind, Norfolk begged the government to remember that he could not be expected to rule the winds and that it was not his fault if a bridge had collapsed drowning five of his men, or that nineteen soldiers, reduced to drinking puddle-water, had died. The Earl of Southampton concurred, and concluded that never had so great an enterprise been so ill provisioned.[59]

Henry was not pleased, and marvelled that his commanders should be blaming inferior wagons and lack of beer for what was obviously an ineptly led expedition. Much to Norfolk's alarm he growled that 'surely it shall be nothing to our honour but rather to the glory of the Scots that we have levied so great armies as we have done and been at so importable charges, and in fine to do them no greater damage than is like to ensue ... '[60] The campaign was every bit as inglorious as the King feared and, though the generals sought to save face and spoke of the incredible destruction of corn, the English retreated homeward after an invasion which lasted scarcely a week. They had managed to hang eight Scots for horse-stealing, to burn possibly thirty towns, and never once to lay eyes on the enemy's army.[61] It was little wonder that Henry grumbled and wanted to know why such an expensive campaign had not been 'more displeasant' to his enemies.[62]

What the Duke of Norfolk failed to achieve, James V of Scotland managed for him. In a single day Scotland was neutralized as a military power and the dishonour of Haddon Ridge was avenged. Once the English were safely back in winter quarters, James, 'like a young and spirited prince' whose honour was just as tender as his uncle's, sent his armies to pillage north-western England in retaliation for Norfolk's attack. The result was Solway Moss, where on November 24th 3,000 hurriedly assembled English troops met some 14,000 to 20,000 Scots who turned tail and ran without a fight. Exactly what happened will never be known. Suffice it to say that from the start the Scottish leaders had little stomach for the fight. They detested the man whom James had placed at their head, and the defeat at Flodden Field was still vivid in every mind. Scottish morale snapped, and in the confusion the army found itself trapped between the English on one side and a tidal bog on the other. In the middle were a swarm of Scottish Borderers who hated the Lowland Scots just as much as they loathed the English and were in part responsible for the disaster. By the end of the day, James's splendid army had vanished into the Solway Moss or back across the frontier or into the hands of the English, who captured 3,000 horses, 24 cannons, 4 cartloads of spears, 30 clan-standards, 10 pavilions and 1,200 prisoners, including 500 gentlemen, 5 barons and 2 earls.[63]

Henry was jubilant; once again God had smiled upon his affairs, and, as Chapuys noted, the sadness which had been upon him 'since he learnt the conduct of his last wife' disappeared. Again the court resounded with banqueting and music and the King was in such good spirits that the Ambassador suspected he might be thinking of trying yet another wife.[64] The joyous news had an equally salubrious effect on Sir William Paget: it cured a bad attack of sciatica. Francis, however, sighed; he perceived that his good brother meant to divide France and Scotland by fair means or foul and having once destroyed his northern neighbour would launch himself against France.[65] The French King was quite right, but Henry had yet to finish securing his back door before turning his attention to the Continent. Even after Solway Moss it was thought that further military action would be necessary the following spring, and Lord Lisle was of the opinion that southern Scotland should be annexed, reasoning that such a conquest would be 'an acceptable deed before God, considering how brutely and beastly the people now be governed'.[66] Lisle wrote on December 12th; three days later James V died, and Henry suddenly found his mouldy feudal overlordship to be no longer diplomatic window-dressing but an attainable political goal. Only a week-old baby girl, whose life-expectancy was almost nil, stood between him and the throne of Scotland.[67]

Never did a more confident innocent reach for the honey-pot only to find a hornet's nest; never did a sovereign so certain of his legal rights try to do business with a breed so skilled in befuddling the issue or bewildering outsiders with Celtic political craft and pragmatism. Like the man who lacks the patience to crush each kernel of grain separately but in his haste flings his hammer at the entire bin only to see it disappear from sight for ever, Henry rushed in his usual impetuous fashion at the chance to settle the Scottish problem once and for all. The source of the subsequent debacle was partly psychological, partly geographical: the King in Westminster regularly over-reacted to matters which were presented to him in isolation and out of political context, and no one in London was adequately informed about a kingdom whose political, emotional and geographic configurations no Sassenach could fathom. Henry was literally without maps, and few people in southern England had the faintest notion, except for the obvious landmarks, where important clans and political strongholds were located.[68] The entire realm was regarded as a damp and squalid fastness engulfed in mist and dotted with chilly lochs and mountains inhabited by 'dissimulating Scots'.[69] One point, however, was not lost upon the English: they did perceive that they were dealing not with a unified kingdom but with three largely independent regions—the Border counties, the Lowlands whose political life centred in Edinburgh, and the Western Highlands and Isles. Moreover, it was understood that all three areas were liberally mixed with a host of even more particularistic and predatory clans, most of which cherished grudges to the point where rival members would rather see one 'another's throat cut' than go to the door 'to save their neighbour's goods'.[70]

If there was any sense of Scottishness, it consisted in an atavistic devotion to the few square miles upon which a man had been born and an unreasoning distrust of everything English. James V had imposed a semblance of discipline, but on his death the kingdom fell to pieces. The Border clans moved into the English orbit. The Highlands and Western Isles broke away completely, resurrecting that Nordic curiosity, the Lordship of the Isles—claimed by a middle-aged gentleman whose father was a bastard, whose mother had been raped, and whose life had been largely spent in an Edinburgh jail. The Lowlands were the most complex of all, for they splintered into six warring factions manœuvring for control of the infant Queen of Scots and what was left of political Scotland.[71] There was the Queen Dowager, Mary of Guise, a shrewd and patient lady, who with French help ultimately triumphed over all her rivals; James Hamilton, Earl of Arran, cousin to the Queen and heir presumptive, who was made governor of the kingdom and protector of the realm in January 1543; David Cardinal Betoun, leader of the aggressively pro-French Church party; Matthew Stuart, Earl of Lennox, a cousin of Arran and regarded by the French as Mary's legal heir; Archibald Douglas, Earl of Angus, the hated stepfather of James V, who with his brother George had been living in exile in England; and finally a group of ten slippery, if occasionally embarrassed, noblemen, Henry's 'assured' Scots, captured by the English at Solway Moss and sent back to their homeland sworn to promote the dynastic union of the two countries. Into this potpourri of personalities, prejudices and determination to settle Celtic politics according to time-honoured Scottish methods, both Henry and Francis poured quantities of gold. In the end French assertions that their intentions were strictly honourable were more convincing than similar English declarations, largely because the proposition could be measured in terms of mileage from the Scottish border.[72]

The total collapse of Scotland proved highly inconvenient to the industrious Imperial Ambassador, who was busily reminding the English sovereign of his Christian duty to punish the unprincipled King of France and of the honour to be won on the fields of Picardy. Chapuys was afraid that Henry had 'derived so much glory' from the 'unexpected and miraculous' victory at Solway Moss that he no longer had 'need of his neighbours', and that he might 'forget other affairs' in his effort to grasp the Scottish crown.[73] Indeed, why shouldn't Henry have dreamt of another sceptre? By feudal law he was overlord of Scotland; by blood he was the grand-uncle of a month-old baby who should have been his ward; and he was sure he had in hand the means to fulfil his ambitions—the Scottish captives of Solway Moss.

Cynics scoffed at the picture of a gaggle of 'assured' Scottish lords returning to their barren outcroppings, loaded with handsome gifts and bound by solemn promises to be totally English in all their actions. Money and expediency had purchased their oaths to work for the marriage of Mary Stuart and Prince Edward and, in case of her death, to set forth to 'the uttermost of their powers' Henry Tudor's paramount title to the Stuart throne. It was only to be expected that when English money and military influence ran out, honour, no matter how strictly pledged, would give way to self-interest. The French court found the entire proposal comical, and Paget felt obliged to defend his master by indignantly pointing out that his sovereign was 'a Prince of so good faith that he thinketh every other man of honesty to be of the same'.[74] Doubtless the Ambassador was gilding the lily for foreign consumption, but Henry knew himself to be a man of honour and, like Charles, was ready to accept the word of a gentleman, even if he were a Scot. Moreover, he had little to lose. Scottish lords and gentlemen were of no use in London except for their ransom money, but in Scotland there was no end to their potential as the nucleus of an English party sworn to the policy of dynastic union with England.

From the optimistic perspective of London it all seemed quite tenable, but Henry was not as naïve as sometimes painted. He informed Lord Lisle, when the Earl of Arran was appointed Lord Protector of Scotland in January 1543, that he really did not think his prisoners would be able to keep their promise to seize the person of the young Queen and ship her to England without military help.[75] The election of Arran by the Scottish estates was a serious blow to English policy and prestige, for Henry indignantly maintained that he, as feudal overlord, should have made the choice, but everyone assured him that the Earl was a weak and pliable man, greedy of gold, secretly favourable to Scripture, and easily bullied into co-operation with the pro-English party. As always, the English sovereign was liberal with his advice and with detailed instructions to his 'assured' lords: they must work closely with the Governor; Cardinal Betoun and all his 'unholy angels' must be imprisoned and God's Word proclaimed from every pulpit; the child Queen must immediately be taken and surrounded by officers and educators friendly to England; the old alliance with France must be severed; and at all costs the schemes of the French King and his papal chaplain must be countered and defeated.[76]

Henry's territorial vision was no more imperial than the Emperor's; neither sovereign could conceive of the modern Leviathan which demands total subservience and systematically seeks to destroy the least vestige of political independence. At heart both were medieval dynasts who saw state aggrandizement in terms of historic rights, and they sought to extend their suzerainty over lands to which they laid claim by the accident of family history. Scotland was never seen as another Wales—a province of an enlarged Britain —but as a subordinate realm, an appanage of the English Crown, the exact limits and control of which were open to negotiation. Scotland south of the Forth was to be governed indirectly either through the young Queen and a staff of English advisers or by a governor closely related to the Stuart line. North of the river Henry was less demanding, and at one point 'by force of his title and superiority' he offered the area to the Earl of Arran as a satellite kingdom with full regal dignity. Significantly, the Earl was not in the least scandalized at such a proposition but politely indicated that most of his family estates lay south of the Forth.[77] As for the Western Isles, which could launch 180 armed galleys and muster 8,000 amphibious troops, the King graciously recognized their independence under the Lord of the Isles.[78]

Throughout January and February 1543 expectations kept abreast of dreams. Betoun was jailed and his papist clappers silenced; Arran asked for a truce and showed himself enthusiastic about the marriage of the Queen to Prince Edward. Even better, it was reported that cartloads of English Bibles, primers and psalters could be used in Scotland, such was the demand for God's truth; and John Drummond wrote that 'all things is like to come to the King's Majesty's pleasure' and that the Earl of Angus was so dutiful that whenever he spoke the English King's name he never failed to pull off his cap and say 'the King's Majesty, my master, God save his grace'.[79] It was an excellent beginning, and in February the Governor graciously returned Robert Bowes and the other prisoners of Haddon Ridge, while Henry, as behoved a prince of honour, insisted that they pay their ransom money.[80] A King of honour and conscience who expected his 'assured' lords to live up to the exact conditions of their oath had to conform himself and his subjects to the very letter of the code of chivalry.

All along, Henry had been bombarding Arran with the benefit of his experience, and for once he abridged with his own pen the verbosity of his Council's draft advising the Governor to publish the scripture so that his people might 'learn by it how they may direct their manners, living and true worshipping of God'. The path to the Earl's soul, the King thought, was through his pocket-book, and he outlined with great care, as he had done three years before for James's benefit, the strategy of a successful reformation—a royal commission to investigate the economic facts of monastic life with secret orders to examine and gather evidence of the abominable and immoral living practised by monks and nuns; collusion with the chief nobles of the realm to redistribute abbey lands; assurance to the more pliable and politic abbots and priors that they would receive enlarged revenues and new offices; arrangement for monks to be pensioned off or sent as poor scholars to a university; and finally the nationalization of all remaining monastic estates for the benefit of the Crown. Henry Tudor's prescription for a thoroughly moral commonwealth was not without a financial potion: if Arran would cut away the evil wasters who spent 'their time in all idleness and filthiness' he would assuredly be walking in the path of good business as well as godliness.[81] The King's estimate of the Governor's approach to religion was not far off the mark. Arran could indeed be reached with gold, but unfortunately he eventually opted for a handsome Catholic pension in the hand in preference to lavish Protestant promises in the bush. For the moment, however, the Governor seemed so friendly and success so near that the King decided to eat his cake and have it too. Now that his son was to marry Mary of Scotland and his northern frontier was secure, the time had come to display the honour of England and punish his dishonourable brother the King of France. On February 11th a secret understanding was reached with the Emperor Charles, and within the fortnight the English Council was writing to Sir John Wallop at Guisnes inquiring how to get in 'the first buffet' before the French became aware that war had been decided upon.[82]

As usual Henry was being too precipitate and too sanguine, for the ungrateful Scots began to display an alarming talent for procrastination and deceit. The Queen Dowager warned of the 'great dissimulation of the Governor'; the 'assured' lords used their master 'slenderly' and 'obeyed with their lips but not with their hearts'; and Cardinal Betoun, though behind high walls, could not be silenced, for he placed the entire kingdom under an interdict: no marriages, no burials, no baptisms, no masses.[83] In the midst of Scottish sophistry and confusion it was becoming depressingly apparent that no one, except possibly a handful of the 'assured' lords, had any intention of parting with their infant Queen or permitting Henry to name the members of her household.[84] To make matters worse, French money and troops were giving renewed hope to the anti-English elements, and during the first week of April the Earl of Lennox, with his pockets full of gold and a handful of French troops, succeeded in avoiding the English navy and landed on the western coast.[85] The Pope sent his special representative lest Scotland be taken from the Catholic fold, and in mid-April, contrary to Henry's most dire commands, the Cardinal was mysteriously set free. Throughout May and June Arran moved steadily closer to the Church and the pro-French party, a development made less painful by the offer of a thousand-pound ecclesiastical annuity for his bastard son.[86] Henry alternately howled with frustration, threatening the most dreadful reprisals, and purred with sweet reason, offering concessions and money to anyone who looked in the least corruptible, which included almost everybody except the Cardinal.[87]

After considerable back-tracking and to the surprise of many, the English King eventually got his way. The rejoicing was great when the two kingdoms signed a treaty of eternal peace and a marriage alliance providing for the removal of the Queen to England at the age of ten.[88] The settlement was accepted by the Scottish parliament on June 8th; two weeks later Henry declared war on France; and nine days thereafter he signed the Treaty of Greenwich divorcing Scotland from her ancient ally and establishing her future dynastic union with England.[89] Despite obvious Scottish reluctance, mounting French financial and military pressure, and the mutterings of the English commanders along the northern frontier, nothing had happened to make Henry change his mind or go back upon his word given in February to the Emperor. Moreover, Sir Ralph Sadler, the English resident Ambassador, reported on June 6th exactly what the King wanted to hear: only fear of war with England had held the Scottish factions together, and the moment peace was established on the frontier the kingdom would fall apart.[90] Henry had not got his hands on his grand-niece or established his authority beyond the border, but surely it was a safe assumption that Scotland would give him no further trouble. No prophecy could have been less accurate, for a French fleet of sixteen ships and five thousand soldiers was already preparing to sail for Aberdeen, using as its excuse Francis's desire to convey his greetings to the Dowager Queen.[91] The hint of such an expedition was enough to make Arran wax cold, and not even the offer of a royal title and a Tudor bride for his son could tempt him back into the English camp. In July Sadler was already writing: 'Such malicious and despiteful people, I think, live not in the world'; and by September Henry's Scottish door, so carefully sealed with marriage vows and promises of peace, was flung wide open.[92]

During August it became evident that the political balance was swinging towards Cardinal Betoun, and Henry had to keep five thousand men ready to rescue the Governor and prevent the Cardinal from kidnapping the Queen and bundling her off to France.[93] Possibly nothing could have prevented the deterioration of the English position in the face of mounting pressure from Francis, who required, it was said, nothing of the Scots 'but friendship', whereas Henry sought to bring them under his subjugation, but the King's handling of the Scottish crisis was not designed to win friends or placate his enemies.[94] Invariably Henry Tudor sacrificed long-term diplomatic gain for short-run military objectives, and, as his frustration grew, he sought to dynamite the lock with a show of force instead of patiently learning the diplomatic combination. Henry, of course, was a man in a hurry. He was now committed to full-scale war against France and was making ready his plans for a really 'notable exploit' the following summer.

As Sadler had predicted, Scotland seemed to the Council in London to be breaking up, but this in itself posed an awkward problem. Henry was at peace with the official but unpopular government at

Edinburgh under the Governor, but Arran was only nominally in control. There also existed a powerful rebel faction under Cardinal Betoun committed to the eviction of all English influence—both religious and political—which openly sought military aid from France and sent out privateers under the guise of merchantmen to plunder English shipping. Henry's solution was militarily sound but diplomatically catastrophic. He ordered the interception of all Scottish vessels unless they could prove authorization from the Governor. The policy was perfectly reasonable: Scottish ships were violating his blockade of France, operating in defiance of their own legal government, and therefore were pirates. Unfortunately the action antagonized the single element in Scotland still friendly to the English cause, the commercial classes, who became so indignant that they threatened to lynch the King's Ambassador. Henry answered with more force and assured the merchants of Edinburgh that if a finger of Sadler's hand 'should ache by their means, all Edinburgh shall rue it for ever after'.[95]

Affairs in Scotland had been moving at a bewildering pace. On August 25th Arran actually got round to ratifying the peace treaty with England and three days later he obliged Henry by outlawing the Cardinal. But on September 3rd he quietly slipped away from Edinburgh and joined forces with his enemy, and on September 9th he and Betoun together crowned the Queen at Stirling Castle. Arran had had no choice: French gold and English blunders had heavily tipped the military and psychological scales against him, and it was reported that if the Governor could raise ten thousand men, the Cardinal could muster three times that number. Henry was enraged; his 'assured' lords had played him false, the Governor had taken his money, and failed in his word, and now all his enemies were united against him. Sadler agreed that never under the sun lived a 'more beastly and unreasonable people than here be of all degrees'.[96] Only fear could discipline such a people, and the English monarch made immediate plans for a lightning thrust of eight thousand mounted troops to burn Edinburgh. The 'chief and principal' cause for such an act was self-evident: to avenge honour. The Scots and especially their Governor had cheated his expectations and failed to observe their treaty obligations; they must now be taught the wages of disobedience and dishonour.[97]

The weather made the threat impotent and the Duke of Suffolk wrote that he could not possibly muster such an expedition in late September. Though the punishment was delayed, everybody realized that some retaliatory action would be necessary unless England were to face war on two fronts. In fact, after a year of listening to the

Scottish siren, Henry's policy was totally wrecked, and he was back where he had started. Matters, however, were even more pressing than before, for in eight months' time the King was planning to launch the largest and best equipped English army ever sent against France. Instead of a chastened neighbour at his back, he had an enemy which had moved back into the French orbit. Mary Stuart was for ever beyond his reach, and by December Betoun was boasting that shortly an army of ten thousand Scots and six thousand French-paid mercenaries would invade England.[98] Alas, Henry had it all to do over again, but at least he had learned his lesson: henceforth he would treat the Scots as they deserved and teach them to 'fear the hand of God' and 'fear the power of the prince able to daunt' them. His anger was majestic. He declared war on Scottish perfidy and deceit. 'Ye should remember with whom ye have covenanted ... Ye have covenanted with a prince of honour, that will not suffer your disloyalty unpunished and unrevenged; whose power and puissance, by God's grace, is and shall be sufficient against you to make you know and feel your own faults and offences.'[99] His Scottish interlude was over; hereafter the King would return to his original purpose: neutralize Scotland by fire and sword; honour his agreement with his ally the Emperor; and give teeth to his challenge to the King of France—'the sole cause and source of the evils that afflict Christendom at large'.[100]

9

Youth Renewed

Heaven is high; the earth is deep;
a king's heart is unsearchable.
Prov. xxv 3

A shabby and gouty Emperor, a mercurial and disintegrating King of France, a broken titan of England, sick of body and melancholic of mind, and a septuagenarian Pope who suffered from a 'flux of blood' and a weak stomach: the leaders of Christendom were indeed a scruffy lot. Sickness hung over them like a cold fog through which good health shone with increasing rarity. Methodically the Emperor Charles had kept a calendar of his gout—eleven attacks in sixteen years—but by 1544 anxiety and gluttony had made a travesty of the documentation; the pain had become so frequent that he gave up recording it. Nothing, however, could curb his appetite. He knew that live oysters, pickled eels, spiced Spanish sausages and German ale would be the death of him, but he could not stop, and in desperation his physicians cried out that 'kings must think that their stomachs are not made like other men's'. In later life matters became even more desperate, for a cleft lip made chewing difficult and the Emperor preferred to wash down his food with great draughts of Rhenish wine. Over-indulgence was not without the sharp reminder of conscience. All the world knew that the lash of gout was administered by God to punish the rich and mighty, and Charles like his 'good uncle' of England was wont to listen to that inner voice which ordered him 'in no event and for nothing in the world' to 'act against duty and conscience'.[1]

Of the three sovereigns, the worn and unassuming Charles, who had lived as many years as the century and had perambulated the length and breadth of Europe—nine times to the Lowlands and Germany, seven times to Italy and Spain, four times to France and twice to England—had the toughest and most resilient personality. True, he lacked the flamboyance and outward self-confidence of Francis or Henry, his household was as threadbare as his cloak, and his caution sometimes bordered on irresolution; but he possessed the

CHARLES V, 1500–88. *Titian*

FRANCIS I, 1494–1547.
School of Clouet, c.1544

HENRY VIII'S ARMOUR

left

This armour, for foot combat, was made *c.*1512. The marks of the Milanese
Missaglia armourers are stamped on the helmet. The rest was perhaps made by
Italian craftsmen working in England.

right

Made *c.*1535-40, this suit of armour belongs to a group of large
armours made for the king during the later years of his reign.

indispensable gift of laughter tempered by determination. Though he took his office with deadly seriousness and might, when set upon the road of righteousness, be as inflexible as Henry Tudor, he could always laugh at himself. Charles was no legalist holding obstinately to precise definitions or appealing to historic authority; nor did he profess to be an expert, except in matters of war, where he classed himself as one of the three best generals of his day. Elsewhere he stood aside to listen to the specialist in law, diplomacy, theology, music and art. Ultimately, however, in his ponderous fashion he made his own decisions and acted upon them, confessing that he was by nature stubborn in the defence of his own opinions. When Cardinal Contarini answered that this was not wilfulness but firmness, Charles laughed and replied: 'Ah! but I sometimes stick to bad ones.' Even the Emperor's mulishness could be touched with humour, and though he dedicated his life to the defence of Christendom, he could still remark to the Pope that he was beginning 'to fear that God intends us all to become Mahometans, but I shall certainly put off my conversion to the very last'.[2]

Tortoise-like, Charles managed to get where he wanted while carrying his ramshackle empire on his back, and somehow he contrived, even when gulping down his food or, as it was said, rushing from 'mass to mess', to appear dignified and civilized. In 1541 he was an imposing man, more sure of himself and his purpose than he had ever been, and his enemies conceded that 'he is imperial in word and deed, in look and gesture, even in the greatness of his gifts'.[3] Disappointment, further attacks of gout and ultimate failure to reconcile or purge the enemies of God eventually exhausted and destroyed him, but when he died in 1558 the words of his confessor were uniquely appropriate: 'Thus ended the greatest gentleman there ever was, or ever will be'[4]—an epitaph which could not have been written for the King who swore only by the 'foi de gentilhomme' and styled himself the first gentleman of France.

The big-nosed Valois King, who happily sacrificed ten years of his reign to the recovery of Milan, was visibly disintegrating in 1542, eaten up with what the Imperial Ambassador at varying times called 'a gathering under the lower parts', an 'ulcerated bladder', or chauvinistically the 'French disease'.[5] Henry's junior by three years, but six years older than the Emperor, Francis I had come to the throne at twenty-one determined to enjoy what God and Louis XII's inability to sire a male heir had given him. Tall and muscular like his Tudor cousin but far less massive, he was the international glass of princely fashion, as elegant in dress and melodramatic in behaviour as Charles was dowdy and self-controlled. Contemporaries enjoyed

G

comparing Francis I and Henry VIII. The Admiral of France remarked to Sir William Paget in 1542 that their masters were much alike, 'not only in personage but also in wisdom and affection, delighting both in hunting, in hawking, in building, in apparel, in stones, in jewels, and of like affection one to another'.[6] There was always, even when they raged at one another, a rapport between the two sovereigns, but the Tudor cub grew into the English lion who referred to himself as the 'old man' and wore his advancing years and spreading girth with majesty, while the Valois prince withered into an embarrassing and undignified roué. The once brilliantly articulate speaker fell victim to dental decay, mouthing his words between toothless gums; his face grew puffy and pustular; and men no longer laughed at the jest that the King's obsession for the hunt was so great that when old and sick he would be carried to the chase and when dead would go in his coffin. The older Francis grew the more restless and listless he became, wandering aimlessly from one 'peevish village' to the next, and ruling his kingdom *ad lib.* without bothering to write his orders down or concerning himself with the routine of government. He fluctuated wildly between gaiety and despair, tearing out his hair, wringing his hands and breaking into loud lamentations.[7]

Francis could be devastatingly charming or gracefully insulting as the occasion required, and when the Imperial herald bearing his master's declaration of war pompously referred to the French King as his 'sacred majesty', Francis acidly told him: 'Claive me not where I itch not with thy sacred majesty, but go to thy business and tell me thy errand in such terms as are decent betwixt enemies, for thy master is not my friend.'[8] But for all his wit and versatility, Sir William Paget found him undignified and thought his casual ways unbecoming a king, while Nicholas Wotton, the English resident Ambassador, was shocked by the vicious intriguing and female-ridden atmosphere of his household.[9]

If foreign ambassadors found the Emperor imponderable and his purpose inscrutable, they were even more perplexed by the vagaries of Valois policy, which responded as much to the ambitions and vindictiveness of the two ladies of the court as to the realities of international politics. Henry Tudor's household also bubbled with rival factions and political intrigue, and his ministers knew the value of a pretty young partisan in the King's bed, but Henry's policies were his own. The English King was jealous of any man who might seek to usurp his authority, and when the Duke of Norfolk in August 1544 entered into private peace negotiations with the French without consulting his master, the King was dangerously offended.

As Chapuys carefully explained to the Emperor, 'secret communication' was 'a thing which those of the Council are not accustomed to do even in matters of no such importance or suspicions'.[10] Francis, on the other hand, exercised almost no control; his views were constantly being shaped and his plans secretly modified by two tough-minded and middle-aged females—his mistress, Anne Duchesse d'Estampes, and her detested rival, Diane de Poitiers, who ruled from the Dauphin's bed. Between the two ladies raged a war of invective which, when it touched foreign policy and military affairs, sometimes amounted to treason. Equally bitter, if somewhat less verbal, was the rivalry between the King's two sons—Charles Duc d'Orléans and his elder brother, the taciturn and moody Dauphin, the future Henry II. Madame d'Estampes, in alliance with the King's sister the Queen of Navarre, favoured reform in religion and supported Orléans in the family squabble in the expectation that the Duke would defend her interests once Francis was in his grave and the hated Diane ruled at court. The Dauphin's mistress was as pro-Catholic as the Duchess was pro-Protestant. She was also aggressively anti-Imperial in diplomacy and vehemently supported her lover against any dynastic alliance which might have elevated young Orléans to the dignity of an independent prince.[11]

'The world', as Gardiner noted, 'laboureth now chiefly' to make 'by secrecy all things uncertain',[12] and in Paris boudoir diplomacy and sibling politics were incomprehensible save for a single point: no matter how sacred or holy his oath to maintain the peace, Francis would sell his soul and his whole kingdom to regain Milan. In 1542 he saw his chance, for in Hungray and North Africa the Emperor Charles had met with disastrous defeats at the hands of the Sultan. In international politics it might not be moral, but it was generally regarded as astute, to kick an opponent when he was down.

During the summer of 1541 Suleiman the Magnificent pushed almost to the gates of Vienna, smashing a Christian army of 25,000, occupying the city of Pest, and forcing the Archduke Ferdinand to pay tribute for the remaining Hungarian lands under his control. In October it was Charles's turn to taste defeat. Hoping to relieve pressure on Hungary and avenge his brother's defeat, the Emperor sailed with 155 vessels and 20,000 men for Algiers, Barbarossa's naval headquarters in the western Mediterranean. Unfortunately the winds blew Muslim. The day after his army landed his fleet was demolished by storm, and the crusaders stranded without food, munitions or retreat. Charles was magnificent in defeat and managed to extract the remnants of his battered forces, but he returned to Valladolid in January 1542 to discover that Francis had been busy spinning a web of alliances against him in preparation for a war which he officially declared on July 12th. France, Sweden, Denmark, Scotland, Venice, the Emperor's rebellious vassal the Duke of Cleves, the might of the Ottoman Empire and even his Holiness in Rome were aligned in varying degrees of hostility against the man who, despite every setback, could say: 'We must thank God for all, and hope that after this disaster He will grant of His great goodness some great good fortune.'[13] Charles, however, rarely left diplomacy or war solely to the divinity. Despite the gout which raged in his foot, neck and hands, he was determined to defend his inheritance, punish the disloyalty of Cleves, and if necessary league with the devil himself to achieve his purpose.

Thus it was that throughout 1542 the Most Christian King of France and an Emperor of Catholic descent began their courtship of a sovereign who only four years before had officially been proclaimed accursed in the eyes of God and man, whose kingdom had been cut off from the body of Christ, and whose subjects had been placed under an interdict—their marriages void, their wills illegal, their burials unconsecrated and their children illegitimate.[14] Both Francis and Charles were fulsome in their attentions and generous in their offers, especially with one another's property, the Emperor tempting Henry with Boulogne, Montreuil and Ardres, which lay to the south and east of the Calais pale, and the French countering with Dunkerque, Gravelines and Bourbourg to the north.[15] In return the English King entered upon an elaborate charade in which the ambassadors of Europe tried to guess who, if anybody, was seriously intent upon marrying the Princess Mary. The correct answer, of course, was nobody, for that unfortunate lady was a declared bastard, a technical disability which dampened nuptial ardour. Moreover, even had the Duc d'Orléans been willing to overlook her doubtful pedigree in order to marry a lady second in line to the Tudor throne, neither his brother nor his potential father-in-law had any intention of permitting it. The Dauphin disliked his brother far too much to sanction a marriage which might have transformed the young Duke into a real sovereign. As for Henry, he had no desire for such a powerful son-in-law and refused absolutely to consider legitimizing Mary, announcing that he 'loved his daughter well and esteemed her honour ... but he loved and regarded himself and his own honour more'.[16] More than honour was involved when it came to the Emperor's suit, and the King informed the French Ambassador that he 'might count him demented' if he ever let Charles through marriage get his hands on Catherine of Aragon's child.[17] The endless negotiations were never taken seriously by either side, and the

twenty-seven-year-old Princess knew that 'it was foolish to suppose
that they would marry her out of England, or even in England, as
long as the King her father lived'.[18]

Behind the endless discussions about dowries and delivery-dates
lay a crucial decision: would England re-enter the European arena
and if so, on whose side? Under the circumstances Henry found
marriage negotiations a useful delaying tactic, especially since the
international situation had changed for the better. The pursuer had
become the pursued, and as early as January 1542 Chapuys felt quite
certain that the English King would 'temporize with both parties' to
'obtain more advantageous conditions'. Henry, he concluded, knew
how to 'profit by the times'.[19] In the end England opted for Charles.
Possibly the old unreasoning enmity with France tipped the scales;
possibly the commercial ties with the Lowlands were too profitable
to break; but of the two Ambassadors jockeying at the English
court Chapuys was clearly the better negotiator. Though de Marillac
knew his Henry almost as well as his rival and could tell that when
the King grumbled the most he was in fact getting ready to concede
a point,[20] it was the cagey Imperial Ambassador who best understood
the monarch's diplomatic style.

The war-hawks had been gathering all winter but they were
scarcely united. Norfolk was strongly French; the Earl of Southampton, Sir Anthony Browne and Thomas Wriothesley were equally inclined towards the Imperial cause. Neither side, however, cared to
be caught negotiating with a foreign power, and Southampton was so
discreet that he even refused to be seen speaking to Chapuys at
court.[21] The crux of the matter, as always, was the King, and the
Imperial Ambassador wisely allowed himself to be guided by the
Earl and Bishop Gardiner, both of whom, he remarked, knew their
master's nature better than any other men in England. Southampton
counselled flattery and the call of honour; the Bishop suggested an
appeal to conscience.[22] Accordingly, Chapuys dropped all reference
to marriage alliances, commercial advantages and power-politics and
called upon 'a prince so virtuous, learned, reasonable and experienced' to take upon himself the burdens of Christendom. It was the
King's moral duty to use his riches and wisdom to 'the pacification
and repose of Europe and the chastisement of France'. Adroitly the
Ambassador angled for his man, 'praising his prudence and experience', presenting the King with openings to indulge in his passion for
lecturing, and dazzling him with the prospects of seizing Boulogne,
Ardres and Montreuil. Then he dangled the most tempting bait of
all: not only was it the King's moral obligation to save Christendom
but by doing so Henry would 'obtain the good will, great renown and

fame of all the world and also deserve reward of God'.[23] The argument was irresistible; the English monarch was always seeking renown in this world and a favoured position in the next, and clearly Francis deserved punishment for having allied himself to God's historic enemy, the unspeakable Turk.

By late June and early July Henry seemed to be caught, hook, line and sinker, but the moment the long-expected war broke out, the negotiations fell apart, for the English King upped his price.[24] Henry was deliberately stalling, seeking to strike at Scotland while Francis was engaged against the Emperor, but the delay also reflected the King's innate caution and his approach to diplomacy: every detail had to be debated, every ambiguity clarified, every possibility investigated. 'He would rather', he informed Chapuys in November, 'remain in his neutrality than enter an imperfect treaty.'[25] War, as the whole world knew, was easy enough to enter into and fair-weather allies were plentiful, but 'to come honourably out thereof' could be 'full painful and very dangerous for the soul and body',[26] especially if you were a monarch of high conscience and honour obliged to place trust in brother sovereigns who regarded you as a moral leper and religious outcast. Experience and instinct warned Henry to be careful, and he gravely told Chapuys that 'he had been so often deceived in treaties and had found so many interpretations and cavillations that henceforth he meant to treat so amply that there might be nothing to gainsay'. When it came to good faith, common sense told him always to insist upon 'the literal sense ... without any other interpretation'.[27]

The price the King demanded was a measure of his insecurity: recognition by the Emperor that Henry's conscience had been in the right and that his actions in putting Catherine aside, defying the Pope and assuming the supremacy of the Church of England were justifiable in the eyes of God and man. The haggling went on for months. Henry was engrossed in the correspondence, underscoring, making marginal comments to himself and carefully noting the exact cost and size of the Emperor's military effort. The English King was for ever laying semantic traps; Charles and his sister, the Regent of the Lowlands, were equally zealous in avoiding them. When Henry demanded that his full title as Defender of the Faith and Supreme Head of the Church be recognized and refused to accept that convenient subterfuge 'etc.', Charles politely but firmly continued to address his 'good uncle' only as King of England, France and Ireland. The English insisted that each side guarantee to return all rebels, recognize one another's laws and ally with no one, secular or spiritual, who was the enemy of the other—meaning, of course, the Pope.

Imperial negotiators sought specifically to exclude the pontiff and refused to accept any obligation to turn loyal Catholics over to Henry's tender care, and the Emperor's sister adamantly declined to sanction 'any laws contrary to our faith'.[28] By November, Chapuys had almost given up hope that Henry would ever sign, and wrote the Regent that the English were deliberately temporizing and had no intention of joining the war.[29]

From the start the courtship had been as intricate and ritualistic as the dance of two scorpions set upon matrimony, but eventually the monarchs got together—Charles listening to the politic advice of his sister and Henry making pencil jottings to himself on 'which way to redub the pact with the Emperor'.[30] As in most mutually advantageous negotiations, a compromise was reached, and, with the aid of a great deal of linguistic imprecision to gloss over the difficult issues, an agreement was signed on February 11th, 1543. The Emperor backed down on the matter of the Pope, promising not to treat with 'any other prince or potentate or with any other person whatsoever', and Henry gave in completely on the question of his title. Each party was to style the English King as he saw fit. Military objectives were left in studied vagueness, the English contracting only to invade France within two years for a period of four months, with 20,000 foot-soldiers and 5,000 cavalry. In contrast political aims were flamboyantly clear: the chastisement of Francis for his detestable alliance with the Sultan, and the dismemberment of his kingdom in the name of the Emperor's rights to Burgundy and Henry's claim to Normandy, Aquitaine, Guienne and the Valois Crown.[31]

Chapuys could scarcely believe his ears; against every prognostication Henry had decided to launch himself into a 'sea of difficulties' when he could have 'easily passed along in the midst of the storm'; but the Ambassador had underestimated his man.[32] The decision to wage war against France had been made at least as early as June 1542, when Henry took the bait and began detailed discussions as to the size of the army necessary to seize Montreuil. Thereafter it was simply a matter of timing, or, as the King bluntly put it, 'to determine whether the journey overseas may be this year or not'.[33] As all the world knew, Henry Tudor was 'far from reckless', and he delayed until he thought his Scottish back door was secure, until he had extracted from the Emperor all that he could reasonably expect, and until he was convinced that he would be on the winning side. By February 1543 he was ready to sign; Scotland appeared to be his for the taking, the French offensives in Luxemburg and Navarre had ended in disaster, and Charles's prospects looked bright for the forthcoming military season. Even so, he hesitated before

committing himself to a declaration of war. The Council explained
to the Emperor that 'all things have remained for a time in such
suspense and stay' that a firm decision had been impossible.[34] In May
all doubts were cast aside, and on the last day of the month Henry
drew up his formal defiance of France. On June 22nd, 1543, two days
after the Scottish parliament had accepted the marriage of their
young Queen to Prince Edward, he officially demanded satisfaction
from Francis for all his abominable actions against God and the
princes of Christendom.[35]

Throughout most of the summer the King was in a genial and
expansive mood, and punctiliously he fulfilled his treaty obligations,
dispatching in early July a small but magnificently equipped expeditionary force to help defend the Flemish frontier and participate (at
the Emperor's expense) in the siege of Landrécy, which the French
had captured the month before.[36] It not only satisfied his taste for
the bizarre to receive news of the fantastic mortars used to destroy
the town's defences and the 'strange and dreadful' sight of shells
exploding in the air and 'spouting fire on every side', but, best of all,
it was splendidly flattering that Henry's own plan for the bombard-
ment should have been well received and put into immediate operation. The English sovereign's penchant for delivering expert counsel
was one of the crosses which Charles had to bear for the sake of his
'good uncle's' friendship, but when the royal strategist intimated
that the Emperor had promised to 'attack France wherever Henry
thought best', the Regent felt this was too much and quickly pointed
out that the King had taken 'as an engagement what was meant only
as politeness'.[37]

Henry's amiable spirits were sufficient even to weather the collapse
of his Scottish policy. Instead of depressing him, Celtic perfidy
shocked and angered a prince who had already gone on record as
stating that there was 'no faith in the world' save in himself.
Charles, however, was alarmed that the prospect of war on two
fronts would dampen the King's ardour for glory in France, and in
December he sent Don Fernando de Gonzaga, Viceroy of Sicily, to
London to ascertain whether there were 'any doubts or scruples in
the King's mind'. The Emperor was fearful lest his ally withdraw his
troops to Scotland at the last moment, leaving Charles 'single-
handed to fight the French'. The Viceroy was ordered to inquire
particularly into Scottish affairs, to discover whether England was
likely to achieve a peaceful settlement or would have to go to war
again, and also to 'calculate what English force may be required next
year on the border against the Scotch'. If, as Charles anticipated, the
English Council argued that their master would have to give 'first

place to the war with Scotland', then Gonzaga was to answer that
trouble in the north was the 'very reason why the King should assist
with all his power to the undertaking against Francis because ... it
stands to reason that by attacking him at home and invading his
kingdom', Henry could prevent further French aid to Scotland.[38]

Charles did not belabour the rather fragile argument that the
swiftest path to Edinburgh was through Paris, for if Henry had really
been set upon conquering his northern neighbour, his surest policy
would have been to keep France neutral and embroiled on the Continent while English armies struck on the Scottish frontier. Instead,
he appealed to the King's imagination and proved himself to be a
master of psychology. First he delivered a cannonade of the most
flagrant flattery, deferring to Henry's 'great wisdom, long experience,
singular and clear understanding of all matters and especially in
military affairs'. Then he painted a marvellous picture of a faithless
and insane French monarch loathed by his subjects, detested by the
Christian world, and compelled 'to acknowledge publicly his faults'.
Now was 'the proper season', he said, for the two allies to prevent
Francis 'from doing further mischief' by attacking on both sides;
Paris would be theirs within the fortnight and the whole of northern
France would fall. Finally, Charles played his trump card. The
Emperor knew his Henry, and Gonzaga was ordered to remark con-
versationally: 'We have no doubt that Our dear brother, the King of
England, would wish to attend personally the proposed invasion. We
firmly believe that the step would be a very important one, and
contribute greatly to the success of the war, not only on account' of
Henry's 'personal qualities, magnanimity, reputation and experience
in military affairs, but because it would undoubtedly terrify the
King of France and his subjects. Yet on the other hand, considering
the present state of England and everything else concerning Our
common affairs, We should not dare to propose it.' Then, as savoury
to an already delicious meal, the Viceroy was instructed to add
casually that the Emperor 'intended leading Our army in person'.[39]
If King Hal ever had any notion of backing out, Charles had
dexterously scotched it. Thereafter the proud picture of a conquering
Tudor hero leading his troops into battle never faded; Henry would
go to war in person.

The Emperor's shafts at Henry Tudor's need to excel were well
aimed but unnecessary. The King had already been touched where
he was most sensitive. No matter how attractive it might be to forsake his ally and concentrate on a Scottish enemy, honour stood
squarely in the path of temptation. He had bragged too often of his
good faith, his dependability and his sacred oath; and, as he liked to

say, he was now too old to change. It was essential to his own image to be known in a world of Catholic sovereigns as a 'prince of such honour that he would no wise be reproached with having failed to observe any treaty or promise'.[40] A pope, an emperor and a Valois king might barter honour, compromise conscience and forswear an oath, but a ritualistic old rebel such as Henry, who had placed his own conscience above conformity to the common mores of Christianity, had to be above reproach once he had given his word to an agreement. As was written in a book on which Henry was an expert: 'It is an abomination to kings to commit wickedness: for the throne is established by righteousness' (Proverbs, xvi 12). Moreover, the English sovereign was angry, and when fully aroused he could be extraordinarily stubborn. He was determined both to wreak a punishment upon the Scots which would 'remain for ever a perpetual memory of the vengeance of God' and also to chasten Francis for being in league with Satan and the Infidel. The French were 'very much mistaken', he said, 'if they think that their intrigues in Scotland will prevent him from crossing over'; on the contrary, the King himself would go into France 'with a more considerable force than that which he intended to take at first'.[41] He was morally bound to chastise Francis, and, as Chapuys remarked, when the King 'decides for an undertaking he goes the whole length'.[42] Henry, of course, was boasting, for he had no real intention of increasing the size of his military commitment to the Emperor, which had been finally settled with Gonzaga in December after days of acrimonious bargaining; but in bragging of his military might he was dramatizing what every true knight knew—glory was to be earned upon the fields of Picardy and Normandy, not on the dreary slopes of the Cheviot hills. A single town added to the Calais foothold, a hundred acres of territory trod by the heroes of Agincourt and restored to England, was worth all the lochs and moors of Scotland.

As befitting a chivalric sovereign intent upon honouring his oath, Henry gave his word to the Emperor that during the summer of 1544 he would personally invade France at the head of 35,000 foot- and 7,000 horse-soldiers. He somewhat soiled the gesture, however, by haggling stubbornly over two vital points—the exact time of the invasion and the commitment to strike at Paris. Charles's strategy called for a double thrust to be launched no later than May 15th in order to catch Francis by surprise. The English, with a realistic eye on Scotland, announced that they were sorry but they could not be ready before June 20th at the earliest. The change in date jeopardized the entire invasion and must have raised doubts as to Henry's sincerity, but the Emperor had no choice; he had to accept the new time-table. Worse, Charles failed to extract an unconditional promise that the English army would push on to Paris; he had to make do with an extremely vague statement that each prince would diligently seek in all good faith to arrive at Paris but could modify his march according to the dictates of war, the behaviour of the enemy and the availability of supplies.[43] Under the circumstances, the Emperor was probably wise to move with caution, for matters had been so arranged that a King of scrupulous honour could keep his word yet do exactly as he pleased.

There were, of course, a series of altercations as the two allies got to know one another better,[44] but, for all the bickering, preparations moved along relatively smoothly. Siege guns were cast, costs were estimated, provisions gathered, musters taken and money extracted from a kingdom depicted by Thomas Becon as teeming with loyal subjects 'so desirous to defend their country' that they neglected 'their private businesses' and disregarded 'their dear wives and sweet children'.[45] Henry, with his literal attitude to an obligation, was careful to give no cause for reproach. Over and over again Chapuys reported how unfaltering seemed the King's determination to go beyond the seas in person, and how industriously he was collecting huge piles of provisions.[46] In the midst of such activity Henry was at his infuriating best—supervising, detailing, lecturing. His health was good, his spirits ebullient, and he made the only recorded royal joke of the reign: when informed that Francis was suffering pangs of conscience for his nefarious alliance with the Turks, the King remarked that whosoever might give him absolution, he and the Emperor would dictate the penance.[47]

Before the monarch's blue-coated soldiers with their red and blue hose could administer punishment in France there was further retribution to be meted out in Scotland, where in April the Earl of Hertford was sent as scourge and executioner of the King's wrath. Of all Henry's military ventures, Hertford's amphibious assault on Edinburgh was the most ruthless in conception and efficient in execution. The Earl himself was anxious that the operation should be more than a punitive campaign, and his advice was a projection of his later policies under Edward VI: seize and fortify the port of Leith, garrison certain strategic points within the kingdom, and cultivate the political and military friendship of the pro-English elements and all those weary of a losing war. His argument was extremely persuasive and had at one time been the government's plan for the spring invasion, but after the King had 'considered and weighed' the issue and consulted with his Council, he vetoed the proposal as being too costly and too dangerous. Moreover, every available soldier was needed for the summer invasion of France. Hertford was therefore to put Leith and Edinburgh to the sword and wherever he went was to post the thought-provoking reminder: 'You may thank your Cardinal' for bringing 'you to sorrow and trouble'.[48] The decision was brutal but in accord with the image of a God who could say 'I will break the pride of your power'; and 'I will bring seven times more plagues upon you according to your sins' (Lev. xxvi 19, 21). Henry knew his Leviticus and the wages of evil. Moreover, he disagreed with his lieutenant that destruction would breed greater desperation and resistance; rather he believed in the calculated carnage of the civilian population so that 'the sound of a shaken leaf' would so terrify the survivors that they would 'flee, as fleeing from a sword' (Lev. xxvi 36). Given his purpose—the protection of his back door while invading France—the King was probably correct.[49] Accordingly, Hertford arrived at Leith on May 3rd with 212 vessels and 10,000 men, while 4,000 mounted troops raced northward from the border. For once the timing was perfect. Lord Evers's horsemen burned and devastated their way to Edinburgh; the city was stormed and put to flames; the countryside was set ablaze; and on the 16th the English soldiers returned whence they had come, part by land and part by sea, pillaging every port, hamlet, chapel, castle and town in their path. So ended the Earl's 'prosperous adventures' into Scotland, and he returned just in time for the largest invasion any English sovereign had ever sent against the Continent.[50]

The logistic and strategic account of the French campaign is best left to the military experts.[51] Suffice it to say that Henry approached the adventure with all the strengths and deficiencies of his character —compulsively cautious yet overly enthusiastic, fearful of failure yet desirous of glory, and always enthralled by detail and the immediate objective. Almost at once the Emperor's concessions made the previous December were put to the test, and the King began to talk about the need to protect his flank and secure his supply depots, and about the futility of burning Paris or expecting Francis's subjects to rebel.[52] Henry had cause to be wary, for two decades before, and much against his better judgment, he had allowed enthusiasm to overcome prudence and had opted for a dramatic thrust on the French capital in preference to a conservative siege of Boulogne and a war 'of small prickings'. Caution in 1523 had warned him what to expect: 'wet weather and rotten ways', flooded rivers and cannons stuck deep in mud; hopelessly indefensible supply lines; towns easily captured by armchair strategists which turned overnight into impregnable arsenals; and tarnished honour as English armies retreated faster than they had advanced. Ten thousand soldiers under the Duke of Suffolk had miraculously marched to within fifty miles of Paris, then all the King's predictions had come true: his allies had played him false, the weather had turned so cold that his soldiers lost their 'fingers, hands and feet', the Imperial forces under Floris d'Egmont, Count de Buren, had picked up and gone home, and to Henry's eternal shame his own wretched army had ignominiously bolted for safety.[53]

Twenty years later, history, it would appear, was resolved to repeat itself. Again the King was urged by his Imperial ally to think big and told that Ardres, Montreuil and Boulogne could easily be cut off and must inevitably fall if his armies made a dash for Abbeville, the River Somme and Paris. Again he was asked to place his trust and honour in the hands of an Imperial army under the command of another Count de Buren, this time Maximilian d'Egmont, Floris's son. And again the skies augured a wet and dreary summer.[54] Henry Tudor had a long memory and more than sufficient reason to hesitate, especially at the incredible spectacle of a gouty old Emperor and an obese monarch carted across the French countryside in a Blitzkrieg attack on the capital. Certainly the Duke of Suffolk, who was again in command, and the rest of the military were appalled at the thought of hauling their prince in a litter into the heart of France, and the Council secretly approached Chapuys, explaining that the security measures required to safeguard the King were delaying the entire operation. They begged the Ambassador to write to the Emperor, who alone, they said, could 'excuse his going' in person. Chapuys agreed and reported that the King was so fat and his legs so bad* that 'those who have seen them are astonished that he does not stay continually in bed'.[55] In fact, the Ambassador thought it was ridiculous for either sovereign to attempt such a campaign, but he no more dared make the suggestion directly to Charles than Paget did to Henry.

Each monarch had promised to lead his troops in person and each found it impossible to back out. A comic opera scenario ensued in which both kings sang lustily about honour and made *sotto voce* comments about the other's ill health. The Emperor explained that he was honour bound to confront Francis face to face, for that chivalric prince, sick as he was, had challenged Charles to 'meet in mortal combat' and had sworn an 'unadvised oath' to seize all of Artois in person 'else it shall cost him his life'. Henry, of course, was an old man and might reasonably remain on the sidelines. Moreover, the

---

* The records are vague as to whether Henry suffered from ulcers on one or both legs. Most sources, however, refer to only one leg.

Emperor intimated that possibly it would be best if he did so, since his leg was so painful and there was small likelihood of a major encounter, because Francis was far better at eating than fighting. In his turn, the English King pointed out that Charles's gout was a chronic ailment guaranteed to return during the autumn months, while his own trouble with his leg was merely a matter of chance. Moreover, he had information that Francis was marvellously reinforced and therefore it was folly to risk the person of an emperor upon such a hazardous expedition.[56] As a matter of fact both princes had set their hearts on campaigning in France and no amount of gout or avoirdupois was going to stop them. The two creaky warriors were strangely alike when it came to camp life—the 'grave and severe' Emperor becoming 'alive, active and mirthful' and 'doing the work of a subaltern or inferior captain'; the fat old King busy 'foreseeing and caring for everything' and in better health than he had been for the past seven years.[57]

The issue between the two was not whether to campaign but where. The English, Chapuys bitterly complained, 'wanted everything exactly their own way',[58] and it became increasingly evident that the King had decided on one of three limited objectives: the inland town of Montreuil which was the gateway to Abbeville, Amiens and the valley of the Somme; the coastal city of Boulogne only twenty-five miles south of Calais, whose capture would have almost doubled the size of the Calais pale; or the prickly border fortress of Ardres almost within gunshot of the English bastion at Guisnes. At first Henry offered a compromise. Each monarch would remain sensibly in his own territory—Henry at Calais, Charles in Artois—with a reserve force strong enough to seize any fortress town, while their main armies, each thirty thousand strong, would push on to Paris as planned. Charles, however, politely refused any modification of the original proposal, and Henry grumpily answered that he would consult his Council. By then it was June 18th and neither sovereign was on schedule, the Emperor still at Metz and Henry acknowledging that the main English force would probably not leave England before July 8th.[59]

The van of the King's army under the Duke of Norfolk arrived in Calais during the second week of June, and immediately recriminations, complaints and 'plain writing' began. There was no beer or bread, the price of food anticipated by the Council in London bore no relation to the inflated costs demanded by usurious Flemish merchants, the wagons supplied by the Emperor were too few, too small and too weak, the weather was 'strange and horrible', the English horses were so scrawny that it took fifteen to pull the portable ovens which kept falling apart during the march, there was no local grain to be had, and the Imperial leaders were lying knaves who urged Norfolk on to Montreuil but failed to supply him with the necessary transportation, food or soldiers. In total exasperation the Duke wrote that Charles's Flemish officials had no desire whatever for the English to advance on Paris; their sole purpose was to relieve poor Englishmen of as much money as possible and to keep them close to the frontier in case of French attack. It was, concluded Lord John Russell, a 'wild war' much to the King's dishonour, for they did nothing except wander about.[60]

In the face of this barrage, Henry retreated into a citadel of inscrutability so impregnable that when the Duke of Suffolk arrived in Calais on July 3rd with the main army the King's ultimate purpose was still unknown, at least to the military chiefs, and much to Suffolk's indignation Norfolk accused him of deliberately concealing their master's true design. When highly secret orders from London finally arrived on July 7th the Duke of Norfolk was no better off than before, since the Council took the unrealistic position that the Duke, as a consequence of calculated Imperial misdirection, had inadvertently been manœuvred into a siege of Montreuil. Now that he was there, he was to do what he could to capture it, but he would have to do so on his own, for the King had settled upon Boulogne as the main target for the English expeditionary force. Even then, the Council's wording was so vague that Norfolk was not absolutely certain whether Montreuil and Boulogne were to be spring-boards for a strike at Paris or military trophies sufficient unto themselves. The frustrated commander continued his loud lamentations: he had been left in the dark; he was dependent for supplies upon faithless allies; he was having difficulty with de Buren's troops, and he had been given insufficient soldiers either to go on or to surround Montreuil, which had turned out to be a veritable porcupine of fortifications defended by four thousand French troops. The older he got the more Norfolk bemoaned his stars and harped on the military obstacles of the moment, and finally Paget had to order him to stop nagging and exaggerating the number of the defending army and the impregnability of the city's defences. The King, the Secretary said, had definitely decided, not to attempt a crossing of the Somme but to 'enlarge his Pale and make a great and profitable conquest' by seizing Montreuil, Boulogne and Ardres. He then warned the elderly commander that should Henry return home without victory it would be neither to the King's honour 'nor [to] the reputation of those that have charge of such things under his Majesty'.[61]

The King's reputation demanded a really notable exploit but it also had to be swift, cheap and sure. The decision to avoid the dangerous attack on Paris had been admitted as early as June 13th when Paget informed Lord Cobham, the deputy lieutenant of Calais, that the King's armies would always 'be so near Calais' that the city needed no extra forces to defend it, and in fact Henry probably never seriously considered the proposal.[62] Gonzaga's description the previous December of two monarchs in brilliant armour administering God's retribution upon a feckless Francis had no doubt inflamed the King's imagination, but old complaining Norfolk, whose massive invasion of Scotland only the year before had petered out in seven days, and Winchester, who knew exactly how difficult it was to supply a sixteenth-century army, along with Hertford, Paget, Wriothesley and Browne, had done the staff-work and had insisted on that crucial safeguard—each army would act as it saw fit.[63]

Exactly when and why Boulogne was selected as the primary English objective is a mystery. Militarily Montreuil was more important, for it was the main French staging-area for Boulogne as well as Ardres, and if it were taken, the entire French defence system for north-east France would have collapsed. Unfortunately, to seize Montreuil Henry had to rely on the Emperor for supplies, and Norfolk's howls about Flemish perfidies were enough to scare anyone. Doubtless Boulogne seemed both tactically and financially more desirable, for it appeared to be the cheapest trophy available to a prince who 'bet only on a sure thing' and 'attempted nothing which he did not bring to a successful conclusion'.*

Whatever the logic or illogic of the decision, Boulogne was selected, and at the same time Henry pared down his expectations by reducing Suffolk's summons to all people 'within the realm of France to come in and acknowledge their duties of allegiance to his Majesty' to only those 'within Picardy and the county of Boulogne'.[64] Henry might dream, but in the end he was usually willing to settle for what he could get at a reasonable price, and by July 21st, when Chapuys began nagging him about Paris and his promises to the Emperor, he coldly refused to elaborate on what the Ambassador could see for

---

* Possibly there were military considerations, for it has been argued that Boulogne threatened French sea lanes to Scotland. Strategic objectives, however, are suspect. If Boulogne was so essential to the war in Scotland, then its capture certainly did not have the desired effect; French supplies and troops to Scotland increased during the period of English control (1544–50), and in the end English defeat in Scotland led to her withdrawal from Boulogne. As a port, the city was in no way the equal of Calais, and if Henry really wanted a second staging-area for an invasion of France, Étaples at the mouth of the Canche, not Boulogne, would have been infinitely more desirable.

himself—his troops were besieging Montreuil and Boulogne and he could not advance till they had been taken because his soldiers, 'even at the very threshold of the Emperor's countries, had suffered extreme want of victuals'.[65] Seeing his 'look and resolution', Chapuys wisely decided not to push the matter, if only because Charles himself was in no position to complain. Much to Henry's secret delight, the Emperor's invasion had also bogged down before St Dizier, where he had been repulsed with such great loss that he could not 'with honour now depart'.[66]

Henry was meticulous about his military commitment, assuring Charles that just as soon as Montreuil and Boulogne had fallen he would sweep on to Paris. He refused to listen to any French offers of peace and sanctimoniously informed the Emperor of each new French concession, but Chapuys was morally certain that the English King would never cross the Somme even if both cities were captured. He wrote his master that Henry would remain in France only the stipulated four months, that he was far more concerned with the mounting cost of war than with the glory, and that once he had Boulogne he would pull out completely. The Ambassador was quite sure of his prognosis when on August 7th he dexterously led the King from one topic to the next to 'declare that when all was said it would ultimately be well to come to a good peace'.[67] Unfortunately, however, Boulogne continued to elude its besiegers and despite 'enough cannons to conquer hell' remained defiantly French. To make matters more embarrassing, St Dizier capitulated on August 17th and Charles was now in a position to demand the fulfilment of Henry's treaty obligations.

Exactly what the Emperor had in mind was beyond the English Ambassador's understanding, and the research of a dozen historians has failed to make the matter any more lucid. Possibly Charles was not clear himself, for as he marched he negotiated, always keeping open the alternatives of peace and war. In three weeks he covered eighty-five miles, moving steadily along the left bank of the Marne to Château-Thierry, his advance cavalry reaching to within thirty miles of Paris itself. If Boulogne had fallen, if the Emperor had been more confident of his ally, if his efforts to cross the Marne had not been repulsed, if he could have got at the French army which was cautiously pacing him on the opposite side of the river, if, as Henry had predicted, the first twinges of gout had not appeared in September, if his financial resources had been greater, if Paul III had not lashed out against his godless dealings with the heretical princes of Germany and the schismatic King of England, if a host of unguessed strategic, personal and religious pressures had not advised caution, then European history might have been very different. As it was, he made peace even as he held Francis by the throat.[68]

Charles was weary of the senseless duel for prestige which had been going on for almost thirty years, and he hoped that Francis at the eleventh hour would begin to ponder his soul's welfare and that of Christendom. He demanded no concessions, no compensations, no territorial adjustments, even though the French had been the aggressors and were now the losers. Instead, at the Treaty of Crêpy on September 18th, 1544, both princes restored their conquests. Francis publicly eased his Christian conscience by promising sixteen thousand soldiers for use against the Infidel, and granted his son Charles Duc d'Orléans in marriage either to the Emperor's daughter, who would bring as her dowry the rich estates of the Lowlands, or to the Archduchess Anna, whose wedding gift from her Imperial uncle would be the treasured city of Milan. The concessions were apparently to be made by Charles, but the Emperor had achieved his purpose, for in one of the best-kept secrets of the century Francis signed a secret codicil guaranteeing to help Charles reform the Church, call a General Council, return the heretics of Germany to the Catholic fold, and 'at the Emperor's command' permit the troops allocated to quell the Turks to be used for the chastisement of Christian sinners. As for Henry Tudor, the wording was ominous: Francis swore to make no peace without including the Emperor and 'if, because of their treaty, the King of England should wish to quarrel with or make war upon the Emperor', then Francis promised to assist Charles.[69] The Emperor must have known that any agreement with Francis was as fragile as the French King's life, for the connubial terms of the treaty benefited only the Duc d'Orléans, and the Dauphin protested that he signed solely 'pour la crainte et révérence paternelle'.[70] But Charles was willing to take the chance that Francis Valois would live long enough to fulfil his Christian mission and to roll back the Reformation in Germany.

Honour among sovereigns was a flexible commodity, and the Emperor accepted the principle that treaties must be regarded 'in conjunction with what is possible' and that allies could not be expected to 'run risks for the sake of groundless scruples'.[71] He had sent the Bishop of Arras on September 7th to inform Henry of the conditions on which the French were willing to negotiate, but he singularly failed to mention that he and Francis had in fact settled the terms, and he ordered the Bishop to assure his 'good uncle' that the Emperor had not yet committed himself either 'to war or peace, but rather suspends all' until he had heard from Henry.[72] The English monarch was not impressed. He told the Bishop that in private negotiations the French had already offered not only to pay all that was owing him but were willing to turn over Ardres, Boulogne and Montreuil as assurance of payment and to force the Scots to fulfil their marriage treaty with England. Henry's advice was that Charles should retire into his own territory without signing anything, and if he needed assistance in his retreat the English would send a small diversionary force into France. He concluded by assuring the Emperor that Charles could treat with the enemy as much as he liked, so long as nothing which was prejudicial to their friendship or to the terms of their treaty was decided.[73] On the day that Henry spoke to Arras, he wrote to his own Ambassador with Charles 'in what sort we mind to agree to the peace and in what things we desire to have for our own satisfaction without the which we would not willingly agree to a peace'. Only if his pensions were paid up in full, if satisfaction were given for damages incurred during the war, if hostages were offered for all future pensions, if Ardres were ceded and the Scots ordered to make peace, and if Francis renounced all claims to the counties of Boulogne and Guisnes, only then would the English King consider the peace to be honourable.[74]

Henry was greedy, but he was also ill-informed; he accepted Arras's word when the Bishop said that Charles would make no peace without Henry's consent. Boulogne had finally fallen on September 13th, and in his elation Henry refused to believe that the French negotiators with the Emperor were any closer to a settlement than were those treating separately with his own ministers. He did not realize the concessions which Charles was willing to make for the sake of exterminating heresy in Germany. It was a disastrous miscalculation. Charles had already determined on peace with or without the English, and calmly wrote into the Treaty of Crêpy Henry's approval of peace, as reported by the Bishop of Arras, without bothering to add the conditions on which that consent had been granted.[75]

Charles anticipated an explosion and Chapuys was carefully instructed to watch the King's countenance when delivering the news of the treaty; but Henry was unexpectedly restrained, receiving the news passively 'with none of his usual boastful manner'.[76] The King was saving his histrionics for another matter. What incensed Henry was not his partner's perfidy—that was only to be expected, and he sadly told Charles that God would judge between them and give him 'force to withstand the malice of all our enemies'. What he could not abide was the thought of the public ridicule that a King of England should consent to such a dishonourable treaty and that the word of a mere bishop had been accepted over that of a prince.[77] The sovereign who took such pains correcting and annotating his ministers' sentences and who prided himself on diplomatic exactness was not pleased by the suggestion that he could be guilty of an inadvertent diplomatic indiscretion. Long after the issue had ceased to have real significance, Henry continued to belabour the point and to 'mutter between his teeth'; it was, he said, a matter which touched his honour and self-esteem and could not be dismissed lightly. A year later he was still repeating that he could not understand how Charles had 'deserted him on the mere word of a minister', and he pompously informed Van der Delft, the new Imperial Ambassador, that 'he was getting to be an old man, having been forty years a king and no person could ever truly say that he had acted otherwise than sincerely and straightforwardly'.[78]

The monarch who sailed home for Dover on September 30th was very different from the prince who seventeen days before had reviewed the surrender of Boulogne amidst the blare of trumpets, the tramp of wheeling regiments and the glint of polished steel. During those two weeks he had learned 'that all good faith is almost banished out of the world'. God himself seemed to have turned away His face, for storms of unheard-of violence tore at the English camp, toppling tents, transforming trenches into canals, and bringing in their wake disease, filth and plague. Boulogne and Guisnes became charnel-houses, their streets like jakes fit only as 'a swine stye'.[79] Even his glorious trophy, Boulogne, was being besmirched by French rumours that he had won the city dishonourably, and had purchased treason for '150,000 nobles à la rose'.[80] Moreover, the military situation was desperate, for at Montreuil de Buren's troops packed up and went home, leaving the English in danger of being cut off from Calais by a French army of fifty thousand. Most ignoble of all, it must now look to all the world as if a deflated and ridiculous English sovereign were scurrying home for safety as fast as his great ships could carry him. It made but little difference that Henry's departure had been planned long before he learned of Charles's treachery,[81] and it took all of Paget's powers of persuasion to convince him that he could withdraw with honour, for he had achieved his 'enterprise of Boulogne' and Francis 'was not coming in person' to recover it.[82]

On top of military crisis and diplomatic disaster, the King's health collapsed. Early in January he sadly confessed to Chapuys that he had felt ten times better at the camp before Boulogne than he did now, and the Ambassador agreed that he looked old and shaken, sick and depressed.[83] The fleeting interlude when youth and good health had been recaptured was over; henceforth only two issues remained: how to survive in the face of the French menace, and when the King would die. In the minds of his ministers the two questions were intimately related, and Gardiner told Paget in November 1545 that if they did not labour diligently to preserve and maintain their sovereign's honour 'to the repose of his mind', he might die before 'my lord prince may come to man's estate' which would be 'more ruin to the realm than any war could engender'.[84] As usual, however, Henry had his own views on the subject and, tired as he was, he returned from France determined no matter what the cost to cling to Boulogne and to life. The old man was still in charge, a fact which commanders and councillors forgot at their peril.

Fortunately for the King, the French army set upon recapturing Boulogne turned out to be smaller than reported and beset by the usual French bad luck. Instead of risking a frontal attack on the citadel, the Dauphin launched a surprise night-assault on the port where the walls were still unrepaired. Clad in white shirts over their armour in order to distinguish friend from foe, six thousand French troops quickly massacred the camp-followers and labourers who were sleeping in the ruins of the town and discovered great piles of cannon-shot, casks of corselets and heaps of provisions which the English had not bothered to take into the citadel. English negligence was retrieved by French greed. Confronted with mountains of booty, the French troops began to loot and were unable to defend themselves from the English garrison, which sallied forth, routing the dis-organized attackers and killing six hundred. For once the awful weather played into Norfolk's hands, for thunderstorms and floods prevented the Dauphin from following up his night-attack. Checked at Boulogne, he turned on Guisnes, where he encountered the main English army and, as the English commanders reported, hopping and leaping hither and thither, he eventually retreated to Paris to await the coming of spring and the siege of England itself.[85]

Norfolk's troops were triumphant, Henry's honour sustained, and the Dauphin along with his brother, 'with all their glory and thousands upon thousands' of soldiers, had only succeeded in pulling down two churches; but even so Henry was in a vile mood. He accused Norfolk and Suffolk of incompetence, disobedience and even cowardice in the face of the enemy, and scolded them for having left Boulogne inadequately fortified and their war-material unpro-tected.[86] As the military and diplomatic crisis deepened, tension mounted; the King fussed and fumed throughout the winter, and greater and greater sacrifices were expected of his subjects. A new tax was levied on beer, parliament voted the largest subsidy in history (£196,000), and landowners and merchants were relieved of a further £119,581 in benevolent loans. War consumed it all, and to save the government from bankruptcy Henry turned to that 'holy anchor', debasement of the currency. Bishop Gardiner grumbled that it seemed to be a general rule that the government was expected to buy dear and sell cheap; everything cost twice what was anticipated, and the price of defending Boulogne, which had been optimistically set at £6,000 a month, jumped to £13,000. Chancellor Wriothesley described himself as weary of life and at his wits' end to meet the government's monotonous demand to 'pay, pay, prepare for this and that', and the King's loving subjects began to grumble that Boulogne was turning into 'a second Milan'.[87] The exhausted and frustrated Bishop of Winchester spoke for the entire kingdom when he lamented that it was his fate to live 'in an unreasonable world' where reason and learning 'prevaileth not'.[88]

Across the Channel things were no better. Boulogne and Calais were unable to get supplies from the Emperor's territories, and it was discovered that not 'so much as an egg, a chicken or a sparrow', those dainties which made the life of an officer and a gentleman endurable, could be purchased in Flanders.[89] Those vultures and 'consumers of prince's treasuries', the German mercenary troops, were eating up the King's money, threatening his commissioners and moonlighting on the side. Stephen Vaughan, his cheeks lean, his head spinning and his fingers weary with letter-writing, was having increasing difficulty raising funds on the Flemish money-market. Gold was scarce, England's chances in the war against France were considered risky, and interest-rates soared: 12 per cent in June, 14 per cent in August and the possibility of 16 per cent by September.[90]

Throughout the winter and spring lurid reports began to flood in describing the extent of the French military effort. Francis was preparing by land and sea to win back his city of Boulogne. The French and the Scots, it was said, were planning a joint invasion from the north with 30,000 men, 6,000 of whom were to be supplied by the Pope; Mediterranean galleys were being shipped overland to Dieppe and Le Havre; an armada of 300 sail was being made ready to invade England; Spanish and German mercenaries were flocking to the service of the Valois King; and Francis intended to liberate Boulogne in person at the head of 40,000 soldiers.[91] As the rumours grew, exhausted councillors prepared for the worst. Bell-metal was turned into cannon-barrels; a warning system of beacons was constructed throughout the coastal counties so that 25,000 men could be mustered the moment the French invaders were sighted; the gentlemen of the King's Chamber were alerted to superintend the mobilization; itemized reports were made directly to the King on the state of the defences of Boulogne, Calais and the coast; an army of 30,000 was spoken of to counter a possible French landing in the north of England; every second chalice throughout the parishes of the realm was dedicated to the war effort; and finally, as a gesture that the English meant to stay in Boulogne, Henry ordered 420 flock beds at a price of £70 12s. 10d. to be sent over for the comfort of his troops.[92]

Psychologically late February and early March were the most difficult months. Destitute of allies and surrounded by enemies who boasted that they would soon 'beat Englishmen as dogs', Henry was confronted with evidence that English soldiers could be routed by barbaric Scottish clansmen. In February a sizable English force under Sir Ralph Evers was defeated at Ancrum Muir. Fourteen hundred English soldiers were slain or captured and Sir Ralph along with Sir Brian Layton were left dead as the English fled in confusion. As at Haddon Ridge, it was not the number of English dead or the multitude of prisoners but the quality of those killed which mortified the King and delighted his enemies.[93] In military fact the defeat changed nothing, for the Scots were too exhausted, even with French help, to follow up the victory with a full-scale invasion of England, but in the eyes of Europe and the English monarch the kingdom had been disgraced. Henry swore that Arran and Cardinal Betoun would 'have no great cause to rejoice' at the death of his captains, but he had to admit that revenge would have to be deferred 'for a season'.[94]

Diplomatically it was an equally cold spring. Henry's one-time ally the Emperor moved steadily from friendly neutrality to secret hostility, and by March it was clear to the most sanguine observer that Charles did not care whether his late friend sank or swam so long as he kept on fighting the French. Chapuys, as always, put Imperial policy in its most succinct and witty form: Anglo-French peace should not take place too soon since 'it will be preferable that they should both tire somewhat and become more tractable than they are'.[95] To add to the King's unhappiness there was the mystifying matter of the second and secret Treaty of Crêpy. The English never did find out for certain what Francis and Charles had settled between them, but they suspected the worst and lived in constant fear that the Emperor's hatred of his German Protestants and Francis's obsession to recover Boulogne would draw the two old rivals into a mutual enterprise against schism throughout Europe. As Bishop Gardiner explained in November 1545, the problem was simply a question of whether the 'glue pot' of self-interest was hot enough to hold such an alliance together, and of that no one could be certain.[96] Under the circumstances Nicholas Wotton was scarcely exaggerating when he noted: 'There may peradventure some scorpion be hidden under the [Imperial] stone.'[97]

Blatant self-interest on the part of the Emperor could be accepted as a diplomatic constant, but in war, as Henry was wont to recite, 'fortune is not always one',[98] and fate now proceeded to make a mockery of all military forecasts and to prove that wind, tide and the bloody flux were solidly English. Balked in their efforts to assault or starve Boulogne into submission, the French high command concluded that the city could only be reconquered if the citadel of England itself were assailed, and they settled upon a three-pronged attack—a diversionary Franco-Scottish army moving down from the north, an amphibious operation aimed at naval control of the Channel and the seizure of the Isle of Wight, and a direct frontal attack on Boulogne itself. By July 15th all was ready, and Francis with his entire entourage came to Le Havre to bid godspeed to his splendid armada and to dine on board the flagship *Carraquon*. The dinner was scarcely propitious, for just as his majesty, his wife and sister were sitting down to eat, the vessel burst into flames—the King's chef, it was said, was not used to cramped naval quarters and had been careless with the galley fires—and the royal family, along with the expedition's treasure, were evacuated just before the *Carraquon* exploded, sending red-hot cannon-balls into the anchored fleet. D'Annebaut, the French admiral, immediately shifted flagships, and two days later the armada of 200 sail and 60,000 soldiers and sailors weighed anchor and headed for the Solent, Portsmouth and the Isle of Wight.[99]

Across the Channel the English King was also dining on board his flagship, the *Great Harry*, a thousand-ton hulk as overweight, clumsy and old-fashioned as the monarch himself. All the previous week Henry had been lumbering down the coast to inspect his ports and harbours. The Council had been sent post-haste into the shires to levy troops and alert the countryside, and precise instructions had been issued to the Lord Admiral on how to handle the French galleys when they appeared in English waters. Dinner on board the *Great Harry* was as close as Harry of England ever got to a real battle. When the English cavalry had triumphed at the Battle of the Spurs in August 1513 and captured six French standards, a duke, a marquess and a vice-admiral, Henry had been well in the rear, leading his regiments from behind; victory over the Scots at Flodden Field and Solway Moss were achieved by lieutenants; and the siege of Boulogne, though pleasant to watch, had scarcely been dangerous. Now at Portsmouth the King prudently retired ashore, leaving the battle to Lord Lisle and the vagaries of wind and current, which prevented either fleet from getting within musket-shot of the other. Courage and optimism there were aplenty; results, however, there were none, except that D'Annebaut's second flagship ran aground, sprang a leak and had to be sent home; the *Great Harry*, according to French reports, received a direct hit; the *Mary Rose*, an ungainly man-of-war of six hundred tons, sank with all hands because her crew had forgotten to close her gunports when she heeled over in the breeze; and the French landed a few hundred men for a few hours on the Isle of Wight and pillaged the Sussex shore in order to shame Henry into activity. If the elements and Henry's caution prevented his ships from ever reaching the enemy, nothing could stop the plague. It raged through the stinking ranks of sixty thousand French, packed into ships which had been at sea for almost a month, and by the time the Admiral sailed his dying fleet into Le Havre, his men, it was reported, would rather have been hanged than remain on board.[100]

On land the story was the same. Francis's great army of thirty-five thousand sent to storm Boulogne dissolved and died, helpless in the face of pestilence, quarrelling commanders and English supply ships sent to relieve the city. By September both England and Boulogne were quite safe, and Henry was of a mind to retaliate. Honour and conscience required that he break the pride of the invader's power, making their 'heaven as iron' and their 'earth as brass'. Lord Admiral Lisle made a punitive raid along the Normandy coast north of Dieppe, and the following year the King argued acrimoniously with his captains in favour of an amphibious assault on the French harbour of Étaples, the seizure or even the destruction of which Henry claimed would more than avenge D'Annebaut's landings on the Isle of Wight and the Sussex coast and would again threaten Montreuil.[101] But it was in Scotland that Henry demanded the greatest exploit: clearly God had ordained that the English should teach the faithless Celts 'to do their allegiance and fealty' to the King of England.[102] Not even French gold and two thousand reinforcements had been able to put new stomach into the Scots, and Hertford planned his second invasion as he had executed his first: systematic burning and destruction but no pitched battles. The expedition which marched forth from Newcastle on September 5th was sixteen thousand strong, and its triumphs are a catalogue of atrocities: the places 'burnt, razed and cast down' ran the gamut from seven great abbeys to 243 villages, with sundry 'piles, huts and stone houses' thrown in for good measure. The crops had just been gathered, the grain stood bundled in the fields and the harvest had been the best in years, but all was scorched and wasted by an army set upon making it impossible for the Scots to mobilize or to supply an attack on the English frontier.[103]

Henry was extremely busy and even more pleased with himself. The French armada had been hurled back, Boulogne was still English, the Scots had paid for their perfidy, on all fronts the sovereign's honour had been defended and embellished, and the King was delighted by the loyalty and affection shown by his subjects. Despite his unpredictable health, he had been poring over diplomatic reports, fortification plans, schedules of supply and muster-sheets. Throughout 1545 and 1546 his lieutenants and ambassadors were flooded with advice, criticism, orders and grudging praise: 'his majesty required', he 'savoryth meetly the grosse and platt of the matter', he remembers, he answers, he 'is well pleased', he signifies, marvels and desires his lieutenants to 'suck out the secrecy and bottom of the matter', he 'hath devised an article', he 'much desires to know the certain number of all his men', he has made 'additions and alterations' to the plan of fortifications, and he 'must needs think that no due order has been taken' with his supplies.[104] As the victories rolled in, his bellicosity increased, and he bluntly told Van der Delft that he had honourably won Boulogne 'at the sword's point and he meant to keep it'.[105] Francis was equally adamant. All summer he had been boasting that no matter the expense he would recapture Boulogne and now he could not with honour back down. It was, as Stephen Gardiner wearily observed in November 1545, 'a troublesome case to meddle' with an adversary who was both proud and poor.[106]

Bishop Gardiner was far too loyal to suggest that it takes two to make a fight or that his own master was also a proud and impecunious prince, but now that the King had defended his realm with so much repute there was a growing element at court which sought to stem his martial zeal and persuade him that peace was both honourable and an economic necessity. The civilians on the Council were for peace at almost any price. Sir William Paget wrote Gardiner that 'I would we had peace or truce, I care not by whom,' and the Bishop answered that 'the worst peace is better than the best war'.[107] The peace party discovered an uncomfortable political bedmate in the Duke of Norfolk, whose fervent pro-French sympathies led him to write sharply in late September to his son the Earl of Surrey not to animate 'the King too much for the keeping of Boulogne', and to warn him that he would receive little thanks at court if he did. A month later he was still grumbling that what the Council managed to do for peace in six days his son undid in six hours by his jingoistic letters to the King.[108] Surrey was a chivalric hawk whose daredevil behaviour appealed to his master. The Earl delighted in writing his sovereign that he should visit Boulogne to see 'the willingness of his men', and he urged the King to take the field again so that he could perceive for himself how ineptly Francis constructed his defences and how easy it was to supply the city.[109]

Once committed to a course of action, Henry was a Juggernaut, and the Council had to move cautiously lest he become suspicious of their motives or their actions be distorted by the war party. Months after peace negotiations had started, Paget was informed that his prince was not pleased by his constant harping on the benefits of peace, and Sir William felt obliged to beat his breast, assuring his 'sovereign and most benign and gentle master' that all his knowledge had come from conversing with his monarch and that he would never for his life favour a peace which was not to the King's Majesty's satisfaction and honour.[110] In the end, a monarch who had once remarked that 'to enter into war it needeth no counsel, but how to end war with honour and profit men must needs study',[111] proved tractable, if at times extremely mercenary in his approach to a settlement. Henry was convinced that his ambassadors would be going to the peace table with far better cards than the French, for it was reported that France was exhausted, her soldiers near mutiny, and her King broken-hearted and sick unto death with the French disease.[112] Despite all Francis's fine words about blowing Boulogne into powder, the fight had gone out of him when his best-loved son, the twenty-three-year-old Duc d'Orléans, died of the plague on September 9th, 1545, while strutting and play-acting before the walls of the city.[113] It took, however, another nine months of hard bargaining and intermittent warfare before two stubborn old men were willing to stand as godparents to the peace which was finally born on June 7th, 1546.

As the war ground to its costly and inconclusive end, the creaky structure of diplomacy took over with a consequent change of emphasis, if not of subject. The complaints remained the same, ambassadorial grumbling about 'evil-flavoured lodging and worse bedding' replacing military nagging about sour beer, loathsome food and foul weather. Throughout the autumn and winter the Emperor continued to play the dishonest broker. For months Imperial officials had been pointing out to the French that a truce might be to their advantage, on the cold-blooded demographic premise that Henry was old and 'a prince of short life', his heir was a sickly minor, and therefore Boulogne might be regained without a fight.[114] Charles's motives are far from clear, but so long as Francis followed the bait of Milan and hoped to marry his son to a Habsburg princess, the

Emperor could afford to urge peace among Christian kingdoms. Unfortunately, just when Charles had decided to destroy the military power of the Lutheran princes, the Duc d'Orléans died. Suddenly the Habsburg hold over Francis was broken and it became essential to keep France at war with England. The Emperor, however, did not wish to antagonize Henry lest England make her own peace with Francis, and he resolutely turned down all Franch bids to join a holy war against the English.[115] To make matters even more complex, the German Protestants were desperately seeking to end the Anglo-French war if only to save their own skins, and both Francis and Henry were showing signs that they might accept a settlement mediated by the German heretics. The one disaster Charles had to avoid was an unholy alliance between his Valois rival, his schismatic uncle and his sinful subjects.

The Emperor's discomfort was Henry's delight, and throughout the autumn and early winter of 1545 he stage-managed a semantic display so overwhelmingly wordy that if phrases alone could have brought peace, the war would have been smothered in verbiage. In October Bishop Gardiner travelled to Bruges to re-negotiate the Anglo-Imperial military alliance and informally to discuss peace terms with the French Lord Admiral, who also held a double commission—to negotiate with the English and at the same time urge Charles to join in the war against England. The following month Secretary Paget, complaining furiously the whole way, ventured across the Channel to meet the German Protestants and French representatives in a damp tent outside Guisnes. The results of both missions were meagre. Sir William 'lied, said truth, spoke fair', promised gifts and did 'all that may be done or said', but the negotiations got so involved in matters of religion and speculation as to whether Francis could be persuaded by his sister and mistress to forsake the Pope that the English Ambassador at length declared himself hopelessly confused. He was, he said, a plain man who spoke in a 'rude and plain fashion': if the French wanted peace they would have to give up Boulogne and pay their debts. This, of course, Francis had no intention of doing; neither his honour nor his exchequer would permit it.[116]

At Bruges Gardiner was no more successful, and concluded that the peace terms suggested by the French were so miserable that he feared for the King's health. Even the Bishop considered it too much to expect Henry 'after so long travail in honour, in rule and government of the world' to give back Boulogne and leave Scotland alone 'only for a little money, not paid but promised'. Boulogne remained the diplomatic and military heart of the issue. Francis could not with honour make peace without it; Henry could in honour discuss peace only with it. Francis was willing to buy the city back for two million crowns, but, as Gardiner noted, his King had already spent five million to keep it. Francis said that his English brother had won the port with honour and could now return it with even greater honour; the Bishop coldly parried that the French offered too much honour, too little money and absolutely no guarantee that they would keep their promises. Francis already owed Henry, according to English calculations, 1,600,000 crowns in unpaid debts and pensions and was currently so short of cash that he could not pay his own troops, and Winchester dourly warned his master to 'consider how naughtily the world faileth him in all degrees'.[117] Since the world had in Henry's opinion always been delinquent in good faith, the Bishop's words could scarcely have come as a surprise, and he ordered Gardiner to cease treating with an enemy so obviously wanting in honour and good intentions.

Just as the disgruntled Bishop was concluding his talks with the French Admiral, Secretary Paget was commencing his parley at Guisnes. No one except possibly the German Protestants expected any better results, but Henry found the negotiations a useful form of blackmail to strengthen Gardiner's bargaining position with the Emperor. In this he was successful, for a month after the Secretary began his discussions Charles signed the Treaty of Utrecht, reaffirming the non-military sections of the Anglo-Imperial Alliance of February 1543.[118] What the Emperor hoped to achieve by guaranteeing England and Calais against further French attack is obscure. Possibly he thought that Henry, as the weaker sovereign, needed his support to continue the struggle and to help counter the growing peace party at court. Possibly he was concerned by the Anglo-French-Protestant negotiations and feared that, unless the English were injected with new bellicosity, a peace would be established by which both Henry and Francis would guarantee the Lutheran princes from Imperial attack.[119] Or possibly renewed *rapprochement* with Henry simply reflected a growing rift with Francis after the death of the Duc d'Orléans: if Charles had to choose one or the other as an ally, Henry Tudor was more of a gentleman than Francis, or at least he could be more easily manipulated.

Whatever his motives, the results could not have been what Charles desired, for in May Henry unexpectedly went directly to the conference table without benefit of Imperial or Lutheran good services and gouged out of Francis almost everything he wanted. The end of Anglo-French hostilities was bad enough, but the timing was even worse, for peace was concluded at Camp on June 7th, 1546, too late for Charles to call off the war in Germany. All he could do was to assure Henry that he was delighted by the settlement, inquire tactfully whether his uncle bore 'any rancour' for having been left alone in the war, and explain that his enterprise in Germany was aimed at disciplining disobedient subjects, not at enforcing religious conformity.[120]

In the end peace was made because England and France were exhausted, their kings were elderly and in poor health, and a happy honour-saving device was discovered which satisfied both men. Francis continued in theory to own Boulogne but left Henry in possession; Henry in principle gave up the city but remained its conqueror. Once honour had been salved, the two sovereigns could settle down to hard bargaining. Henry's diplomatic style was neither deft nor imaginative but he generally got what he wanted. He haggled like a street-vendor over the price Francis would have to pay to get his city back and started the bidding at eight million crowns on the legal ground that in any action at law to recover a debt a man also received his costs, and the war, he claimed, had cost him that amount. The French were aghast—'Eight million! quoth they; you speak merrily. All Christendom have not so much money'—and countered with 200,000 crowns.* Henry was adamant; he was determined that Francis should pay for the war, and on paper at least he did. A financial settlement was worked out which, if it had ever been paid in full, would have gone a long way to recompense King Hal for the cost of defending his honour. Francis granted his royal brother 104,736 crowns annually in pensions and salt taxes and gave Boulogne as hostage for his promise to pay two million more within eight years.

Henry got his gold but he had to purchase it with land. At first he demanded the entire Boulonnais but eventually he settled for the area immediately north of the port, adjacent to the Calais pale and extending inland to the headwaters of the Liane river on which Boulogne stood. Weeks were spent arguing over the exact course of the upper Liane, which was so swampy that poor Paget and his French confrère got lost in the brackish water trying to locate its source. Further hours were spent worrying over the south bank and the point of highest tide which Henry claimed as part of the harbour of Boulogne. As always, his methods were laborious and technical; he read each word of every article twice over, adding phrases to cover every eventuality, even the bothersome question of whether French vessels using Boulogne should pay port fees and custom duties. But, as he said, he liked 'to treat so amply that there might

* The crown varied, but in 1546 it was worth five shillings (A.P.C., I, p. 266).

be nothing to gainsay' and he urged his negotiators on to ever greater 'stoutness'.[121]

When the final document with all its financial and geographic clauses was finally ratified in August 1546 everyone was reasonably satisfied. Honour had been saved; Boulogne remained French in theory, English in fact; and the two monarchs were perfectly aware of the significance of Paget's parable—offered to persuade his master to accept the French terms, based as they were on only an eight-year mandate. Once upon a time, Louis XI of France had condemned a man to die, but the rascal promised to teach the King's ass how to talk within a year if his life were spared. Louis accepted the proposal. When it was pointed out to the culprit that he had scarcely made a good bargain since he could not possibly do as he promised, the man answered: 'Hold thy peace'; in twelve months, either 'the king will die, or the ass will die, or the ass will talk or I will die'.[122] As Sir William explained, 'in time many things [are] altered', and time was running out for both Francis and Henry. Slowly Boulogne, Ancrum Muir, Calais and Solway Moss receded into the mist of time; new contours and tensions began to emerge, configurations based on two overriding considerations: when would Henry die, and who would pick up the heavy mantle of his majesty and rule in the name of a boy King?

10

The King Must Die

In old age most people become to some extent caricatures of themselves.

Anthony Storr, 'The Man', *Churchill Revised*

Death had always been a demographic possibility; now it was a personal reality and Henry was frightened. Age had been 'coming fast on' and for almost a decade he had known that 'time slippeth and flyeth marvellously away'. Confronted with his own mortality, Henry Tudor sadly acknowledged that time 'is of all losses the most irrecuperable, for it can never be redeemed with no manner [of] price nor prayer'.[1] Twenty years before, there had been no rush, and time had been told to stand still while Henry sought what he desired most—'heart's ease' and 'quietness of mind' in the company of Anne Boleyn.[2] For that vision of connubial bliss he had risked losing paradise, only to discover that the gods had devised a worse punishment on earth: they had granted his wish and Anne had become his wife. Thirty-nine months and a revolution later, he had tried again with Mistress Jane Seymour, and this time the deities were more merciful. The King's third wife survived marriage by only 511 days; long enough to bear him a son, short enough to enshrine a memory which a sentimental old monarch took to his grave. Henry never forgot the mother of his only legitimate son. Twice, in 1539 and again in 1543, he paid nostalgic pilgrimages to the cramped medieval manor-house of Wulfhall in Savernake Forest where Sir John Seymour had served his daughter her betrothal feast, and in his will he ordered 'the bones and body of our true and loving wife Queen Jane' to be added to his own in the tomb.[3]

Thrice more the King had sought happiness and domestic peace in that 'high and blessed order ordained of God in paradise' and twice more he had felt the sting of the adage: 'He that invented this knot and tie of marriage had found a goodly and beautiful means to be revenged of man.'[4] Anne of Cleves had proved repulsive but tractable, content to become her husband's 'beloved sister', but with Catherine Howard the gods had mocked the King, and he had

224

CATHERINE PARR, 1512–48. *Attributed to William Scrots*

HENRY HOWARD, EARL OF SURREY, *c*.1517–47.
Wrongly inscribed 'Thomas, Earl of Surrey'. *Holbein*

bitterly told his councillors that never again would he endure another wife. For two years grief and injured pride consumed him, but in the end, such is the triumph of hope over experience, he was willing to risk the lesson of the three married men who sought to enter the gates of heaven. To the first, who had had but a single spouse, St Peter said: 'Thou art worthy to have a crown of glory' for his suffering on earth; to the second, who was twice married, he offered 'a double crown'; but to the third, who had endured matrimony three times over, he cried out: 'What! thou has been once in trouble and thereof delivered, and then willingly wouldst be troubled again and yet again thereof delivered, and for all that couldst not beware the third time—but enterest willingly in trouble again! Therefore go thy way to hell, for thou shalt never come in heaven for thou art not worthy.'[5] What St Peter might have said to a sovereign six times married is better left to the imagination, but as the story goes, Henry was at least cautious enough to select his final spouse with an eye to his old age, and he informed his council that he had had enough of young fillies and had resolved upon an honourable and modest widow, the lady Catherine Parr.[6]

Though St Peter might have slammed the doors of paradise in Henry's face, legend has been more considerate, and traditionally the King's sixth and final matrimonial venture has been presented as that 'heart's ease' and 'quietness of mind' which had so long been denied. There were ugly moments—the Queen's apartments ransacked for heretical books, Anne Askew tortured on the rack, the poet Henry Howard led like a common criminal through the streets of London, and Dr Edward Crome 'canting, recanting and decanting' at Paul's Cross—nevertheless, it is possible to picture a grey and tired old man, the volcano of his personality slowly subsiding, intent on 'loving rest and fleeing trouble' and set upon preparing himself and his kingdom for death.

If, as Chancellor Wriothesley assured the Duke of Suffolk, the King had never had 'a wife more agreeable to his heart' than the new Queen,[7] it was because Catherine Parr was a lady uniquely experienced in the role expected of a Christian wife: 'If she saw her husband to be merry, then was she merry; if he were heavy or passionate, she would endeavour to make him glad; if he were angry, she would quickly please him, so wisely she demeaned herself towards him.'[8] Only the King's 'beloved sister', Anne of Cleves, was unkind enough to comment openly upon the spectacle of Catherine in bed with that great sack of royal flesh. 'A fine burden Madame has taken on herself!' was her caustic comment, an opinion which seems to have stemmed more from pique than disgust, for she was

H

not willing to admit that the attractions of a twice widowed and childless lady of thirty-one could possibly be greater than her own Germanic charms.⁹ Whatever ribald thoughts the rest of the court may have had, dutiful subjects kept them to themselves, and they loyally prayed God to send the royal couple 'long life and much joy together'.¹⁰ Doubtless the sixteenth-century admonition that 'we are to speak nothing but good of the princes of the people' explains much, but by and large subjects wished their sovereign well, and William Thomas reckoned that 'amongst all the happy successes' which Henry had achieved this one was special, for 'after so many changes, his glorious chance hath brought him to die in the arms of so faithful a spouse'.¹¹

Catherine plighted her troth on Thursday July 12th, 1543. Though she later confessed that she had followed the wishes of God and not her heart in marrying her sovereign, her letters to her lord and husband are filled with endearments, and when Henry was parading before the walls of Boulogne in the summer of 1544 she wrote to say that she knew his absence was necessary for the good of the kingdom 'yet love and affection compelleth me to desire your presence'. As she said, her words were not 'only written with ink but most truly impressed in the heart', and no one has ever been cynical enough to disbelieve her¹² Possibly the Catherine Parr of legend—the wife who brought domestic peace into the old King's house, who reconciled him to his daughter Elizabeth, befriended the Princess Mary and mothered the little princeling—is too good to be true, and it is gratifying to know that she experienced a wholesome, if politic, desire to bite the Earl of Hertford and wished his wife in hell, and that she indulged in some singularly unqueenly activities in the company of her fourth and final husband, young Thomas Seymour, and her fourteen-year-old stepdaughter, the Princess Elizabeth; but for all that she probably merits her reputation as a pleasant, witty, cultured woman who generally took to heart the medieval recommendation: 'Take care thou dost on no account say to him, "my advice is better than thine".'¹³

Catherine was the perfect companion to Henry's final years. Whether they actually sat together, his sore and bandaged leg in her lap, is immaterial; she knew how to divert his attention and ease the pain that was in him. In the ingenuous but compelling words of the Spanish chronicler, she was 'quieter than any of the young wives the King had had, and as she knew more of the world, she always got on pleasantly with the King and had no caprices, and paid much honour to madam Mary and the wives of the nobles.'¹⁴ What they talked about as man and wife has not been totally lost, for

Catherine was a fervent and well-read devotee of Erasmian piety. The subject was safe enough, for Henry had no dispute with the central religious tenet of the Queen's faith—that a true comprehension of the charity which stands at the root of God's universe begins in the hearts of men. The King's own *Book*, that necessary and sufficient doctrine to assure salvation, had defended good works not as outward acts alone or 'superstitious works of man's own inventions' but rather as 'inward spiritual works ... as the love and fear of God, joy in God, godly meditations and thoughts, patience' and humility.[15] Henry himself had lamented in his tearful farewell speech to parliament that 'the special foundation of our religion, being charity between man and man, is sore frigerate' and that meaningless name-calling 'devised by the devil' had caused his subjects to forget St Paul's words: 'Charity is gentle, charity is not envious, charity is not proud.' He longed to see the day, he said, when his people 'by unity, concord and charity between themselves may be [accounted] among the righteous of the world.'[16] What caused trouble was not the Queen's pietism, for her devotional poem *The Lamentacion of a Sinner* was aglow with tactful praise for her 'godly and learned King', but her religious enthusiasm which led her to forget that nature had formed her husband's 'lineaments' to superiority and 'set the print of government in his face'.[17] Henry considered that he had cause to complain, for 'you are become a doctor, Kate, to instruct us (as we take it) and not to be instructed or directed by us'. Catherine forgot at her peril that when her spouse urged his subjects 'to be in charity one with another, like brother and brother', he also added the sharp reminder to 'love, dread and serve God (to the which I as your supreme head and sovereign lord, exhort and require you) and then I doubt not but that love and league, that I spake of ... shall never be dissolved or broken between us'.[18]

The King's wrath with his wife may have stemmed from an underlying fear of the dangerous social conclusions of humanistic pietism, which placed a high premium on inner devotion and played down the organizational and sacramental aspects of religion, or from irritation at Catherine's unwifely lecturing, or it may have been reflex action on the part of a frightened and suspicious old man intent upon humiliating and testing the motives of his councillors. Perhaps all three impulses led to the Queen's dramatic encounter with the heresy laws when her apartment was searched for illegal books and the yeomen of the guard came to carry her to the Tower. The story has already been told—how the plan was disclosed to the Queen, how Catherine received her pardon, and how Chancellor Wriothesley, not the Queen, became the victim of the plot when he sought to carry out his master's orders—but Catherine's performance bears restatement, if only because it reveals the extent of that worldliness and tact of which the Spanish chronicler spoke, and of her ability to manipulate a king who was also a man and a husband. When Dr Wendye revealed to the Queen the full extent of the enterprise against her and counselled her to 'frame and conform herself unto the King's mind', Catherine went to her husband's bedchamber. Henry welcomed her courteously and blandly proceeded to ask her to resolve a number of religious doubts which of late had been bothering him. The Queen was far too wise to fall into such an obvious trap and be drawn into a dangerous debate, and she tactfully answered that since God had endowed man with 'special gifts of perfection' so that he could contemplate heavenly matters, it was not for woman to meddle in such affairs. 'How then', she demurely inquired, 'cometh it now to pass that your majesty, in such diffuse causes of religion, will seem to require my judgment, which when I have uttered and said what I can, yet must I, and will I, refer my judgment in this, and in all other cases, to your majesty's wisdom, as my only anchor, supreme head and governor.' The words were nectar to Henry's thirsty lips, but he was not completely mollified and remarked that she had not been so meek and reverent in the past. No, Catherine answered, the King did her wrong. She had been bold to differ with him not to maintain her own opinions but in order to take his mind away from his infirmities and to improve her own knowledge.[19] For a sovereign who by definition had to be right and whose 'nature and custom hath been in such matters, ever more to pardon them that will not dissemble, but confess their faults',[20] the Queen's submission was eminently satisfactory. Dismissing any lingering doubts, Henry graciously announced: 'And is it even so, sweetheart, and tended your arguments to no worse end? Then perfect friends we are now again, as ever at any time heretofore.' It was this sudden volte-face which the King failed to make known to his Lord Chancellor, who arrived with forty yeomen the following afternoon to arrest the Queen but received instead a verbal thrashing from his master.

Wriothesley was bruised and humiliated but Catherine's credit was high. Her good will was manifest throughout the court, though Henry warned her that she was courting disaster to ask him to forgive the Lord Chancellor, who was 'an arrant knave' and wished her only evil. Possibly Mr Francis Goldsmith overstated the case when he said that 'her rare goodness' had made 'every day like Sunday', but then he was a patron-seeker looking 'for the smallest coin out of the rich treasure of her grace'.[21] Even so, the Queen's cultured and humanistic influence was felt in every sector of the palace, and for the first time the royal children found in their newest stepmother a lady sufficiently educated and tactful to be their friend and mentor. Six wives, whose marital calamities have been neatly caricatured in the cruel little jingle—'divorced, beheaded, died; divorced, beheaded, survived'—had left their scars. Elizabeth had been only eight years old when Catherine Howard, her third stepmother, was beheaded for adultery, but her shock was voiced in the prophetic cry: 'I will never marry.'[22] Mary at twenty-seven was moody and melancholic, loving yet hating the father who had broken her pride and forced her to confess that her mother's marriage had been 'incestuous and unlawful' in the eyes of God and man[23] In the years after 1543 Catherine was able to reach both her stepdaughters; it was, she said, her pleasure as well as her duty.[24] She interested the Princess Mary in Erasmus's *Paraphrases* and Elizabeth in his *Dialogus Fidei*, and on New Year's Eve, 1544, the little Princess proudly presented her with a translation in her own hand of Margaret of Navarre's humanistic verse-treatise, *The Mirror of a Sinful Soul*.

The Spanish Ambassador noticed the change at court, but so also did that 'little manikin' Prince Edward, who priggishly wrote to his stepmother in May 1546 asking her to beseech his dear sister Mary 'to attend no longer to foreign dances and merriments which do not become a most Christian princess'.[25] Whose moral affectations the nine-year-old boy was spouting is not recorded; possibly it was that stern and egregious moralist Dr Richard Cox, who pointed out the Prince's failings and drilled him in the book of Proverbs, 'wherein he delighteth much and learneth there how good it is to give ear unto discipline, to fear God, to keep God's commandments, to beware of strange and wanton women, to be obedient to father and mother, [and] to be thankful to them that telleth him his faults'.[26] Edward was well on the road to becoming that 'godly imp' so important to Anglican myth, but as yet he was no Protestant Josiah. Instead, the documents suggest something both sadder and more terrible: a precocious and fatuous little boy mouthing the stilted language of his elders, devoid of compassion and obsessed with his own deficiencies. He shuddered at the thought of what his father expected of him, for all his life he had been drilled in the single pedagogical principle: 'Learn, oh boy, what is likely to be of use to you when a man.'[27] He had been carefully schooled to beware 'the wiles and enchantments of the evil one', and had learned how to thank his father for his lavish and costly gifts: 'You grant me all these, not that I should be proud and think too much of myself,

and fancy I excel others; but that you might urge me to the pursuit
of all true virtues and piety, and adorn and furnish me with all the
accomplishments which are fitting a prince ... '[28] With extraordinary
speed the princeling who played with sandbox and hoop became the
sterile scholar who heeded 'every notable sentence' in a sermon,
'especially if it touched the King'. He congratulated his stepmother
on her progress in the Latin tongue and in *belles-lettres*, but rather
like his father marred the effect by delivering a lecture on the subject:
literature is conducive 'to virtuous conduct, but ignorance thereof
leads to vice; and, just as the sun is the light of the world, so is
learning the light of the mind'.[29] What Catherine thought of such
pomposity she mercifully kept to herself, but in his letters to her
alone a real little boy emerges. To her he wrote in his terror at the
thought of having to address the French Ambassador-extraordinary
in Latin; to her he said that 'it seemed an age since I saw you'; and
to her he prayed God that 'I may be able in part to satisfy the good
expectations of the King's Majesty, my father'. To bring out the
fearful child behind the starched façade of the prince was no mean
accomplishment, and he offered her his passionate and most 'un-
common thanks'.[30]

The year of Catherine's marriage had found the King ebullient
and self-satisfied. The tonic of Solway Moss in November 1542 had
done him a world of good, and with his new spouse he had to make
no youthful pretensions. Admittedly he was old, but he was still
a mighty prince bent on winning a crown in Scotland for his son
and honour for himself in France, and he found in his sixth wife a
companion to his elderly tastes. Catherine, it was true, might not
conform perfectly to the mirror of womanly excellence as an 'ape
in the bed', but she fulfilled the prescription as 'a shrew in the
kitchen, a saint in the church [and] an angel at the board'.[31] She
ran his kingdom with quiet efficiency when he journeyed to France
in the summer of 1544; she could be trusted to perceive that 'in the
time of their harvest' was the moment for the King's troops to lay
waste the Scottish frontier 'as much as may be'; and in his absence
she cared for the royal progeny, carefully reporting on their health
and welfare.[32] Towards the end, however, not even his 'sweetheart',
as he was wont to address his Kate, could stave off age and melancholia. The betrayal of his Imperial ally and the prolonged defence
of his precious city of Boulogne had exhausted him. The old malady
in his leg returned with renewed pain, and even the victorious peace
of the summer of 1546 failed to revive his spirits.

Sickness rarely elicited the best in Henry Tudor. Ever since
March 1541, when his ulcerated leg had brought him to the brink

of the grave and in his pain he had flared out at his thankless subjects and their disloyal grumbling against his religious policies, his
health had been deteriorating. His medical record became a steady
chart of rising costs, diminishing returns and recurrent colds, headaches, colics, agues, rheums, fevers and indispositions.[33] In spite of
industrious investigation and reporting by foreign ambassadors,
surprisingly little is really known about Henry's health, or the ultimate cause of his death. Compared to the clinically accurate picture
of the progress of Francis I's disease, descriptions of the English
monarch's illness are amateurish and imprecise, rarely going beyond
vague references to his *mal de jambe* or his *mal d'esprit*. The King's
health was a carefully guarded secret, and foreign observers had to
judge by his countenance or from the reports of spies, who carefully
watched to see whether he rose from his bed, remained in his chamber
gaming with his friends, dressed to go to mass or rode to the hunt.[34]
What ailed Henry Tudor is still debated, and medical speculation
ranges inconclusively from malaria, syphilis and alcoholism to osteo-
myelitis, gout and cardiac infection.[35] There is also the possibility
of brain damage sustained in 1536 when the King, at the age of
forty-four, fell from his horse while jousting and lay unconscious
for two hours. The evidence is circumstantial but the increasing
headaches, serious trouble with his leg and mounting irascibility
do appear after 1536. Moreover, that was Henry's last tournament.[36]

The legend that the King suffered from syphilis is a flamboyant
bit of historical gossip treasured by everyone who has ever heard
the name of the eighth Henry; but it is of modern origin, having first
been suggested in 1888.[37] Since then the medical profession has
sought to salvage King Hal's reputation, emphatically denying that
he had the great pox, or what the English called the French disease,
the French named the Italian pox, the Italians referred to as the
Spanish complaint and the Spanish, completing the circle, styled the
English disease. Historians have generally concurred: there is not
a scrap of documentary evidence for the claim, and foreign ambassadors were paid to discover exactly this kind of intimate information.
The story might possibly have quietly withered away had not a
Danish physician reopened the debate by arguing that Henry's
portraits indicate a deformity on his nose which suggests a syphilitic
gumma.[38] Whether this be evidence of syphilis or a slip of the artist's
brush is anybody's guess. Enough sins have been laid at Henry
Tudor's door without adding a social disease to the list. Moreover,
if he actually did have syphilis, it must have been arrested, for there
is one thing on which the evidence is clear: the old man was fully
and dangerously in control of those who were quietly asking them-

selves when he would be dead. Senility was never the danger; egotism, distrust, fear and depression were Henry's demons. No matter what the cost, the King was set upon disproving the young man's prophecy that 'old men are out of date'.

There is no need to posit venereal degeneration of mind and body to explain the Henry of later life; far more likely age itself was the villain. Senescence strips the personality of its protective coating and leaves the unadorned man to face mounting pain and disability, real or imagined rejection by a world geared to youth and good health, and the spectre of the tomb. The results, according to the specialist, are depression, hypochondriasis and panic.[39] Whether the King channelled his fright into an excessive concern for the ailments of his unwieldy body is not recorded. Henry had always exhibited an intense medical curiosity, and the manuscripts are heavy with ointments devised by the monarch to take away inflammation and 'make good digestion', plasters to 'retain the humours' and 'comfort the member', and various balms and unguents consisting primarily of rose and honeysuckle water, white wine, calf's marrow and ground pearls.[40] Possibly his attention to hygiene is psychologically important, especially his oft-noted timidity in the face of that silent killer the plague, which could reduce the lustiest flesh to ashes in hours and had taken six of his advisers in two years. But it is equally probable that his concern for the cure of the various ruptures, gravels, wheezing lungs, tetters, corns, raw eyes, toothaches and haemorrhoids which assailed Tudor society was evidence more of his engrossment in technology than of mental disorder.

Melancholia, which can erupt into excessive suspicion and delusion, is somewhat better documented. Every minister knew the King's emotional instability: the tears which trickled down his face as the royal pedant sharply lectured his subjects on their lack of charity; the sudden spasms of rage which the foreign ambassadors took care to deflect by tactfully changing the subject; the 'sinister opinion' which he might suddenly form of his chief advisers; but after 1541 and Catherine Howard's treason against his manhood as well as his divinity, a change began to take place. The tears, the indisposition and the pain were more pronounced; so were the reports of depression, moodiness and alternation between heavy lassitude and frenzied activity, when he would move restlessly from palace to palace, pore endlessly over diplomatic dispatches and watch his councillors with baleful eyes. Again and again observers remarked that he was sad, nostalgic, depressed or harking back to better days. In 1541 de Marillac had noted the King's *mal d'esprit*; five years later the Imperial Ambassador was mentioning his 'melancholy' and

strange refusal to leave his chamber even for mass or his daily walk
in the garden.[41] Thereafter the deterioration in his health was so
marked that any report of Henry's mental condition was submerged
in a flood of depressing comments on the dangerous state of his body
—he looks 'greatly fallen away', the King 'is very ill and in great
danger and the physicians despair', the King is 'so unwell considering
his age and corpulence he may not survive', the King is 'seriously ill
with a pain in the leg which caused a high fever', the King is 'so
ill for the past fifteen days that he was reported dead and many
people here still believe him so', and the final prophetic reference
written on January 10th, 1547: 'Whatever his health, it can only be
bad and will not last long.'[42]

Age and agony walked hand-in-hand in a century which believed
that the more painful a prescription the more efficacious the cure,
and which did not recognize the aged as a problem at all. Society was
geared to youth; the activities which it most admired—the joust, the
hunt and war—were young men's occupations; the stories it told
were of youths and maidens and enterprises of great heroism and
virtue. The young were everywhere; possibly 45 per cent of Henry's
subjects were children; 70 per cent of all households were likely to be
populated with the young, and even at court children abounded—
scullery boys, pages, ushers, rascals and sweepers.[43] At the centre of
this great youthful household the sovereign who watched and
waited seemed even older than he was. As Henry reached his last and
fifty-fifth birthday in June 1546 Surrey was twenty-nine, the
Queen's brother was thirty-three and Catherine herself a year older;
Petre, Paget and Wriothesley, those three indispensable Tudor
work-horses, were barely forty; the Seymour brothers were thirty-
eight and forty; Lisle, Gardiner, Denney, and Sir William Herbert
the Queen's brother-in-law, were still under fifty, while Sir Richard
Riche had just turned the half-century mark. Only Cranmer, Browne
and Russell were of an age with the King, while two—Bishop Tunstal and old Norfolk—were in their seventies.

The gulf between Henry at fifty-five and Hertford and Paget at
forty was greater than it would have been two decades earlier, for
those twenty years had seen a political and spiritual upheaval. In
1526 Henry had been a magnificent specimen of thirty-five with five
wives and a revolution still in front of him, while Hertford and Paget
had been twenty-year-olds whose entire careers would be set by the
King's 'Great Matter' and whose memories scarcely went back to the
days when Christendom had never heard of Martin Luther. By 1546
they were the sovereign's chief ministers, but they had no history;
they were essentially post-Reformation creatures who looked towards

the future, not the past. Henry was not just medically old; he belonged to another generation, and courtiers found him outmoded in a society which maintained a surprisingly high life expectancy of forty-five, but which still wrote:

> When forty winters shall besiege thy brow,
> And dig deep trenches in thy beauty's field,
> Thy youth's proud livery, so gaz'd on now,
> Will be a tatter'd weed of small worth held ... [44]

Whatever the root cause—mental, physical or social—the results were appalling. Walking became an agony, but it was a greater anguish to curtail the food and drink that had become the King's sole pleasure; so filled was the bloated body with pain and sickness that it was said that Henry was 'often of one mind in the morning and of quite another after dinner', and 'at the last, by reason of his sore leg (the anguish whereof began more and more to increase), he waxed sickly, and therewithal froward and difficult to be pleased'.[45] He could abide no whispering behind his back, and his 'accustomed patience' sharpened. Diseased and frightened, Henry became the most dangerous kind of tyrant, secretive, neurotic and unpredictable. As the promise of renewal and the potency of youth receded, there was no softening, no amused and stoical acceptance, no relaxing into weary semi-retirement, not even the search for distractions in music, art or the hunt. The pattern of his life did not change; it simply sharpened: there was a steady ripening of suspicion and fear, an increasing need for power, a mounting reliance on external sources to replenish self-esteem, and above all an absolute determination to control those closest to his throne.

Kings, be they Tudor, Habsburg or Valois, are but men, and they die in many ways according to their nature. The Emperor Charles passed away in quiet stages, first giving his son Philip meticulous instructions on how to rule, then abdicating and retiring to the monastery of San Jerónimo de Yuste and finally depreciating his attainments and role in life: 'I have done what I could, and am sorry that I could not do better. I have always recognized my insufficiency and incapacity.' Ultimately, modesty and self-control gave way to immoderate penance, anguished fear and a consuming necrophilia.[46] He scourged himself till he bled, sang hymns the night through, wept uncontrollably, and awoke the Jerónimite monks lest they miss a single second of their midnight vigil for his soul. And finally he celebrated his own obsequies; lying in his coffin and participating in the prayers for the dead, he was carried to the high altar where he received the last benediction. A few days later, on September 21st, 1558, he was dead, aged fifty-eight, and the funeral was re-enacted in earnest.

Francis Valois died more secularly but no less fearfully. It was said that the unfortunate sovereign could chart the course of his malady by the countenances of those around him; if they frowned he was recovering, if they smiled he was dying, such was the impatience of a younger generation to be done with the decrepit roué.[47] Henry Tudor, as he lay *in extremis*, thought of his old rival and maliciously sent him a farewell note remarking that his French brother was also mortal.[48] When word of the English King's death arrived in Paris, Francis ordered a full funeral service at Notre Dame as if it were a dress rehearsal for his own. Near the end his resentment against the living exploded, when word was brought to his bedchamber that the Dauphin and his friends were sitting drunkenly at table redistributing the great offices of state and boasting of what they would do once the King had joined his ancestors at St Denis. Enraged, Francis ordered out the Scottish guard and rushed to his son's apartment only to find it empty but for dirty plates, soiled linen and terrified servants. What ensued was symbolic—the helpless, frustrated anger of old age against youth, and the wanton satisfaction of hurling chairs, beds, mirrors and lackeys out of the window.[49] Francis was too sick, too old and too mercurial for sustained emotion, and eventually he forgave his son his cruel impatience, but as Charles Habsburg turned in his final moments to necrophilia, so Francis Valois turned to nostalgia, nervously revisiting the places he had once loved, the bedrooms where he had once conquered, and the forests where he had once ridden after boar and deer. As the King slipped into a euphoria of restless perambulation, hauling his diseased body from one hunting-lodge to the next, government, never one of his consuming interests, lapsed into a paralysis of waiting. The end came in March 1547; by the last day of the month, to the intense relief of everyone except possibly Madame d'Estampes, he was gone, three years younger than his English brother, who had already been in his coffin sixty-one days.

In Westminster a similar drama had taken place, but with a difference; Henry Tudor was not content to put his affairs in order and fade quietly away, or to cushion his fear and sickness in an orgy of hunting, allowing power to slip from his feeble grip. Instead, he refused to have anything to do with death, and, as John Foxe reported, 'was loath to hear any mention' of it.[50] Doggedly he sought to live, and in living to hold in absolute subjugation those about him, as if by wielding power he could forestall the inevitable and close the door to the knowledge that history was getting ready to do without him.

Protestant legend has a more pleasant version of those grim, unloving months. Henry appears as the prudent and prescient sovereign intent upon mapping out his son's future and tidying up unfinished diplomatic and political business. The final acts of his reign—the brilliant diplomatic display; the destruction of the Howards, those 'proud beasts' who stood in the way of a nine-year-old sapling; the selection of sixteen carefully screened but 'well-beloved' councillors to govern in his stead; the dismissal of that opinionated ecclesiastic, Bishop Stephen Gardiner; and the touching deathbed farewell—are all part of the same romance which places the King firmly on the side of the Protestant heroes. As it is told, Henry sought to die secure in the knowledge that his Church and his son would inherit his kingdom in peace and tranquillity. Indomitable and clear-headed to the end, he cast down the sole surviving dynastic threat to young Edward's succession: Thomas Duke of Norfolk and his son, Henry Earl of Surrey, whose feudal resources and Plantagenet blood made them security risks for the new reign. The wilful and conservative Bishop of Winchester was read out of the council of regency because none but the dying sovereign himself could control him, and the clairvoyant old King placed his son's future in the hands of newly erected men who were economically and spiritually committed to the Henrician Reformation and could be depended upon to defend a small boy against both magnate and prelate. Then with unerring dramatic sense he enacted the culminating scene; on January 27th he called his daughter Mary to his side, most uncharacteristically apologized for not having found her a worthy husband, and begged her to become a mother to his son, 'for look, he is very little yet'. The Princess burst into tears and pleaded with her father not to leave her thus 'an orphan so soon'. When she left his bedside the King bade farewell to his Queen and granted Catherine leave to remarry and presented her with an income befitting his widow. And so, having arranged for the future as best he could, 'he left the kingdom and took his rest with the dead'.[51]

Alas, the image of Henry Tudor winding up his days in the odour of domestic tranquillity and statesmanlike concern for the future is as psychologically distorted as it is polemically dramatic. The story bears the outward appearance of truth, but shift the interior lighting by a fraction of an inch and the picture is lost in the dark uncertainty of judging human motives. Indisputably, death, and his ugly stepchildren sickness, suffering, suspicion and fear, were the central figures of the scene. The King must die; that fact was self-evident to every chancery in Europe and sensed by every scullery boy in the royal kitchen; but when would he die? Would he linger on in agony, alert but body disintegrating, or would he slip into childish senility and infantile helplessness? Would he die today, tomorrow or next month, or would life endure in one form or another for years to come? Could he be controlled, influenced by sly innuendoes or deliberately goaded into anger? Or would he simply be treated like a child? Was he preparing himself and his kingdom for death or had he in fact closed his mind to the inevitable? And the most crucial question of all: would he go gracefully and quietly or would he fight back, striking at the living to prove his 'absolute power and independence' and driving his bloated carcase until it dropped?

The events of those final weeks had little to do with death, except for the accident of timing, but they had a great deal to do with life. They were the instruments by which the King sought to govern and intimidate the living, not to rule from the grave. Accept the proposition that a frightened, neurotic and desperately ill old man, who did 'not choose that any one shall have it in his power to command' him,[52] was psychologically incapable of acquiescing in death, that he had no intention of relaxing his grasp over younger men who were planning for a future which he could not share, and the entire scene changes. In place of tranquillity and 'heart's ease' there is mounting tension; instead of statesmanlike and calculated policies are unreason and panic; in place of rational control is fear—fear of the King's death, fear of his continued life, fear of whispering, fear of the unknown.

11

Preparing for the Worst

Better is a poor and a wise child than an old and foolish
king, who will no more be admonished.

Eccles. iv 13

For the twentieth century Henry's death is merely an oft-recorded
fact—2 o'clock on the morning of January 28th, 1547—for his contemporaries, however, it was a deeply frightening proposition, something between an intellectually accepted possibility and an emotionally explosive probability. To within a month of his death, the
King was still goading his great body into action, riding to the hunt,
appearing in his chair, being carried from palace to palace, and ignoring his doctors' pleas for rest and quiet. It was difficult to imagine
that such a sovereign was really dying, but if ministers were to survive they had to prepare for the political vacuum which would inevitably follow the old King's death. A legal heir to the throne
existed, but the source of human power was terminating and no one
as yet had clear authority to step into the breach. This fact alone
added an almost Stalinesque quality to the final scene.* No plan was
secure, no prediction reliable, no friendship dependable so long as
the unknown at the core of political life remained: exactly when
would Henry die? Only when the central question had been answered
could its corollaries—who would speak for the boy King and what
changes would ensue—be meaningfully stated, for both propositions
were dependent upon the men who managed to retain their positions
by the side of a dying but unpredictable monarch.

Tension was endemic in a regime which recognized neither the
heterogeneity of religious truth nor the possibility of a loyal political
opposition, but which was in fact torn by rival creeds and factions.
Security may make cowards of us all, but Stephen Gardiner and
Edmund Lee, the Archbishop of York, voiced no more than the car-

---

* The similarity between the last years of Henry's reign and those of Stalin's
rule deserve study. In neither case was the heir apparent the real successor to
power. Moreover, it was extremely dangerous to mention or in any way be
associated with the ruler's approaching death (note the fate of Stalin's doctors).

238

dinal principle of survival in the midst of ideological revolution, when the one advised that a clergyman should write his sermon down beforehand and give it to 'the chiefest man there that can read' so that no one could distort what had been said, and the other asked if anyone thought him 'so simple [as] to utter anything in the pulpit' that he could not 'well avow'.[1] When a society demands pure hearts as well as clean hands and accepts as sound politics Sir Richard Riche's famous words to Sir Thomas More—'Even though we should have no word or deed to charge against you, yet we have your silence, and that is a sign of your evil intention and a sure proof of malice'—then men must walk warily and wonder about even their closest friends.[2]

Stephen Vaughan thought he had cause for alarm when the government began inquiring as to 'what are my manners, my opinions, my conversation, my faith', even though the Treason Act of 1534 had not yet become law.[3] That engine of orthodoxy went into effect on the first day of February, and thereafter it was judged high treason 'if any person or persons ... do maliciously wish, will or desire, by words or writing or by craft imagine, invent, practise, or attempt any bodily harm ... to the King's most royal person' by denying his supremacy, pronouncing him heretic or in any way seeking to deprive him of his royal estate.[4] Anthony Waite's reaction was to remark jocularly that 'it is rumoured that a person should be committed to the Tower for saying that this month will be rainy and full of wet, next month, death, and the third month, war' until 'experience shows the truth of his prophecy',[5] but Richard Hilles's laconic words to Henry Bullinger in 1541 revealed what seven years of the Treason Act had wrought: tyranny had become an ordinary fact of life. 'To confess the truth,' he wrote, people did not inquire much, as it was no novelty 'to see men slain, hung, quartered or beheaded, some for trifling expressions which were explained or interpreted as having been spoken against the King'.[6] The French Ambassador concurred: 'When a man is prisoner in the Tower none dare meddle with his affairs, unless to speak ill of him, for fear of being suspected of the same crime.'[7]

It is easy enough to prove that the times were difficult and that a man could 'neither speak nor be silent without danger',[8] but examples taken out of cultural context are misleading; men learn to countenance tyranny, and what for one subject was despotism for another was security and a well-ordered commonwealth. Very possibly Sir John Mason spoke for most of Tudor society when he said that 'the worst act that ever was done in our time' was the repeal of the treason laws by the Lord Protector. In other countries, he ex-

plained, liberty was possible because 'men were content with talking,
not doing', but in England it was otherwise, 'for there talking is
preparatory to doing'.[9] Mason spoke after the event, when the
memory of a King who had once been described as 'the most dangerous and cruel man in the world' had softened and only the legend
of his regal presence remained.[10] Moreover, neither Sir William Paget
nor the future Lord Protector agreed with him. They both had cause
to know at first hand the price paid for too much majesty. Sir
William remembered that the rule of his late master had been 'too
straight' and it was then 'dangerous to do or speak though the
meaning were not evil'; as for Hertford, he could scarcely wait to
abrogate laws which he said were 'almost iniquitous in their
severity'.[11] As long as Henry lived, however, the treason laws remained and men learned to survive by following Sir William Petre's
prudent advice: 'Provide for the worst, the best will serve itself.'[12]
Unfortunately, the price of providing for the worst, if you were
caught out at it, could be death, and tension steadily rose as men
played at political roulette, seeking always to guess the precise
moment when the King would die.

Had no man feared the King's passing or projected his own fears
and aspirations about a dissolving present into an evolving future,
no one would have cared a farthing whether Henry lived or died. As
it was, a single refrain sounded: May God long preserve his Majesty
in good health 'and then come what will I fear not but there shall be
good'.[13] As the numbered days of the King's reign slipped by, tension
mounted. Emotional control declined, and for a moment not just
England but all of Christendom seemed to be in a state of panic,
terrified that time was running out. Francis I, always so volatile and
debonair, suddenly turned into a religious fanatic, butchering and
burning the entire pseudo-Protestant population of Merindol and
Cabrières, and such was the strange delusion of his mind that even as
he sent encouragement to Charles's heretical subjects in Germany,
he sacrificed his own people as a blood-offering to purchase peace of
mind for having allied with the Infidel.[14] The Emperor himself,
generally so methodical and judicious, cast caution aside, 'abandon-
ing his usual phlegmatic mode of proceeding'. His Catholic conscience
seemed unexpectedly to awake, and he determined to save his Low
Countries from spiritual error and once and for all to root out the
heresy which choked the states of Germany.[15] Almost at once, lurid
reports began to spread: seven hundred men had been sent by the
Pope and the Emperor to poison the wells and slaughter the cattle of
the Protestant faithful; Spanish and Italian soldiers, unsurpassed 'in
cunning and deceit', boasted that the war was to exterminate

heresy; and Catholic troops carried with them papal indulgences for any kind of atrocity, 'provided that they fall in this war against the heretics'.[16]

In England the same mania was apparent, and conservatives and reformers alike were swept by hysteria. The usually level-headed Bishop of Winchester suddenly began to prophesy ill. He was certain that the broad, non-denominational pietism in Catherine Parr's private chamber must of necessity lead to treason, for those who were bold enough to criticize their prince in words would ultimately translate sinful thoughts into treasonous actions.[17] Gardiner's warning to his sovereign to protect himself and his Church ere 'the faction was grown already too great' was not simply an astute appeal to Henry's latent paranoia; it was also a reflection of the growing insecurity which led thoughtful men to believe in the conspiracy theory of history.

The events that ensued—the attack on the Queen, the arrest and incredible escape of George Blagge, the frantic heresy hunt which started with the elegant and highly favoured court preacher, Dr Edward Crome, and touched even the ladies of the Queen's household —were all symptoms of the emotional strain within a court dominated by a suspicious and unstable monarch who was far more concerned with demonstrating his absolute power over his ministers than with shaping a consistent religious policy.

The attack on Catherine flared melodramatically and just as unexpectedly receded; the only person who seems in any way to have enjoyed or profited from the eruption was the King himself. Even more improbable was the assault on George Blagge, an intimate of the Privy Chamber. Suddenly and without warning he was accused of heresy, hauled off by order of the Lord Chancellor, and tried and found guilty of having defiled the sacrament of the mass by impudently asking 'what if a mouse should eat the bread' and answering 'then they should hang up the mouse!' Blagge denied the charge but confessed to an equally coarse impiety. After one of Dr Edward Crome's less satisfactory recantation sermons he had been asked whether the preacher had in fact said that the mass profited neither the living nor the dead. 'No', replied Blagge, no one denied the value of the mass; it was excellent 'for a gentleman, when he rideth a hunting to keep his horse from stumbling'. The jury thought his humour quite sufficient to warrant burning. Wriothesley unaccountably failed to inform the King that the law had dared enter the sovereign's closet; at least this is what we are told, and Henry, when he discovered the fate awaiting his servant, was 'sore offended', not at Blagge's outspoken religious opinions but with a Lord Chancellor who had presumed to enforce the King's law against a member of the Privy Chamber. In the nick of time the King sent for Wriothesley and ordered him to draw up a pardon with his own hands. His 'pig', as Henry was wont to call Blagge, escaped burning, but possibly our sympathies should be with the Lord Chancellor who once again must have received a different kind of roasting.[18]

The onslaughts on Blagge and the Queen were part of a concerted effort to establish guilt by association if not by actual doctrine. If the conservatives could show that the humanistic pietism preached in the Queen's chamber led to the 'obstinate and heady' opinions of an avowed heretic such as Anne Askew, the King's unpredictable reactions might be sufficient to upset the entire structure of household politics, and it was a measure of the mounting hysteria that the rack should have been used on Mistress Anne. Torture was unusual in religious interrogations, and unprecedented when applied to a gentlewoman who had already been convicted of heresy, but so also was the suspicion that Anne was receiving financial aid and spiritual comfort from Lady Denney and my ladies of Suffolk, Hertford and Sussex, and that she might have benefactors on the Privy Council as well. For that reason 'they did put me on the rack because I confessed no ladies or gentlewomen to be of my opinion, and thereon they kept me a long time; and because I lay still and did not cry, my Lord Chancellor and Master Riche took pains to rack me with their own hands till I was nigh dead'.[19] Wriothesley and Riche turned the handle of the rack but Lisle, Paget, Gardiner and the Queen's own brother were all involved as inquisitors, seeking we know not what—to save her from the fire? to lead her back to the fold? to use her as a weapon against their colleagues on the Council? or to discern the truth whatever it might have been? Anne Askew divulged nothing, except to reiterate endlessly that she would rather die than break her faith with God.

No such confidence sustained those who were determined to go on living. Time was short, and each man, alone or in league, sought to survive as best he could in a world which lived by the axiom: 'Slippery is the place next to kings'; and where every enemy knew the rule: 'Whom thou lovest not, accuse: for though he heal the wound, yet the scar shall remain.'[20] How much religion had to do with the constantly shifting galaxy of factions whirling in orbit about the sovereign is questionable. In terms of sixteenth-century political theory, the answer is 'none'; the very concept of factions, each harbouring secret malice and warring policies, was anathema to a generation which cherished the social ideal of a kingdom filled with right-thinking subjects inspired solely by God's grace and His

Grace's express desires. At least in public Chancellor Wriothesley was absolutely clear on this point: 'Rather than I would have consented in my heart to any party, tumult or faction in the realm, if I had had a thousand lives I would have lost them all one after another.'[21] In actual fact, of course, factional alliances had always existed.

While Henry lived there was little room for rival religious theories, only for a gnawing concern about the changes that would inevitably be introduced once the King was gone. Beyond this, religion had little to do with whom a man invited to dinner or to whom he confessed his political faith and anxieties. Thomas Wriothesley did as he was told, turning the rack on Anne Askew and organizing the arrest of Catherine Parr and George Blagge; he was no friend of the Earl of Hertford, who jettisoned him as soon as he could manage it after the King was dead, but the Lord Chancellor had been a protégé of Thomas Cromwell, was a good friend of Archbishop Cranmer, and the tone of his final testament was well to the left of religious centre.[22] Henry Howard, Earl of Surrey, was even more inconsistent. Politically he was an anachronism, harking back to a golden, if mythical, age of divine-right aristocracy. He detested Hertford both as a social parvenu and a military rival, but in religion he may have been even more radical than his adversary. His brother Thomas Howard had been severely reprimanded for adopting the ribald manners and language of Erasmian humanism, and the Earl himself was a religious iconoclast and good friend of that outspoken gentleman, George Blagge, to whom he wrote: 'But now my Blagge mine error well I see; such goodly light King David giveth me.'[23] A single couplet is scarcely evidence of anything, least of all the faith of a man as emotionally unstable as Surrey, but the words almost suggest a conversion, and the Imperial Ambassador was convinced that the Earl was infected with Lutheranism.[24] Politics and personality, however, not religion, stood at the root of Henry Howard's furious hatred of Hertford, and gouty old Chapuys, writing from semi-retirement, placed religion in its proper political perspective when he observed that both Hertford and Lord Lisle were confirmed in their incurable religious malady because of 'their plans to obtain the government of the prince'.[25] Control of a small boy was what led Surrey to destruction, divided the Seymour brothers from Chancellor Wriothesley, and forged the efficient alliance between Lisle, Paget and Hertford.

The political situation had been tense and changeable ever since the execution of Thomas Cromwell in the early summer of 1540. No new political impresario had emerged to control access to the throne or monopolize royal patronage; no longer was there an effective shield to deflect the King's wrath or the enmity of those deprived of the fruits of political power. Instead, ministers, still bitter from the factional strife which had culminated in Cromwell's fall, confronted a foxy and suspicious sovereign directly. Shortly it was being predicted that the Council would destroy itself, for 'others have arisen who will never rest till they have done as much to all who supported Cromwell, and afterwards God knows whether there will be any others who will recommence the carnival'.[26] Ralph Sadler, Sir Thomas Wyatt and Wriothesley himself had each felt the sting of slander, and all three knew the truth of Wyatt's terrible exposé of Henrician politics: even the most devoted and astute of the King's servants could not for ever guard himself from the malicious report of treason manufactured by quoting words out of context. Truth could be made into error simply by the 'altering of one syllable either with pen or word'.[27]

By 1546 the 'carnival' was reaching its climax, and Henry in his misery was willing to believe the worst of all men. Under the circumstances, Sir John Mason's prescription for political longevity under four monarchs rings true: 'Few things would save a man', he said, unless he was 'intimate with the exactest lawyer and ablest favourite', 'spoke little and writ less', sought to be of service to each party, and 'was so moderate that all thought him their own'.[28] The advice was excellent politics, but it bedevils history, concealing the factional war which was being waged in preparation for the King's demise and a new reign. Two men, however, stand out as the poles around which the fearful, the ambitious, the spiteful and the prudent could gather —Edward Seymour, Earl of Hertford, and Henry Howard, Earl of Surrey. As political personalities both men were unsatisfactory, for their leadership stemmed from neither talent nor charisma, but from the accident of birth—one was the senior uncle of the young prince and the other was heir to the ranking dukedom in the kingdom and in his own right a potential claimant to the throne.

Henry Howard was a poet of great sensitivity who felt deeply the contrast between the shadows of a man's inner existence and the bright sensuousness of his outer world, but as a statesman he was a dangerous neurotic with little sense of reality. He was firmly committed to the anti-social creed that a nobleman's honour has its own privilege. There was a strange rapport between the sulky Earl and a sovereign old enough to be his father, and the King put up with a degree of incompetence, irresponsibility and histrionics which would have outraged him in anyone less talented. Surrey was the sole member of his clan to escape untarnished in 1542 from the disgrace of his first cousin, Catherine Howard, and within two months of her execution he was honoured by being elected to the Order of the Garter. The following July his temper got him into trouble with Sir John a Leigh, the King's servant and justice of the peace, whom he challenged to a duel, and at the monarch's command he spent the month learning self-control in the Fleet. Leigh had not been the first victim of the Earl's anger; five years before he had struck Hertford in the face, risking the loss of his hand in punishment for violence committed within the precincts of the court. He escaped with nothing worse than two weeks at Windsor Castle, but Surrey never seemed to learn.

Henry Howard remained untamed and unreasoning, and the 'fury of his reckless youth' finally landed him in really serious difficulty when in March 1543 during a midnight escapade he insulted the worthies of London with obscenities and broke their windows.[29] Again he did penance in the Fleet and found it sufficiently cold and damp to promise grudgingly to bridle his 'heady will'. His actions, he said, had been motivated by the highest principles: he had thrown his stones at the windows only of those he took to be secret papists, so that they might learn from 'the stones passing noiselessly through the air and breaking in suddenly upon their guilty secrecy' the 'suddenness of that punishment which the scriptures tells us divine justice will inflict on impenitent sinners'.[30] Even when making his excuses, Henry Howard succeeded in suggesting that he was more sinned against than sinning, and possibly Chapuys was not too far off the mark when he noted that the wayward but haughty Earl was not only Lutheran in religion but 'also French in his living'.

Fortunately for Surrey, the King accepted his behaviour as more French than Lutheran, and by the middle of May he was at liberty, seeking action more pleasing to his sovereign. In July he was permitted to join the English contingent at the siege of Landrécy, thereby acquiring the secrets of war from the hands of the Emperor himself. Howard doubtless learned a great deal, and the English commander was lavish in his praise, but the Earl was also up to his usual tricks: if he wasn't throwing stones in the name of religion, he was risking his life by deliberately exposing himself to French cannon-fire in the name of chivalry.[31] The same infantilism was exhibited the following year before the walls of Montreuil where his father's army was bogged down in flooded trenches and logistical inefficiency. He grew frantic with the delays, pettiness and discomforts of siege warfare, and nearly got himself killed storming the Abbeville gate in an attempt to end the frustration by a single spectacular assault.[32] Finally, late in September 1545 his great moment came; he was appointed the King's Lieutenant on land and sea in charge of the defence of Boulogne. Henry had been vastly impressed by Howard's martial zeal and heroic posturing, but the cautious Principal Secretary was not, and prudently reminded Surrey that he was both an earl and the King's Lieutenant General and that he should not expose himself to unnecessary danger. Paget was too politic not to wish the new commander well and concluded by assuring Surrey that the 'wise and happy proceeding' expected of him would shortly be realized, considering his 'grace, courage, knowledge of war, liberality and good luck'.[33]

Alas, the Earl of Surrey was neither lucky nor gracious. He antagonized the Privy Council by melodramatic accounts of his feats at Boulogne which encouraged Henry in his determination to continue the war, and he exposed his command to the accusation of treasonous misappropriation of supplies and general inefficiency.[34] Then early in January 1546 he met with what chivalric society could only judge to be a serious defeat. Just when victory, in an engagement against the French outside the walls of Boulogne, seemed certain, his troops bolted, leaving their captains to be cut down by enemy fire. It was scarcely a total rout. The cavalry won a spectacular victory, and strategically the engagement might even be accounted a success, but by the standards of Surrey's world it was a disaster; fourteen English captains died and English emblems were captured. In his frenzy, the Earl dramatically called upon his officers to 'stick their swords through his guts and make him forget the day'. Later he tried to make the best of it, pointing out that 'there was loss and victory on both sides' and placing the blame squarely on the shoulders of the common soldier. 'We assure your Majesty there was no default in the rulers, nor lack of courage to be given them, but a humour that sometime reigneth in Englishmen.'[35] One of those Englishmen had his own unflattering explanation: defeat had come 'chiefly because of the Earl their leader, whose head and heart were swollen with pride, arrogance and empty confidence in his own reasoning bravery'.[36]

Henry Tudor did not take kindly to failure, especially when his honour was touched; but for a time the magic surrounding the Earl's life still held, and Paget, that master of practices, wrote soothingly that the King, being 'a prince of wisdom', knew full well that he 'who plays at a game of chance must sometimes lose'.[37] It was a measure of the Principal Secretary's finesse as well as of Surrey's political potentialities that Sir William should have sought to deflect Henry's wrath and that a month and a half later, when he sent the distasteful news that my Lord of Hertford was to replace the Earl at Boulogne, he should have offered his friendship, urging Surrey to curb his pride, leave his post gracefully and seek a lesser position where he might renew his honour. 'If it please you', he concluded 'to use me as a means to his Majesty, I trust so to set forth the matter to his Majesty as he shall take the same in gracious part and be content to appoint you to such a place as may best stand with your honour. And this counsel I write unto you as one that would you well ... '[38] Had a stiff-necked and insolent nobleman, in whose aristocratic veins coursed a dangerous quantity of Plantagenet blood, been able to humble his pride for the sake of political convenience and ally himself to a mere parvenu, Surrey would have fulfilled at least one of Sir John Mason's prescriptions for political success. He would have been intimate with the most exact lawyer and ablest favourite at court. Unfortunately he failed to grasp until too late the crucial fact that Sir William Paget, despite his doubtful ancestry, was the brains behind the succession. This point, however, did not escape the more astute Earl of Hertford.

Edward Seymour, Earl of Hertford, was blessed with a multitude of advantages. He was in tune with the mild Protestant breezes which blew at court, but like Mr Mason he was 'so moderate that all thought him their own'. He was an excellent soldier—even old Norfolk had thought him the only man fit to command in the north—and supremely fortunate at war, for not only did he personally lead two highly successful raids into Scotland, but handsome victories came flooding in during his administration. Twenty-four days after he replaced Norfolk as commander of the King's armies in the north came the unexpected triumph of Solway Moss, and a week after taking temporary command of Guisnes and Boulogne in January 1545 a massive French attack was brilliantly thrown back.[39] But the Earl's most useful advantage was his friendship with Sir William Paget. Seymour was neither a gracious nor a popular courtier, and almost from the moment that he took command in the north Wriothesley scolded him for his lack of charity and his efforts to shift the blame to Norfolk when the fault lay with both men.[40] Five months later, despite the Earl's successes in Scotland, Paget felt obliged to deliver a short sermon on political tact. 'I would ... if you fortune to find things amiss ... you should rather amend them ... than to signify hither that they be amiss.' Such 'advertisements' offended his friends at court and hurt the Earl's reputation. Then Sir William added a cogent postscript: 'Your lordship shall do well to salute now and then, with a word or two in a letter my Lord of Suffolk and my Lord Wriothesley and such others, as you shall think good; forgetting not Mr Denney.'[41]

Even before he left court for the northern counties, Seymour had wisely promised to accept with a good heart whatever the Principal Secretary wrote, for of all men Mr Paget was the minister who knew best how to set matters before the King. Hertford never did develop real political acumen, and in the next reign Paget was to deliver a far sharper warning about his friend's ineptness and remind him that he had once promised 'to follow mine advice in all your proceedings more than any other man';[42] but while the old King lived the Earl was thankful and tractable, and a solid political and personal friendship developed between the two men.[43] Neither minister could do without the other: Paget held absolute control over the sovereign's closet and Hertford had the indispensable blood link with the young prince. There was no other man, as Chapuys observed, better fit by age, birth or military experience to govern in the name of a boy king.[44] Stephen Gardiner had the most incisive mind of all but also the most biting tongue, and he was far too ready to 'nip a man' for his faith.[45] Moreover, he was a bishop, an office detested by many. Lord Chancellor Wriothesley was clever and ingratiating but essentially a follower, friendly to both sides but trusted by almost nobody and making up in industry what he lacked in social standing.[46] Norfolk was too old, too grumbling and too versatile to be relied upon. John Dudley, Lord Lisle, was not a man who inspired confidence, especially in the art of politics, and he confessed that he found the problems of war easier to solve than those of peace.[47] Finally Surrey, for all his brilliance and social standing, was unable to divorce politics from family megalomania.

As for the Principal Secretary, he had every political virtue save the cardinal one. He was flexible without being an opportunist, cautious without being a cipher, popular without being a sycophant, generally correct without saying 'I told you so.' He 'never loved extremes' or precipitant actions, could joke at his own expense, baffled everybody as to the true nature of his religious beliefs and was able to manage his lonely and unapproachable sovereign during those last desperate months.[48] In fact, he alone of all the King's councillors secured his economic future before, not after, Henry died. For his 'special good service' he paid only £6,040 for estates worth £10,320, a handsome reward which he prudently arranged to have verified by private Act of Parliament. Sir William was strategically placed, for he saw to it that his parliamentary bill received the royal signature within hours of his master's death by means of that useful instrument, the dry stamp kept by his three good friends Messrs Denney, Clerk and Gate.[49] As Surrey spitefully remarked, however, Paget for all his talents was a 'catchpole' and a civilian, who could never hope to stand *in loco parentis* to a king.[50] Only the young Prince's uncle, the Earl of Hertford, could aspire to such a distinction, and Sir William was content to leave the limelight to his friend and political pupil.

The shifting alliances which emerged during the twilight of the King's life were shy affairs, tentative agreements based more on personality, propinquity and profit than on ideology. Lisle, Hertford and Paget co-operated, wrote friendly, gossipy letters and did one another little favours,[51] but there were always other pressures and associations which transcended politics. Paget, an Imperialist, was closer to Gardiner in foreign policy than to Hertford or Lisle, who preferred the French. Wriothesley, Paget and Winchester were doves, while Lisle, Surrey, Norfolk and Hertford were hawks by instinct if not always by policy. Then there were family ties. Wriothesley and Gardiner were related by marriage; so also were Sir Anthony Browne and the Suffolk family. The Queen during the years of her ascendancy was able to build up a profitable family entourage around the King: her brother was created Earl of Essex and a Privy Councillor, both her brother-in-law and the husband of her close friend, Elizabeth Billingham, were appointed to the Privy Chamber, her uncle Lord William Parr was made chamberlain of her household, Mistress Billingham became mother of her maids, and her sister Lady Herbert, her stepdaughter Margaret Neville and her cousin Lady Lane all found positions in her chamber. The predominant cohesive force, however, was not family affection or religious creed, but political survival as the old King's ministers prepared for the new reign, and Van der Delft correctly diagnosed English politics: self-interest and fear held men together.[52]

All was focused on the old man, and the moths of politics had no choice but to flutter about the flame, endure the heat while it lasted, and protect themselves as best they could from the fire. As the flame spluttered and flared, agitation increased and tempers blazed, each councillor fearful that his enemy might indeed blind the King's 'eyes with mists' and slander. There was a long back-log of enmity to be forgiven or revenged. The Seymour brothers were on bad terms with almost everybody except possibly the tolerant Principal Secretary. Not only did Hertford irritate the Lord Chancellor by tactless criticism of the Duke of Norfolk's doubtful organizational abilities and exacerbate the friction between military and civilian by seeking to blame Bishop Gardiner for the breakdown of war supplies, but in March 1544 he also clashed violently with John Russell, the Lord Privy Seal, for his failure to advance Hertford's economic interests with the King.[53] The Earl wrote that Russell bore him 'malice or grudge', and he growled that he would 'rather have an open enemy than a feigned friend'. In his turn the Lord Privy Seal thought Hertford's letter insufferably arrogant and 'princely written', and it took all Paget's tact and Wriothesley's attention to smooth over the quarrel. As for Sir Thomas Seymour, his holier-than-thou attitude towards the Earl of Surrey's imprisonment for breaking windows and eating meat during Lent was scarcely designed to ease the strain between the Seymour and Howard families. Sanctimoniously, Sir Thomas advised a harsher punishment, arguing that 'a secret and unobserved contempt of the law is a close undermining of authority' and that 'liberty knows no restraint, no limit, when winked at'.[54] If the Seymour brothers, whom Surrey despised as disgusting caterpillars of the commonwealth, were actually preaching this kind of righteousness at the Earl's expense, possibly Henry Howard had cause for resentment.

It was not long before the foreign ambassadors were commenting on the atmosphere of growing anxiety. Odet de Selve complained about the spiralling cost of espionage. He was unable to ferret out information, for everyone was in a state of panic lest he be accused of treason if found speaking to the Frenchman. Not even great quantities of gold could unlock fearful tongues, and de Selve warned that 'there is no certainty which way the English will take'. The Ambassador was rarely in agreement with his Imperial confrère, but on the mutability of Tudor politics they were in perfect accord. Van der Delft reported that affairs 'change almost daily', and the Frenchman exclaimed that fickleness was an English characteristic.[55] As the autumn days shortened so also did tempers, and factional rivalry erupted into harsh words and violent acts. Lord Admiral Lisle flared up against the Bishop of Winchester, striking him 'in full council meeting', and was expelled from court for most of October. Hertford had 'violent and injurious words' with the Lord Chancellor; Bishop Tunstal quarrelled with the Principal Secretary over the sale of ecclesiastical lands; and Surrey lashed out against Lisle, used insulting language towards Sir Richard Riche, and announced that my Lord of Hertford 'should smart' for replacing him in France.[56]

In an environment where it was high treason to 'imagine' the King's death but impossible not to do so, and where men lived by Sir Ralph Sadler's thoughtful dictum never to communicate a secret to two, Henry's ministers walked a tight-rope between doing too little and being forgotten by their master or doing too much and arousing the suspicions of a sovereign well aware of the whispering and bickering going on behind his back.[57] Successful intrigue must by definition remain hidden, and precisely what the Seymours and their friends were conspiring can only be surmised, but Chapuys was convinced that they had 'plans to obtain the government of the prince'. Those plans consisted largely of trying to discredit their opponents, monopolize the remaining hours left to the King, and persuade him to indicate by some signal honour that he regarded the Earl of Hertford as the only man of 'fit age and ability' to rule in his stead.[58]

In the first two designs the Seymours were supremely successful. Surrey was ultimately destroyed by his own folly, but the nails of his coffin were systematically driven in by a working alliance between Hertford, Wriothesley and Paget. United by the newness of their pedigrees, they set about ruining a nobleman who would just as surely have destroyed them had he managed to secure control of the regency. War, the King's sickness and his restlessness all played into Hertford's hands, for as the monarch mused more and more about revenge on Scotland, dreamt of leading his troops in person against that thankless race, and spoke of past victories and future campaigns, the men to whom he turned were the warriors, especially Hertford and Lisle whose military reputations were at their height. The previous March when Henry had been critically ill, as now he so often was, he chose to pass his days at cards with Lord Admiral Lisle. By September the Imperial Ambassador was deeply disturbed at the constant presence of Seymour sympathizers about the King; and during the autumn and early winter when Henry hauled his great body in a restless odyssey between Hampton Court, Guildford, Windsor, Oatland and London, the civilians—Wriothesley and Gardiner—were left behind, while Hertford, Lisle, Russell, Browne and, of course, Mr Secretary Paget commanded the all-important access to a sovereign who demanded that 'such as came now to court' be 'specially sent for'.[59]

Where Hertford failed was in shaping his sovereign's mind, for to the very end Henry retained his independence. Whatever hopes Edward Seymour may have had that his master would name him governor of the young prince and present him with a dukedom were thwarted by the Lord Chancellor, who later claimed he had argued Henry out of such an idea.[60] Not even Sir Thomas Seymour's appointment to the Privy Council on January 23rd, four days before the old King died, was much consolation, for, if we are to believe Lord Lisle, Henry, 'being on his deathbed, and hearing his [Seymour's] name among those elected to the council, cried out "No, no," though his breath was failing him', and only Hertford's pleading had persuaded him.[61] The Seymour brothers are a perplexing lot: the Earl so naively generous in his social theories yet so petty and tyrannical in his political behaviour; Sir Thomas so Surrey-like in the violence of his ambitions and easily wounded pride; and Henry, the only brother to escape the axe, of whom nothing at all is known. Under their old master, Edward and Thomas had co-operated, but the younger was always resentful of the elder's fame and title, and his rancour exploded in the new reign when his brother was created Lord Protector and governor of the young King. He furiously argued that one uncle should not hold both positions and he claimed that such had not been Henry's intention.[62] Sir Thomas was never one for moderate policies or diplomatic phrases, and the instant the old monarch died he was all for packing the Lord Chancellor and the Princess Mary off to the Tower.[63] Possibly it was the sheerest luck and simply a mark of his inferior political status that while Henry still lived, Thomas Seymour's furious temper did not land him, with Henry Howard, upon the execution block.

Howard's intriguing is the better documented for having failed but no less mystifying for having been exposed. The entire enterprise has most of the attributes of a thriller replete with international espionage, heraldic riddles, hidden pictures and a desperate escape from the Tower down a Jacob's-ladder, but, despite imaginative frills, the story seems to be essentially true. Without a doubt Surrey and Norfolk were 'imagining' the King's death, a risky undertaking at best and fatal when conceived by a man who was pathologically incapable of controlling his temper or keeping his mouth shut. At no time did father and son work as a team, for the Duke wasted little love on the Earl's chivalric bragging or the religious company he kept. Old Thomas Howard never made any bones about his own religious tastes: he did exactly what the King his master ordered. He distrusted anything un-English, including the papacy, but he thoroughly disliked humanistic reformers and babbling Bible-readers.[64] Of the two men, the father was less dangerous than the son. He was old, his military reputation had been smashed by chronic complaining and ineptitude in Scotland and France, he had antagon-ized both friend and foe on the Council by attempting to go behind their backs directly to the sovereign, and, as he bitterly observed, his enemies had been successful in barring him from the 'privy privy council'. Like Gardiner and Wriothesley, no place was reserved for him beside his monarch's bed, and he felt himself to be highly vul-nerable, for, he said, the King did not love him because he was too popular in the shires.[65]

The times were critical and the Duke's future uncertain, but Nor-folk was a master of political survival. He had lived to see Wolsey and Cromwell destroyed; he had extricated himself from the 'abominable deeds' committed by his two nieces; and he had managed to profit from the calamities that had beset his fellow peers. Now that the King was 'sickly and cannot long endure', it behoved the Duke to mend his political fences and bend with the wind. For all his hereditary titles, Mowbray ancestry and 204 great horses, 88 oxen, 115 steers, 407 sheep and 420 hogs which lived upon his immense estates,[66] Thomas Howard could not compete with the political strength of the Seymours and he knew it. His methods, however, were the opposite of his son's: 'if you can't beat them, join them,' and during the spring of 1546 he asked Henry's permission for a series of weddings to link Howard and Seymour children. His daughter, the widow of the King's illegitimate son, Henry Fitzroy, Duke of Richmond, was to marry Sir Thomas Seymour, and a bevy of Nor-folk's grandsons were to wed Hertford's daughters.[67] This amicable proposal seems to have been agreeable to nearly everybody except Surrey, who adamantly refused to permit his sons to degrade them-selves by taking Seymour wives.

If the documents are to be credited, the Earl preferred methods less demeaning than marriages of convenience to first-generation political upstarts in order to secure his position at court. He was socially disgusted and politically outraged at the idea of such con-nubial misalliances, and suggested that his sister, whose widowed reputation was not without its scandal, would be more useful as the King's concubine than as Sir Thomas's wife. Chapuys had been quite right: Surrey was exceedingly French in his ways, and his crude advice to the Duchess was that she use her proposed marriage to Seymour as a pretext to charm her sovereign, and 'thus, by length of time, it is possible the King should take such a fantasy unto you that you shall be able to govern like Madame d'Estampes' in France. Henry Howard's cavalier handling of his sister's virtue, doubtful though that may have been, did nothing to promote sibling affection, and the Duchess furiously replied that she would rather her entire family should perish and would 'cut her own throat [rather] than consent to such a villainy'.[68]

It seems that the Duchess of Richmond did in fact take her brother's advice and influence the King, but not exactly as he sug-gested, for it is told that she went to Henry's privy chamber and revealed to him the secret of her brother's treasonous armorial pre-tensions.[69] Mary of Richmond was quite capable of betraying her brother, but whether she did so is immaterial; Surrey's heraldic boasts were known to many besides his sister. The Earl scorned his father's reticence and political dealings, but he was even more vulnerable than the Duke because more than Mowbray blood coursed in his veins. He inherited all the instability and emotionalism of his mother's family along with her Plantagenet blood. Elizabeth Stafford, who quarrelled so frantically with her husband that he had to sit on her till she spat blood, was the daughter of the last Duke of Buckingham, executed in 1522 largely because he was a direct male descendant of that source of so much genealogical and dynastic confusion—Edward III. Surrey was something more than the heir to the highest-ranking title in the kingdom; he was regarded by many as a prince in his own right. Only three years before, in 1543, the Council had suspiciously probed into the meaning of London gossip which referred to him as a 'prince' and claimed that 'if ought came at the King and my lord Prince [but good], he would be king after his father'.[70]

Unfortunately, Henry Howard turned what might have been a political asset equal to Hertford's avuncular relation to Prince Edward into his greatest peril. He could not refrain from dramatizing the distinction between his own pedigree and the common ancestry of the Seymours. In displaying the arms of Edward the Confessor joined with those of his Mowbray forefathers he advertised for all to see that the Howards had a claim to the throne equal to that of the Tudors themselves. Such pretensions would have come to the King's attention regardless of the Duchess of Richmond's visit, for Surrey was a master at making enemies. Hertford and Lisle he insulted as parvenus. Russell, Browne, Gardiner and Wriothesley he disliked for their part in his interrogation during his sojourn in the Fleet after the stone-throwing episode of 1543. He sorely irritated the doves within the Council by his warlike letters to the King during the Boulogne campaign; he was barely on speaking terms with his sister or his father's mistress; and he ended up antagonizing his good friend George Blagge by suggesting that Norfolk was the man most meet to rule the Prince[17]. It was scarcely astute to think that a gentleman who regarded the Catholic mass as a piece of superstitious nonsense would welcome the prospect of the conservative Duke of Norfolk as lord protector of the realm, and in no uncertain terms Blagge told his friend that he would thrust his dagger into him rather than see the government in the hands of either Surrey or his father. The Earl snapped back that he was 'very hasty and that God sent a shrewd cow short horns'. Blagge's reply was prophetic: 'Yea, my lord, and I trust your horns also shall be kept so short as you shall not be able to do any hurt with them.'[72]

This conversation took place during the spring of 1546 and by the following autumn Surrey's family pride was ready for cropping, horns, neck and all. During the summer he indulged his heraldic imagination, decorating his new palace at Mount Surrey with escutcheons, and designing a badge which prominently displayed the letters H and R on either side of a broken pedestal with the royal arms at the top and the Howard arms at the base. Was it, as the Earl later maintained, a reference to the royal displeasure which he felt to be crushing his house, the H and the R standing for *Hereditas Restat* because he had nothing left but his family inheritance on which to stand; or was it, as the government argued, treason, the H and the R standing for Henricus Rex, the broken pillar signifying a ruined commonwealth destroyed by the Tudors but re-established in the end by the Howards? Not even a Tudor jury could be persuaded that such heraldic fantasy was tantamount to secret treason. What they did find, however, was evidence of 'conspiracy of murder'.[73]

Exactly what was going on in 'the busy head of the father and the pride of the son' is obscure. It was certainly not a carefully laid plot, as the government gave out, to murder the Council, depose the monarch, seize the young Prince 'with the intention of subsequently treating him like his father, and take possession of the kingdom'.[74] On the other hand, there was more than enough circumstantial evidence to make any Tudor jury suspect the worst. When the King was desperately ill in November and everybody thought he was dying, Surrey had acted in a way which might give any councillor cause for thought. He had announced that his malice reached to the very top of the government, trusting some day to make them all 'very small'.[75] That the Earl actually contemplated a coup d'état, as his enemies claimed, is doubtful, but there is evidence to suggest that he was distributing high offices of state in anticipation of the King's death, and that he sought, somewhat belatedly, to lure Mr Secretary Paget away from his political friends by offering him the Lord Chancellorship.[76]

Henry did not die, which was fatal for the Howards, and on December 1st the axe discreetly but efficiently fell. Surrey was at Westminster Palace, and on direct orders from the throne he was quietly arrested as he came out from dinner. Scarcely a courtier was aware that he had been whisked off to the house of the Lord Chancellor for intensive questioning. Twelve days later the velvet gloves were laid aside and the Earl was publicly paraded through the streets of London, a prisoner bound for the Tower, where his father was already imprisoned.[77] Every imaginable political facet was then probed. What had Surrey meant by offering his sister to be the King's concubine? Had he ever defamed the King's Council? Had he considered fleeing the realm? Had he secretly sought to surrender Boulogne to the French? Had he thought himself ill treated by the

King after his defeat outside the city? What had he written to his father at the time of the King's sickness? Had he been in secret correspondence with Cardinal Pole? Had he planned to call in Imperial troops to help in his coup d'état and had he an understanding with the Emperor dating back to their meeting before the walls of Landrécy? And what about his heraldic display? What had he meant by it? How long had he borne such royal arms? By what authority did he do so? And most sinister of all, why did he 'bear them at this time more than ... at other times before'? What plans had he for the Prince and why did he think his father best suited to govern a young king? What degree did he take himself to be within the realm and did he regard himself to be a 'true subject'?[78] And so it went on and on, with the father's interrogation added to that of his son: What about the Duke's clandestine meetings with the French Ambassador? Had he known about a secret cipher? Had he been in treasonous intercourse with the Pope five years before when Gardiner and Henry Knyvet had been inquiring into the possibility of a *rapprochement* with Rome through the Emperor's good graces?[79]

Clearly the government was searching for a conspiracy, a pattern, and the Lord Chancellor jotted down some varied but suggestive notes to jog his memory. Nothing was too obscure, nothing too coincidental to warrant a place in his memorandum.[80] Sir Henry Knyvet's death in France the previous August was carefully noted and joined to 'my lord of S. dissembling'. Thomas Clere, who had died saving Surrey's life, was mentioned and so was 'Dr Butts and the matter of Mr Denney'. Then followed the mysterious remarks 'that Mr P. should be chancellor of England' and '400 marks every bishop'. Richard Fulmerston and Thomas Hussey, Howard family retainers, and 'a packet of letters to the duke' did not escape notice, nor did 'my lord of Surrey's pride and his gown of gold'. Stephen Gardiner's priory of St Mary Overey came under scrutiny. Surrey's street-brawling was studied as well as his dangerous statement: 'They will let me alone as long as my father lives and after, I shall be well enough.' And finally came the most baffling notation of all: 'things in common. Paget, Hertford, [lord] Admiral, Denney'. What, besides their inferior blood, the Lord Chancellor, or for that matter Surrey, thought the men had in common is impossible to say, but whatever it was, all the evidence had to be submitted to the King who was said to be 'much perplexed' by the entire affair. He had a right to be, and he gave the matter his devastating editorial attention.[81]

During the interrogation Henry had again been desperately ill, this time suffering thirty hours of fever, but on December 24th he recovered sufficiently to incarcerate himself in his closet with three or four of his councillors and privy gentlemen and personally weigh the Earl's treason. With his own hands he annotated the legal and heraldic charges, and he obviously enjoyed himself hugely. There was no loss of control, only the aggravated display of his worst characteristics—pedantry and suspicion—and the absolute conviction that he was 'too old to allow himself to be governed' by anybody. As usual, he wanted the argument presented in every particular, no matter how unpleasant the details might be, and after carefully editing the evidence he added the crucial question: 'How is this man's intent to be judged?' There was no doubt in the King's mind as to the answer, and he settled down to rewriting the main case against the Earl. Where the Council had been satisfied to say: 'If a man compassing to govern the King should for that purpose advise his daughter or sister to become his harlot what this importeth,' Henry had redundantly inserted: 'If a man compassing with himself to govern the realm do actually go about to rule the King and should for that purpose advise his daughter or sister to become his harlot thinking thereby to bring it to pass and so would rule both father and son, as by this next article doth more appear: what this importeth.' Then followed a brutal summary of the evidence against Surrey, heavily annotated by Henry himself:

If a man say these words, 'If the King die, who should have the rule of the Prince, but my father, or I,' what it importeth.

The depraving of the King's Council.

If a man shall say these words of a [nobleman] or woman of the Realm, 'If the K[ing] were dead, I should shortly shut him up'; what it importeth.

If a man, provoked and compelled by his duty of allegiance, shall declare such matter as he heareth touching the King, and shall after be continually threatened by the per[son] accused, to be killed or hurt for it; [what] it importeth.

If a man take upon him to use [liberties] in his Lordship, or to keep pleas [or to make] himself free warren in his groun[ds, without] licence; what it importeth.

If a subject presume without li[cence to] give arms to strangers; what it imp[orteth].[82]

What indeed did it import? Henry gave his unequivocal answer less than a month later, when on January 13th Henry Howard was tried in an ordeal lasting eight hours. Such was the magic of the Earl's name and the magnificent insolence of his defence—which rested on the single assertion that a true nobleman would never lie but that the Hertfords, Pagets and Lisles of this world would condemn their fathers for a piece of gold because they lacked honour—that the jury hesitated, and for five hours debated whether blood was thicker than the evidence. The Principal Secretary had been called a 'catchpole', and he waited to hear the decision; at ten o'clock he slipped away, it was said, to seek his master's advice. An hour later he was back and a verdict was immediately brought in: 'Guilty and he should die.'[83] The outcome was no surprise; only the hesitation of the jury was remarkable, for Surrey, like his cousin Catherine Howard, was guilty on the basis of intent. As Sir Thomas More himself had once said, 'a deliberate design to commit a crime is equal to the fact itself'.[84]

If heraldic presumption and wild words had not been sufficient to prove evil intent, there was the matter of Surrey's effort to escape before the trial; innocent men, it was pointed out, should have nothing to fear. Howard's room in the Tower overlooked the river and his privy was a shaft which was filled with water except at extremely low tide. The Earl arranged with a trusted servant to have a boat on the Thames at midnight when the tide was out, planning to slip down the shaft while his guards were on their rounds. Unfortunately he was caught half-way down. It was not only a humiliating position but also manifest evidence of guilt, and when Lord Lisle, during the trial, asked him, if he were innocent, why had he sought to escape, Surrey's answer compounded his treason. 'I tried to break out', he savagely said, 'to prevent myself coming to the pass in which I now stand ... They always find the fallen guilty.'[85] Only an arrogant and malicious heart would have ever suggested that the King's law was fixed or that innocent men could be found guilty.

When Henry Howard broke he shattered like fine crystal into a thousand pieces. He shouted that he knew his sovereign wanted 'to get rid of all noble blood around him and to employ none but low people', and as they led him back to the Tower with the edge of the axe turned towards him, he continued to rant against the 'conjured league' which had destroyed him.[86] Execution came on January 19th; he was marched to the scaffold to learn that 'one had a little pain in the head and heart, then all is over'. The son broke, but versatile old Norfolk was not so easily destroyed. He bent; he ate humble pie; he pleaded for his life; and he confessed that he had known and concealed the Earl's treason and had 'given occasion that His

Highness might be disturbed, destroyed and interrupted in fame, body and title'.[87] In the end he was attainted and sentenced to die, but even in defeat the Duke found means to disappoint his foes, for he wrote to Henry suggesting that his estates and offices be reserved for the young Prince and his forthcoming creation as Prince of Wales and not be divided among his enemies.[88] Norfolk's attainder, which was signed at the last minute by dry stamp on January 27th, 1547, confiscated everything, even his mistress's beads, buttons, girdles and pearls which were carefully inventoried.[89] Henry always liked treason handled methodically and accurately, but what fate the King had in mind for the old Duke is anything but certain. Court gossip was divided, one group opting for the theory that Norfolk's execution had been set for January 28th and only the monarch's death saved his life. The other held to the theory that Henry would have pardoned a man who so humbly confessed his faults and begged forgiveness, and years later it was hinted that the Hertford faction, not the sovereign, who was already past caring, had affixed the royal signature to the attainder.[90]

If Hertford and Paget really did arrange that Norfolk's attainder receive their master's signature by dry stamp, possibly Henry, whose 'infantile omnipotence' was divinely ordained, had cause to fear and detest the whispering behind his back. Less difficult men than the King would react neurotically to the inexorable contraction of power, and the man who became his successor responded in much the same way. When Edward Seymour saw his authority falling away, he 'could scarcely see two councillors speaking together without suspicion', and Sir William Paget bitterly observed that power had not improved his friend's character, for 'of late your grace is grown into great choleric fashions wheresoever you are constrained in that which you conceived in your head'.[91] In Henry Tudor it aroused his worst instincts; the living were slipping from his grasp and temporizing for their own profit, and it became all the more important to devise means to hold his 'well-beloved' servants in subjugation to his will.

12

The 'Old Fox'

> He is a man to be marvelled at and has wonderful people
> about him ... He is an old fox, proud as the devil and
> accustomed to ruling.
>
> *Correspondance Politique de MM. de*
> *Castillon et de Marillac* (1537–42)

The sovereign whose ministers were busily preparing for his death
was disturbingly interested in matters of this world, not the next.
Illness consumed more and more of Henry's hours, but so did France,
Scotland and the promise of the new year. During the late summer of
1546 he put on a spectacular diplomatic display for the French
Admiral, who arrived in England to represent Francis I at the
official signing of the peace treaty. Young Prince Edward, his Latin
oration firmly fixed in his mind and accompanied by eighty gentlemen resplendent in cloth of gold, was sent on his first state mission
to meet the Admiral as he rode to Hampton Court. The French were
fêted and feasted in two new banqueting houses adorned with
tapestries wrought in gold and precious jewels, and sent home bur-
dened with gifts of horses, dogs, silver cups and an entire sideboard
of gold plate.[1] It was the least Henry could do, for in Paris his good
brother had been even more generous: in a loud voice and in the
presence of a multitude of bishops and at least six cardinals, that
Most Christian King of France had sworn eternal friendship with a
sovereign who in defiance of every papal anathema styled himself
Supreme Head of the Church of England and Ireland.[2] Much to
Henry Tudor's satisfaction, Henrician Anglicanism had finally come
of age; the King's conscience had been accepted as one of the ingredients of European diplomacy.

Farther afield, the King immersed himself in that web of rumours,
intrigues, half-truths and deceptions which passed for diplomacy
among the princes of Christendom. Dexterously he balanced
Lutheran Dr Hans Bruno and the suggestion of yet another alliance
with the Protestant princes of Germany against papist Guron
Bertang and Catholic efforts to seek a reconciliation between England

and Rome. When the Emperor began the disciplining of his disobedient subjects in Germany, Henry hinted at the possibility of a
diplomatic revolution whereby everybody would switch sides but,
like the Mad Hatter at his tea-party, only the English sovereign
would receive a clean cup and saucer. His proposal was to cut
Charles back to size by a Franco-English-German military alliance,
and in July 1546 Europe was rocked by a nicely timed rumour that
the English were ready to offer Boulogne and Calais to France in
return for the marriage of Mary Stuart to Prince Edward and the
virtual union of England and Scotland. Fernando de Gonzaga refused
to believe that Francis would ever give up his Scottish pistol aimed
at England's back door, and it is doubtless idle to speculate whether
Charles's military successes would ever have been sufficient to bring
those two dilapidated old rivals together, for the 'closer amity' and
'league defensive' of which Henry spoke on January 17th, 1547, died
with the King two weeks later.[3] Possibly Henry was up to his old
tricks, amusing himself by suggesting an Anglo-Protestant-French
alliance just to worry his Imperial nephew. Possibly he was putting
pressure on the Emperor to make him more tractable with English
merchants in Spain. Possibly he was entangling Francis in great
coils of diplomacy so that he would not 'slip away to the Emperor';
possibly, like the wise politic prince of Foxe's *Martyrology*, he was
trying to safeguard his kingdom against the day when a Catholic
Emperor might heed the Holy Father's urgent appeals to exterminate
heresy in England as well as in Germany; or possibly he was simply
seeking to neutralize France before once again waging war on Scotland.

Only the previous May, the King had announced his intention of
campaigning in person against his northern neighbour so lacking in
feudal respect and fealty.[4] That same month the assassination of
Cardinal Betoun, carefully arranged so as not to disturb the monarch's conscience, had opened up new vistas of diplomatic and
military intrigue. The Cardinal's body was hung from his castle
window, suspended by sheets tied to foot and wrist, and his murderer
invited the people to behold 'their god', a foolish prelate who had
defied the English King and had placed his trust in French gold and
papal interdicts.[5] Now that Francis I had sworn perpetual peace, the
time seemed ripe to renew the war in the north. Throughout the
autumn Henry made great preparations on land and sea, borrowing
on the Antwerp money-market, hiring foreign mercenaries, and
mustering an army rumoured to be between forty and sixty thousand
strong. By the second week in January both the Imperial and the
French Ambassadors were reporting that Henry, who had scarcely

two weeks to live, was set upon war, one commenting that the English were 'taking the Scottish war very much to heart', the other writing that the King was set upon war unless 'distracted by the ambassadors of the Protestant princes'. What de Selve could not fathom, however, was whether all this activity was really directed at the Scots or was a cover for further aggression against the French, and he warned his master that Henry was intensely irritated by new French fortifications across the river from Boulogne. Probably the French Ambassador had cause to suspect that the English had 'some evil fantasy of surprising us somewhere', for Henry secretly ordered the destruction of the French bastion, and the last command he ever sent to his captains in Boulogne and Calais was to be particularly on their guard against both the Emperor and the French King.[6]

Henry was extraordinarily belligerent for a dying man; he was also supremely optimistic, ordering for his garden French trees and grafts which could not have borne fruit for another decade.[7] In fact, what emerges is not the picture of a careful ruler preparing his kingdom for a new reign but the image of an obstinate old man who had no intention whatsoever of dying on the prescribed date. The issue is a matter of organizational legerdemain: if the King's life is told in terms of its final conclusion on January 28th, 1547, then every earlier event is tainted by association and the eye sees only the tidy order of causation leading to death and a new monarch; if, however, the tale is reorganized so that death drops in unexpectedly, leaving ragged ends and upsetting a host of schemes, the atmosphere changes —life with all its meanness and confusion becomes the central theme.

It is easy enough to find rational purpose in Henry Tudor's decision to place his son's future in the hands of Hertford, Paget and Lisle in calculated preference to Norfolk and Bishop Gardiner, but his emotional outbreaks against Chancellor Wriothesley and his unexpected rage at the Bishop of Winchester scarcely fit the portrait of a sovereign deliberately purging his Council on the basis of a statesmanlike concern for tomorrow. Until almost the very end Winchester had been in high favour, and in mid-August the Imperial Ambassador spoke of Wriothesley, Paget and Gardiner as the King's chief advisers;[8] yet within two and a half months only the Secretary retained his master's confidence and both the Chancellor and the Bishop were in a state of near-panic. As early as Michaelmas Wriothesley sensed the danger and wrote Mr Secretary that no matter how hard he and his colleagues laboured, their efforts seemed 'to be otherwise taken than we trust we have or shall deserve'. By October there was no doubt about it; his interests and his office were in jeopardy. Again he communicated his fears to Sir William in the

hope that the King would relent: 'I shall have cause to be sorry in my
heart, during my life, if the favour of my most gracious master shall
so fail that ... he do not somewhat of his clemency temper it.'[9]

A month later Stephen Gardiner felt the lash of the King's displeasure. Possibly, as Foxe suggests, Henry was irrationally furious
that the Bishop should have helped persuade him to distrust his
wife's religious opinions; possibly, as the most vocal Imperialist on
the Council, he was a victim of the growing international tension
and emotionalism which followed in the wake of triumphant
Catholicism abroad; possibly, as the richest prelate in the kingdom,
he had spoken out too strongly against growing court sentiment to
nationalize the chantry lands and use the episcopal wealth of the
Church to finance the massive attack on Scotland which the King
was busily preparing for the spring; or possibly the difficulty was
neither diplomatic, nor religious, nor political, but was exactly what
Henry coldly stated it to be: Gardiner had been an unloving subject.[10]
The issue was the exchange of episcopal lands which Paget, Wriothesley and Sir Richard Riche had demanded of the Bishop at the King's
request. Gardiner had not actually refused, but he presumed upon
his sovereign's favour by insisting that he first discuss the matter
with Henry himself. When the King heard of this presumption, he
had some very unpleasant things to say, remarks which 'confusedly'
trickled back to Gardiner as word that his 'doings should not be
well taken' at court. Immediately he took pen to paper to apologize
for his boldness and beg his master to accept both his apologies and
the disputed estates in 'gracious part', and to permit him to come in
person to explain.[11]

Henry dictated his answer on December 4th, and it was a marvellous balance of cold disdain and sulky outrage to which he added
further insult by not bothering to sign it. Had 'your doings', he
wrote, 'been agreeable to such fair words as ye have now written ...
neither you should have cause to write this excuse nor we any occasion to answer the same. And we cannot but marvel at this part of
your letter, that you never said nay to any request made unto you
for those lands, considering that this matter ... [was] debated with
you as well by our Chancellor and Secretary as also by the Chancellor
of our Court of Augmentations, both jointly and apart, [and] you
utterly refused to grow to any conformity in the same, saying that
you would make your answer to our own person: which we can be
well contented to receive, and will not deny you audience at any
meet time when you shall make suit to be heard ... [but] we must, in
the meantime, think that if the remembrance of our benefits towards
you had earnestly remained in your heart ... you would not have

been so precise in such a matter, wherein a great number of our subjects ... dealt both more lovingly and more friendly with us. And ... if you be yet disposed to show that conformity you write of, we see no cause why you should molest us any further therewith ... '[12]

It seems incredible that a simple matter of the exchange of land could have warranted the fury behind the King's words, and one instinctively looks for deeper and more weighty explanations for the abrupt slamming of the door in the face of a servant so experienced in discerning his master's nature and so in tune with his approach to religion. Surely Henry must have detected some basic deficiency in the Bishop's character, or sensed some danger to his son's succession, to warrant an anger which was still so intense at the end of the month that he absolutely refused to mention Gardiner in his will or name him to his son's council of regency. Yet Henry's own explanation, reported four years later when Hertford, Paget and the rest were industriously seeking to paint Stephen Gardiner as a dangerous security-risk whom the King had deliberately jettisoned for reasons of religious and political policy, only adds to the mystery. When Anthony Browne begged him to include the prelate in his will, Henry peremptorily cried out: 'Hold your peace! I remember him well enough, and of good purpose have left him out: for surely, if he were in my testament ... he would cumber you all, and you should never rule him, he is of so troublesome a nature. Marry, I myself could use him, and rule him to all manner of purposes as seemed good unto me; but so shall you never do.'[13] For those who wish to see a prince of foresight and prudence, the King's words are evidence of a secure and rational mind, concerned with the future and seeking to rule from beyond the grave; but it is equally possible to see only the angry, emotional phrases of a man who bore a grudge, was determined to 'show his absolute power and independence of everyone', and, as Lord Herbert of Cherbury noted, was suspicious and willing to think the worst on the basis of 'impressions privately given him by any court-whisperer'.[14]

How a man approaches death is immensely revealing; it is, after all, the last word to be said about his personality. Having flung off his many titles and dignities, the Emperor Charles, the evening before he left the Lowlands for his monastic tomb at Yuste, conversed late into the night with Vice-Chancellor Seld. As Seld rose to leave, Charles rang the bell for a servant to light the Chancellor out. No one came, and the Emperor sardonically commented on the mortality of power. See how soon, he said, 'they have found out that I am no longer master'. Then picking up the torch himself he ushered Seld out, saying: 'Let this be a monument to thee, dear Seld, of the

Emperor Charles, whom thou hast so often seen surrounded by the most brilliant court and victorious armies, and now seest alone, forsaken even by his menial servants; he whom thou hath served faithfully so many years, now takes the place of a servant in waiting on thee.'[15] True or not, the story is in character, as it would not have been with a Tudor king who never laughed at himself, never relaxed or set aside the mask of kingship and who all his life meant exactly what he said: 'I do not choose anyone to have it in his power to command me, nor will I ever suffer it.' Henry VIII would never be reduced to lighting his servants home.

At no time was the King more dangerous; had he been dying of syphilis or slipping into his dotage, it would have been safer for those who served and counselled him. As it was, he lived and governed as he always had, by the rule that 'fear begets obedience', and he spent his final days testing friend and foe alike for the hidden fear and malice in every heart. If it is possible to believe the knowledgeable Principal Secretary, Henry held the whip firmly even over his wilful Bishop of Winchester. It was not enough to banish Gardiner from his will or peevishly cut him out of the bequests presented to his good and faithful servants. There was also a 'certain writing touching the said Bishop' which the King ordered Paget to fetch and keep in a safe place so 'that he might have it when he called for it'.[16] The document dealt with some 'just and sore matter of old' which an ever-suspicious sovereign with almost total recall had never forgotten. Henry spoke the plain truth when he asserted that only he could rule the prelate 'to all manner of purposes as seemed good unto me'.[17] The King, however, was nothing if not just, and it was reported that another writing existed which was also safely stored away, for 'many men's names were gathered and enrolled together in a catalogue, and at that time accused unto the King by the Bishop of Winchester and other prelates'.[18] The sovereign who informed Sir William Paget that he 'opened his pleasure' to him alone, and then promptly told Messrs Denney and Herbert exactly 'what had passed between them', was quite capable of having two whips—one for Winchester and those suspected of papacy, another for Hertford and his more radical friends. There is a ring of truth in the story that towards the end not a single councillor dared advise him honestly or 'tell him his mind' for fear 'a snare had been laid for him'.[19] Paranoid suspicion gave birth to a thousand fears, until finally, though his servants continued to serve him, he was more isolated from the living than even the Emperor in his abdication.

Fear without hope leads straight to treason, and the King's control was neatly balanced by great expectations. He was lavish with promises but stingy with rewards, for a gift once given is irretrievable and its receiver no longer beholden. Expectations ran high, especially when Henry informed his Principal Secretary that the Howard estates would 'be liberally dispersed and given to divers noble men and others his Majesty's good servants'. Together the sovereign and the secretary devised who should be advanced in honour and rewarded with estates, and Sir William drew up a 'book' of such as his master 'did choose to advance', wherein, Paget later said, the King had determined among other creations to present Hertford with a dukedom, Lisle and Wriothesley with earldoms and Seymour and Riche with baronies. Then, on the Secretary's advice, Henry ordered Paget to 'tot upon each man's head' the Howard incomes, lordships and offices as an economical means of financing the new dignities and rewarding his loyal ministers. Hertford was to receive lands worth 1,000 marks a year, Seymour £300, Lisle £200, and Wriothesley had to make do with a beggarly £100. Paget thought the amounts far too little. Moreover, he noted that the King had forgotten the excellent Sir Anthony Denney and his 'painful service'; so the obliging monarch ordered Sir William to consult with his colleagues to discover the revenues each thought suitable to his new honour. In so doing, Henry opened Pandora's box: some were outraged that they had been passed over, others grieved that they had not received more, and almost everyone thought the lordships allotted them were too little.

Alas, a far greater disappointment was in store. When Paget returned to his master, he discovered that the King had decided, on the Duke of Norfolk's recommendation, to keep all of the Howard estates for himself and his son. The Secretary then tried to salvage the situation by urging his sovereign at least to agree upon the list of new titles and the yearly incomes to sustain them, and thereafter to worry about where the money was to come from, but Henry would not have even this. Praising his advisers as men whom he 'trusted and loved above all others', he began to stall, and said he 'must consider them more'. 'Divers devices' then were drawn up, but significantly not one was ever implemented. Instead, when the final list was settled upon, the King took the document, 'put it in his pooke of his nightgown' and told Paget that he could inform his friends of their expectations.[20] Nobody ever seems to have seen the list again. After Henry was dead Paget had to tell the entire story from memory, and on the strength of the Secretary's intimate knowledge those who survived to the end of the reign rewarded themselves with lands worth £107,712.[21]

There was only Paget's word for Henry's promised generosity.

Considering how little a King who disliked signing and loved his treasures had actually parted with, it seems most uncharacteristic that he had any intention of fulfilling those pledges. Except for the favoured Paget, no councillor or privy servant managed to extract important pecuniary favours from a master who was well aware of the power of the purse. Lord Russell and Dr Wendye managed annuities of £40 each; Sir Thomas Darcy of the Privy Chamber received a small yearly grant of £1 1s. 4d., the industrious Mr William Clerk who watched over the dry stamp was presented with a pension of £30, and Anthony Browne received lands with an annual rent of £36 2s. 0d., 5 cocks, 25 hens and 11 pounds of pepper. Lord William Parr, Philip Hobey, Sir William Herbert, Edward Billingham, Dr Owen and Messrs Cawerden and Gate received small estates on extremely favourable terms, and Anthony Denney, George Blagge, and Thomas Henneage latched on to highly profitable licences, but in all the cost was less than the King's generosity to Secretary Paget, and the Seymour brothers, despite Henry's grandiose promises and Paget's hard work, received nothing at all.[22]

Of all the weapons at the King's disposal with which to cudgel his servants, the cruellest but most effective was his last will and testament, for it united both fear and greed: dread of being excluded from the council of regency, and hope of a handsome legacy. The will stands at the heart of the story if only because it is the most mysterious and controversial document of those final days. It was revised on or shortly after December 26th, 1546; it clearly stated that 'we have signed it with our own hand, in our palace of Westminster the 30 day of December'; and it was witnessed by eleven members of the Privy Chamber.[23] There is, however, overwhelming presumptive evidence that Henry's testament was not in fact signed until almost a month later and bore not the King's signature but a dry stamp facsimile, for in the list of documents signed with the dry stamp by William Clerk in the presence of Messrs Denney and Gate during January 1547 is a most perplexing entry. Number 85 reads: 'Your Majesty's last Will and Testament bearing date at Westminster the thirty day of December last past, written in a book of paper, signed above in the beginning and beneath in the end, and sealed with the Signet in the presence of the Earl of Hertford, Mr Secretary Paget, Mr Denney and Mr Herbert, and also in the presence of certain other persons whose names are subscribed with their own hands as witnesses to the same. Which testament Your Majesty delivered then, in our sights, with your own hand, to the said Earl of Hertford, as your own deed, last will and testament, revoking and annulling all others ... ' The entire list is signed by William Clerk at the end, but to make it doubly certain that he knew the importance of what he was doing, he signed a second time beneath the 85th entry.[24] Despite the date of December 30th, there seems no doubt that during January Clerk technically forged the King's signature by affixing the dry stamp at the top and bottom. Moreover, the position of the 85th entry, placed as it is next to the last item on the list and located immediately above the Duke of Norfolk's attainder, which received the stamp on January 27th, suggests that the testament also was signed close to the hour of Henry's death.

The 85th entry is no mere historical riddle. It exploded into a red-hot, if somewhat theoretical, political issue a generation later, when the will became a source of considerable dynastic embarrassment to the proponents of the Stuart claim to the English throne, for in establishing the order of succession Henry signally failed to mention the descendants of his elder sister Margaret, the wife of James IV of Scotland. Instead, the succession jumped from Edward, Mary and Elizabeth to the Suffolk family, the children of the King's younger sister, Mary Duchess of Suffolk. Therefore it behoved the advocates of Mary Stuart to throw out the will, which they sought to do on the technical ground that the document had not been signed by Henry's own hand but by dry stamp. The highly respected Elizabethan lawyer, Edward Plowden, wrote categorically that he had heard Sir William Paget admit that the stamp had been used and that Sir Henry Nevell, one of the witnesses, could confirm the statement. Other Stuart advocates claimed that Sir William Clerk had sought and received under Mary a pardon for his technical forging of his master's signature.[25] Legally the type of signature—holograph or facsimile—made no difference, for no one, not even wily Winchester or those proficient legalists Wriothesley and Riche, questioned the validity of the document, and years later the Stuart party lost their argument when they took their case to court.[26] The mystery, however, is not whether the King literally signed with his own quill, but concerns two other matters involving Henry Tudor's character: the substance and therefore the purpose of the will, and the possibility that it was not signed until January 27th.

The contents of the testament have always embarrassed those who wish to place Henry on the side of progressive Protestantism and regard him as a far-sighted statesman. The document is not only exceedingly Catholic in its phraseology, but as a serious instrument of government to expedite his son's minority it is preposterous.[27] The King placed his soul squarely in the hands of 'the holy company of Heaven', called to God's attention the 'good deeds and charitable works' which he had done for 'the honour and pleasure' of the Lord, 'required and desired the blessed Virgin Mary' to pray for him, dutifully instructed his executors to give a thousand marks in alms to the deserving poor, and optimistically ordered masses to be said for the sake of his soul 'for ever perpetually'. Having arranged for everlasting life, Henry turned his attentions to more secular and political concerns. The succession was worked out in great detail. It covered every eventuality, patently ignoring both the Stuart and Douglas descendants of his elder sister Margaret and carefully barring the children of Mary and Elizabeth should either princess marry without the consent of his son's Council. Then he turned to the matter of Edward's minority and appointed sixteen of his own 'well-beloved' ministers to form a council of regency with full powers to govern in the name of a boy king who was commanded by his father never 'to change, molest, trouble nor disquiet' his legally appointed advisers. As usual the King could not leave well enough alone; not only did he emphasize the equality of each of his son's councillors but he also imposed upon them a rigid majority rule without creating any machinery by which the council could recruit new members. Since Edward could not come of age until he was eighteen, the personnel of the council would have to remain constant for almost a decade. Finally, to compound the constitutional confusion, he proceeded to name a second list of advisers to guide and assist his son's councillors, but left their function in studied vagueness.

As a realistic basis of sixteenth-century government the will was totally inadequate and utterly out of touch with prevailing political notions, which were authoritarian to the core and insisted that nature had decreed that there should always be a single head of state. If, as has been suggested, Henry sought to rule from the grave and forestall the ambitions of 'wicked uncles' who might seek to destroy his dynasty, his posthumous reign lasted scarcely a week.[28] Before the life was out of his body, plans were afoot to jettison the testament and promote the Earl of Hertford to the office of Lord Protector. Sir Anthony Browne was no admirer of the Earl or of his religious sympathies, but he voiced what was obviously the overwhelming sentiment of the Council when he agreed that a protectorate was 'both the surest kind of government and most fit for this commonwealth', and, despite the bitter political animosity within the Council, Hertford was unanimously elected Lord Protector within four days of Henry's demise.[29] If the old King really had believed that his will would be law and his dead hand could control the government of his son, he must have been bitterly disappointed, for the document itself fared no better than its provisions. One copy ended up in a basket of dirty linen and another, discovered years later among the effects of Bishop Tunstal, was dismissed as of no interest or importance.[30]

Under the circumstances it is extraordinary that an experienced and autocratic sovereign, wise in the realities of politics and aware of the adage 'Woe to the land where the king is a child,' should have foisted on to his son a structure of government almost guaranteed not to work. In fact, history is faced with two mysteries, not one: why the conflicting evidence over the signing of the will, and why the obvious inadequacies of its provisions? Neither riddle can be solved objectively, and the historian must again return to Henry's personality. If the predominant picture is that of a monarch systematically preparing for death, putting his affairs in order, rationally selecting his son's councillors on the basis of their religious sentiments and administrative qualities, screening out the disrupting influence of a Gardiner or a Surrey and guaranteeing a majority of religious reformers, and above all projecting his own fierce personality into the new reign, then the political testament with its awkward majority-rule and clumsy guarantees against 'wicked uncles' and over-mighty magnates becomes perfectly understandable and characteristic of a far-sighted prince.

Change the profile, imagine the old man sick but clinging to life, searching for fetters with which to hold the living to him, and the will emerges as something very different. Instead of a rather ineffectual excursion into political theory, it becomes an instrument of power politics and a sword to be held in readiness over the head of any councillor who failed to toe the line. It was a maxim of the century that the 'very day that the heir apparent is published, you may say, *Ecce rex alter Angliae*'.[31] The one thing Henry dared not do was to name his son's guardian; if he had, he would have appointed his own successor and signed his own political death-warrant.[32] He could not indicate to whom he was willing to bequeath his rule even though that authority was only *in loco parentis*, for fear that loyalty and control would gravitate to the power which held promise of the future. A monarch who knew his Malory as well as Henry did could not have failed to perceive the lesson of Arthur's failure to dominate his court. As the ageing hero lost control, fratricide destroyed the Round Table, and though no mirror of the past could have foretold the future tragedy of the Seymour brothers, Henry well knew the tensions, hatreds and jealousies which ebbed and flowed about his chamber. The sovereign who warned his Queen of the hatred harboured by his Lord Chancellor, probed the 'intent' of Surrey's heraldic claims, watched the unsatisfied greed of his councillors as they sought to plunder Norfolk's estates, flared out at the land-speculators and could distinguish between the good servant and the flatterer, was quite aware of the envy which consumed the younger Seymour. To have designated a Lord Protector would have endangered his entire Council as well as his own control. On the other hand, to name a council of 'well-beloved' equals and assign them handsome legacies was to make it brutally clear that their political futures depended on their good conduct today. So long as the testament remained unsigned, the King's servants lived in bondage to their own fears and expectations.

John Foxe tells the story of the revising of the will in a straightforward fashion. On the night of December 26th, Henry was feeling better and ordered Sir Anthony Denney to fetch his testament. Sir Anthony brought the wrong version, which the King immediately spotted, saying: 'That was not it, but there was another of a later making,' written three years before by Lord Wriothesley when he was Principal Secretary. The correct document was eventually located and Henry had it read to him and was amazed how out of date it had become. He thereupon announced that he was determined to name some 'whom, he said, he meant to have in, and some [who were] in, whom he meant to have out'.[33] Henry spent a considerable time culling the list of his son's councillors as well as the register of their advisers. He was enjoying himself immensely, and he made it painfully evident that a man's place in the testament was strictly conditional upon his obedience. When Sir Anthony Browne begged that Gardiner's eviction be reconsidered, the monarch crossly retorted: 'Have you not yet done' molesting 'me in this matter'? Then he silenced Sir Anthony once and for all by warning him: 'If you will not yet cease to trouble me, by the faith I owe unto God, I will surely dispatch thee out of my will also; and therefore let us hear no more of the matter.'[34] It was said that 'when the King took a fancy to anyone he carried it to extremes', and once an opinion had entered his head not all of his Council could dislodge it.[35] At this particular juncture he was thoroughly outraged with Gardiner and set upon destroying Surrey, and no one dared dissuade him.

There were other omissions from the will which are not so easily explained. Bishop Thirlby was dismissed as being too much like the irascible Bishop of Winchester; Secretary Petre received no bequest; nor did the King's old friend Sir Francis Bryan, or Dr Huycke, or, strangest of all, Sir Thomas Henneage, the chief gentleman of the King's Privy Chamber. Then there is the story of an unknown gentleman at whom the King 'made some stick' but eventually relented upon the united suit of the rest of the Council.[36] Whatever Henry's reasons for favouring or barring a man, they were based as much on emotion as on rational calculation. Moreover, they might be changed without warning. Henry declined to sign his will for exactly the same reasons that he never got around to fulfilling his promises about lands and titles. True, he was always 'loath to sign' and preferred to 'sleep and dream upon the matter and give an answer upon the morning'; but as long as the document was unsigned his ministers lived in a constant state of anticipation. The door stayed open; Gardiner was still a member of the Privy Council and had survived worse storms;[37] Norfolk's fate had not been settled; Thirlby might yet redeem himself; and, if the way were open for names to be added, they could also be removed.

As the days slipped by, Henry lived on, but so accustomed had his ministers become to their chains and so powerful was the magnetism which held them that there was no indecent haste, no drunken hopes to be done with the malicious old man who bedeviled their lives. Such behaviour might be expected in Paris, but not in Westminster where to the last moment Henry maintained his extraordinary hold over the imaginations of those who served him.

The French and Imperial Ambassadors saw the King on January 16th, and de Selve noted that he seemed 'now fairly well'. Three days later plans for the installation of young Edward as Prince of Wales were still being pushed,[38] and to the very end no one thought to bring the boy close to Westminster in expectation of his father's death. On the 23rd appeared the first sign that Henry was losing control when he gave up the battle to keep Sir Thomas Seymour off the Council and despite his cries of 'No, no,' Hertford had his way. By the 27th it was clear that death was near, and the Council ordered the closure of all ports within the kingdom. The King had waited too long; he could no longer sign his will even had he wished to do so, and his ministers were confronted with the appalling probability that he would die intestate. By the last day, though life remained, power had passed to the men of a new reign, and suddenly William Clerk and his dry stamp became the crucial instrument by which the living could speak for a dying sovereign. During those final hours, Mr Clerk was unusually busy. Not only were there a King's testament and a Duke's attainder to be signed but there was a small personal matter to attend to: a fat wardship for himself also received the dry stamp.[39] Subjects could now afford openly to 'temporize for their own profit'!

A facsimile signature was better than no signature, and Hertford and Paget did the best they could, arranging that Henry's hand should be made to deliver his last will and testament to the Earl as the only possible man to inherit his authority. The situation, nevertheless, was far from auspicious. It was little wonder that Hertford and Sir Anthony Browne were 'in some doubt' whether their powers were 'sufficient under the will', or that Sir William Paget considered how much of the testament it was necessary to publish, or that he and the Earl whispered together in the gallery, or finally that all the new councillors were so anxious to transfer the basis of their authority from the old King's will to letters patent issued by their new prince.[40] Henry's servants knew their master, and they must have realized that his testament was far more a reflection of his personality than a serious basis for future government. All the facets of Henry Tudor were focused on those twenty-eight pages of parchment: his love of pedantry and detail; his concern for conscience and his self-confident alliance with God; his ritualistic approach to religion; his emotional precipitousness; his innate caution and deep insecurity; his discomfort with final decisions and his dislike of signing; and above all his need to 'show his absolute power'.

So Henry died, refusing unto the end to consider that life was finished. When asked whether he desired a priest to ease the burden that weighted upon his Christian conscience, he answered as usual that he would 'take a little sleep' and then decide.[41] But it was later than he thought, for indifference and coma followed sleep, and Henry, whose sense of the dramatic so rarely failed him, drifted quietly and uncharacteristically into oblivion. Fiction demands something more appropriate, some gesture rich with meaning, but the dissolution of the human body is too clinical, the end of life too biological to conform to the requirements of imagination. The symbolic details—the dying handshake offered the faithful Cranmer, the defiant demand for a bowl of white wine, the cry: 'All is lost'—are later poetic additions.

The 'old fox' was gone; all that remained of that 'serene and invincible prince' was a cold and swollen carcase to be sponged, disembowelled, spiced, wrapped, labelled and coffined as quickly as possible. The dead remains were cast aside and in their place was fashioned a great wax effigy so like the late sovereign in all points that it almost appeared as if death had been cheated and Henry granted a few extra hours of life, for 'he seemed just as if he were alive'. But reality was already buried; fakery and history had taken over. A great hearse was devised nine storeys high and so unwieldly that the road from Westminster to Windsor had to be repaved and 'the noisome boughs' cut down ere the great vehicle, upon which a wax king sat in majestic state, could begin its final progress to Windsor Chapel.[42] It took over two weeks to paint the escutcheons of the monarch's ancestry and many marriages, build the canopied chariot, garnish the image with sceptre, orb and crown imperial and place upon the plaster leg a golden garter. An army at least a thousand strong attended upon the funeral march: two hundred and fifty paid mourners; the children, clerks and priests of the Chapel Royal; the Yeomen of the Guard dressed in black, three abreast, their halberds pointed to the ground; the King's nine youthful henchmen with their master, Sir Francis Bryan; the Privy Council; the twelve aldermen of the city of London; the foreign ambassadors; the heads and sergeants of the household and a host of others. It was a triumph of organization, perfectly timed and gorgeously appointed. As always, Henry's servants served him well; there were no embarrassing breakdowns, no unseemly behaviour, no shoddy showmanship. The magnificent idol and the still-vital memory of the King continued if only for a fortnight to rule from the grave. Eventually living memory receded but the image remained: the Bluff Prince Hal of romantic fiction, the Titan whose will had wrenched England from popery, the Bluebeard who went through six wives and spent his hours wenching and wining, the architect of an island kingdom unified and strong in its Protestant faith, and the sovereign of whom it had been said that he 'does not desire gold or gems or precious metals but virtue, glory, immortality'.[43] If immortality was Henry's goal, he achieved it in his own majestic fashion, for the King's fabled reputation is assured as long as there are men to dream, critics to condemn and historians to write. Apothecary, chirurgeon, wax-chandler, carpenter and painter had done their work well: the great wax image, so lifelike that it seemed to breathe the air of royalty, eventually became the man preserved in the imagination of history. In the meantime, reality had been decently interred in a great leaden chest and laid to rest on February 16th, 1547, in the floor of St George's Chapel. There it is best to leave that 'very rare spectacle of humanity' which once had contained multitudes and was judged 'the rarest man that lived in his time'.[44]

MANUSCRIPT CITATIONS AND ABBREVIATIONS

British Museum	B.M.
Cotton MSS	
Caligula E IV	Calig.
Cleopatra E IV, V, VI	Cleo.
Galba B X	
Titus B I, II, F III	
Vespasian C VII, XIV	Vesp.
Vitellius B X III, XXX	Vit.
Additional MSS	Add. MSS
Egerton MSS	
Hargrave MSS	
Harleian MSS	Harl. MSS
Lansdowne MSS	Lans. MSS
Royal MSS	
Sloane MSS	
Stowe MSS	
Public Record Office	P.R.O.
State Papers, Henry VIII	S.P. 1
Signature by Stamp	S.P. 4
Theological Tracts, Henry VIII	S.P. 6
State Papers, Domestic, Edward VI	S.P. 10
State Papers, Elizabeth I	S.P. 11
Royal Wills	E. 23
Treasury Receipt, Miscel.	E. 36
Lisle Papers	
Northampton Record Society—Paget Letters	Northamp. Rec. Soc.

ABBREVIATIONS OF
PRINTED BOOKS

American Historical Review	*A.H.R.*
Acts of the Privy Council	*A.P.C.*
Calendar of State Papers, Foreign, Edward VI,	*Cal. St. P. For.,*
1547–53	*Edw. VI*
Dictionary of National Biography	*D.N.B.*
Early English Text Society	E.E.T.S.
Household Ordinances	*H.O.*
Journal of British Studies	*J.B.S.*
Journal of the History of Ideas	*J.H.I.*
Letters and Papers, Foreign and Domestic, of	*L.P.*
the Reign of Henry VIII (1509–47)	
Proceedings of the Privy Council	*P.P.C.*
Calendar of Letters ... Relating to the	*Span. Cal.*
Negotiations between England & Spain	
State Papers during the Reign of Henry VIII	*State Papers*
Strype, *Ecclesiastical Memorials*	Strype, *Ecc.*
	Memo.
Calendar of State Papers ... Preserved in the	*Ven. Cal.*
Archives of Venice	

In most cases spelling and punctuation of manuscript quotations have been modernized.

NOTES

Full titles, names of editors and details of publication are given in the bibliography of printed books. Certain well-known authors and editors, such as Burnet, Foxe, Kaulek and Nott, are cited under names only.

CHAPTER I

1   Moriemini, *A Profitable Sermon*, p. 19.
2   Boorde, *Dyetary of Helth*, pp. 246, 302.
3   Copeman, *Doctors and Diseases*, p. 88, quoting from Boorde, *The Breviary of Helthe*.
4   Shakespeare, *Twelfth Night*, I.i
5   *L.P.*, XXI (2), 768; *The Wisdom of Andrew Boorde*, p. 51.
6   Foxe, V, p. 689.
7   Copeman, *Doctors and Diseases*, p. 121, quoting from Ambrose Paré.
8   Godwin, *Annals*, p. 207.
9   *Spanish Chronicle*, p. 152. The title given to this work by its editor, M. A. S. Hume, is *Chronicle of King Henry VIII*. Its authorship is unknown, but the chronicle was probably written largely from memory by one of the Spanish mercenary captains in Henry's pay during the last years of the reign. It is a fascinating if exceedingly dangerous document.
10 Foxe, V, p. 689.
11 Halliwell, *Letters*, II, pp. 25–6.
12 B. M., Hargrave MSS 311, f. 125; cf. Sanders, *Anglican Schism*, p. 164.
13 Dickens, *Child's History of England*, p. 324; Elton, *Henry VIII*, p. 15; Oman, 'The Personality of Henry VIII', *Quarterly Review*, CCLXIX, p. 97; Brinch, 'The Medical Problems of Henry VIII', *Centaurus*, V, p. 365.
14 Pollard, *Henry VIII*, p. 440.
15 *L.P.*, XIV (1), 194. Thomas Wriothesley made this statement five years before he became Lord Chancellor.
16 Edwardes, *Castra Regia*, pp. 17–18.
17 Thomas, *The Pilgrim*, pp. 78–9.
18 Quoted in James, *Religious Experience*, p. 119.
19 *Spanish Chronicle*, p. 151; *L.P.*, XXI (2), 713; *Span. Cal.*, IX, p. 2.
20 See for example Gardiner, *De Vera Obedientia*, p. 89; and Bp Shaxton to Cromwell, *L.P.*, XIII (2), 214.
21 *L.P.*, XIX (2), 726.
22 There is no published biography of Paget. Still the best is Gammon's thesis, 'Master of Practices. A Life of William Lord Paget'.
23 Beer, 'Rise of John Dudley', *History Today*, XV, pp. 274–5; *L.P.*, XVIII (1), 701; XX (2), 391.
24 Nott, I, p. xcvii.
25 *Cal. St. P. For.*, *Edw. VI*, p. 196.
26 *Span. Cal.*, VIII, 386, p. 557.
27 This is an old story and can be found in one form or another in most biographies of Francis. See Pardoe, *Francis the First*, II, p. 555.

28 *L.P.*, XXI (2), 756.
29 Foxe, VIII, p. 33.
30 Gardiner, *Letters*, 79, p. 161.
31 *Span. Cal.*, VIII, 347, p. 502; IX, p. 495.
32 Op. cit., IX, p. 492.
33 Wilbraham, *Journal*, p. 57.
34 *A.P.C.*, II, pp. 15–20; P.R.O., S.P. 10, vol. 1, ff. 41–54. See also Chapter 12.
35 Foxe, VI, p. 163; *Span. Cal.*, IX, pp. 30–31.
36 P.R.O., S.P. 10, vol. 1, f. 1.
37 *L.P.*, XXI (2), 760.
38 Both B.M., Harl. 1419, no. 34, f. 416 and Add. MSS 46348, ff. 9–27 are dated January 27th, 1547, the day before Henry died. The details listed on these pages come from Harl. 1419A, ff. 189, 223 and Add. MSS 46348, ff. 89–775. See also *L.P.*, XXI (2), 754.
39 *State Papers*, I, 136, pp. 627–8.
40 Gardiner, *Letters*, 124, p. 307; Strype, *Ecc. Memo.*, II, pt ii, p. 309.
41 Kaulek, 418, p. 422.
42 Ellis, *Letters*, 1st Ser., II, 163, pp. 149–51.
43 Halliwell, *Letters*, II, p. 15.
44 Op. cit., pp. 1–4, 13–14.
45 Op. cit., pp. 15–16.
46 Du Bellay, *Mémoires* (ed. Bourrilly and Vindry), IV, p. 333.
47 B.M., Cotton MSS Titus B II, 25, ff. 51–2.
48 *L.P.*, XXI (1), 330.
49 English and Pearson, *Emotional Problems of Living*, p. 449.
50 James, *Religious Experience*, p. 42.
51 Leonardo da Vinci, *Treatise on Painting*, I, p. 104.
52 Chesterton, *Heretics*, p. 15.
53 Storr, 'The Man', *Churchill Revised*, p. 273.

CHAPTER 2

1   Becon, *Early Works*, p. 245.
2   Tytler, *England under Edward and Mary*, I, p. 169.
3   B.M., Sloane MSS 1523, f. 36.
4   B.M., Cotton MSS Titus F III, f. 276 (279); or P.R.O., S.P. 10, vol. 8, f. 4.
5   Ibid.
6   Eccles. viii 4.
7   Gardiner, *Letters*, 124, pp. 301, 308.
8   *State Papers*, I, 9, p. 393.
9   Cranmer, *Writings*, p. 104.
10 Edwardes, *Castra Regia*, p. 31.
11 *State Papers*, I, 70, p. 513.
12 Giustinian, *Four Years of the Court of Henry VIII*, I, p. 237.
13 *Span. Cal.*, VIII, 367, p. 530; 386, p. 555.
14 Cornwallis, *Discourses*, f. A2.
15 The dating is obscure, but the most likely is April–May 1543. The story is in Nichols, *Narratives of the Reformation*, pp. 254–8 and originated with Cranmer's secretary, Ralph Morice. Foxe, VIII, pp. 24–6, has a somewhat embroidered version.
16 Foxe, V, pp. 690–91.

17 Chapuys specifically mentions Hertford and Dudley (*Span. Cal.*, VIII, 386, p. 556), and Gardiner himself named Cranmer, congratulating himself that he had never sought revenge (*Letters*, 125, p. 326).

18 Chapuys thought that the Duke of Norfolk was the source of the leak. *Span. Cal.*, VIII, 386, p. 556.

19 Foxe, V, pp. 553–61.

20 For Gardiner's difficulties see *Span. Cal.*, VIII, 386, p. 556. Cranmer's troubles are well documented (*L.P.*, XVIII [2], 546, and Ridley, *Cranmer*, ch. xv); and throughout 1546 there were persistent rumours that Catherine Parr was in danger and about to be divorced (*Span. Cal.*, VIII, 204, p. 318; 238, p. 373).

21 Foxe, V, p. 557.

22 Edwardes, *Castra Regia*, p. 38.

23 Kaulek, 306, p. 273; Henry VIII, *Letters*, p. 224.

24 Stapleton, *Sir Thomas More*, p. 77.

25 *Span. Cal.*, VIII, 364, p. 523.

26 Hall, *Henry VIII*, I, p. 177.

27 Foxe, V, p. 564.

28 Nicolas, *Privy Purse Expenses*, pp. xxx–xxxi, 64, 168.

29 Foxe, VI, p. 36; Gardiner, *Letters*, 121, p. 287.

30 *A.P.C.*, II, pp. 16, 19–20.

31 Cranmer, *Writings*, p. 341.

32 Wilson, *The State of England*, pp. 42–3.

33 Nott, II, p. 338.

34 Cavendish, *Thomas Wolsey*, p. 230.

35 Grey, *Commentary on William Lord Grey*, pp. 1–9. See also *L.P.*, XXI (2), 149, 254.

36 Foxe, VI, p. 36; Gardiner, *Letters*, 121, p. 287.

37 Doernberg, *Henry VIII and Luther*, p. 32; Scarisbrick, *Henry VIII*, p. 29; B.M., Harl. MSS 282, f. 43 (*L.P.*, XIV [1], 92); Henry VIII, *Assertio Septem Sacramentorum*, p. 450.

38 *L.P.*, XXI (1), 654 (41); 716 (5), 963 (83, 86).

39 Elton, *Revolution in Tudor Government*, p. 383; *L.P.*, I. 4103.

40 Kaulek, 401, p. 397; *L.P.*, XVI, 1459.

41 *L.P.*, XVI, 312; XX (2), 737.

42 Henry VIII, *Letters*, pp. 73–4, 201; *Span. Cal.*, VIII, 255, p. 391. Cranmer's famous interview with the King by which he escaped his enemies was conducted very late at night (see Nichols, *Narratives of the Reformation*, p. 254).

43 *L.P.*, XIV (1), 1181.

44 *State Papers*, I, 70, p. 518. The compliment to Cranmer is quoted in Bowle, *Henry VIII*, p. 261.

45 *L.P.*, XXI (1), 1537 (31–4) describes the procedure. There are 17 lists of documents signed by dry stamp: P.R.O., S.P. 4, vol. 1 (*L.P.*, XX [2], 418, 706, 909, 1067; XXI [1], 148, 301, 650, 963, 1165, 1381, 1536; XXI [2], 199, 331, 475, 647, 770). The lists are all William Clerk's copies except for one which is the original and carries Henry's signature: S.P. 4, vol. 1, September–October 1545 (*L.P.*, XX [2], 706 [1]).

46 P.R.O., S.P. 4, vol. 1, January 1546 (*L.P.*, XXI [1], 148 [51, 124]); *L.P.* XXI (1), 149 (35).

47 P.R.O., S.P. 10, vol. 1, f. 69 (58).

48 P.R.O., S.P. 1, vol. 224, f. 95 (*L.P.*, XXI [2], 54); *State Papers*, III, 348, pp. 580–5. Occasionally Henry actually helped to draft the Council's

letters when he felt himself personally involved or his honour touched. See *State Papers*, X, 1063, pp. 161–5.

49 *A.P.C.*, I, pp. 15–48, 148.
50 *State Papers*, I, 243, p. 844.
51 Op. cit., 156, pp. 310–12.
52 Nichols, *Literary Remains*, I, pp. xxvii–xxx; *H.O.*, p. 139. For the King's economic interests see *Seymour Papers*, pp. 92, 96, 99.
53 The *L.P.* are rich with examples. Outside the original documents in the Public Record Office and the British Museum, the best places to study Henry at work are *State Papers*, I and X, and Henry VIII, *Letters*, especially pp. 180–260.
54 *State Papers*, IX, 773, pp. 157–63.
55 B.M., Cotton MSS Cleo. E V, f. 319 (*L.P.*, XIV [1], 869 [9]).
56 Cranmer, *Writings*, p. 105.
57 B.M., Cotton MSS Cleo. E V, ff. 10, 23. The entire volume is filled with Henry's corrections.
58 P.R.O., S.P. 1, vol. 194, ff. 92–7 (*L.P.*, XIX [2], 592). See also 216, ff. 75–6 (*L.P.*, XXI [1], 507).
59 Op cit., vol. 169, ff. 90–94 (*L.P.*, XVII, 140 [3]).
60 B.M., Cotton MSS Cleo. E V, ff. 327, 328; Cranmer, *Writings*, p. 89.
61 Scarisbrick, *Henry VIII*, p. 45.
62 The King's corrections of the Ten Articles are in Burnet, ed. Pocock, IV, p. 272 n (see also *L.P.*, XI, 1110). His comments on *The Bishops' Book* are in Cranmer, *Writings*, pp. 83–114, and more extensively in B.M., Royal MSS 17 cxxx, ff. 1–135, and also in P.R.O., S.P. 6, vol. 3, f. 9 ff. and vol. 8, f. 95. The Tunstal correspondence is in B.M., Cotton MSS Cleo. E IV, ff. 131 ff. The King's notes on the sacraments are found throughout Cotton MSS Cleo. E V, but see especially ff. 39v and 42. His corrections of *The King's Book* are op. cit., ff. 8 ff. Cleo, E V makes impressive if heavy reading, and almost anybody would be inclined to agree with Professor Scarisbrick that 'for one who was not addicted to writing ... the hundred-odd often lengthy corrections and additions he [Henry] made to the text of this sizable work [*The Bishops' Book*] must stand as a monument to his theological enthusiasm' (*Henry VIII*, p. 403).
63 Brown, *Foreign Policy of Henry VIII*, p. 68, n. 27.
64 P.R.O., S.P. 1, vol. 201, f. 98 (*L.P.*, XX [1], 784).
65 *L.P.*, XX (2), 884.
66 P.R.O., S.P. 1, vol. 195, ff. 208–11 (*L.P.*, XIX [2], 724); 206, f. 232 (XX [2], 217); 207, f. 173 (XX [2], 364); 213, ff. 136–7 (XXI [1], 105); 215, ff. 19–22 (XXI [1], 347); ff. 52–5 (XXI [1], 367); B.M., Harl. 283, ff. 218b–219a (XXI [1], 349).
67 B.M., Cotton MSS Vesp. C VII, ff. 71–83 (esp. f. 79).
68 Erasmus, *Epistles*, I, p. 424. See also *State Papers*, X, 1063, pp. 161–5.
69 Read, *Secretary Walsingham*, I, p. 439.
70 *L.P.*, X, 76; 141, p. 50.
71 P.R.O., S.P. 1, vol. 195, f. 134 (*L.P.*, XIX [2], 629).
72 Op cit., vol. 193, f. 45 (*L.P.*, XIX [2], 366) and f. 77 (XIX [2], 384).
73 Both the French and the Imperial Ambassadors were well aware that Henry was reluctant to be parted from his treasures. *L.P.*, XIV (1), 1091; XVII, 759; XVIII (1), 266; (2), 39; XIX (1), 799.
74 Kaulek, 126, p. 107.
75 P.R.O., S.P. 1, vol. 211, f. 22 (*L.P.*, XX [2], 845).

76   Op. cit., vol. 217, f. 153 (*L.P.*, XXI [1], 724).
77   Op. cit., vol. 214, f. 131 (*L.P.*, XXI [1], 254).
78   *L.P.*, XIX (1), 441.
79   Norfolk wrote from Abbeville on February 17th, 1540; the King gave his answer on the 21st and the Duke replied on the 23rd (*L.P.*, XV, 233, 253). Paget wrote to Henry on December 29th, 1545, from Calais and was answered by the Council the next day (*L.P.*, XX [2], 1057, 1060).
80   Kaulek, 146, p. 128.
81   Gerth and Mills, *From Max Weber*, pp. 88–9, 236–9, 248–51.
82   Thomas, *The Pilgrim*, pp. 78–9.
83   Huizinga, *Erasmus*, p. 251.
84   B.M., Add. MSS 4729, ff. 1–24.
85   *L.P.*, IV, 4858.
86   Henry VIII, *Letters*, pp. 122, 353–91, 426–7.
87   P.R.O., S.P. 1, vol. 216, ff. 1, 31, 91, 102 (*L.P.*, XXI [1], 471, 488, 520, 529).
88   Gurney-Salter, *Tudor England*, p. 28.
89   P.R.O., S.P. 1, vol. 216, f. 88 (*L.P.*, XXI [1], 517).
90   Haynes, *State Papers*, p. 52.
91   P.R.O., S.P. 1, vol. 216, ff. 38–9 (*L.P.*, XXI [1], 494).
92   *Span. Cal.*, IV (1), 160, p. 221.
93   Roper, *Lyfe of Moore* (E.E.T.S.), p. 11.
94   Erasmus, *Opus Epistolarum*, VIII, 2143, p. 129.
95   Halliwell, *Letters*, II, pp. 11–12.
96   Strype, *Ecc. Memo.*, I, pt ii, p. 392.
97   Tjernagel, *Henry VIII and the Lutherans*, p. 12.
98   Hall, *Henry VIII*, II, pp. 328–38.
99   B.M., Cotton MSS Titus B I, ff. 136–8.
100   Cited in Doernberg, *Henry VIII and Luther*, p. 118, and Tjernagel, *Henry VIII and the Lutherans*, p. 19.
101   *State Papers*, VI, 114, p. 417.
102   Dunne, *Mr Dooley Remembers*, p. 158.
103   Sadler, *State Papers*, I, p. 8; *L.P.*, XIX (2), 21; *Span. Cal.*, VIII, 140, p. 251; P.R.O., E. 36, vol. 118, f. 151 (p. 300).
104   Foxe, V, p. 554.
105   Cranmer, *Writings*, p. 117.
106   Gardiner, *Letters*, 125, p. 336.
107   *L.P.*, XX (1), 426.

CHAPTER 3

1   B.M., Harl. MSS 4990, f. 1 (*L.P.*, XVII, App. A, 1).
2   Gardiner, *Letters*, 125, p. 321.
3   Febvre, *Le Problème de l'incroyance*, pp. 471 ff.
4   Hall, *Henry VIII*, II, p. 299.
5   There is no full treatment of this critical subject. Huizinga, in *Waning of the Middle Ages*, had much to say; so has Ferguson, in *Indian Summer of English Chivalry* (pp. 26–7) and Erickson, in *Young Man Luther* (p. 187). I am particularly indebted to Brandt, *Shape of Medieval History*, pp. 33–4, 79, 129–30, 145–6.
6   *State Papers*, VI, 114, p. 417.
7   Castro, *Structure of Spanish History*, p. 591.
8   Crotch, *Prologues and Epilogues of William Caxton*, p. 66.

9   P.R.O., S.P. 1, vol. 191, f. 25 (*L.P.*, XIX [2], 19 [2]).
10 Op. cit., vol. 77, ff. 175–6b (*L.P.*, VI, 775).
11 Cruttwell, 'Physiology and Psychology in Shakespeare's Age', *J.H.I.*, XII, pp. 75–80.
12 Hall, *Henry VIII*, II, p. 356.
13 Sadler, *State Papers*, I, p. 7.
14 Sir Thomas Wyatt was explicit on this point:

> The pompous pride of state and dignity
> Forthwith rebates repentant humbleness;
> Thinner vile cloth than clotheth poverty
> Doth scantly hide and clad his nakedness.
> Nott, II, p. 105)

15 Lyly, *Complete Works*, II, p. 45.
16 Nott, II, p. 324.
17 P.R.O., S.P. 1, vol. 212, ff. 111–13 (*L.P.*, XX [2], 1030 [2]).
18 Becon, *Early Works*, p. 219.
19 *L.P.*, IX, 74.
20 Nicolas, *Privy Purse Expenses*, p. 251. See *L.P.*, XVIII (1), 231 for one of the few hints of assassination.
21 Becon, *Early Works*, p. 218.
22 Henry VIII, *Letters*, pp. 78, 237, 418.
23 Koebner, ' "The Imperial Crown of this Realm" ', *Bul. Inst. His. Res.*, XXVI, p. 31.
24 P.R.O., S.P. 1, vol. 57, f. 112 (*L.P.*, IV, 6401).
25 Murray, *The Divine King*, pp. 179–83; Legg, *English Coronation Records*, p. 21.
26 Parsons, *Three Conversions* (1603–4), I, pt 2, ch. XI, sec. 17, p. 564 (italics mine).
27 P.R.O., S.P. 1, vol. 195, f. 213–14 (*L.P.*, XIX [2], 726).
28 Febvre, *Le Problème de l'incroyance*, pp. 473–4.
29 Hole, *Mirror of Witchcraft*, pp. 108–9; Wriothesley, *Chronicle*, I, pp. 120, 156; Holinshed, *Chronicle*, IV, p. 431.
30 Hole, op. cit., p. 87; Holinshed, op. cit., V, p. 234; Meadows, *Elizabethan Quintet*, p. 187.
31 Cranmer, *Writings*, p. 100.
32 Ibid.
33 Op. cit., p. 235.
34 *L.P.*, XXI (2), 417; *Span. Cal.*, VIII, 293, p. 430.
35 Hughes, *Reformation*, I, pp. 341–2.
36 Gardiner, *Letters*, 119, p. 274.
37 Becon, *Early Works*, p. 218.
38 *L.P.*, XIV (1), 237.
39 P.R.O., S.P. 1, vol. 167, f. 159 (*L.P.*, XVI, 1339).
40 Becon, *Early Works*, p. 248.
41 P.R.O., S.P. 1, vol. 116, f. 92 (*L.P.*, XII [1], 479); *L.P.*, XII (1), 478.
42 Cited in Erickson, *Young Man Luther*, p. 236.
43 *Sir Thomas More*, p. 28.
44 Becon, *Early Works*, p. 249.
45 Wriothesley, *Chronicle*, I, pp. 162–3; *L.P.*, XVII, 362 (65).
46 *Original Letters*, I, 108, pp. 236–7; *L.P.*, XVI, 625, 632.
47 Stow, *Annales*, pp. 581–2; *L.P.*, XVI, 903.
48 Wriothesley, *Chronicle*, I, p. 137.

49 Puttenham, *Arte of Poesie*, p. 245.
50 Fiddes, *Life of Wolsey*, I, p. 174; Foxe, V, p. 691.
51 *L.P.*, XVI, 931.
52 P.R.O., S.P. 1, vol. 166, ff. 73–4 (*L.P.*, XVI, 932); Hall, *Henry VIII*, II, pp. 312–13.
53 *L.P.*, XVI, 941, 954.
54 Pollard, *Henry VIII*, p. 433.
55 Sander, *Report to Cardinal Moroni*, p. 39.
56 Rastel, *Le Liver des Assises*, 'the Prologue'.
57 Becon, *Early Works*, p. 286.
58 Cornwallis, *Discourses*, f.A4; Watson, *Shakespeare and Renaissance Honor*, p. 92.
59 Cornwallis, *Discourses*, f. A4.
60 Rastel, *Le Liver des Assises*, 'the Prologue'.
61 Hall, *Henry VIII*, II, p. 357.
62 Frazer, *English History in Contemporary Poetry*, III, p. 9.
63 These are all familiar anecdotes of the French court. See Williams, H. N., *Henri II*, pp. 166–70.
64 Hall, *Henry VIII*, I, p. 175.
65 Wriothesley, *Chronicle*, I, p. 125; *A.P.C.*, I, p. 289; *L.P.*, XVII, 28 (9).
66 B.M., Harl. MSS 78, ff. 24–5 (20–21) (*L.P.*, XVII, 542); see also Anglo, *Spectacle, Pageantry and Early Tudor Policy*, chs III–VII.
67 Hall, *Henry VIII*, I, p. 320; *L.P.*, X, 200; 427, p. 172.
68 *Original Letters*, I, 105, p. 206; also *L.P.*, XII (1), 126.
69 *Span. Cal.*, IV (2), 1061, p. 638.
70 Flugel, 'The Character and Married Life of Henry VIII', in *Psychoanalysis and History*, p. 148.
71 *L.P.*, X, 908, p. 378.
72 Stubbs, *Seventeen Lectures*, p. 284.
73 Kaulek, 99, pp. 80–81.
74 Puttenham, *Arte of Poesie*, p. 225; Rowley, *When You See Me, You Know Me*, f. L3.
75 *State Papers*, IX, 777, p. 182.
76 Baldwin, *Treatise of Moral Philosophy*, p. 109.
77 Du Bellay, *Mémoires* (ed. Bourrilly and Vindry), IV, p. 104.
78 P.R.O., S.P. 1, vol. 112, ff. 184–9 (*L.P.*, XI, 1271).
79 *A.P.C.*, I, pp. 474–5.
80 Wriothesley, *Chronicle*, I, p. 84.
81 P.R.O., E. 36, vol. 121, p. 23 (*L.P.*, XI, 1175).
82 The most literate statement of these ideas can be found in Heilbroner, *The Future as History*.
83 Nott, II, p. 118.
84 Henry VIII, *Letters*, p. 69.
85 Rye, *History of Norfolk*, p. 57.
86 Quoted in Owst, *Literature and Pulpit*, p. 560 from Harl. MSS 4894, f. 182.
87 *Sermons or Homilies in the Time of Elizabeth*, p. 469.
88 Strype, *Ecc. Memo*, I, pt ii, pp. 188–93.
89 Tyndale, *Doctrinal Treatises*, p. 174.
90 P.R.O., S.P. 1, vol. 56, f. 147b (*L.P.*, IV, 6111).
91 Kelso, *Doctrine of the English Gentleman*, p. 39.
92 P.R.O., S.P. 1, vol. 109, pp. 227–8 (*L.P.*, XI, 894).
93 Aske's ultimate fate is not clear. He did, however, beg a reprieve from

the full horrors of a traitor's death: P.R.O., S.P. 1, vol. 120, f. 134 (*L.P.*, XII, 1224 [3]). Dodds, *Pilgrimage of Grace*, II, pp. 222–5 does not mention hanging in chains but Wriothesley (*Chronicle*, I, p. 65) does.

94 *L.P.*, XVII, 880 (ii).
95 *A.P.C.*, I, p. 418.
96 Owst, *Literature and Pulpit*, p. 295.
97 Hall, *Henry VIII*, II, p. 284.
98 Op. cit., p. 282.
99 Nott, II, p. 268.
100 A.P.C., I, p. 390.
101 For a fuller discussion see Stone, *Crisis of the Aristocracy*, pp. 29–42.
102 Wriothesley, *Chronicle*, I, pp. 150–51.
103 Oxley, *The Reformation in Essex*, pp. 143–4.

CHAPTER 4

1 Kaulek, 242, p. 211.
2 *L.P.*, XVI, 106.
3 Gardiner, *Letters*, 91, p. 198.
4 P.R.O., S.P. I, vol. 221, ff. 98–9 (*L.P.*, XXI [1], 1201).
5 *Span. Cal.*, VIII, 115, p. 219.
6 Puttenham, *Arte of Poesie*, p. 245.
7 Ibid.
8 Gardiner, *De Vera Obedientia*, p. 89.
9 Segar, *Honor, Military and Civill*, II, p. 51.
10 Smith, *De Republica Anglorum*, p. 41.
11 Nicolas, *Privy Purse Expenses*, pp. xxiii, 5, 156, 193, 267, 277; *L.P.*, XVI, 380, f. 114b.
12 *L.P.*, XVI, 380, ff. 108b–111.
13 Stow, *Survey of London*, pp. 81–2. Derby's generosity is a guess. According to Stow he fed 60 aged persons every day, all comers twice a week, and 2,700 with 'meat and drink' on Good Fridays.
14 The studied vagueness of this estimate reflects the difficulty of establishing any certain sum for charity over and beyond the 37s. 11d. weekly offerings, 6s. 8d. donations on Sunday, 33s. 4d. presented on Twelfth Night, and £5 given the 'heralds-at-arms for their largesse' (*L.P.*, XVI, 380, p. 180). Edward VI's yearly offerings came to £38 6s. 8d., but his annual alms amounted to £447 17s. 1d. (B.M., Add. MSS 30198, f. 33). It is even more risky to translate money into buying power. The rather doubtful premise has been used that a penny was more than sufficient to feed a beggar in a 'royal style'.
15 Quoted in Kelso, *The Doctrine of the English Gentleman*, p. 90.
16 Stow, *Survey of London*, p. 81; Stone, *Crisis of the Aristocracy*, pp. 207–8.
17 Chastellain, *Œuvres*, vol. VI, pp. 416–17.
18 *L.P.*, XV, 617; Wriothesley, *Chronicle*, I, p. 118.
19 *Spanish Chronicle*, p. 110.
20 *H.O.*, p. 165; B.M., Cotton MSS Vesp. C XIV, f. 92 (*L.P.*, XXI [1], 969). Even at this restricted level the court is difficult to compute. *L.P.*, XVI, 394 (3) gives 80 Yeomen of the Guard plus 24 for the Queen's side, but the total for the entire palace seems to have varied from year to year. In 1545 it was given as 122 (B.M., Lans. MSS 2, ff. 34–5). Besides the regular guards there were at least 81 'guards extraordinary', bringing the total to 203 (*L.P.*, XXI [1], 1424), but by the end of the reign only 150

guards were recognized by the Lord Protector (B.M., Royal MSS 7 cxvi, ff. 92–5). Eventually by 1552 the number rose to 207 (Add. MSS 30198, f. 32).

21 *Seymour Papers*, pp. 5–7; *L.P.*, XVIII (2), 530 has the smaller figure of 179.

22 *H.O.*, p. 198.

23 Op. cit., p. 142.

24 There are a number of descriptions of court life and royal palaces. The best are Dunlop, *Palaces and Progresses of Elizabeth I*, Williams, N., *Royal Residences*, Brook, *The Story of Eltham Palace* and Law, *The History of Hampton Court Palace*.

25 P.R.O., E. 36, vol. 233, f. 23.

26 *H.O.*, pp. 153–4.

27 Most of what follows comes from Elton, *Revolution in Tudor Government*, ch. VI, and Woodworth, *Purveyance for the Royal Household*. I am particularly indebted to Robert Braddock, 'Royal Household 1540–1560'.

28 *L.P.*, XV, 599 (2, 3); Nicolas, *Privy Purse Expenses*, p. 364; P.R.O., E. 36, vol. 231, p. 196.

29 Nott, I, p. 49.

30 Dunlop, *Palaces and Progresses of Elizabeth I*, p. 117; Woodworth, *Purveyance for the Royal Household*, p. 71.

31 Jordan, *Chronicle and Political Papers of Edward VI*, pp. 124, 137.

32 *Seymour Papers*, p. 7.

33 Woodworth, *Purveyance for the Royal Household*, pp. 55, 57, 62, 65–6.

34 Quoted in Dunlop, *Palaces and Progresses of Elizabeth I*, pp. 79–80.

35 *L.P.*, XVIII (2), 542; XXI (2), 329; B.M., Cotton MSS Vesp. C XIV f. 277; *H.O.*, pp. 147–8.

36 *H.O.*, pp. 139, 143, 154.

37 B.M., Harl. MSS 41, ff. 16–16b; P.R.O., S.P. 10, vol. 1, ff. 10–23.

38 *H.O.*, pp. 148–9, 155–6; *L.P.*, XVI, 127.

39 B.M., Royal MSS 7 cxvi, ff. 92–6; Add. MSS 30198, ff. 30–31; *L.P.*, XIV (1), 781, f. 58; XVIII (2), 530.

40 Braddock, 'Royal House 1540–1560', ch. V.

41 *H.O.*, p. 157.

42 *L.P.*, XVI, 127.

43 Foxe, V, p. 606; B.M., Hargrave MSS 31, 'Rise and Growth of the Anglican Schism', f. 124. The printed version is somewhat different—see Sander, *Anglican Schism*, p. 162.

44 *L.P.*, II (1), 1495.

45 Puttenham, *Arte of Poesie*, p. 245.

46 *State Papers*, V, 530, pp. 456–7; *L.P.*, XVIII (2), 45; XIX (1), 481.

47 Cranmer, *Writings*, p. 414.

48 P.R.O., S.P. 1, vol. 217, f. 46 (*L.P.*, XXI [1], 633); vol. 207, ff. 64–5 (*L.P.*, XX [2], 268); *L.P.*, XX (2), 412, 427, 496; XXI (1), 26.

49 *L.P.*, XIX (2), 331; P.R.O., S.P. 1, vol. 198, ff. 176–7 (*L.P.*, XX [1], 268).

50 P.R.O., S.P. 1, vol. 228, ff. 45–6 (*L.P.*, XXI [2], 694).

51 Op. cit., vol. 197, ff. 228–9 (*L.P.*, XX [1], 131).

52 Op. cit., vol. 213, f. 130 (*L.P.*, XXI [1], 95); f. 167 (XXI [1], 127); ff. 180–1 (XXI [1], 142 [1]).

53 Nott, II, p. 422.

54 P.R.O., S.P. 1, vol. 214, f. 168 (*L.P.*, XXI [1], 291).

55 Gardiner, *Letters*, 101, p. 220.

56 Op. cit., 125, p. 326.

57 Foxe, VIII, p. 34.
58 *L.P.*, XVII, App. B, 22; 23, p. 736.
59 *State Papers*, IX, 293, pp. 301–2.
60 Op. cit., VIII, 502, p. 51.
61 The full story on Sir Thomas Seymour can be found in Nichols, *Narratives of the Reformation*, pp. 260–63.
62 *L.P.*, II (1), 1653; *Ven. Cal.*, III, 493.
63 *Span. Cal.*, VI (1), 244, p. 493; VIII, 2, pp. 4, 6; 216, p. 33.
64 *L.P.*, X, 908.
65 Op. cit., XVI, 1426; *P.P.C.*, VII, pp. 352–3.
66 *Span. Cal.*, VI (1), 84, p. 185; VI (2), 94, p. 223; *L.P.*, XVII, App. B, 13, p. 723.
67 *State Papers*, VI, 70, pp. 201–11; 76, pp. 233–9.
68 Scarisbrick, *Henry VIII*, p. 136.
69 *State Papers*, I, 61, pp. 490–91.
70 *L.P.*, IV (2), 5028, 5050, 5053. By far the best study of Henry's handling of the divorce diplomacy is in Scarisbrick, *Henry VIII*, ch. VIII.
71 *L.P.*, VI, 1427.
72 Scarisbrick, *Henry VIII*, ch. VII.
73 Roper, *Life of More* (ed. Campbell), p. 255.
74 Strype, *Ecc. Memo.*, I, pt ii, App. xcviii, p. 391.
75 Henry VIII, *Letters*, p. 82; Scarisbrick, *Henry VIII*, pp. 110–11.
76 Wriothesley, *Chronicle*, I, pp. 109–10.
77 Scarisbrick (*Henry VIII*, pp. 105–13) argues that Henry was a bored man and that Wolsey suggested he write *The Defence of the Seven Sacraments* in order to use up some of his excess energy.
78 *L.P.*, X, 909.
79 *Span. Cal.*, VI, 13, p. 37.
80 Doernberg, *Henry VIII and Luther*, conveniently summarizes the subject, p. 21.
81 Henry VIII, *Assertio Septem Sacramentorum*, pp. 316, 320.
82 Tjernagel, *Henry VIII and the Lutherans*, p. 21.
83 Henry VIII, *Letters*, p. 367.
84 *Span. Cal.*, VII, 161, p. 264.
85 *State Papers*, I, 3, pp. 2–3.
86 P.R.O., S.P. 1, vol. 101, ff. 57–8 (*L.P.*, X, 76).
87 *State Papers*, VI, 114, p. 417.
88 *L.P.*, IV, 4858; XI, 80; Cavendish, *Life of Wolsey*, p. 225.
89 Quoted in Erickson, *Young Man Luther*, p. 241.
90 *L.P.*, XVII, App. B, 22, p. 731.
91 *Span. Cal.*, IV (2), 1061, p. 643; Kaulek, 242, p. 212.
92 Erasmus, *Opus Epistolarum*, VIII, ep. 2143, p. 129.
93 Kaulek, 131, p. 114.
94 Hall, *Henry VIII*, I, p. 128; *Span. Cal.*, IV (1), 250, p. 423.
95 Scarisbrick, *Henry VIII*, chs I–VI, gives impressive evidence that Wolsey kept his master well informed.
96 Kaulek, 307, p. 274.
97 *L.P.*, XVI, 1426.
98 B.M., Sloane MSS 1523, f. 36.
99 Cranmer, *Writings*, p. 401.

CHAPTER 5

1 Constant, *Reformation*, I, pp. 385–6.
2 Scarisbrick, *Henry VIII*, pp. 405–20, is the clearest and most perceptive
   sketch available. For the Catholic view see Hughes, *Reformation*, II,
   pp. 22–60. Two Lutheran interpretations are Doernberg, *Henry VIII and
   Luther*, and Tjernagel, *Henry VIII and the Lutherans*, ch. XIII. Hughes
   concludes that 'Henry, whatever he is, is not a Catholic' (p. 56).
3 James, *Religious Experience*, p. 259.
4 Quoted in Baumer, *Early Tudor Theory of Kingship*, p. 104 from the
   Homilies of 1547.
5 Owst, *Literature and Pulpit*, pp. 293, 571; Petry, *Christian Eschatology*,
   p. 301.
6 Henry VIII, *Letters*, p. 5.
7 Salter, 'Skelton's Speculum Princepis', *Speculum*, IX, pp. 27–9; Herbert,
   Henry the Eighth, p. 2; Coulton, *Medieval Panorama*, p. 698; Erasmus,
   Opus Epistolarum, VIII, ep. 2143, p. 129; Huizinga, *Erasmus*, p. 251.
8 *Ven. Cal.*, II, 1287, p. 559.
9 John Bouge, 'Letter to Katheryn Manne', in Nugent, *Thought and Culture
   of the English Renaissance*, p. 548.
10 Owst, *Literature and Pulpit*, pp. 294, 551; Patch, *The Other World*, p. 321;
   Petry, *Christian Eschatology*, pp. 112–13, 316, 347.
11 Owst, *Literature and Pulpit*, p. 297.
12 Becon, *Early Works*, p. 55; Petry, *Christian Eschatology*, p. 282.
13 Cranmer, *Writings*, pp. 100–1.
14 Op. cit., p. 106.
15 Henry VIII, *Letters*, p. 78.
16 Cranmer, *Writings*, pp. 84, 89, 106.
17 Erasmus, *The Education of a Christian Prince*, p. 181; Nichols, *Literary
   Remains*, I, p. clx.
18 Hall, *Henry VIII*, II, p. 146.
19 P.R.O., E. 36, vol. 118, f. 153 (p. 305) (*L.P.*, XI, 957).
20 James, *Religious Experience*, p. 87.
21 Op. cit., pp. 83, 112–13, 116–17.
22 Op. cit., p. 85; Clark, *Psychology of Religion*, p. 156.
23 Henry VIII, *Letters*, p. 68.
24 James, *Religious Experience*, p. 42.
25 Op. cit., p. 382.
26 Vetter, *Magic and Religion*, p. 166.
27 *Ven. Cal.*, I, 751, p. 261.
28 Mosher, *Louis XI*, pp. 63, 128–30.
29 Quoted in Williams, P., *Life in Tudor England*, p. 141; Owst, *Literature
   and Pulpit*, p. 147.
30 *Span. Cal.*, II, 43, p. 38.
31 Nichols, *Literary Remains*, I, p. clix.
32 *L.P.*, I, 4461–2; Ellis, *Letters*, Ser. 1, I, p. 90; *Span. Cal.*, II, 141, p.
   165.
33 Henry VIII, *Letters*, p. 55.
34 James, *Religious Experience*, p. 259.
35 Henry VIII, *Assertio Septem Sacramentorum*, p. 320.
36 Cranmer, *Writings*, p. 91.
37 Op. cit., p. 105.
38 Henry VIII, *Letters*, p. 62.

39 P.R.O., Lisle Papers, IX, f. 6 (*L.P.*, XIV [1], 967); Gardiner, *Letters*, 121, p. 290.
40 Sander, *Anglican Schism*, p. 161.
41 Cranmer, *Writings*, p. 414.
42 Ostow and Scharfstein, *The Need to Believe*, p. 85.
43 Tyndale, *Doctrinal Treatises*, pp. 174–5.
44 *L.P.*, VI, 1501.
45 B.M., Add. MSS 15387, ff. 88–90 (*L.P.*, III, 1297).
46 *L.P.*, II (2), 3163.
47 Cranmer, *Writings*, p. 88.
48 Cavendish, *Life of Wolsey*, pp. 111–12.
49 Op. cit., p. 117.
50 P.R.O., S.P. 1, vol. 77, f. 175 (*L.P.*, VI, 775 [1]).
51 Op. cit., vol. 56, f. 139 (*L.P.*, IV, 6111).
52 Mattingly, *Catherine of Aragon*, p. 246.
53 Pollard, *Henry VIII*, pp. 184, 206.
54 Erasmus, *Opus Epistolarum*, VII, ep. 2040, p. 471.
55 Neale, *Elizabeth I and her Parliaments*, II, pp. 139–40.
56 *State Papers*, V, 539, p. 470 and n. 1.
57 Greene, *James the Fourth*, p. 211.
58 *L.P.*, IV (3), 6627.
59 Cavendish, *Thomas Wolsey*, p. 117.
60 *Span. Cal.*, VI, 9, p. 15; 13, p. 37.
61 B.M., Cotton MSS Vit. B XXI, f. 122 (133).
62 Mattingly, *Catherine of Aragon*, p. 235; *L.P.*, IV, 667.
63 Mattingly, op. cit., p. 242.
64 Hall, *Henry VIII*, I, p. 320.
65 Op. cit., II, p. 38.
66 *L.P.*, III, 1073, 1187, 1193, 1275, 1294.
67 Pollard, *Henry VIII*, p. 209.
68 Gurney-Salter, *Tudor England*, p. 73.
69 Mattingly, *Catherine of Aragon*, pp. 304, 311; Elton, 'King or Minister? the Man Behind the Henrician Reformation', *History*, XXXIX, pp. 221–32.
70 *Span. Cal.*, IV (2), 1057, p. 626.
71 P.R.O., S.P. 1, vol. 77, ff. 175–66 (*L.P.*, VI [1], 775).
72 Quoted in Henry VIII, *Letters*, p. 86.
73 Quoted in Erickson, *Young Man Luther*, pp. 241–2.
74 B.M., Cotton MSS Vit. B XIII, ff. 171–2 (the original is badly burnt; see Burnet [ed. Nares], IV, 42, p. 62).
75 Hughes, *Reformation*, I, p. 341, n. 2 places Henry firmly in hell.
76 *Span. Cal.*, IV (2), 1061, p. 636.
77 'Henry VIII to Luther' (1526), in Nugent, *Thought and Culture of the English Renaissance*, p. 408 (*L.P.*, IV, 2446).
78 *L.P.*, V, 148; Hall, *Henry VIII*, II, p. 355.

CHAPTER 6

1 *L.P.*, XVI, 106.
2 Lloyd, *Formularies*, p. 52.
3 *King's Book*, p. 3.
4 Quoted in Bainton, *Here I Stand*, p. 45.
5 More, *English Works* (1557), pp. 207–8.
6 Quoted in Bainton, *Here I Stand*, p. 65.

7 Foxe, IV, p. 635.
8 Tyndale, *Doctrinal Treatises*, pp. 56, 228.
9 *King's Book*, p. 28.
10 Op cit., p. 7; see also Hall, *Henry VIII*, II, pp. 356–7.
11 Bale's Preface to Gardiner, *De Vera Obedientia* (1553), n.p.
12 Gardiner, *Detection of the Devils Sophistrie*, f. cxxxii.
13 *Corpus Reformatorum*, III, 1790, pp. 676–9.
14 Cranmer, *Writings*, p. 415.
15 Foxe, VIII, p. 407.
16 Foxe, V, pp. 544 and 545 n. 2.
17 Foxe, V. p. 547; VI, p. 48; *Span. Cal.*, VIII, 386, p. 555; *Original Letters*, I, p. 256; Jordan, *Edward VI*, pp. 206–7.
18 Foxe, V, p. 545. For a full discussion of Cheke and Cox see Smith, 'Henry VIII and the Protestant Triumph', *A.H.R.*, LXXI, pp. 1245–50.
19 Quoted in Ridley, *Cranmer*, p. 83, which is a liberal translation from Sampson's treatise on papal supremacy, Strype, *Ecc. Memo.*, I, pt ii, pp. 162–75.
20 Gardiner, *Letters*, 124, pp. 300–1.
21 *Span. Cal.*, IV (1), p. 719.
22 B.M., Cotton MSS Cleo. E VI, f. 216 (*L.P.*, V, App. 9).
23 Quoted in Doernberg, *Henry VIII and Luther*, p. 118.
24 The best works on the theological and diplomatic events of these years are Tjernagel, *Henry VIII and the Lutherans*, chs IX–XI, and Scarisbrick, *Henry VIII*, pp. 355–423.
25 Erasmus, *Epistles*, III, p. 361. For a discussion of the relationship between humanism and the English Reformation see Gelder, *The Two Reformations*, chs IV, V, X; McConica, *English Humanists and Reformation Politics;* and Trinterud, 'The Origins of Puritanism', *Church History*, XX, and also his paper read at the American Historical Association meeting, December 1966.
26 Latimer, *Sermons*, pp. 61–2.
27 B.M., Royal MSS 17 cxxx, ff. 67–8; cf. Cranmer, *Writings*, p. 98.
28 Cranmer, *Writings*, p. 103.
29 *L.P.*, XVI, 733, 737.
30 Foxe, V, p. 692.
31 Foxe, V, p. 562; Cranmer, *Writings*, pp. 414–15.
32 Henry VIII, *Assertio Septem Sacramentorum*, p. 312.
33 *L.P.*, IV (1), 40.
34 More, *English Works* (1557), p. 258; Smith, *Tudor Prelates and Politics*; pp. 94–5, 103–4, 235–9.
35 Foxe, V, p. 261.
36 Burnet (ed. Nares), IV, 16, p. 107.
37 Foxe, VIII, p. 24.
38 Foxe, V, p. 556.
39 Cranmer, *Writings*, p. 110.
40 Op. cit., p. 103.
41 Op. cit., p. 108.
42 B.M., Royal MSS 17 cxxx, f. 85; cf. Cranmer, *Writings*, p. 108.
43 Rymer, *Foedera*, XV, p. 111.
44 Gardiner, *Declaration of True Articles*, ff. xxix, lxxiiii, cxli.
45 Cranmer, *Writings*, pp. 84, 93–4.
46 *King's Book*, p. 162.
47 *L.P.*, XVIII (2), 546, p. 307.

K

48 Harpsfield, *Pretended Divorce*, p. 297; Kaulek, 241, p. 210.
49 Ellis, *Letters*, ser. 3, III, p. 303.
50 *Cal. St. P. For., Edw. VI*, p. 559.
51 P.R.O., S.P. 1, vol. 103, f. 235 (*L.P.*, X, 804).
52 Gardiner, *Letters*, 124, p. 308.
53 *L.P.*, XVII, 537.
54 Oxley, *Reformation in Essex*, pp. 145–7.
55 Hughes, *Reformation*, II, pp. 27–9.
56 B.M., Cotton MSS Cleo E V, f. 312.
57 Gardiner, *De Vera Obedientia* (tr. Janelle), p. 205.
58 *L.P.*, IX, 611.
59 Hooper, *Early Writings*, p. 466.
60 B.M., Harl. MSS 425, ff. 4–7.
61 Turner, *Rescuynge of the romishe fox*, Sig. Diiii.
62 Gardiner, *Letters*, 97, pp. 206–7; *Declaration of True Articles*, f. cli–clii.
63 P.R.O., S.P. 1, vol. 103, f. 235 (*L.P.*, X, 804).
64 *Original Letters*, I, pp. 200–1.
65 Turner, *Rescuynge of the romishe fox*, Sig. cv; *huntyng of the Romyshe foxe*, p. 86.
66 Hooper, *Early Writings*, p. 276.
67 Parker, *Correspondence*, p. 9.
68 *Hundred Merry Tales*, pp. 92–3.
69 Op. cit., pp. 124–5.
70 *L.P.*, IV (3), 6179.
71 P.R.O., S.P. 1, vol. 241, f. 3 (*L.P.*, Add. MSS 1209); Foxe, IV, p. 688.
72 B.M., Cotton MSS Cleo. E V, ff. 313–26 (*L.P.*, XIV [1], 868 [1]). Much of this is in Henry's own hand.
73 Cranmer, *Writings*, p. 469.
74 Henry VIII, *Assertio Septem Sacramentorum*, pp. 182, 208.
75 Henry VIII, *Letters*, p. 315.
76 Foxe, V, pp. 229–36.
77 Gardiner, *Letters*, 125, p. 350.
78 *Journal of the House of Lords*, I, p. 105.
79 P.R.O., S.P. 1, vol. 152, f. 102 (*L.P.*, XIV [1], 1157); *L.P.*, XIV (1), 1040.
80 B.M., Cotton MSS Cleo E V, ff. 327–36 (printed with the King's corrections in Henry VIII, *Letters*, pp. 252–4).
81 Quoted in Doernberg, *Henry VIII and Luther*, pp. 115, 120.
82 P.R.O., Lisle Papers, vol. 12, no. 75 (*L.P.*, XIV [1], 1004).
83 *L.P.*, XIV (1), 1092.
84 Tjernagel, *Henry VIII and the Lutherans*, ch. XIII; Maitland, *Essays*, chs XI–XIV.
85 Foxe, V, pp. 443–51.
86 Hughes, *Reformation*, II, pp. 17–18; Foxe, V, pp. 464–94; *L.P.*, XVIII (2), 241 (6), 327 (9); *A.P.C.*, I, pp. 96–7; Hall, *Henry VIII*, II, pp. 343–4.
87 Tjernagel, *Henry VIII and the Lutherans*, pp. 234–5.
88 *King's Book*, p. 5.
89 Op. cit., p. 137.
90 Op. cit., pp. 115–16.
91 Op. cit., p. 124.
92 P.R.O., S.P. 1, vol. 158, ff. 124–5 (*L.P.*, XV, 414).
93 *L.P.*, XVIII (1), 538; Foxe, V, App. XII.
94 Foxe, V, App. XII.

95 *A.P.C.*, I, p. 479.
96 Hall, *Henry VIII*, II, p. 357.
97 Quoted in Bainton, *Here I Stand*, p. 186.
98 *Span. Cal.*, VIII, 196, p. 305; 197, p. 306.
99 P.R.O., S.P. 6, vol. 6, no. 17, pp. 219–23 (*L.P.*, XI [2], 987).
100 P.R.O., S.P. 10, vol. 8, f. 4; Foxe, VIII, p. 110.
101 Hughes, *Reformation*, I, p. 368 n. 3.
102 Hughes, *Life of Fisher*, p. 160; *L.P.*, XIII (1), 981.
103 Gardiner, *Letters*, 95, p. 204.
104 Foxe, VIII, p. 33.
105 *L.P.*, XIII (1), 713; XXI (1), 1215.
106 *Span. Cal.*, VIII, 221, p. 339.
107 Pastor, *History of the Popes*, XII, p. 460.

CHAPTER 7

1 Kaulek, 62, p. 50.
2 £799,310 was the total value of land alienated between 1538 and 1547. The lion's share or £520,324 was sold between 1543 and 1546. See Dietz, *Public Finance*, I, p. 149.
3 Foxe, V, p. 103; Slavin, *Politics and Profits* pp. 80–83.
4 More, *Correspondence*, 197, pp. 498–9.
5 Brandi, *Charles V*, p. 112.
6 See for example *State Papers*, VIII, 560, p. 249; 563, p. 258.
7 *L.P.*, XVII, 748.
8 Batiffol, *Century of the Renaissance*, pp. 71, 73; Brandi, *Charles V*, pp. 235–6, 242.
9 B.M., Cotton MSS Vesp. C VII, f. 80 (82). See also Vit. B XXI, f. 64, and Harl. MSS 282, f. 73.
10 *L.P.*, XVII, 63; for the root of the King's dilemma see Gardiner, *Letters*, 62, p. 97.
11 *L.P.*, XIII (1), 274; the Wriothesley quotation is XIV (1), 433; see also XX (2), 496 (47).
12 Royal incomes are largely guesswork. Wernham (*Before the Armada*, p. 12) gives £1,100,000 for Charles, but Brandi (*Charles V*, pp. 463–5), Elliott (*Imperial Spain*, pp. 196–204) and Tyler (*Charles the Fifth*, p. 242) suggest half as much. Batiffol (*Century of the Renaissance*, p. 98) gives 3 million crowns or £675,000 for Francis but Wernham prefers £800,000. For Henry's revenues, see Dietz, *Public Finances*, I, pp. 137–50 and *L.P.*, XX (2), 366, 558.
13 *L.P.*, XVII, 759; XVIII (1), 266; (2), 39.
14 Gardiner, *Letters*, 62, pp. 98–9.
15 The figures come from Dietz. *Public Finance*, I, pp. 166–77, but they are reliable only in a general sense. Cf. Elliott, *Imperial Spain*, p. 203; Tyler, *Charles the Fifth*, p. 242, and Brandi, *Charles V*, pp. 463–6.
16 Brandi, op. cit., pp. 342–3.
17 Harpsfield, *Pretended Divorce*, p. 278; *L.P.*, XIV (2), 400. For opinions on Edward see *Span. Cal.*, VIII, 36, p. 78; *L.P.*, XVII, 248.
18 Kaulek, 430, p. 436.
19 *State Papers*, VIII, 558, p. 241; 560, p. 249.
20 Nott, II, p. 380.
21 *L.P.*, X, 965.
22 P.R.O., S.P. 1, vol. 215, f. 17 (*L.P.*, XXI [1], 346).

23   *L.P.*, IV (2), 3137.
24   *L.P.*, VIII, 874, 909.
25   P.R.O., S.P. 1, vol. 219, f. 51 (*L.P.*, XXI [1], 894).
26   Quoted in Doernberg, *Henry VIII and Luther*, p. 115.
27   *Span. Cal.*, VIII, 203, p. 315.
28   *State Papers*, X, 1061, p. 158.
29   Op. cit., XI, 1331, p. 84; P.R.O., S.P. 1, vol. 214, f. 114 (*L.P.*, XXI [1], 246).
30   *State Papers*, XI, 1378, p. 201 n.
31   Op. cit., IX, 1277, p. 179; see also *L.P.*, XVII, 534.
32   *Span. Cal.*, VIII, 95, p. 173.
33   Op. cit., 297, p. 436; *L.P.*, III (2), 2958.
34   *L.P.*, II (1), 1902, 1923.
35   *L.P.*, III (1), 432; Williams, H. N., *Henri II*, p. 8.
36   Brandi, *Charles V*, pp. 413–17; *L.P.*, XIII (2), 310–11.
37   Tyler, *Charles the Fifth*, pp. 25, 40.
38   Williams, H. N., *Henri II*, pp. 31–2; Brandi, *Charles V*, pp. 223–36.
39   *State Papers*, X, 1276, p. 777.
40   *L.P.*, XIV (1), 92; XVI, 449, pp. 221–2; 712; Herbert, *Henry the Eighth*, p. 94.
41   For instance see *L.P.*, XIX (1), 712; 978; XX (1), 531.
42   Rymer, *Foedora*, XV, pp. 53–7; Herbert, *Henry the Eighth*, pp. 513–15.
43   *Span. Cal.*, VIII, 101, p. 190; 104, p. 198.
44   Wernham, *Before the Armada* (esp. ch. XII), is the best comprehensive study of Henry's foreign policy. See also Bowle, *Henry VIII*, p. 270; Pollard, *Henry VIII*, pp. 328–30; and Scarisbrick, *Henry VIII*, pp. 434–6, 445–8.
45   *Span. Cal.*, VI, 13, p. 37; Kaulek, 444, pp. 461–3.
46   Elton, *Reformation Europe*, p. 79.
47   *L.P.*, XIX (1), 65.
48   *L.P.*, XVIII (1), 288.
49   P.R.O., S.P. 1, vol. 244, ff. 140–43; *State Papers*, IX, 847, pp. 388–91; *L.P.*, XVIII (1), 606.
50   Keen, *Laws of War*, pp. 68–9.
51   Ascham, *Whole Works*, III, p. 159; Gardiner, *Letters*, 118, p. 271; More, *Utopia* (ed. Campbell), p. 25; *L.P.*, III, 1165; XIX (1), 678.
52   *State Papers*, XI, 1344, pp. 115–16.
53   Gardiner, *Letters*, 83, p. 180.
54   Brandi, *Charles V*, p. 365; *L.P.*, XIX (1), 324, 529, 530; Romei, *Courtiers Academie*, p. 78.
55   Quoted in Kelso, *Doctrine of the English Gentleman*, p. 98, from Gervase Markham, *Honour in his Perfection*, p. 4.
56   For example, Henry VIII, *Letters*, pp. 147, 378; *State Papers*, X, 1009, p. 19.
57   The literature on the subject is extensive. I have relied heavily on Brandt, *Shape of Medieval History* (esp. chs 3 and 4); Ferguson, *Indian Summer of English Chivalry*; Bryson, *Point of Honor in Sixteenth-Century Italy*; Ernle, *Light Reading* (esp. pp. 77–105); Borst, 'Das Rittertum im Hochmittelalter—Idee und Wirklichkeit', *Saeculum*, X; and Huizinga, *Men and Ideas* (esp. 'The Political and Military Significance of Chivalric Ideas').
58   Brandi, *Charles V*, pp. 28–31, 77, 89; Gardiner, *Letters*, 99–102, pp. 211–27.
59   Ferguson, *Indian Summer of English Chivalry*, pp. 23–4, 70.

60 Ascham, *Whole Works*, III, pp. 7–8.
61 Brandt, *Shape of Medieval History*, pp. 85, 164.
62 Castiglione, *Book of the Courtier*, p. 70.
63 Vergil, *Anglica Historia*, p. 161.
64 *L.P.*, I, 4284, p. 624.
65 P.R.O., S.P. 1, vol. 194, f. 222 (*L.P.*, XIX [2], 549); 195, f. 39 (580); f. 61 (588).
66 *Span. Cal.*, VIII, 184, p. 292. For details of the battle see Nott, I, pp. 198–201 and *State Papers*, XI, 1303, p. 17.
67 Henry VIII, *Letters*, p. 355; see also Keen, *Laws of War*, p. 225.
68 *L.P.*, XVII, 672–4.
69 *State Papers*, V, 416, p. 250 n.
70 *Hamilton Papers*, I, 189, p. 240; 204, p. 261; *L.P.*, XX (1), 781.
71 *State Papers*, V, 407, p. 229; 408, p. 230.
72 *L.P.*, XVIII (2), 13; Nott, I, App. X, p. xxxvi.
73 Du Bellay, *Mémoires* (ed. Bourrilly and Vindry), IV, pp. 265–6.
74 Nott, I, p. 183.
75 Quoted in Williams, H. N., *Henri II*, p. 19, from Brantôme, *Vie des grands capitaines*.
76 *Hamilton Papers*, I, 261, p. 342.
77 *L.P.*, XXI (1), 940.
78 *L.P.*, XIX (1), 533; Hall, *Henry VIII*, II, p. 348.
79 *State Papers*, IX, 980, p. 688.
80 Op. cit., IV, 15, p. 26. See also Brandt, *Shape of Medieval History*, pp. 132–3, and Keen, *Laws of War*, p. 243.
81 *L.P.*, XX (2), 306; P.R.O., S.P. 1, vol. 194, f. 113 (*L.P.*, XIX [2], 500).
82 P.R.O., S.P. 1, vol. 216, ff. 65–72 (*L.P.*, XXI [1], 505); *Span. Cal.*, VIII, 143, p. 256.
83 Langsam, *Martial Books*, p. 52.
84 Castiglione, *Book of the Courtier*, p. 41.
85 Op. cit., p. 96.

CHAPTER 8

1 Kaulek, 401, p. 397; 275, p. 247.
2 *Spanish Chronicle*, p. 77.
3 Quoted in Camden, *Elizabethan Woman*, p. 100, from J. C. Jeaffreson, *Brides and Bridals*.
4 Kaulek, 306, p. 273.
5 Ibid.
6 Op. cit., 345, pp. 309–10, 350, pp. 317–20; 359, pp. 334–6; 361, pp. 337–8.
7 Op. cit., 361, pp. 337–8.
8 *State Papers*, I, 156, p. 680; *L.P.*, XVI, 1131.
9 *P.P.C.*, VII, pp. 352–3; Kaulek, 369, pp. 350–51.
10 The story can be read in Smith, *Tudor Tragedy*, from which this account has been taken.
11 P.R.O., S.P. 1, vol. 168, f. 60 (*L.P.*, XVI, 1409 [1], sec. 4); ff. 64–5 (1409 [3], secs. 1, 7, 8, 10).
12 Op. cit., vol. 167, f. 129 (*L.P.*, XVI, 1320).
13 Op. cit., vol. 167, f. 130; f. 161 (*L.P.*, XVI, 1339); Burnet (ed. Nares), IV, 71, p. 505; *Cal. Marquis of Bath MSS*, II, 9.
14 *L.P.*, XVI, 1469.

15 Burnet (ed. Nares), IV, 71, p. 505; *L.P.*, XVI, 1414; P.R.O., S.P. 1, vol. 167, f. 161 (*L.P.*, XVI, 1339).
16 Kaulek, 376, p. 363.
17 *Original Letters*, I, 108, pp. 226–7.
18 *P.P.C.*, VII, p. 353.
19 Op. cit., pp. 354–5.
20 Op cit., p. 355; Kaulek, 380, p. 370.
21 *Span. Cal.*, VI (1), 211, pp. 410–11.
22 P.R.O., S.P. 1, vol. 167, f. 159 (*L.P.*, XVI, 1339).
23 Kaulek, 380, p. 371.
24 *Statutes of the Realm*, III, cap. 21, p. 859; *Span. Cal.*, VI (1), 232, p. 473; Ellis, *Letters*, ser. 1, II, 147, pp. 128–9.
25 Kaulek, 380, p. 370; *Journal of the House of Lords*, I, p. 171.
26 *State Papers*, VIII, 703, p. 636; *L.P.*, XVI, 1396, 1448, 1453; XVII, 19.
27 Kaulek, 401, p. 397.
28 *L.P.*, XVII, 415; 568; 1258, p. 693; XIX (1), 531 (2).
29 *L.P.*, XVII, 235; 746; 770.
30 *L.P.*, XV, 21; XVI, 394, 449, 660, 678 g. 41, 578 g. 28, 1391 g. 18; XIX (1), 275; XX (2), App. 2; XXI (1), 969.
31 *L.P.*, XV, 616–17.
32 Elton, *Revolution in Tudor Government*, pp. 382–4, 387; *L.P.*, XV, 179.
33 Henry VIII, *Letters*, p. 173.
34 Thomas Cawaden, Thomas Paston, Peter Mewtas, Anthony Denney and Philip Hobey were knighted in 1544 (*L.P.*, XIX [2], 334). Thomas Seymour, Richard Long, Thomas Darcy, Maurice Barkley, Anthony Browne and George Carew, not to mention Hertford and Lisle, all received important military posts.
35 P.R.O., S.P. 1, vol. 193, ff. 126–7 (*L.P.*, XIX [2], 416).
36 *L.P.*, XXI (1), 498, 939, 951; XXI (2), 58, 62, 116, 289, 316, 319, 347.
37 A.P.C., I, p. 406.
38 Waggoner, 'Elizabethan Attitudes toward Peace and War', *Philological Quarterly*, XXXIII, pp. 22, 31; Langsam, *Martial Books*, pp. 10, 14; Raleigh, *Works*, VIII, p. 257.
39 *Literae Cantuarienses*, III, 1079, pp. 274–85.
40 Hughes and Larkin, *Proclamations*, I, 250, p. 352; *L.P.*, XX (2), 305.
41 Kaulek, 293, p. 263.
42 Cranmer, *Writings*, p. 110.
43 Shanley, *Spencer's Gentleman*, p. 24; Langsam, *Martial Books*, p. 147.
44 *L.P.*, XX (1), 97–8, 129, 381; Wriothesley, *Chronicle*, I, pp. 151, 153.
45 Raleigh, *Works*, VIII, p. 258.
46 *L.P.*, XVII, 178, 261, 279.
47 Kaulek, 416, pp. 420–21.
48 Op. cit., 421, p. 426.
49 *L.P.*, XVII, 559, 571, 639, 729; Kaulek, 436, p. 448; 439, p. 456; 444, p. 462.
50 *L.P.*, XVII, 580, 586, 643.
51 Op. cit., 540, 574, 650–51, 663, 759, 1072.
52 Op. cit., 778.
53 Op. cit., 862, 865, 886, 906, 942.
54 Op. cit., 806, 835.
55 Henry VIII, *Letters*, p. 299.
56 Op. cit., pp. 296–7, 301; *L.P.*, XVII, 898; see also Mackie, 'Henry VIII and Scotland'. *Trans. Royal His. Soc.*, XXIX, pp. 93–114.

57 *State Papers*, IX, 797, pp. 244–5.
58 *L.P.*, XVII, 754, 771, 804, 809, 813, 820, 836, 846, 940.
59 Op. cit., 828, 894, 946, 969, 975.
60 *Hamilton Papers*, I, 223, p. 282.
61 *L.P.*, XVII, 994, 996, 998.
62 Op. cit., 1001; *Hamilton Papers*, I, 231, p. 297.
63 *L.P.*, XVII, 1110, 1117, 1121, 1130, 1137, 1142; XVIII (1), 44; Makinson, 'Solway Moss and the Death of James V', *History Today*, x, pp. 106–15,
64 The Ambassador was correct but premature; Henry married Catherine. Parr on July 12th, 1543. *Span. Cal.*, VI, 84, p. 185.
65 *State Papers*, IX, 798, p. 248.
66 *L.P.*, XVII, 1034; *Hamilton Papers*, I, 255, p. 331.
67 *L.P.*, XVII, 1193, 1213–14, 1249.
68 Op. cit., 1194.
69 Gurney-Salter, *Tudor England*, p. 75.
70 *L.P.*, XVIII (1), 141. See Grant, *Social and Economic Development of Scotland* and also *The Lordship of the Isles*; Dickinson, *Scotland to 1603*; and Donaldson, *Scotland: James V to James VII* (esp. pp. 3–84).
71 *L.P.*, XVIII (2), 42, 677.
72 Op. cit., 323.
73 *Span. Cal.*, VI (2), 94, p. 216.
74 Wriothesley, *Chronicle*, I, pp. 140–41; Henry VIII, *Letters*, p. 313; *Span. Cal.*, VI (2), 89, pp. 191–2; 90, p. 193. For Paget's defence see *State Papers*, IX, 802, p. 269.
75 *Hamilton Papers*, I, 275, p. 363.
76 Op cit., 275, pp. 365–6; 276, pp. 367–76; 348, pp. 498–503. I have relied heavily for the narrative of these complex doings on Slavin, *Politics and Profit*, especially ch. VI. Our views as to Henry's purpose, however, are not the same.
77 Sadler, *State Papers*, I, pp. 248, 256.
78 *L.P.*, XX (1), 273; XX (2), 40–42; *A.P.C.*, I, pp. 174, 240, 243.
79 *Hamilton Papers*, I, 301, p. 426; for the reception of the Bible see op. cit., 316, p. 445.
80 *L.P.*, XVIII (1), 153, 741, 779.
81 *Hamilton Papers*, I, 348, pp. 499–500.
82 *L.P.*, XVIII (1), 144, 170, 194–5.
83 Sadler, *State Papers*, I, pp. 84–90, 101–3, 108–12; *Hamilton Papers*, I, 330, pp. 462–7; *State Papers*, V, 427, p. 271; 428, pp. 271–80.
84 Sadler, *State Papers*, I, pp. 142–50.
85 *L.P.*, XVIII (1), 316, 325, 334, 374.
86 Slavin, *Politics and Profit*, p. 118.
87 *L.P.*, XVIII (1), 400, 402, 410, 418, 455, 468, 479, 482.
88 Op. cit., 804, 865.
89 Op. cit., 671, 754.
90 Sadler, *State Papers*, I, p. 216.
91 *L.P.*, XVIII (1), 796, 810.
92 Sadler, *State Papers*, I, p. 235.
93 Op. cit., pp. 242–6.
94 Op. cit., pp. 325–9.
95 *L.P.*, XVIII (1), 849, 867, 902, 905, 935, 952; XVIII (2), 42, 133, 155.
96 *Hamilton Papers*, II, 27, p. 34.
97 Op. cit., 31, p. 43.
98 Op. cit., 99, p. 161.

99 *State Papers*, V, 473, p. 351.
100 *Span. Cal.*, VI (2), 97, p. 235.

CHAPTER 9

1   Armstrong, *Emperor Charles*, II, pp. 367, 376, 382; Bradford, *Correspondence of Charles V*, p. 365; see also *State Papers*, IX, 774, p. 167; 779, p. 191.
2   Brandi, *Charles V*, pp. 313, 450; Tyler, *Charles the Fifth*, pp. 26–7; Armstrong, op. cit., II, p. 374; Bradford, op cit., pp. 436–9, 470.
3   Brandi, op. cit., p. 502.
4   Tyler, *Charles the Fifth*, p. 285; Bradford, *Correspondence of Charles V*, pp. 383–4.
5   *Span. Cal.*, VIII, 36, p. 76; 104, p. 196; 115, pp. 219–20; 186, p. 295.
6   *State Papers*, VIII, 710, p. 661.
7   Op. cit., IX, 801, p. 258. There is no adequate biography of Francis I in any language, and most of the biographies are romantic potpourris of court gossip, taken from Du Bellay, *Mémoires*, Montluc, *Commentaires*, Brantôme, *Œuvres*, and *Chronique du roi Francois premier*.
8   Puttenham, *Arte of Poesie*, p. 228.
9   *L.P.*, XVII, 400; *State Papers*, XI, 1412, p. 278.
10   *L.P.*, XIX (2), 105.
11   *L.P.*, XVII, 935; Williams, H. N., *Henri II*, pp. 90–91, 116, 126–8.
12   Gardiner, *Letters*, 60, p. 89.
13   Brandi, *Charles V*, p. 459. The story can be followed in *L.P.*, XVI, 1031, 1199, 1228, 1303, 1431, 1453; XVII, 487, 492.
14   *L.P.*, XIII (2), 1087; Pastor, *Lives of the Popes*, XII, pp. 460 ff.
15   Gardiner, *Letters*, 62, pp. 96–100; Burnet (ed. Nares), IV, p. 512.
16   *State Papers*, VIII, 712, p. 678; 719, p. 710; *Span. Cal.*, VI (2), 2, pp. 6–7; see also *L.P.*, XVII, 145, 164, 182, 248, 415.
17   Kaulek, 420, p. 424.
18   Op cit., p. 422.
19   *L.P.*, XVII, App. B, 4.
20   Kaulek, 428, p. 433.
21   *L.P.*, XVII, App. B, 13, p. 720. 'The King lately dismissed a gentleman of his chamber for being too familiar with the French Ambassador' (XVII, 780).
22   Op. cit., App. B, 13, p. 720; B, 22, p. 729; B, 23, p. 736.
23   Op. cit., App. B, 13, p. 720; B, 21; B, 22, pp. 729, 731; B, 23, p. 735; B, 30; *Span. Cal.*, VI, 13, p. 38; Gardiner, *Letters*, 62, p. 97.
24   *L.P.*, XVII, 980, 993, 1017.
25   Op. cit., 1017, p. 575; 1241.
26   Dudley, *Tree of Commonwealth*, p. 50.
27   P.R.O., S.P. 1, vol. 211, f. 100 (*L.P.*, XX [2], 891); *L.P.*, XVII, 1017, p. 571.
28   The critical documents are *L.P.*, XVII, 446, 608, 616, 963, 1008, 1017, 1092, 1212; XVIII (1), 144, 150, 171; *State Papers*, IX, 740, pp. 68–73; 786, pp. 213–16. Henry followed the negotiations with infinite care, pencilling documents and scrutinizing their language. See especially *State Papers*, IX, 773, p. 162.
29   *L.P.*, XVII, 1017, 1212.
30   *Hamilton Papers*, I, 159, p. 197.

31 Rymer, *Foedora*, XIV, pp. 768–76; *L.P.*, XVII, 1017, pp. 572, 574; 1044; XVIII (1), 150, 171.
32 *L.P.*, XVII, 442.
33 *Hamilton Papers*, I, 159, p. 197.
34 *L.P.*, XVIII (1), 534.
35 Op. cit., 622; *State Papers*, IX, 847, p. 388.
36 *L.P.*, XVIII (1), 771, 798, 831, 832.
37 *State Papers*, IX, 921, p. 527; *L.P.*, XVIII (2), 280, 310, 657 (2).
38 *Span. Cal.*, VI, 269, p. 541.
39 Op. cit., VI, 268, pp. 529, 531, 533–4.
40 Op. cit., VI (2), 59, pp. 127–9; VIII, 140, p. 251.
41 Op. cit., VII, 7, p. 24; Henry VIII, *Letters*, p. 346.
42 *Span. Cal.*, VI, 13, p. 37.
43 Op cit., VI (2), 272, p. 544; *L.P.*, XVIII (2), 467 (7); *State Papers*, IX, 941, p. 572.
44 See for example *L.P.*, XIX (1), 105, 127, 284, 312, 381, 400, 472, 578, 767, 770, 802, 832; *State Papers*, IX, 993, pp. 720-21.
45 Becon, *Early Works*, p. 235.
46 *L.P.*, XIX (1), 118, 206, 375.
47 Op. cit., 84.
48 *State Papers*, V, 486, pp. 371–3; Haynes, *State Papers*, pp. 11–12; *Hamilton Papers*, II, 207, pp. 325–7; 217, pp. 338–43. See also *L.P.*, XIX (1), 327.
49 For a full discussion of medieval war of attrition see Hewitt, *Organization of War under Edward III*.
50 For a complete description of the raid, its planning, cost and results, see *L.P.* XIX (1), 140, 366, 472, 483, 510, 531–4.
51 See Davies, 'Provisions for Armies 1509–50', *Eco. His. Rev.*, ser. 2, XVII, pp. 235–48; Oman, *The Art of War in the Sixteenth Century*; Lot, *Les Effectifs des armeés françaises 1494–1562*; Cruickshank, *Army Royal*; Hale, *Art of War and Renaissance England;* and also 'Armies, Navies and the Art of War', *New Cambridge Modern History*, II; O'Neil, *Castles and Cannon*.
52 *State Papers*, IX, 990, p. 711 n. 1; *L.P.*, XIX (1), 730.
53 *State Papers*, I, 75, pp. 135–40; VI, 76, pp. 233–5; *L.P.*, III, 3281, 3284, 3288, 3347, 3516, 3580.
54 *L.P.*, XIX (1), 438, 469, 622, 667, 674, 685–7, 700.
55 Op. cit., 529.
56 *State Papers*, IX, 990, p. 711 n. 1; 980, pp. 682–93; *L.P.*, XVIII (1), 599; XIX (1), 324, 530, 619, 626, 730; Williams, H. N., *Henri II*, p. 48.
57 B.M., Cotton MSS Calig. E IV, f. 55 (*L.P.*, XIX [2], 201); P.R.O., S.P. 1, vol. 191, ff. 233–4 (*L.P.*, XIX [2], 174); Bradford, *Correspondence of Charles V*, p. 450.
58 *L.P.*, XIX (1), 604.
59 *State Papers*, IX, 980, pp. 682–93; *L.P.*, XIX (1), 730, 739.
60 *L.P.*, XIX (1), 654, 674, 694, 701, 709, 738, 741, 763, 836, 849; P.R.O., S.P. 1, vol. 189, ff. 151–2 (*L.P.*, XIX [1], 816); ff. 153–4 (XIX [1], 817).
61 Norfolk's plight is best studied in B.M., Harl. MSS 6989, ff. 127–8 (*L.P.*, XIX [1], 863); f. 129 (XIX [1], 872); P.R.O., S.P. 1, vol. 189, ff. 207–8 (XIX [1], 849); 190, ff. 23–5 (XIX [1], 903).
62 *L.P.*, XIX (1), 691.
63 *State Papers*, IX, 941, pp. 571–3. The Duke of Suffolk, who had led the 1524 fiasco, was busy on the Scottish border.
64 P.R.O., S.P. 1, vol. 190, ff. 78–80 (*L.P.*, XIX [1], 933).

L

65 *L.P.*, XIX (1), 955.
66 *State Papers*, IX, 999, pp. 733–5.
67 *L.P.*, XIX (1), 955; (2), 45, 181.
68 Brandi, *Charles V*, pp. 514–21. The Pope's reprimand (*L.P.*, XIX [2], 134)
    is quoted at length in Froude, *History of England*, IV, p. 337. Nicholas
    Wotton's dispatches for August and September are worth looking at:
    L.P., XIX (2), 109–10, 138–9, 162, 193–4, 267–8.
69 The treaty of Crêpy is *L.P.*, XIX (2), 249. The secret codicil is B.M.,
    Egerton MSS 990, ff. 414–16 (*L.P.*, XIX [2], 260). See also Brandi,
    Charles V, pp. 520–21.
70 Williams, H. N., *Henri II*, p. 159.
71 *L.P.*, XIX (2), 250.
72 Op. cit., 198.
73 Op. cit., 236.
74 *State Papers*, X, 1031, pp. 71–5.
75 *L.P.*, XIX (2), 249.
76 Op. cit., 264, 304.
77 *State Papers*, X, 1109, p. 297; *Span. Cal.*, VIII, 2, pp. 6–8; Henry VIII,
    Letters, p. 392.
78 *State Papers*, X, 1229, p. 623; *Span. Cal.*, VIII, 83, pp. 154–5; 126, p. 236;
    140, p. 251.
79 For the description of the fall of Boulogne see Rymer, *Foedera*, XV, pp.
    52–7. For the aftermath see *State Papers*, I, 201, pp. 767–8, and *L.P.*,
    XIX (2), 259, 306–7, 424.
80 Du Bellay, *Mémoires* (ed. Michaud and Poujoulat), V, p. 550; Vieilleville,
    Mémoires, IX, pp. 49, 64–5; *Span. Cal.*, VIII, 115, p. 223; *L.P.*, XIX (1),
    946.
81 *L.P.*, XIX (2), 258–9.
82 For the English difficulties see *L.P.*, XIX (2), 280, 303, 306, 307, 309,
    377, 380; Du Bellay, *Mémoires* (ed. Michaud and Poujoulat), V, p. 550,
    and *L.P.*, XIX (2), 318; XX (1), 11.
83 *Span. Cal.*, VIII, 2, p. 2.
84 Gardiner, *Letters*, 86, p. 187.
85 P.R.O., S.P. 1, vol. 193, f. 92 (*L.P.*, XIX [2], 395); Nott, I, App. xvii,
    pp. xlviii–li; Montluc, *Commentaires*, VIII, pp. 74–5; Du Bellay, *Mémoires*
    (ed. Michaud and Poujoulat), V, pp. 550–1.
86 For the whole story and the King's state of mind see Nott, I, App. xviii,
    pp. lii–lv; App. xx, p. lvi; P.R.O., S.P. 1, vol. 193, ff. 98–100 (*L.P.*, XIX
    [2], 399); *State Papers*, X, 1045, pp. 106–7; 1050, pp. 117–19; *L.P.*, XIX
    (2), 629.
87 Rising costs and tempers can be sampled in *L.P.*, XIX (2), 689; XX (1),
    984; (2), 324, 366, 453, 472, 729, 769; XXI (2), 59; *A.P.C.*, I, p. 325;
    Span. Cal., VIII, 226, p. 349; and Dietz, *Public Finance*, I, pp. 155–7,
    162.
88 Gardiner, *Letters*, 85, p. 183; 86, p. 186.
89 *L.P.*, XX (2), 971.
90 For trouble with mercenaries see *L.P.*, XX (2), 536, 616, 671; for
    Vaughan's difficulties see op. cit. XX (1), 1194, 1234; (2), 113, 566;
    XXI (1), 211, 264.
91 *L.P.*, XX (1), 87, 153, 541, 630, 682, 925, 952, 1101; *Span. Cal.*, VIII,
    36, p. 77; 115, p. 220.
92 A fair sampling of the war effort can be found in *State Papers*, I, 211,
    pp. 785–7; P.R.O., S.P. 1, vol. 197, ff. 11–16 (*L.P.*, XX [1], 16); 200, ff.

189–98 (*L.P.*, XX [1], 672–4); *A.P.C.*, I, pp. 174, 346; *Span. Cal.*, VIII, 67, p. 130; *L.P.*, XX (1), 513, 555, 557, 845.

93 *L.P.*, XIX (2), 709; XX (1), 253, 280, 285–6, 301, 311–12, 332, 367, 781.

94 *State Papers*, V, 515, p. 431.

95 *Span. Cal.*, VIII, 86, p. 161. For the deterioration of Anglo-Imperial relations see P.R.O., S.P. 1, vol. 198, ff. 207–12 (*L.P.*, XX [1], 302); *State Papers*, X, 1088, pp. 236–7; 1092, pp. 243–4; 1160, pp. 456–7; 1185, pp. 524–9; *L.P.*, XX (1), 871, 933; (2), 19.

96 Gardiner, *Letters*, 87, p. 192.

97 P.R.O., S.P. 1, Vol. 203, ff. 122–3 (*L.P.*, XX [1], 1133).

98 *State Papers*, V, 515, p. 431.

99 For the French misadventures see Du Bellay, *Mémoires* (ed. Michaud and Poujoulat), V, p. 533; *Span. Cal.*, VIII, 104, p. 198.

100 For narratives of the war, both French and English, see Du Bellay, *Mémoires* (ed. Michaud and Poujoulat), V, pp. 552–60; *A.P.C.*, I, pp. 211–17; *State Papers*, I, 230, pp. 818–20; 232, pp. 823–4; *Span. Cal.*, VIII, 91, p. 165; 101, pp. 187, 190–91, 204–5; 104, p. 198; 119, p. 229; 122, p. 232; 136, pp. 247–8; 143, pp. 255–6.

101 *L.P.*, XX (2), 368, 494; XXI (1), 527, 706.

102 Op. cit., XX (2), 533.

103 For Hertford's raid see *State Papers*, V, 568–71, pp. 521–35; *L.P.*, XX (2), 533.

104 P.R.O., S.P. 1, vol. 195, ff. 66–7 (*L.P.*, XIX [2], 592); ff. 134–5 (XIX [2], 629); 210, ff. 171–4 (XX [2], 811); 211, ff. 19–20 (XX [2], 843); ff. 100–3 (XX [2], 891); *State Papers*, X, 1250, pp. 683–7; 1258, pp. 715–16; 1264, pp. 733–7; 1280, pp. 785–6.

105 *Span. Cal.*, VIII, 140, p. 251.

106 Gardiner, *Letters*, 85, pp. 183–4.

107 B.M., Add. MSS 25114, f. 338 (*L.P.*, XX [2], 714); Gardiner, *Letters*, 86, p. 189.

108 Nott, I, p. 178; P.R.O., S.P. 1, vol. 210, ff. 30–32 (*L.P.*, XX [2], 738).

109 *L.P.*, XX (2), 929, 950.

110 *State Papers*, XI, 1354, pp. 138–40.

111 Hall, *Henry VIII*, II, p. 133.

112 *Span. Cal.*, VIII, 71, p. 136; 79, p. 143; 104, p. 196; 115, pp. 219–20; 289, p. 421; *L.P.*, XX (1), 1045; (2), 677.

113 *L.P.*, XX (2), 350; XXI (1), 40, 250.

114 *Span. Cal.*, VIII, 31, pp. 67–8; 130, pp. 241–2.

115 *L.P.*, XX (2), 21, 567; XXI (1), 230–31, 998, 1012.

116 *State Papers*, X, 1270, p. 755; 1278, p. 782.

117 Gardiner, *Letters*, 85, p. 183; 86, p. 186.

118 The agreement was reached on December 20th, 1545, but not ratified until February 16th, 1546. See *L.P.*, XX (2), 741, 786, 790, 792, 821, 871; XXI (1), 71.

119 Francis more than once suggested such a possibility. See *State Papers*, X, 1229, p. 619 n. 1; *Span. Cal.*, VIII, 289, p. 420.

120 *Span. Cal.*, VIII, 280, p. 410; 281, pp. 411–12. See also Smith, 'Henry VIII and the Protestant Triumph', *A.H.R.*, LXXI, pp. 1254–64.

121 *L.P.*, XXI (1), 748, 841, 927, 941, 949, 989, 1014; *State Papers*, XI, 1377, pp. 192–3.

122 *State Papers*, XI, 1362, p. 164; see also *Span. Cal.*, VIII, 277, p. 407, and *L.P.*, XXI (1), 1213.

CHAPTER 10

1   Henry VIII, *Letters*, p. 216.
2   Henry VIII, *Love Letters*, p. 46.
3   Jackson, 'Wulfhall and the Seymours', *Wilt. Arch. Mag.*, xv, pp. 144, 149, 170–71; Rymer, *Foedora*, XV, p. 111.
4   Camden, *Elizabethan Woman*, p. 83.
5   *Hundred Merry Tales*, pp. 85–6.
6   *Spanish Chronicle*, p. 108.
7   P.R.O., S.P. 1, vol. 180, f. 69 (*L.P.*, XVIII [1], 894).
8   Stubbs, *Chrystal Glass*, f. A3.
9   *Spanish Chronicle*, p. 108; *L.P.*, XVIII (1), 954.
10 P.R.O., S.P. 1, vol. 180, f. 69 (*L.P.*, XVIII [1], 894).
11 Thomas, *The Pilgrim*, p. 59.
12 Strickland, *Queens of England*, III, p. 259; Strype, *Ecc. Memo.*, II, pt ii, pp. 331–2.
13 Haynes, *State Papers*, pp. 61, 99–100. There is no adequate biography of Catherine. Gordon, *Katherine Parr*, is a thoroughly unreliable little book of 56 pages, privately printed.
14 *Spanish Chronicle*, p. 108.
15 *King's Book*, p. 158.
16 The words are from Henry's speech given in Hall, *Henry VIII*, II, pp. 354–8, and in Petre's letter to Paget, P.R.O., S.P. 1, vol. 212, ff. 111–13 (*L.P.*, XX [2], 1030 [2]).
17 Strickland, *Queens of England*, III, p. 212; Camden, *Elizabethan Woman*, p. 112. For the Queen's humanistic influence see McConica, *English Humanists and Reformation Politics*, ch. VII.
18 Foxe, V, p. 559; Hall, *Henry VIII*, II, p. 357.
19 Foxe, V, pp. 559–60.
20 Foxe, V, p. 691.
21 *L.P.*, XVIII (2), 531.
22 Jenkins, *Elizabeth*, p. 17.
23 Quoted in Prescott, *Mary Tudor*, p. 79.
24 *Span. Cal.*, VIII, 2, p. 2.
25 Halliwell, *Letters*, II, pp. 8–9.
26 P.R.O., S.P. 1, vol. 195, ff. 213–14 (*L.P.*, XIX [2], 726).
27 Halliwell, *Letters*, II, 22–3; Smith, 'Henry VIII and the Protestant Triumph', *A.H.R.*, LXXI, pp. 1248–60.
28 Halliwell, *Letters*, II, p. 15.
29 Op. cit., pp. 12–13.
30 Op. cit., pp. 15–16; Nichols, *Literary Remains*, I, XIV, p. 13.
31 Puttenham, *Arte of Poesie*, p. 245.
32 *State Papers*, I, 199, pp. 763–5; X, 1005, pp. 12–14; *L.P.*, XIX (1), 1019; (2), 172.
33 See Chamberlin, *Character of Henry the Eighth*, pp. 178–214, for a detailed list of his ailments.
34 *Span. Cal.*, VIII, 216, pp. 330–31; 325, p. 475.
35 Brinch, 'The Medical Problems of Henry VIII', *Centaurus*, v (3), p. 367; MacNalty, *Henry VIII*, pp. 180, 199; Chamberlin, *Character of Henry the Eighth*, pp. 269–71; Shrewsbury, 'Henry VIII, a Medical Study', *Jour. His. of Medicine & Allied Sciences*, VII, p. 183.
36 MacNalty, op. cit., pp. 88–9.
37 Currie, 'Notes on the Obstetric Histories of Catherine of Aragon and Anne Boleyn', *Edinburgh Medical Jour.*, I, pp. 1–34.

38 Brinch, 'The Medical Problems of Henry VIII', *Centaurus*, v, pp. 339–69.
39 English and Pearson, *Emotional Problems of Living*, pp. 448–51.
40 B.M., Sloane MSS, 1047.
41 Kaulek, 306, p. 273; *Span. Cal.*, VIII, 291, p. 426.
42 *Span. Cal.*, 325, p. 475; 370, p. 533; 371, p. 535; Selve, 85, p. 81; 90, p. 85.
43 Laslett, *The World We Have Lost*, pp. 103–4.
44 Shakespeare, Sonnet ii.
45 Foxe, V, p. 555; Kaulek, 307, p. 274.
46 Armstrong, *Emperor Charles*, II, p. 351; Bradford, *Correspondence of Charles V*, pp. 383–4.
47 Coignet, *Francis the First*, p. 339.
48 *Span. Cal.*, IX, p. 62.
49 Vieilleville, *Mémoires*, IX, p. 22; Du Bellay, *Mémoires* (ed. Michaud and Poujoulat), V, p. 567.
50 Foxe, V, p. 689.
51 *Spanish Chronicle*, pp. 151–2.
52 *L.P.*, II, 1991.

CHAPTER II

1   Strype, *Cranmer*, I, p. 164; P.R.O., S.P. 1, vol. 112, f. 227 (*L.P.*, II, 1536).
2   Stapleton, *Life of More*, p. 192.
3   B.M., Cotton MSS Galba B X, pp. 21 ff., quoted *in extenso* by Demaus, *Tyndale*, p. 313.
4   *Statutes of the Realm*, III, cap. 13, pp. 508–9.
5   *L.P.*, VIII, 771, p. 290.
6   *Original Letters*, I, p. 211.
7   Kaulek, 292, p. 261.
8   *L.P.*, VII, 635.
9   Quoted in Jordan, *Edward VI*, p. 175.
10 *L.P.*, XIV (1), 144.
11 Northamp. Rec. Soc., 'Paget Letters', 8; *Span. Cal.*, IX, pp. 197, 205–6.
12 P.R.O., S.P. 1, vol. 224, ff. 53–4 (*L.P.*, XXI [2], 29).
13 Op. cit., vol. 224, f. 52 (*L.P.*, XXI [2], 28).
14 Foxe, IV, pp. 474–507.
15 Armstrong, *Emperor Charles*, II, p. 134.
16 P.R.O., S.P. 1, vol. 225, ff. 135–6 (*L.P.*, XXI [2], 216); 226, ff. 88–9 (XXI [2], 378); ff. 150–3 (XXI [2], 440–41).
17 Gardiner, *Letters*, 125, pp. 319–21; Foxe, V, pp. 555–6.
18 Foxe, V, p. 564.
19 Foxe, V, p. 547.
20 *L.P.*, XIV (2), 750, p. 278; Nott, II, p. 291.
21 P.R.O., S.P. 10, vol. 4, ff. 41–2.
22 *Trevelyan Papers*, pp. 206–16; Rowse, 'Eminent Henrician: Thomas Wriothesley', *History Today*, xv, pp. 382–90, 468–74.
23 Nott, I, p. 80; *A.P.C.*, I, 400–1, 408, 411.
24 *L.P.*, XVIII (1), 390, p. 228.
25 *Span. Cal.*, VIII, 386, p. 556.
26 Kaulek, 293, p. 263.
27 Nott, II, p. 295.
28 B.M., Sloane MSS 1523, f. 40.

29 *A.P.C.*, I, pp. 17, 19; Nott, I, pp. l–liv; Chapman, *Two Tudor Portraits*, pp. 64–5.
30 *A.P.C.*, I, pp. 104–8, 114, 125; *L.P.*, XVIII (1), 327. For his 'confession', see B.M., Harl. MSS 78, ff. 24 (20)–25 (21).
31 *L.P.*, XVIII (2), 243; 266, 310; Chapman, *Two Tudor Portraits*, p. 82.
32 Nott, I, p. lxviii.
33 *L.P.*, XX (2), App. 30.
34 The hint of treason is inescapable, and Surrey's inefficiency is transparent. See *L.P.*, XXI (1), 373, 383, 433, 438, 488; *A.P.C.*, I, p. 366; Nott, I, pp. 227–31.
35 Nott, I, pp. 198–202; *L.P.*, XXI (1), 65; Du Bellay, *Mémoires* (ed. Bourrilly and Vindry), IV, pp. 327–9.
36 *Chronicle of Ellis Gruffydd*, p. 42.
37 *Third Report on Historical MSS*, p. 237.
38 *State Papers*, XI, 1315, pp. 58–9.
39 Hertford took command as Warden of the Marches on November 1st; Solway Moss took place on the 24th. For the defeat of the French see *L.P.*, XX (1), 121, 180.
40 Haynes, *State Papers*, p. 5.
41 Op. cit., p. 7.
42 B.M., Cotton MSS Titus F 3, f. 274.
43 For the details of the Paget–Hertford alliance see Gammon, 'Master of Practices', pp. 166–72, and *Seymour Papers*, p. 92.
44 *Span. Cal.*, VIII, 386, p. 557.
45 It was Paget who commented upon the Bishop's uncertain temperament; see P.R.O., S.P. 1, vol. 194, ff. 201–2.
46 Gardiner, *Letters*, 125, pp. 325–6.
47 *L.P.*, XVIII (1), 68; XX (2), 391; Beer, 'Rise of John Dudley', *History Today*, xv, pp. 274–5.
48 Tytler, *England under Edward and Mary*, I, pp. 24, 191.
49 Gammon, 'Master of Practices', p. 164. Paget's bill was dated October 26th, 1546, but it presumably received the royal signature by dry stamp at the last moment. In the list of documents signed by dry stamp it is numbered 80; the last item is number 86 and is known to have been signed on January 27th (*L.P.*, XXI [2], 770).
50 *Spanish Chronicle*, p. 147.
51 Gammon, *Master of Practices*, pp. 166–72; Slavin, *Politics and Profit*, pp. 184–5.
52 *Span. Cal.*, IX, pp. 19–20.
53 For the Russell dispute see *Seymour Papers*, pp. 96–101. Party rivalry is treated in Slavin, *Politics and Profit*, pp. 152–3. See also Haynes, *State Papers*, p. 5.
54 B.M., Sloane MSS 1523, f. 37.
55 Selve, *Correspondance*, 21, p. 23; 43, p. 43; *Span. Cal.*, VIII, 370, p. 533.
56 Lisle's clash with Gardiner was reported by Selve (op. cit., 50, p. 51); Hertford's argument with Winchester is in *Span. Cal.*, VIII, 386, p. 556 (the *Calendar* confuses the Bishop of Winchester with William Paulet, who did not become Marquis of Winchester until 1551); the Tunstal–Paget quarrel is in Sturge, *Tunstal*, pp. 249, 261; and the Surrey–Lisle discord is referred to in S.P. 1, vol. 221, ff. 181–2 (*L.P.*, XXI [1], 1263); *L.P.*, XXI (2), 555 (7ii) and Burnet (ed. Nares), I, p. 554.
57 B.M., Sloane MSS 1523, ff. 26, 30.
58 *Span. Cal.*, VIII, 386, pp. 555–8.

NOTES

303

59 *State Papers*, I, 261, p. 884; *Span. Cal.*, VIII, 208, p. 320.
60 *Span. Cal.*, IX, pp. 100–1.
61 Op. cit., pp. 340–1.
62 Haynes, *State Papers*, p. 90.
63 *Span. Cal.*, IX, pp. 340–41.
64 For Norfolk's religious prejudices see *L.P.*, XVI, 101; XXI (2), 540, and B.M., Harl. MSS 422, no. 68, f. 87. The Duke's dislike of his son's chivalric posing can be seen in *L.P.*, XX (2), 455 and *Spanish Chronicle*, p. 143.
65 Herbert, *Henry the Eighth*, p. 563; Chapman, *Two Tudor Portraits*, pp. 119–20.
66 Nott, I, pp. cxx–cxxi.
67 Op. cit., pp. xcix–cii.
68 P.R.O., S.P. 1, vol. 227, f. 105 (*L.P.*, XXI [2], 555 [5]).
69 *Spanish Chronicle*, p. 143.
70 *L.P.*, XVIII (1), 73, 315, 351.
71 P.R.O., S.P. 1, vol. 227, f. 76 (*L.P.*, XXI [2], 541); ff. 103–4 (XXI [2], 554 [4]).
72 Op. cit., vol. 227, ff. 103–4.
73 B.M., Stowe MSS 396, ff. 8–9. See also Harl. MSS 297, f. 256; *Third Report on Historical MSS*, App. II, p. 267.
74 *Span. Cal.*, VIII, 367, p. 531; 370, p. 533; 372, p. 536; also *L.P.*, XXI (2), 617.
75 P.R.O., S.P. 1, vol. 227, f. 101 (*L.P.*, XXI [2], 555 [1]); Selve, *Correspondance*, 79, p. 76.
76 P.R.O., S.P., 1, vol. 227, f. 129 (*L.P.*, XXI [2], 555 [18]).
77 *Spanish Chronicle*, p. 144; *Span. Cal.*, VIII, 365, p. 527.
78 P.R.O., S.P. 1, vol. 227, ff. 101 ff. (*L.P.*, XXI [2], 555 [1–14]); Herbert, *Henry the Eighth*, pp. 564–5.
79 Nott, I, pp. xcix–c.
80 P.R.O., S.P. 1, vol. 227, f. 129 (*L.P.*, XXI [2], 555 [18]).
81 *Span. Cal.*, VIII, 367, p. 531; 370, p. 533.
82 P.R.O., S.P. 1, vol. 227, ff. 123–4 (*State Papers*, I, 265, pp. 891–2); Henry VIII, *Letters*, p. 423.
83 *Spanish Chronicle*, pp. 142–8; Wriothesley, *Chronicle*, I, p. 177; *Chronicle of the Grey Friars*, p. 53.
84 More, *Utopia* (ed. White), p. 85.
85 *Spanish Chronicle*, pp. 145–6.
86 Op. cit., p. 148.
87 B.M., Harl. MSS 297, f. 256 (*L.P.*, XXI [2], 696).
88 *L.P.*, XXI (2), 753, 759, 770 (85); *A.P.C.*, II, p. 17, in which Paget refers back to Norfolk's letter to Henry.
89 *State Papers*, I, 264, p. 889.
90 Thomas, *The Pilgrim*, p.73; *Spanish Chronicle*, p. 148; Selve, *Correspondance*, 93, p. 87.
91 *Span. Cal.*, IX, p. 450; B.M., Cotton MSS Titus F III, f. 273b.

CHAPTER 12

1 *Span. Cal.*, VIII, 316, p. 465; Wriothesley, *Chronicle*, I, p. 173; Hall, *Henry VIII*, II, pp. 359–60.
2 *State Papers*, XI, 1356, p. 261.
3 *Span. Cal.*, VIII, 297, p. 436. For a fuller treatment of the diplomatic tangle see Smith, 'Henry VIII and the Protestant Triumph', *A.H.R.*,

LXXI, pp. 1252–64; Salles, 'Une Mediation des Protestants D'Allemagne entre la France et l'Angleterre au milieu du xvie siècle', *Revue d'Histoire Diplomatique*, XIII, pp. 27–46; and Scarisbrick, *Henry VIII*, pp. 467–70.

4 *Span. Cal.*, VIII, 262, p. 394; 266, p. 398.
5 Henry VIII, *Letters*, pp. 349–50; *L.P.*, XX (1), 1106; XXI (1), 948, 1070.
6 Selve, *Correspondance*, 24, p. 26; 76, p. 73; 93, p. 86; *Span. Cal.*, VIII, 377, p. 543; *State Papers*, XI, 1471, p. 404. See also *L.P.*, XXI (2), 36, 91, 348, 408, 444, 455, 651, 662, 743.
7 *L.P.*, XXI (2), 770 (56).
8 *Span. Cal.*, VIII, 308, p. 451.
9 *State Papers*, I, 257, pp. 879–80; 259, p. 882.
10 Foxe, V, pp. 557–61.
11 Gardiner, *Letters*, 112–13, pp. 246–9.
12 Foxe, VI, pp. 138–9.
13 Foxe, V, pp. 691–2.
14 Herbert, *Henry the Eighth*, p. 572.
15 Bradford, *Correspondence of Charles V*, pp. 378–9.
16 Foxe, VI, p. 163.
17 Foxe, V, pp. 691–2.
18 Foxe, V, p. 695.
19 Sander, *Anglican Schism*, p. 160.
20 The whole story is Paget's. See *A.P.C.*, II, pp. 15–20. For further confirmation see *Span. Cal.*, IX, p. 4.
21 Jordan, *Edward VI*, pp. 63–5, 112.
22 The grants are recorded in *L.P.*, XXI (2). Grants for October 1546 (332) were Hobey (7), Owen (26), Henneage (41), Russell (59), Wendye (73) and Darcy (77); for November (476): Bellingham (4), Parr (10) and Blagge (63); for December (648): Clerk (9), Herbert (34), Cawerden (50), Denney (60) and Gate (61); for January 1547 (771): Browne (3).
23 Foxe, VI, p. 163; *Span. Cal.*, VIII, 370, p. 533. The original of the will is in the P.R.O., Royal Wills, E. 23, IV, pt i, pp. 1–17. The most easily available reprint is Rymer, *Foedera*, XV, pp. 110–17. In the various copies the date is highly unstable: December 13th (Harl. MSS 293, ff. 107–15); November 3rd (Harl. 1877, ff. 41–5); December 3rd (Harl. 5805, no. 18, f. 373).
24 P.R.O., S.P. 4, January 1547, list 19, sec. 85 (*State Papers*, I, 266, pp. 897–8; *L.P.*, XXI [2], 770 [85].
25 B.M., Harl. MSS 419, f. 151; 849, esp. ff. 32–3; Add. MSS 4314, ff. 73–90; Burnet (ed. Nares), IV, pp. 147–9. For a full treatment see Levine, *Elizabethan Succession Question*.
26 Smith, 'Last Will and Testament of Henry VIII', *J.B.S.*, II, pp. 21–5; Jordan, *Edward VI*, pp. 54–6 and esp. 55 n. 2; B.M., Harl. MSS 419, f. 151; 849, f. 32.
27 Rymer, *Foedera*, XV, pp. 110–17.
28 Pollard, *Protector Somerset*, p. 2; Pickthorn, *Early Tudor Government: Henry VIII*, pp. 539–40.
29 Tytler, *England under Edward and Mary*, I, p. 169.
30 P.R.O., S.P. 11, vol. 4, f. 93; S.P. 12, vol. 8, f. 71.
31 Edwardes, *Castra Regia*, p. 37.
32 Pollard, *Protector Somerset*, pp. 27–8, suggests that Henry could not legally have named a Lord Protector even if he had wished to do so.
33 Foxe, VI, p. 163.
34 Foxe, V, p. 692.

35 *Spanish Chronicle*, p. 105.
36 On Thirlby see Foxe, VI, pp. 163-4; on Petre see Emmison, *Tudor Secretary*, pp. 66, 69. In one of the versions of Henry's last recorded words he is made to say: 'Bryan, we have lost all' (Sander, *Anglican Schism*, p. 164 n. 2); yet Bryan is not mentioned in the will.
37 Muller, *Gardiner*, pp. 198-200; Foxe, VI, p. 106; Gardiner, *Letters*, 121, pp. 286-7.
38 Selve, *Correspondance*, 96, p. 88; for the coronation see *L.P.*, XXI (2), 723.
39 *L.P.*, XXI (2), 770 (28), 771 §32.
40 P.R.O., S.P. 10, vol. 1, ff. 1, 3; *Span. Cal.*, IX, p. 30.
41 Foxe, V, p. 689.
42 *Spanish Chronicle*, pp. 154-5; Wriothesley, *Chronicle*, I, p. 181; Strype, *Ecc. Memo.*, II, pt ii, pp. 289-311.
43 Erasmus, *Epistles*, I, p. 457.
44 Strype, *Ecc. Memo.*, I, pt i, p. 604; Thomas, *The Pilgrim*, p. 79.

BIBLIOGRAPHY OF PRINTED BOOKS CITED IN THE NOTES

Acts of the Privy Council of England, ed. J. R. Dasent, 32 vols (London, 1890–1907).

Anglo, Sydney, *Spectacle, Pageantry and Early Tudor Policy* (Oxford, 1969).

Armstrong, Edward, *The Emperor Charles V,* 2 vols (London, 1910).

Ascham, Roger, *The Whole Works,* ed. Dr Giles, 3 vols (London, 1864).

Bainton, R. H., *Here I Stand, A Life of Martin Luther* (New York, 1950; London, 1951).

Baldwin, William, *A Treatise of Moral Philosophy* (London, 1564).

Batiffol, L., *The Century of the Renaissance,* trans. E. F. Buckley (London and New York, 1916).

Baumer, F. le Van, *The Early Tudor Theory of Kingship* (New Haven, 1940).

Becon, Thomas, *The Early Works,* ed. J. Ayre, Parker Soc. (London, 1843).

Beer, B. L., 'The Rise of John Dudley, Duke of Northumberland', *History Today,* XV (April 1965).

Boorde, Andrew, *A compendyous regyment or a dyetary of Helth* (originally London, 1542, ed. F. J. Furnivall, E.E.T.S.; extra ser., X, 1870).

— *The Wisdom of Andrew Boorde,* ed. H. E. Poole (Leicester, 1936).

Borst, Arno, 'Das Rittertum im Hochmittelalter—Idee und Wirklichkeit', *Saeculum,* X (1959).

Bowle, John, *Henry VIII, a Biography* (London, 1964).

Braddock, Robert, 'The Royal Household, 1540–1560', unpub. Ph.D. thesis (Northwestern Univ., 1971).

Bradford, William, *Correspondence of the Emperor Charles V and His Ambassadors at the Courts of England and France* (London, 1850).

Brandi, Karl, *The Emperor Charles V,* trans. C. V. Wedgwood (London, 1967).

Brandt, W. J., *The Shape of Medieval History; Studies in Modes of Perception* (New Haven, 1966).

Brantôme, Pierre de Bourdeille, *Œuvres Complètes,* ed. L. Lalanne, 11 vols (Paris, 1864–5).

Brinch, Ove, 'The Medical Problems of Henry VIII', *Centaurus*, v (1958).

Brook, Roy, *The Story of Eltham Palace* (London, 1960).

Brown, Marha, 'The Foreign Policy of Henry VIII, 1536–47', unpub. Ph.D. thesis (Northwestern Univ., 1970).

Bryson, F. R., *The Point of Honor in Sixteenth-Century Italy: An Aspect of the Life of the Gentleman* (Chicago, 1935).

Burnet, Gilbert, *The History of the Reformation of the Church of England*, ed. E. Nares, 4 vols (London, 1839); ed. N. Pocock, 7 vols (Oxford, 1865).

Burton, Elizabeth, *The Pageant of Elizabethan England* (New York, 1958).

Calendar of Letters, Despatches, and State Papers relating to Negotiations between England and Spain preserved in the Archives at Simancas and elsewhere, ed. G. A. Bergenroth, *et al.* (London, 1862–1954).

Calendar of State Papers and Manuscripts relating to English Affairs, Preserved in the Archives of Venice and in other Libraries of Northern Italy, ed. R. Brown, *et al.*, 9 vols (London, 1864–98).

Calendar of State Papers, Foreign, Edward VI, 1547–53, ed. W. B. Turnbull (London, 1861).

Calendar of the Manuscripts of the Marquis of Bath preserved at Longleat, Wiltshire, Hist. MSS Com., 3 vols (London, 1904–8).

Camden, Carroll, *The Elizabethan Woman: a Panorama of English Womanhood, 1540–1640* (London, 1952).

Castiglione, B., *The Book of the Courtier*, trans. Thomas Hoby (London, 1928).

Castro, Américo, *The Structure of Spanish History*, trans. E. L. King (Princeton, 1954).

Cavendish, George, *Thomas Wolsey, late Cardinal, his Life and Death*, ed. R. Lockyer (London, 1962).

Chamberlin, F., *The Private Character of Henry the Eighth* (London and New York, 1932).

Chapman, Hester, *Two Tudor Portraits: Henry Howard, Earl of Surrey and Lady Katherine Grey* (London, 1960).

Charlotte, C. (Lady Jackson), *The Court of France, 1514–1559*, 2 vols (London, 1886).

Chastellain, Georges, *Œuvres*, ed. M. le baron Kervyn de Lettenhove, 8 vols (Brussels, 1863–6).

Chesterton, G. K., *Heretics* (New York, 1919).

Chronicle of Ellis Gruffydd, ed. M. B. Davies *Bulletin of the Faculty of Arts*, XI–XII (Fouad I Univ., Cairo, 1949–50).

Chronicle of the Grey Friars of London, ed. J. G. Nichols, Camden Soc., LIII (London, 1852).

Chronique du roi Francois, premier de ce nom, ed. G. Guiffrey (Paris, 1860).

Clark, W. H., *The Psychology of Religion* (New York, 1958).

Coignet, C., *Francis the First and his Times*, trans. F. Twemlow (London, 1888).

Constant, G., *The Reformation in England, I, The English Schism: Henry VIII*, trans. R. E. Scantleburg (London and New York, 1934).

Copeman, William, *Doctors and Disease in Tudor Times* (London, 1960).

Cornwallis, William, *Discourses Upon Seneca the Tragedian (1601)*, ed. R. H. Bowers (Gainesville, Florida, 1952).

Corpus Reformatorum, ed. C. G. Bretschneider, 3 vols (Halle, 1836).

Coulton, G. G., *Medieval Panorama* (Cambridge, 1938; New York, 1955).

Cranmer, Thomas, *Miscellaneous Writings and Letters*, ed. J. E. Cox, Parker Soc. (Cambridge, 1846).

Crotch, W. J. B., *The Prologues and Epilogues of William Caxton*, E.E.T.S. orig. ser., 176 (London, 1928).

Cruickshank, C. G., *Army Royal, an Account of Henry VIII's Invasion of France, 1513* (Oxford, 1969).

Cruttwell, P., 'Physiology and Psychology in Shakespeare's Age', *Journal of the History of Ideas*, XII (January, 1951).

Currie, A. S., 'Notes on the Obstetric Histories of Catherine of Aragon and Anne Boleyn', *Edinburgh Medical Journal*, I (1888).

Davies, C. S. L., 'Provisions for Armies 1509–50: a Study in the Effectiveness of Early Tudor Government', *Economic History Review*, ser. 2, XVIII (1964).

Da Vinci, Leonardo, *Treatise on Painting*, trans. A. P. McMahon, 2 vols (Princeton, 1956).

Demaus, Robert, *William Tyndale*, ed. R. Lovett (London, 1886).

Dickens, Charles, *A Child's History of England* (London, n.d.).

Dickinson, W. C., *Scotland from the Earliest Times to 1603* (London, 1965).

Dictionary of National Biography, ed. L. Stephen and S. Lee, 63 vols (London, 1885–1900).

Dietz, F. C., *English Public Finance 1485–1641*, 2 vols (2nd edn, London, 1964).

Dodds, M. H. and R., *The Pilgrimage of Grace, 1536–37, and the Exeter Conspiracy, 1538*, 2 vols (Cambridge, 1915).

Doernberg, E., *Henry VIII and Luther* (London, 1961).

Donaldson, G., *Scotland: James V to James VII* (Edinburgh, 1965).
Du Bellay, William, *Les Mémoires*, ed. V. L. Bourrilly and F. Vindry, 4 vols (Paris, 1908–19); and ed. Michaud and Poujoulat, *Nouvelle collection des mémoires pour servir a l'histoire de France*, ser. 1, v (Paris, 1838).
Dudley, Edmund, *The Tree of Commonwealth*, ed. D. M. Brodie (Cambridge, 1948).
Dunlop, Ian, *Palaces and Progresses of Elizabeth I* (London, 1962).
Dunne, F. P., *Mr Dooley Remembers* (Boston, 1963).
Edwardes, Roger, *Castra Regia (1568)*, ed. P. Bliss and B. Bandinel, *Historical Papers*, Roxburghe Club, pt I (London, 1846).
Elliott, J. H., *Imperial Spain 1469–1716* (London and New York, 1963).
Ellis, Henry, *Original Letters Illustrative of English History*, 3 series in 11 vols (London, 1825, 1827, 1846).
Elton, G. R., *Henry VIII: An Essay in Revision*, Hist. Assoc. Pamphlet no. 51 (London, 1962).
— 'King or Minister? the Man Behind the Henrician Reformation', *History*, XXXIX (1954).
— *Reformation Europe 1517–1559* (London and New York, 1963).
— *The Revolution in Tudor Government* (Cambridge, 1953).
Emmison, F. G., *Tudor Secretary: Sir William Petre at Court and Home* (London and Cambridge, Mass., 1961).
English, O. S. and Pearson, G. H. J., *Emotional Problems of Living* (London, 1947; New York, 1955).
Erasmus, Desiderius, *Epistles*, ed. F. M. Nichols, 3 vols (London, 1918).
— *Opus Epistolarum*, ed. Allen, P. S. and H. M., 11 vols (Oxford, 1906–47).
— *The Education of a Christian Prince*, trans. L. K. Born (New York, 1936).
Erikson, E. H., *Young Man Luther* (London, 1959; New York, 1962).
Ernle, R. E. Prothero, Baron, *The Light Reading of our Ancestors; Chapters in the Growth of the English Novel* (London, 1927).
Febvre, Lucien, *Le Problème de l'incroyance au xvie siècle: La Religion de Rabelais* (Paris, 1947).
Ferguson, A. B., *The Indian Summer of English Chivalry* (Durham, 1960).
Fiddes, Richard, *Life of Cardinal Wolsey* (London, 1724).
Flugel, J. C., 'The Character and Married Life of Henry VIII', *Psychoanalysis and History*, ed. B. Mazlish (Englewood, New Jersey, 1963).
Foxe, John, *Acts and Monuments*, ed. G. Townsend, 8 vols (London, 1843–9).

Frazer, N. L., *English History in Contemporary Poetry*, III, 'The Tudor Monarchy' (London, 1930).

Froude, A., *History of England*, 12 vols (London, 1872, 1875).

Gammon, S. R., 'Master of Practices: A Life of William, Lord Paget', unpub. Ph.D. thesis (Princeton, 1953).

Gardiner, Stephen, *A Declaration of suche true articles as George Joye hath gone about to confute as false* (London, 1546).

— *A Detection of the Devils Sophistrie, wherewith he robbeth the unlearned people, of the true byleef, in the most blessed Sacrament of the aulter* (London, 1546).

— *A Discussion of Mr Hopers oversight where he entreateth amonge his other Sermons the matter of the Sacrament of the Bodye and Bloode of Christe* (1550; P.R.O., S.P. 10. vol. 12).

— *De Vera Obedientia*, in *Obedience in Church and State*, ed. P. Janelle (Cambridge, 1930); and 'Roane' edition, trans. John Bale (?) (26 October, 1553).

— *Letters*, ed. J. A. Muller (Cambridge, 1933).

Gelder, H. A. Enno van, *The Two Reformations in the Sixteenth Century* (The Hague, 1966).

Gerth, H. H. and Mills, C. W., *From Max Weber: Essays in Sociology* (Oxford, 1958).

Giustinian, Sebastian, *Four Years at the Court of Henry VIII*, ed. R. Brown, 2 vols (London, 1854).

Godwin, Francis, *Annales of England containing the Reignes of Henry the Eighth, Edward the sixt, Queene Mary* (London, 1630).

Gordon, M. A., *The Life of Queen Katherine Parr* (Kendal, n.d.).

Grant, I. F., *The Social and Economic Development of Scotland before 1603* (Edinburgh, 1930).

—*The Lordship of the Isles* (Edinburgh, 1935).

Greene, Robert, *James The Fourth*, in *The Dramatic and Poetical Works of Robert Greene and George Peele*, ed. A. Dyce (London, 1861).

Grey, Arthur Lord, *Commentary on William Lord Grey*, ed. P. Egerton, Camden Soc., XV (London, 1847).

Gurney-Salter, E., *Tudor England Through Venetian Eyes* (London, 1930).

Hale, J. R., *The Art of War and Renaissance England* (Washington D.C., 1961).

— 'Armies, Navies and the Art of War', *New Cambridge Modern History*, II (Cambridge, 1957).

Hall, Edward, *The Triumphant Reigne of Kyng Henry the VIII*, ed. Charles Whibley, 2 vols (London, 1904).

Halliwell, J. O., *Letters of the Kings of England*, 2 vols (London, 1846–8).

Hamilton Papers: Letters and Papers Illustrating the Political Relations of England and Scotland in the XVIth Century (in the British Museum), ed. Joseph Bain, vol. I (1532–1543), vol. II (1543–1590) (Edinburgh, 1890–2).

Harpsfield, Nicholas, *A Treatise on the Pretended Divorce Between Henry VIII and Catherine of Aragon*, ed. N. Pocock, Camden Soc., ser 2, XXI (London, 1878).

Haynes, Samuel, *Collection of State Papers ... Left by William Cecill, Lord Burghley* (London, 1740).

Heilbroner, R. L., *The Future as History* (New York, 1960).

Henry VIII, *Assertio Septem Sacramentorum*, ed. L. O'Donovan (New York, 1908).

— *Letters*, ed. M. St. Clare Byrne (London, 1968).

— *The King's Book*, see under *The King's Book*.

— *The Love Letters*, ed. H. Savage (London, 1949).

Herbert, Lord Edward of Cherbury, *The Life and Raigne of King Henry the Eighth* (London, 1649).

Hewitt, H. J., *The Organization of War under Edward III* (Manchester, 1966).

Hole, Christina, *A Mirror of Witchcraft* (London, 1957).

Holinshed, R., *Chronicles of England, Scotland, and Ireland*, 6 vols (London, 1807–8).

Hooper, J., *Early Writings*, ed. S. Carr, Parker Soc. (Cambridge, 1843).

(*Household Ordinances*) *A Collection of Ordinances and Regulations for the Government of the Royal Household, made in divers Reigns*, Soc. of Antiquaries (London, 1790).

Hughes, Philip, *The Earliest English Life of John Fisher* (London 1935).

— *The Reformation in England*, 3 vols (London, 1954).

Hughes, P. L. and Larkin, J. F., *Tudor Royal Proclamations*, 3 vols (New Haven, 1964–9).

Huizinga, J., *Erasmus and the Age of Reformation* (New York, 1957).

— *Men and Ideas*, trans. J. S. Holmes (London, 1960).

— *The Waning of the Middle Ages* (London, 1924).

Hume, M. A. S., *Chronicle of King Henry VIII* (London, 1889).

Hundred Merry Tales, ed. P. M. Zall (Lincoln, Nebraska, 1963).

Jackson, J. E., 'Wulfhall and the Seymours', *Wiltshire Archaeological and Natural History Magazine*, xv (1875).

James, William, *The Varieties of Religious Experience* (London, 1952; New York, 1958).

Jenkins, Elizabeth, *Elizabeth the Great* (London, 1958; New York, 1959).

Jordan, W. K., *Edward VI: the Young King* (London and Cambridge, Mass., 1968).

Jordan, W. K. (ed.), *The Chronicle and Political Papers of King Edward VI* (Ithaca, New York, 1966)

Journals of the House of Lords, vol. I (London, n.d.).

Kaulek, Jean, *Correspondance politique de MM. de Castillon et de Marillac (1537–1542)* (Paris, 1885).

Keen, M. H., *The Laws of War in the Late Middle Ages* (London, 1965).

Kelso, R., *The Doctrine of the English Gentleman in the Sixteenth Century*, Univ. of Illinois Studies in Languages and Literature, XIV (Urbana, 1929).

The King's Book or A Necessary Doctrine and Erudition for any Christian Man, 1543, ed. T. A. Lacey (London, 1932).

Koebner, R., ' "The Imperial Crown of This Realm"; Henry VIII, Constantine the Great, and Polydore Vergil', *Bul. Inst. of Historical Research*, XXVI (1953).

Langsam, G. G., *Martial Books and Tudor Verse* (New York, 1951).

Laslett, Peter, *The World We Have Lost* (London and New York, 1965).

Latimer, Hugh, *Sermons* (London, 1926).

Law, Ernest, *A Short History of Hampton Court Palace in Tudor and Stuart Times* (London, 1924).

Legg, L. G. W., *English Coronation Records* (London, 1883).

Letters and Papers, Foreign and Domestic, of the Reign of Henry VIII, ed. J. Gairdner and R. H. Brodie, 21 vols (London, 1862–1910).

Levine, Mortimer, *The Early Elizabethan Succession Question 1558–1568* (Oxford and Stanford, Calif., 1966).

Literae Cantuarienses (The Letter Books of the Monastery of Christ Church, Canterbury), ed. J. B. Sheppard, 3 vols (London, 1889).

Lloyd, Charles, *Formularies of the Faith* (Oxford, 1825).

Lot, F. *Les Effectifs des armées françaises ... 1494–1562* (Paris, 1962).

Lyly, John, *Complete Works*, ed. R. W. Bond, 3 vols (Oxford, 1902).

Mackie, J. D., 'Henry VIII and Scotland', *Transactions of the Royal Hist. Soc.*, XXIX, ser. 4 (1947).

Maitland, S. R., *Essays on Subjects connected with the Reformation in England* (London, 1849).

Makinson, A., 'Solway Moss and the Death of James V', *History Today*, x (1960).

Mattingly, Garrett, *Catherine of Aragon* (Boston, 1941; London, 1942).

McConica, J. K., *English Humanists and Reformation Politics under Henry VIII and Edward VI* (Oxford, 1965).

McNalty, A. S., *Henry VIII, A Difficult Patient* (London, 1952).

Meadows, Denis, *Elizabethan Quintet* (London, 1956).

Montluc, Blaise de, *Commentaires* in *Nouvelle collection des mémoires pour servir a l'histoire de France*, ser. 1, VIII (Paris, 1838).

More, Thomas, *Correspondence*, ed. E. F. Rogers (Princeton, 1947).

— *English Works*, (London, 1557); also ed. W. E. Campbell and A. W. Reed, 2 vols (London, 1931).

— *The Utopia ... including Roper's Life of More and Letters of More*, ed. M. Campbell (New York, 1947); also *Famous Utopias of the Renaissance*, ed. F. R. White (New York, 1949).

Sir Thomas More, ed. A. Dyce (London, 1844).

Moriemini, H. B., *A Very Profitable Sermon Preached before her Majesty* (London, 1593).

Mosher, O. W., *Louis XI as He Appears in History and in Literature* (Toulouse, 1925).

Muller, J. A., *Stephen Gardiner and the Tudor Reaction* (London, 1926).

Murray, M. A., *The Divine King in England* (London, 1954).

Neale, J. E., *Elizabeth I and Her Parliaments*, 2 vols (London, 1953, 1957).

Nichols, J. G., *Literary Remains of King Edward the Sixth*, Roxburghe Club, bound in 2 vols (London, 1857).

— *Narratives of the Days of the Reformation*, Camden Soc., LXXVII (London, 1859).

Nicolas, N. H., 'Descent of Henry the Eighth's Queens', *The Gentleman's Magazine and Historical Chronicle*, XCIX (May, 1829).

— *The Privy Purse Expenses of King Henry the Eighth from November 1529 to December 1532* (London, 1827).

Nott, G. F., *The Works of Henry Howard Earl of Surrey and of Sir Thomas Wyatt the Elder*, 2 vols (London, 1815–16).

Nugent, E. M., *The Thought and Culture of the English Renaissance* (Cambridge, 1956).

Oman, C. W. C., *The Art of War in the Sixteenth Century* (New York, 1937).

— 'The Personality of Henry VIII', *Quarterly Review*, CCLXIX (July, 1937).

O'Neil, B. H. St John, *Castles and Cannon: a Study of Early Artillery Fortifications in England* (Oxford, 1960).

Original Letters relative to the English Reformation, ed. H. Robinson, Parker Soc., 2 vols (Cambridge, 1846–7).

Ostow, M. and Scharfstein, B., *The Need to Believe: the Psychology of Religion* (New York, 1954).

Owst, G. R., *Literature and Pulpit in Medieval England* (Oxford, 1961).

Oxley, J. E., *The Reformation in Essex* (Manchester, 1965).

Pardoe, Julia, *The Court and Reign of Francis the First*, 2 vols (London, 1849).

Parker, Mathew, *Correspondence*, ed. J. Bruce and T. T. Perowne, Parker Soc. (Cambridge, 1853).

Parsons, Robert, *A Treatise of Three Conversions of England, from Paganism to Christian Religion*, 3 vols (St Omer, 1603–4).

Pastor, Ludwig, *The History of the Popes*, 32 vols (London, 1923–40).

Patch, H. R., *The Other World According to Descriptions in Medieval Literature* (Cambridge, Mass., 1950).

Petry, R. C., *Christian Eschatology and Social Thought* (New York, 1956).

Pickthorn, K., *Early Tudor Government: Henry VIII* (Cambridge, 1934).

Pollard, A. F., *England under Protector Somerset* (London, 1900).

— *Henry VIII* (London, 1913).

Prescott, H. F. M., *Mary Tudor* (London, 1953).

Proceedings and Ordinances of the Privy Council in England, 1386–1542, ed. N. H. Nicolas, 7 vols (London, 1834–7).

Puttenham, George, *Arte of English Poesie* (London, 1589).

Raleigh, Walter, *Works*, 8 vols (Oxford, 1829).

Rastel, John, *Le Liver des Assises et plees del corone* (London, 1580).

Read, Conyers, *Mr Secretary Walsingham and the Policy of Queen Elizabeth*, 3 vols (Oxford, 1925).

Ridley, Jasper, *Thomas Cranmer* (Oxford, 1962).

Romei, Count Haniball, *The Courtiers Academie* (London, 1598).

Roper, William, *Life of More*, in *The Utopia of Sir Thomas More including Roper's Life of More*, ed. M. Campbell (New York, 1947); and *The Lyfe of Sir Thomas Moore*, ed. E. V. Hitchcock, E.E.T.S., 197 (London, 1935).

Rowley, Samuel, *When You See Me, You Know Me* (1605), Old English Drama Facsimile edition (1912).

Rowse, A. L., 'Eminent Henrician: Thomas Wriothesley', *History Today*, xv (June–July 1965).

Rye, Walter, *A History of Norfolk* (London, 1850).

Rymer, Thomas, *Foedera, Conventiones, Literae et Cujuscunque Generis Acta Publica, inter Reges Angliae*, 20 vols (London, 1727–35).

Sadler, Ralph, *The State Papers and Letters*, ed. A. Clifford, 2 vols (Edinburgh, 1809).

Salles, Georges, 'Une Mediation des protestants D'Allemagne entre la France et l'Angleterre au milieu du xvie siècle', *Revue D'Histoire Diplomatique*, XIII (1899).

Salter, F. M., 'Skelton's Speculum Princepis', *Speculum*, IX (1934).

Sander, Nicolas, 'Report to Cardinal Moroni on the Change of Religion in 1558–59', ed. F. A. Gasquet, *Catholic Record Soc.*, I (1904–5).

— *Rise and Growth of the Anglican Schism*, trans. D. Lewis (London, 1877).

Scarisbrick, J. J., *Henry VIII* (London and Berkeley, Calif., 1968).

Segar, William, *Honor, Military and Civill* (London, 1602).

Selve, Odet de, *Correspondance politique 1546–49*, ed. G. Lefèvre-Pontalis (Paris, 1888).

Sermons or Homilies Appointed to be Read in Churches in the Time of Queen Elizabeth (Oxford, 1802).

Seymour Papers 1532–1686, Report on the Manuscripts of the Most Honourable the Marquess of Bath preserved at Longleat, IV, ed. M. Blatcher, Hist. MSS Com. (London, 1968).

Shakespeare, William, *The Histories and Poems*, ed. W. J. Craig (London, 1912).

Shanley, J. L., *A Study of Spenser's Gentleman* (Evanston, Illinois, 1940).

Shrewsbury, J. F. D., 'Henry VIII: A Medical Study', *Journal of the History of Medicine and Allied Sciences*, VII (1952).

Slavin, A. J., *Politics and Profit: a Study of Sir Ralph Sadler, 1507–1547* (Cambridge, 1966).

Smith, L. B., *A Tudor Tragedy, the Life and Times of Catherine Howard* (London, 1961).

— 'Henry VIII and the Protestant Triumph', *Am. Hist. Review*, LXXI (1966).

— 'The Last Will and Testament of Henry VIII: A Question of Perspective', *Journal Brit. Studies*, II (1962).

— *Tudor Prelates and Politics* (Princeton, 1953).

Smith, Thomas, *De Republica Anglorum*, ed. L. Alston (Cambridge, 1906).

Spanish Chronicle, see Hume, M. A. S., *Chronicle of King Henry VIII*.

Stapleton, Thomas, *The Life and Illustrious Martyrdom of Sir Thomas More*, trans. P. E. Hallett (London, 1928).

State Papers during the Reign of Henry VIII, II vols (London, 1830–52).

Statutes of the Realm, ed. A. Luders *et al.*, 11 vols (London, 1810–28).
Stone, Lawrence, *The Crisis of the Aristocracy 1558–1641* (Oxford, 1965).
Storr, Anthony, 'The Man', *Churchill Revised* (London and New York, 1969).
Stow, John, *Annales, or A General Chronicle of England*, ed. E. Howes (London, 1631).
— *The Survey of London* (Everyman's Lib., London, n.d.).
Strickland, Agnes, *Lives of the Queens of England*, 8 vols (London, 1851–2).
Strype, John, *Ecclesiastical Memorials*, 3 vols in 6 (Oxford, 1822).
— *Memorials of Archbishop Cranmer*, 3 vols (Oxford, 1854).
Stubbes, Philip, *A Chrystal Glasse for Christian Women* (London, 1630).
Stubbs, William, *Seventeen Lectures on the Study of Medieval and Modern History* (Oxford, 1887).
Sturge, C., *Cuthbert Tunstal* (London, 1936).
Taylor, A., *The Glory of Regality: a Treatise on the Anointing and Crowning of the Kings and Queens of England* (London, 1820).
Third Report of the Royal Commission on Historical Manuscripts (London, 1832).
Thomas, William, *The Pilgrim: a Dialogue on the Life and Actions of King Henry the Eighth*, ed. J. A. Froude (London, 1861).
Tjernagel, N. S., *Henry VIII and the Lutherans* (St Louis, 1965).
Trevelyan Papers prior to A.D. 1558, ed. J. P. Collier, Camden Soc., LXVII (London, 1857).
Trinterud, L. J., 'The Origins of Puritanism', *Church History*, xx (1951).
Turner, W., *The huntyng and fyndyng out of the Romyshe foxe, which more then seven yeares hath bene hyd among the bisshoppes of Englande* (Basle, 1543).
— *The Rescuynge of the romishe fox otherwise called the examination of the hunter devised by Steven gardiner* (Zurich (?), 1545).
Tyler, Royall, *The Emperor Charles the Fifth* (London and Fairlawn, New Jersey, 1956).
Tyndale, William, *Doctrinal Treatises*, ed. H. Walter, Parker Soc., XLII (Cambridge, 1848).
Tyler, P., *England under the Reigns of Edward VI and Mary*, 2 vols (London, 1839).
Vergil, Polydore, *Anglica Historia*, ed. D. Hay, Camden Soc., LXXIV (1950).
Vetter, G. B., *Magic and Religion* (New York, 1958; London, 1959).

Vieilleville, Mareschal de, *Mémoires de la vie* in *Nouvelle collection des mémoires pour servir a l'histoire de France,* ed. Michaud and Poujoulat, ser. I, IX (Paris, 1838).

Waggoner, G. R., 'An Elizabethan Attitude toward Peace and War', *Philological Quarterly,* XXXIII (1954).

Watson, C. B., *Shakespeare and the Renaissance Concept of Honor* (Oxford and Princeton, 1960).

Wernham, R. B., *Before the Armada: The Growth of English Foreign Policy, 1485–1588* (London, 1966).

Wilbraham, Roger, *Journal,* Camden Soc., ser. 3, IV (London, 1902).

Williams, H. Noel, *Henri II: His Court and Times* (London and New York, 1910).

Williams, Neville, *Royal Residences of Great Britain* (London, 1960).

Williams, Penry, *Life in Tudor England* (London, 1964).

Wilson, Thomas, *The State of England,* ed. F. J. Fisher, Camden Soc., ser. 3, LII (London, 1936).

Woodworth, A., 'Purveyance for the Royal Household in the Reign of Queen Elizabeth', *Transactions of the Am. Philosophical Soc.,* XXXV (1945–6).

Wriothesley, C. A., *A Chronicle of England,* ed. W. D. Hamilton, Camden Soc., 2 vols, new ser. vols XI, XX (London, 1875, 1877).

INDEX